EAST OF EDEN
Finding Our Way Home
A Study of the Book of Genesis

Stan Key

OTHER TITLES BY STAN KEY

The Last Word (2015)

Marriage Matters (2017)

Jeremiah: Fire in His Bones (2017)

Face to Face (2019)

Journey to Spiritual Wholeness (2019)

EAST OF EDEN
Finding Our Way Home

A Study of the Book of Genesis

Francis Asbury Press
Wilmore, Kentucky

Copyright ©2022 Stan Key. All rights reserved. No part of this publication may be reproduced, stored in a retrieval system, or transmitted in any form or by any means—electronic, mechanical, photocopy, recording, or any other—except for brief quotations in printed reviews, without the prior written permission of the publisher. For this and all other editorial matters, or to purchase additional copies of this book, inquire about distribution, or for all other sales-related matters, please contact:

The Francis Asbury Society
PO Box 7
Wilmore, KY 40390
859-858-4222
800-530-5673
fas@francisasburysociety.com
www.francisasburysociety.com

Unless otherwise noted, scripture quotations are from the Holy Bible, English Standard Version® (ESV®), copyright ©2001 by Crossway, a publishing ministry of Good News Publishers. Used by permission. All rights reserved.

Scriptures marked NASB are taken from the Holy Bible, New American Standard Bible® (NASB), Copyright © 1960, 1962, 1963, 1968, 1971, 1972, 1973, 1975, 1977, 1995 by The Lockman Foundation. Used by permission. www.Lockman.org

Scriptures marked NIV are taken from the Holy Bible, New International Version®, NIV® Copyright ©1973, 1978, 1984, 2011 by Biblica, Inc.® Used by permission. All rights reserved worldwide.

Scriptures marked NKJV are taken from the Holy Bible, New King James Version®. Copyright © 1982 by Thomas Nelson. Used by permission. All rights reserved.

Scriptures marked NLT are taken from the Holy Bible, New Living Translation, copyright ©1996, 2004, 2015 by Tyndale House Foundation. Used by permission of Tyndale House Publishers, Inc., Carol Stream, Illinois 60188. All rights reserved.

Scriptures marked KJV are taken from the King James Version (KJV): King James Version, public domain.

Scriptures marked MSG are taken from *THE MESSAGE*, copyright © 1993, 2002, 2018 by Eugene H. Peterson. Used by permission of NavPress. All rights reserved. Represented by Tyndale House Publishers, Inc.

ISBN 978-0-915143-42-9
Cover design by Jennie Lovell
Printed in the United States of America

To Robert A. Traina
In your classroom I gained a love for God's
Word and a method for studying it that has
defined my life and ministry. Thank you!

Contents

Preface 9
Introduction 13
Chapter 1: Designer Universe 23
Chapter 2: The Way Things Ought to Be 35
Chapter 3: There's a Snake in the Garden! 47
Chapter 4: The Emperor's New Clothes 61
Chapter 5: Spoiler Alert 75
Chapter 6: Why Can't We All Just Get Along? 89
Chapter 7: Rotten to the Core 105
Chapter 8: Deep Waters 119
Chapter 9: Daddy's Drunk! 135
Chapter 10: The City of Man 149
Chapter 11: The Call 163
Chapter 12: A Lot to Remember 177
Chapter 13: The Obedience of Faith 191
Chapter 14: How to Birth a Donkey 203
Chapter 15: An Old Man Gets a New Start 217
Chapter 16: Is Anything Too Hard for the Lord? 231
Chapter 17: Abraham Had Two Sons 247
Chapter 18: Abraham's Final Exam 261
Chapter 19: Hatched, Matched, and Dispatched 275
Chapter 20: The Man in the Middle 289
Chapter 21: Jake the Snake 303
Chapter 22: Heaven's Gate 317
Chapter 23: The Deceiver Is Deceived 331
Chapter 24: The Magnificent Limp 345
Chapter 25: #MeToo 359
Chapter 26: The Pits 373
Chapter 27: Here's to You, Mrs. Potiphar 387
Chapter 28: Faith@Work 403

Chapter 29: Finding the Way Home 417
Chapter 30: Eden's Gates..433
Chapter 31: The Last Words of Joseph..447
            Bibliography..463

Preface

The book you are holding is not easy to classify. It lies somewhere in the middle of the spectrum between a commentary and a devotional book. The chapters may at times read like sermons directed to serious-minded seekers after truth. This book's purpose is both to engage the mind *and* warm the heart. More than that, the author (who happens to be a preacher!) hopes that these chapters will inspire, convict, and motivate the reader to put into action the truths that are learned.

The material covered in Genesis is intended to do more than inform us about the ancient world. Its purpose is to transform our minds, hearts, families, communities, and world! This book, therefore, aims to provoke theological and spiritual reflection at a deeper level than most contemporary students of Scripture are accustomed to. Ultimately, its purpose is to send the reader back to the original biblical text again and again asking the question, "Is that what it *really* says?" If I succeed in this endeavor, I will be deeply satisfied.

The best use of this book will be found by those who use it for a combination of purposes:
- Personal Bible study
- Theological reflection
- Spiritual growth
- Small group study and discussion (see questions at the end of each chapter)
- Supplemental material for one's ministry of teaching and/or preaching

The observant reader will notice that several chapters of Genesis are not treated in this volume. Because of the sermonic nature of this work, I have chosen to give little or no attention to chapters of Genesis that deal with genealogies (Gen 10:1–32; 11:10–32; 36:1–43), redundancies (Gen 20:1–18), and matters that have been treated in other ways elsewhere in the text (Gen 25:1–18; 35:1–29; 38:1–30).

For those who desire a fuller and more scholarly treatment of Genesis and its message, I'm happy to share a short list of the books that have been most helpful to me:

- *The Book of Genesis* (Eerdmans, two volumes): *Chapters 1–17* (1990) and *Chapters 18–50* (1995) by Victor P. Hamilton. If you buy just one commentary on Genesis, this is the one you want.
- *The Beginning of Wisdom: Reading Genesis* (University of Chicago Press, 2003) by Leon R. Kass. This is the most insightful treatment of Genesis I've read. Physician, scientist, and professor of Social Thought at University of Chicago, Kass does not profess to be a believer. He describes himself as someone who is "still in the middle of my journey . . . between Athens and Jerusalem" (p. xiv).
- *Creation and Blessing: A Guide to the Study and Exposition of Genesis* (Baker Academic, 1998) by Allen P. Ross. This work is basic, straightforward, and sound.
- *In the Beginning: The Opening Chapters of Genesis* (InterVarsity Press, 1984) by Henri Blocher. This is an excellent resource for the first eleven chapters of Genesis.

Although it would be impossible for me to thank everyone who played a role in making this book possible, I would be remiss to fail to mention:

- Dr. Dennis Kinlaw, Dr. Victor Hamilton, and Dr. John Oswalt who, in classrooms and college chapel services, first introduced me to the beauty and wonder of the Old Testament in general and to Genesis in particular.
- Dr. Robert Traina who gave me the tools (inductive Bible study) with which to dig for the gold in the English text of Scripture.

I took as many classes from him in seminary as I could. It changed my life!
- The congregation of Loudonville Community Church (Albany, NY) where I served as senior pastor from 1994–2012. My sermon series on Abraham and then Joseph were my first attempts to transmit the message of Genesis to the current generation.
- The Tuesday night Bible study group at the Francis Asbury Society (Wilmore, KY) who listened patiently and encouraged me as I spent an entire year teaching the book of Genesis. This book is a distillation of that study.
- My wife Katy who graciously offered support and encouragement as I labored many long hours to produce the manuscript that has become this book.

Stan Key
Spring 2022

Introduction
Once Upon a Time . . .

Have you ever arrived for a movie twenty minutes late? The images on the screen are riveting but nothing makes sense. The characters are unknown, as is the location and the time-period. There is no discernable plot. You are watching what seems to be a series of randomly arranged events with no coherent meaning. What can be more frustrating than that? And yet for many today, this describes what reading the Bible is like. The stories are interesting, even meaningful: David and Goliath, Jesus and the leper, Noah and the ark, Jonah and the whale. But how these stories fit together and whether there is some master narrative tying them all together remains an enigma.

Ignorance of the book of Genesis accounts for much of the contemporary inability to understand the Bible. Without Genesis, the basic storyline of the broader narrative simply cannot be fully grasped. It is like missing the first twenty minutes of a movie. While other parts of the Bible may hold great interest and meaning, the full impact of the story God is telling needs Genesis for it all to make sense. Here, in the first book of the Bible, we meet the main characters, are introduced to the most prominent themes, and discover God's overarching purpose for men and women on planet Earth.

To understand Genesis, however, demands first that we recognize what kind of literature it is. While it cannot be classified as philosophy, science, sociology, psychology, or religion in the modern sense of those terms, it has much to say concerning all those disciplines. Above all else, Genesis tells a story. While other cultures of the ancient Near East told myths and legends, the Hebrews wrote history. The people, the places, the dates, and the events are real, firmly rooted in time and space.

As we will see, the stories in Genesis awaken the imagination, nourish the soul, and stimulate the intellect. Those who say the book is boring only reveal the poverty of their own spirits. Whether we are talking about Cain and Abel, the tower of Babel, Jacob's wrestling match with the angel, or Joseph and his many-colored coat, these ancient stories fascinate and enthrall both young and old alike.

But just as important as the stories themselves, Genesis encourages us—no, *forces* us—to wrestle with the most fundamental questions of human existence:

- Is there a God? If so, what is he (she? it? they?) like?
- Where do I come from?
- Who am I? Who are my people?
- Why am I here?
- What is good and what is evil and how can I discern the difference?
- Where is my home?
- What's wrong with the world?
- Why are families so dysfunctional?
- Is history going somewhere?

Taken from the Greek *geneseos*, the word "genesis" can mean "birth," "genealogy," or "history of origin." The first book of Bible is, therefore, about beginnings. Here we read about the origin of the heaven and the earth, human life, wickedness and sin, languages, worship, and the nation of Israel. Perhaps the greatest genius of the book is that it tells ancient history in a way that makes it intensely personal and relevant to our situation today. As Leon R. Kass says in his excellent book *The Beginning of Wisdom*:

> The stories cast powerful light, for example, on the problematic character of human reason, speech, freedom, sexual desire, the love of the beautiful, shame, guilt, anger, and man's response to mortality. The stories cast equally powerful light on the naturally vexed relations between man and woman, brother and brother, father and son, neighbor and neighbor, stranger

and stranger, man and God. Adam and Eve are not just the first but also the paradigmatic man and woman. Cain and Abel are paradigmatic brothers. Babel is the quintessential city. By means of such paradigmatic stories, the beginning of Genesis shows us not so much what happened as what *always* happens. And by holding up a mirror in which we readers can discover in ourselves the reasons why human life is so bittersweet and why uninstructed human beings generally get it wrong, Genesis reflectively read also provides a powerful *pedagogical beginning* for the moral and spiritual education of the reader. As a result of what we learn from this early education, when God calls Abraham in Genesis 12, *we* will also be inclined to pay attention.[1]

Therefore, be warned: in your examination of this ancient document, don't be surprised if, in the process, you discover that you yourself are the one being examined!

A Word about Structure

The first eleven chapters of Genesis, stretching from the creation to the tower of Babel, describe universal human history. The focus is broad and generic and tends to relate to humanity in general and no one particular place. The stories of Adam and Eve, Cain and Abel, Noah and the flood, and the tower of Babel teach broad and universal truths based in a history common to all people everywhere. However, beginning with chapter 12, the narrative suddenly focuses on one man (Abraham) and his descendants (the Hebrews) and one place (the land of Canaan). God has chosen to particularize his work in the world in one group of people and in one location in the hopes that, through the Hebrews living in Canaan, he can reveal himself and his purposes to all the other nations of the earth.

---

1   Kass, *The Beginning of Wisdom*, 10. Emphasis in the original.

Genesis 1–11	Genesis 12–50
General: • The place: Mesopotamia • The people: the human race • The time: many generations (centuries) The Problem: Human wickedness and divine judgment. Human attempts to deal with the problem fail miserably.	Particular: • The place: Canaan • The people: Abraham and his descendants • The time: four generations (about 300 years) The Solution: Only God can deal with the problem, and he does so by choosing a man and making a covenant with him and his descendants.

Apart from the major division of the book that occurs with chapter 12, the most obvious indication of Genesis' structure is found in the repeated words, "These are the generations of . . ." Occurring some eleven times, the most important usages serve as a sort of recurring title that introduces the main characters in the book. *These are the generations of*:

- The heavens and the earth (Gen 2:4).
- Adam (Gen 5:1).
- Noah (Gen 6:9).
- Terah, the father of Abraham (Gen 11:27).
- Isaac, the father of Jacob (Gen 25:19).
- Jacob, the father of Joseph (Gen 37:2).

It is immediately apparent that God intends to get his work done in the world through particular persons. Though he does at times accomplish his purposes through cataclysmic events, visions, miracles, and nations, Genesis makes clear that his primary work on earth is done through people and their families. In Genesis, the storyline basically centers around five key individuals, each one highlighting a particular theme:

1. Adam—temptation and sin (Gen 1–5)
2. Noah—salvation from God's wrath (Gen 6–11)
3. Abraham—the walk of faith (Gen 12–25)
4. Jacob—the need for sanctification (Gen 25–36)
5. Joseph—the path of suffering (Gen 37–50)

I have entitled this book *East of Eden: Finding Our Way Home* to remind us how Genesis describes the human condition as a journey. When Adam and Eve sinned, they were cast out of their garden home and compelled to live "east of Eden" (see Gen 3:24; 4:16). An angel with a flaming sword stood guard at the gate making impossible any return to paradise. Alienated from both God and his true home, Cain finally settled in the land of Nod (Hebrew, *wandering*). Ever since, all human history has been lived somewhere "east of Eden." We are all homesick but can't find our way home. The book of Genesis announces the Good News that God has neither forgotten us nor condemned us to wander aimlessly forever. If we listen, follow his call, and walk by faith, he will lead us home!

In describing salvation as a journey, this book can be seen as a prequel to my previous book *Journey to Spiritual Wholeness: How the Map of the Exodus Illustrates our Own Spiritual Journey* (Francis Asbury Press, 2019). That book describes the actual outworking of God's redemptive plan for his people, how he leads them from bondage in Egypt to abundant living in Canaan. The journey described in the Exodus is not just *their* journey but *ours*. Genesis reveals that the journey to spiritual wholeness began long before the book of Exodus. It gives vital background information that enables us to better understand who this God who redeems us really is and how his covenant people ever ended up in Egypt in the first place.

The Message of Genesis in Four Questions

Genesis is more than the history of Israel. At a profoundly personal level, this amazing book is meant to help *you* understand your own origins, your own story, and your own identity. Paul wrote that all Scripture, including Genesis, is "breathed out by God and profitable for teaching, for reproof, for correction, and for training in righteousness" (2 Tim 3:16). Studying Genesis will enable you to answer four life-changing questions so that you can come to a clear understanding of both your true identity and your Creator's purpose for your life.

Question 1: What do you do when things are formless, empty, and meaningless?

In the beginning, the earth God created was "without form and void" and "darkness was over the face of the deep" (Gen 1:1–2). We will leave for others to explore the question of *why* God's first creative act left things an empty, amorphous mass. Our focus here is simply on the fact. At the dawn of creation, everything was chaotic and meaningless, a shapeless mass filled by nothing.

The first chapter of Genesis tells us that God took this empty, shapeless mass and began to create something wonderful and beautiful; something full of meaning and significance. He took what was unorganized and chaotic and gave it structure and form. He created the heavens and the earth and then filled them with stars, birds, fish, and animals. In creating time, he filled it with seasons, days, hours, and minutes.

But *how* did he do it? Genesis wants us to ask this question! He brought order out of chaos and fullness out of emptiness by speaking! "Let there be . . . and there was" (Gen 1:3, 6, 9, etc.). By his sovereign word alone, he brought order and beauty out of the formless emptiness. "In the beginning was the Word" (John 1:1). He spoke, and suddenly there was light and life. "By the word of the Lord the heavens were made . . . for he spoke, and it came to be; he commanded, and it stood firm" (Ps 33:6, 9). Where everything had been dark, mysterious, chaotic, and empty, the cosmos was now flooded with light and life. God did it all through his Word.

Working with what he had made, God began to establish boundaries and make distinctions between the various elements of his creation. He made a clear and distinct separation between light and darkness, day and night, good and evil, male and female. Then he gave names to what he had made. Genesis is all about bringing order out of chaos, filling what is empty, defining boundaries, and giving things their proper names.

Dear reader, if your life feels chaotic, empty, meaningless, this book of Genesis is just what you need. When God speaks into the muddled mess of human existence, he creates order, fullness, and significance.

Question 2: Can the shattered image of God in man be restored?

Genesis tells us that the climax of creation was that moment on the sixth day when God created human persons. The words that describe the event are profoundly simple and simply profound:

> *Then God said, "Let us make man in our image, after our likeness. And let them have dominion over the fish of the sea and over the birds of the heavens and over the livestock and over all the earth and over every creeping thing that creeps on the earth.*
>
> *So God created man in his own image, in the image of God he created him; male and female he created them. (Gen 1:26–27)*

Human persons are unique. They are neither animal nor deity. They alone are made in the image of God. Humans come in two, and only two varieties: male and female. Sexuality and gender thus help to define what the image of God in humans truly is. As stewards over creation, humans are charged to have dominion over the earth. Because God is holy, righteous, and good, to be created in his image means that humans should reflect his character.

Genesis, however, tells the tragic story of how sin came into the world and caused this divine image in man to become damaged, distorted, marred. This explains why humans can be so inhumane. Cain kills his brother, Lamech practices polygamy, the citizens of Sodom are sexually perverse, Shechem rapes Dinah, and much more. The tragic reality of this shattered image is perhaps most poignantly stated in Genesis 6:5: "The Lord saw that the wickedness of man was great in the earth, and that every intention of the thoughts of his heart was only evil continually."

The great question posed by the book of Genesis is, therefore: Can the shattered image of God in man be restored? Must humans be forever condemned to live in their brokenness and sin? Can human nature be changed? Genesis introduces us to God's plan for dealing with the broken image found in every descendant of Adam and Eve. Though giving us only the first hints of God's full plan of redemption, Genesis lets us know that God wants to do more with sin than forgive it. He intends to break its power so that human hearts can be transformed and the image of God can be fully restored! Enoch walked with God (Gen 5:21–24), Noah was blameless (Gen 6:9), Abraham was counted as righteous by faith (Gen 15:6), and Jacob was transformed and given a new identity (Gen 32:22–32). Yes, Genesis promises us that the image of God can indeed be restored (Col 3:10; cf. Rom 8:29).

Question 3: How can we discern the difference between good and evil?

A third message that runs throughout the entire book of Genesis concerns the vital importance of learning to distinguish between good and evil. Genesis teaches us that discerning the difference is harder than you think. We first encounter this theme in the opening chapters of Genesis where we learn of a special tree that God placed in the middle of the Garden of Eden:

> *And the* LORD *God commanded the man, saying, "You may surely eat of every tree of the garden, but of the tree of the knowledge of good and evil you shall not eat, for in the day that you eat of it you shall surely die. (Gen 2:16–17)*

Apparently, God intends for Adam and Eve to discern the difference between good and evil by *not* eating of the tree that promises the knowledge of good and evil! The very act of abstaining from eating the fruit gives them the ability to discriminate what is good from what is evil. The serpent, of course, tempted the couple with just the opposite reasoning. "Eat the forbidden fruit; only *then* will you know the difference between good and evil" (see Gen 3:5). The serpent's strategy was to convince Eve that she must experience evil to know what it is. Taste and see that evil is good! Tragically, Adam and Eve fell for the serpent's lie. Ironically, they lost the ability to discern good from evil when they bought in to Satan's reasoning and ate the forbidden fruit.

Human history tells the tragic story of men and women, all children of Adam and Eve, who make a royal mess of life because they are confused about good and evil. People believe that doing bad is a good thing and doing good is a bad thing. This explains the sequence of tragic events one finds in Genesis and beyond: murder, polygamy, deceit, slavery, idolatry, and all manner of sexual perversions. Welcome to human history. Centuries later the prophet Isaiah will lament; "Woe to those who call evil good and good evil, who put darkness for light and light for darkness" (Isa 5:20) and Jeremiah will bemoan the fact that the heart "is deceitful above all things, and desperately sick" (Jer 17:9).

But there is hope! Genesis shows us that not only can God forgive our bad choices and evil deeds but also he can transform our hearts and renew our minds so that we can rightly discern the difference between good and evil. In what can be considered as the climax to the entire book, Joseph proclaims his discovery that good and evil are not what he originally assumed. God has transformed his heart so that he now can see good and evil in a very different light: "You meant evil against me, but God meant it for good" (Gen 50:20).

Question 4: Who is the seed of the woman?

Careful readers of Genesis will not miss the fact that the story of man's first and greatest failure (Genesis 3) also contains the first and greatest divine promise. In fact, it could be said that Genesis 3:15 is the first announcement of the gospel in the Bible! God himself makes the prophetic promise. To the serpent he says:

> *I will put enmity between you and the woman,*
> *and between your offspring [seed] and her offspring [seed];*
> *he [the seed of the woman] shall bruise your head,*
> *and you shall bruise his heel. (Gen 3:15)*

In the wake of what has happened in the Garden of Eden, God wants everyone to know that human history will now be defined by spiritual warfare, unceasing conflict between the seed of the woman and the seed of the serpent. The "seed" of the woman refers not just to humanity in general but also to a single, specific individual, a coming hero and savior. In Hebrew, as in English, the word "seed" can be either plural or singular. Because of the singular pronouns ("he" and "his") in this verse, the primary reference seems to be to a coming individual who will be born to the woman. This future seed of the woman will enter combat with the serpent's seed and be wounded in his "heel," a superficial wound. But he will give the serpent a fatal blow to his head! In other words, the seed of the woman will be the Serpent Crusher. He will win a final and decisive battle over evil ensuring that goodness, justice, and peace will ultimately prevail.

Readers of Genesis immediately want to know: who is this coming Serpent Crusher? When will he appear? And where? What will he be like? How will we recognize him? And what will the conflict be like when he and the serpent finally fight? As the book of Genesis unfolds, one begins to look in every chapter for hints and clues about who this Serpent Crusher is and when he will appear. One wonders, is it Seth? Enoch? Noah? Shem? Abraham? Ishmael or Isaac? Jacob or Esau? And which of Jacob's twelve sons is the most likely candidate? The book of Genesis closes with the promise of God still unfulfilled. We must wait and keep watching. He's not here yet. But he's coming!

QUESTIONS FOR DISCUSSION

1. Why is it important for Christians, who believe in Jesus as we meet him in the New Testament, to study the book of Genesis?
2. What is the significance of the title of this book, *East of Eden: Finding Our Way Home*?
3. The author summarizes the message of Genesis in four questions:
    a. What do you do when things are formless, empty, and meaningless?
    b. Can the shattered image of God be restored?
    c. How can we discern the difference between good and evil?
    d. Who is the seed of the woman?

    Which of these questions is important for you? Why?

1
Designer Universe
Genesis 1:1–2:3

An often-repeated story of unknown origin tells of a woman who claimed that the world was flat and rested on the back of an elephant. A friend asked her, "And what is the elephant standing on?" Pausing only for a moment, the woman responded, "On a giant turtle." But again, her friend had another question: "And what is the turtle standing on?" Flustered, the woman shot back, "It's turtles all the way down!"

The story is a humorous way to introduce a very serious question: Where does it all begin? "Turtles all the way down" presents us with the conundrum of infinite regress. How far back can we go? Is there a starting point? If there was a Big Bang or a primordial soup, what came before that? Both from a scientific and a philosophical point of view, the question of origins is profoundly difficult. Not only is the question challenging but the answer we choose to believe has implications that touch nearly every area of human life and thought.

Like the opening chords of a great symphony, the first words of the Bible state majestically the Judeo-Christian understanding of ultimate origins: "In the beginning, God . . . ." You simply cannot go further back than that! If someone insists on asking where God comes from, it simply proves that they don't understand the absoluteness of the one we worship. He is the uncaused cause, the uncreated Creator, the absolute Absolute. As stated by the psalmist, "from everlasting to everlasting you are God" (Ps 90:2).

When compared with other creation stories of antiquity, Genesis 1–3 is utterly unique. Rather than a multiplicity of deities working with preexistent materials in obedience to some impersonal force through the instrumentality of sexuality, the opening chapters of Genesis introduce us to a single, omnipotent, personal God who speaks creation into being out of nothing. Perhaps most startling of all, the Genesis record is anchored in time and space and told not as myth but as a fact of history. Nothing like this exists anywhere else in the world.

Non-biblical Accounts of Creation	Genesis 1–2
Myth—time and space are unimportant	History—time and space are very important
Polytheistic—many gods	Monotheistic—one God
Creation out of pre-existent matter	Creation out of nothing—*ex nihilo*
History is cyclical	History is linear
The gods are immoral and selfish	God is holy and loving
The gods submit to fate, an impersonal force	God is absolutely sovereign
Boundaries are blurry	Boundaries are sharp and well-defined
The gods are part of nature	God is wholly "other"—transcendent

Our worldview and basic philosophy of life is determined by how we answer the question, "where does it all begin?" This means that those who shape a culture's understanding of origins are the *de facto* priests of that culture. Our future will be determined by how we understand our past. Origin determines destiny. This is why the Genesis story of creation is so important. It lays the foundation for everything!

Many today say they believe that science alone can answer the question of origins. They assume that faith is irrelevant and that God is nothing more than a convenient hypothesis for the uneducated. They see a conflict between Genesis 1–2 and science. However, such an approach reveals both a misunderstanding of the meaning and role of science and a naivete about faith.

Science is primarily concerned with the questions *How?* and *When?* Genesis is primarily concerned with the questions *Who?* and *Why?* The Bible, in general, and Genesis 1–3, in particular, should not be read as a scientific textbook.

> But that does not mean [the Bible] will have nothing to say which touches the realm of science. The fact that the primary purpose of Genesis is not to instruct us in geology does not exclude the possibility that it says something of relevance to the subject. In the last analysis one cannot make an absolute separation between physics and metaphysics, and religion has to do with everything, precisely because all realms are created by God and continue to depend on him . . . . Faith rests on facts.[1]

John Lennox gives a helpful illustration to show both the purpose and the limits of science. He imagines his Aunt Matilda baking a cake that is taken to a group of the world's top scientists for analysis. They determine the ingredients of the cake and how they relate together. But then Lennox imagines asking them, "But *why* was it made?"

> The grin on Matilda's face shows she knows the answer, for she made the cake, and she made it for a purpose. But all the nutrition scientists, biochemists, chemists, physicists, and mathematicians in the world will not be able to answer the question—and it is no insult to their disciplines to state their incapacity to answer it. Their disciplines, which can cope with questions about the nature and structure of the cake, that is, answering the "how" questions, cannot answer the "why" questions connected with the purpose for which the cake was made. In fact, the only way we shall ever get an answer is if Aunt Matilda reveals it to us. . . . To say with Bertrand Russell that, because science cannot tell us why Aunt Matilda made the cake, we cannot know why she made it, is patently false. All we have to do is ask her.[2]

When it comes to the issue of origins, the real conflict is not between science and religion but rather between two opposite worldviews: naturalism and theism. *Naturalism* claims there is nothing but nature. It is a closed system of cause and effect. There is

---

1 Blocher, *In the Beginning*, 24.
2 Lennox, *God's Undertaker*, 41.

nothing "outside" this universe, no transcendent reality. Carl Sagan famously articulated this philosophy when he said, "The cosmos is all there is, or was, or ever shall be." *Theism*, on the other hand, is an open system because it believes our universe has been created by a Supreme Being. It is summarized in the opening words of Genesis, "In the beginning, God created the heavens and the earth."

It is important to recognize that both Genesis 1:1 as well as the creed of Carl Sagan are statements of faith, not of science. Neither can be proven, only affirmed as a basic assumption. The key issue therefore is *not* some supposed conflict between science and religion but rather the freely made choice of which worldview will inform our scientific exploration.

Examining the Text

The most obvious characteristic of Genesis 1:1–2:3 is its seven-day structure. Regardless of how one interprets the meaning of the word "day," the author beautifully shows how creation was the work of the universe's first week. When all was "formless and void," God began to shape what was shapeless and to fill what was empty. It was this act of forming and filling that constituted God's original work. The symmetry is almost poetic in its beauty:

- On Day One he formed the light; on Day Four he filled it with the sun, moon, and stars.
- On Day Two he formed the heavens and the waters; on Day Five he filled them with birds and fish.
- On Day Three he formed the earth; on Day Six he filled it with creatures and finally with humankind.

The author seems to be motivated almost as much by literary style as he is by chronological order. This does not mean that the passage is therefore non-historical. Rather, it means that we should not press this beautifully crafted text into some sort of scientific textbook.

Several phrases repeated through the passage enhance both its beauty and its message. "And God said" is repeated eleven different times. Unlike the cosmologies of other cultures, God does not make the world out of some pre-existent stuff. Genesis does not support the notion so common in mythological depictions of creation, that matter is eternal. The Bible explains that God majestically spoke matter into being. Out of nothing (*ex nihilo*) he made the universe by his powerful word. "Let there be . . ." and it was! "By the word of the Lord the heavens were made, and by the breath of his mouth all their host. . . . For he spoke, and it came to be; he commanded, and it stood firm" (Ps 33:6, 9).

The text also emphasizes the fact that God gives things their names:

- "And God called the light Day, and the darkness he called Night" (Gen 1: 5).
- "And God called the expanse Heaven" (Gen 1:8).
- "God called the dry land Earth and the waters that were gathered together he called Seas" (Gen 1:10).

In God's created order it is very important that things be called by their proper names. To mislabel something can cause catastrophic harm. We will see in the next chapter how God gave this power of naming things to humans. In fact, to give something its proper name is part of the divine image that resides in men and women. God brought the animals to the man "to see what he would call them. And whatever the man called every living creature, that was its name" (Gen 2:19). It was this authority to give things their proper names that showed man's dominion over the created order.

In a building crescendo of exuberance, God pronounces everything he has made to be good, good, good, and *very* good (Gen 1:4, 10, 12, 18, 21, 25, 31). The text goes to great lengths to make sure the reader understands that God is *not* the author of evil.

Other repeated phrases that help to elucidate the meaning of creation are the terms "and God separated" (Gen 1:4, 6, 7, 14, 18) and "according to their kind" (Gen 1:11, 12, 21, 24, 25). Here we learn of God's intention to keep things in their proper categories. The book of Genesis will give graphic illustration to the damage that occurs when boundaries are blurred between heaven and earth, the divine and the human, animals and man, male and female, and good and evil.

THE *WHO* AND THE *WHAT*

In terms of developing a Christian worldview, it would be difficult to find a more important chapter in the Bible than Genesis 1. Here the foundation is laid for human thought and behavior. As John C. Lennox says in his book, *Seven Days that Divide the World*:

> [The first chapter of Genesis] does something of incalculable importance: it lays down the basis of a biblical worldview. It gives to us humans a metanarrative, a big story into which our lives can be fitted and from which they can derive meaning, purpose, and value.[3]

Though many today examine the opening chapters of Genesis trying to determine the age of the earth (when) and the mechanism by which creation occurred (how), the text seems content to emphasize the who and the what. In the next chapter, we will discover that the real meaning of the creation story is found only when we know the *why*.

Though Genesis 1 certainly does not offer an exhaustive theological definition of God, it does give a surprising amount of information about the deity who created the universe. Who is God? This passage of Scripture gives us our most basic understanding of the uncaused Cause, the ultimate Ultimate, the absolute Absolute, the One who stands behind and before everything.

God is. The Bible does not try to prove God's existence because it assumes that his existence is, at least to some degree, self-evident. "The fool says in his heart there is no God" (Ps 14:1). Every worldview has a starting point. For the atheist, the beginning point is matter, the cosmos. The Bible boldly insists that this material universe is not the ultimate reality, God is. God comes first; then, the cosmos. It is hard to improve on the argument proposed by William Paley over two centuries ago. Describing a hypothetical man walking through the woods and finding a watch lying on the ground, Paley imagines him asking himself, "How did this watch get here? Could it have created itself? Is this the result of chance?" Paley's conclusion is simple yet

---

3 Lennox, *Seven Days*, 91.

profound: If there is a watch, then there must be a watchmaker. If there is a creation, then there must be a Creator.

> *For what can be known about God is plain to them, because God has shown it to them. For his invisible attributes, namely, his eternal power and divine nature, have been clearly perceived, ever since the creation of the world, in the things that have been made. So they are without excuse. (Rom 1:19–20)*

God is eternal. Though we recognize the absurdity of saying, "It's *turtles* all the way down," the Bible encourages us to believe that it's *God* all the way down. You can't go further back than that! To say "God" is to say, "*This* is where it all begins." There is nothing behind God or under him or before him. He is Ground Zero, the uncaused Cause of everything else.

God is omnipotent. Mythological accounts of creation from other cultures of the ancient world typically describe the gods as living under the tyrannical power of some impersonal force, or fate. These gods live in a universe where their lives and actions are limited by a cosmic reality they cannot control. Though having a measure of power, these deities are not sovereign; they can only submit to their predetermined fate. The *Star Wars* saga depicts a similar worldview where an impersonal "Force" or Power, composed of both a good side and a dark side, lies behind and under everything. "May the Force be with you." Not so the God of Genesis. He is sovereign, ruler over all. He has no equal or competition. "But our God is in the heavens; he does whatever he pleases" (Ps 115:3 NASB). "Is anything too hard for the Lord?" (Gen 18:14).

God is transcendent. Other worldviews teach that God is so identified with the world that the two are inseparable, even identical. While others may worship the sun, the stars, or the earth, the Bible invites us to worship their creator! God created the universe, but the universe is neither identical to God nor some sort of emanation from God. He is distinct from what he has made. If the universe suddenly disappeared, God would remain unchanged. And yet Genesis does not suggest that God is remote, a distant deity who started the universe and then went away, leaving the world to run on its own. God is both distinct from the created order and yet very present in it.

God is one. Genesis does not speak of multiple deities but of one, and only one, creator God. "I am the Lord, and there is no other, besides me there is no God" (Isa 45:5). This makes the Bible unique among all the creation stories of the ancient world. "Hear, O Israel, the Lord our God, the Lord is one!" (Deut 6:4).

Yet God is a plurality of oneness. Though God is one, the text of Genesis hints at a plurality in the unity. There are indications that God's unity may be more nuanced than we first imagined, though it falls short of a full-blown doctrine of the Trinity. For one thing, God's Spirit hovers over the waters (Gen 1:2). Does this mean that God *has* a Spirit or that God *is* a Spirit? For another thing, God creates the universe with his word. Is his word distinct from his being or part of his being? Centuries later the Gospel of John will declare, "The Word was with God, and the Word was God" (John 1:1). And finally, we have this intriguing use of the plural pronouns: "Let *us* make man in *our* image" (Gen 1:26). Regardless of how scholars try to explain it, these plural pronouns surely hint at a reality in God that invites us to contemplate the majestic mystery of his being. One would be hard-pressed to find an ancient text more strongly monotheistic than Genesis 1, and yet here on the first page of the Bible, we are introduced to a God who is a plurality of oneness.

God is personal. The fact that God speaks, evaluates what he has made as "good," confers his blessing on parts of creation, and, above all, creates man in his own image, indicates that God is far more than cosmic energy or an impersonal force. Though it would be wrong to call God a human, it is not erroneous to call him a Person. When God interacts with the man and the woman he has created, we see the personal nature of God even more clearly.

God is the source of light. According to Genesis, the sequence of the days of creation begins with, "And God said, 'Let there be light'" (Gen 1:3). Not only is this initial creational act important for the origin of the cosmos but also it speaks to a universal human need for a divine act of enlightenment so that men and women can see clearly and make wise choices. In the New Testament, Paul draws an analogy between the creation of light at the beginning of time and the divine enlightenment that is necessary in human experience: "For God, who said, 'Let light shine out of darkness,' has shone in our hearts to give the light of the knowledge of the glory of God in the face of Jesus Christ" (2 Cor 4:6).

> Paul uses creation as a metaphor for what happens to a person at conversion.... The light that God shines into the human heart that trusts him is not physical, of course, but it is real.... The gospel effects an actual spiritual transformation, as Paul goes on to say in the very next chapter, again using the language of creation: "If anyone is in Christ, he is a new creation. The old has passed away; behold, the new has come" (2 Cor 5:17). It is for this reason that we can have confidence in the Christian message—it brings real illumination, authenticating itself in human experience. It also authenticates itself intellectually, as C. S. Lewis pointed out: "I believe in Christianity as I believe that the sun has risen: not only because I see it, but because by it I see everything else."... The sad irony of the Enlightenment is that it puts the light inside man by making human reason the ultimate arbiter.... We need light from outside.[4]

Not only does Genesis introduce us to the creator, it wants us also to be alert to the basic facts about the creation. For those raised with a Judeo-Christian worldview, these facts may seem self-evident. However, for those unfamiliar with the biblical understanding of reality, these truths are astounding. Their implications are revolutionary.

Nature is real. Some eastern philosophies teach that this universe is an illusion. We are only dreaming. Atheism claims that nature is the only ultimate reality. The cosmos is all there is, ever was, or ever will be. The biblical view of the universe brings great clarity of thought when it teaches that nature is real but not ultimate.

Nature is comprehensible. The universe is not the result of random forces. It is no cosmic accident. Time plus chance cannot account for the world we inhabit. No, nature is orderly and structured because it is the product of a rational God. It is governed by laws that

---

4   Ibid., 102–103, 108, 110.

bring stability and predictability to the world (gravity, seasons, etc.). Albert Einstein said, "The most incomprehensible thing about the universe is that it is comprehensible."[5] Our universe is intelligible. Nature *invites us* to study it. This explains, at least in part, why science arose first in the Western world, where the Judeo-Christian worldview was predominant. It took a worldview rooted in Genesis to make the leap from astrology to astronomy, from alchemy to chemistry. The universe can be and should be studied because it is a uni-verse and not a multi-verse. A single and sovereign creator God put it all together. This means that the same laws that govern the earth, govern the stars.

Nature is good. Though the coming of sin into the world brought catastrophic changes (death, thorns and thistles, pain in childbirth, etc.), the first thing the Bible wants us to know about the world God has made is that it is good, *very* good. God wants us to enjoy it. While other religions have often taught that matter is evil and that we should therefore devote ourselves to that which is spiritual, the Bible boldly affirms the goodness of material existence and invites us to delight in the physical realities all around us. "For everything created by God is good, and nothing is to be rejected if it is received with thanksgiving, for it is made holy by the word of God and prayer" (1 Tim 4:4–5).

Nature reflects the glory of God. Other religions teach that the heavens are god. The Bible says something infinitely more profound: they reflect his glory. Don't worship the stars; worship the One who made them! Whether we use a telescope to look at distant galaxies or a microscope to look at tiny cells, we see God's glory in all that he has made.

> *The heavens declare the glory of God,*
> *and the sky above proclaims his handiwork.*
> *Day to day pours out speech,*
> *and night to night reveals knowledge.*
> *There is no speech, nor are there words,*
> *whose voice is not heard.*
> *Their voice goes out through all the earth,*
> *and their words to the end of the world. (Ps 19:1–4)*

---

5   Quoted in Lennox, *God's Undertaker*, 59.

The earth is specially designed as a home for humans. It's simply amazing how conditions on our planet seem to perfectly match the conditions necessary for optimum human function. The temperature, the tilt of the earth on its axis, the distance from the sun, the speed of the earth's rotation, the amount of water, the food supply, etc. Even the position of our planet in the Milky Way and the clarity of our atmosphere gives us the best possible perspective for gazing into the heavens. It almost seems that the earth was designed just for us!

THEN SINGS MY SOUL

The reason the creation story is included in the Bible is not primarily to turn us into scientists, historians, or even theologians. The primary purpose of this amazing text is to invite us to slow down, look up, and worship. Surrounded by buildings and deafened by noise, many of us are too busy to gaze in wonder at the majestic beauty of God's creation and to hear the call to worship. The old gospel song written originally by Carl Boberg, made famous by George Beverly Shea, and sung at many Billy Graham crusades around the world states the issue well:

> *O Lord, my God, when I in awesome wonder*
> *Consider all the worlds Thy hand hath made.*
> *I see the stars, I hear the rolling thunder,*
> *Thy power throughout the universe displayed.*
> *Then sings my soul, my Savior God, to Thee:*
> *How great Thou art, how great Thou art!*

But many other poets and song writers have helped Christians throughout the ages respond to God's creation in awe and adoration:

> *All creatures of our God and King,*
> *Lift up your voice and with us sing,*
> *Alleluia, alleluia.*
> *Thou burning sun with golden beam,*
> *Thou silver moon with softer gleam,*
> *O praise him, O praise him;*
> *Alleluia, alleluia, alleluia. (Francis of Assisi)*

> *I sing the mighty power of God,*
> *That made the mountains rise;*

> *That spread the flowing seas abroad,*
> *And built the lofty skies.*
> *I sing the wisdom that ordained*
> *The sun to rule the day;*
> *The moon shines full at his command,*
> *And all the stars obey. (Isaac Watts)*

> *This is my Father's world,*
> *The birds their carols raise,*
> *The morning light, the lily white,*
> *Declare their Maker's praise.*
> *This is my Father's world;*
> *He shines in all that's fair.*
> *In the rustling grass I hear him pass,*
> *He speaks to me everywhere. (Maltbie Babcock)*

> *Earth's crammed with heaven,*
> *And every common bush afire with God,*
> *But only he who sees takes off his shoes:*
> *The rest sit round and pluck blackberries.*
> *(Elizabeth Barrett Browning)*

God speaks to us through the grandeur and wonder of creation, but only if we pause to look and listen. The message we receive both reveals God's glory and calls us to worship.

QUESTIONS FOR DISCUSSION

1. Why is it so important to have a right understanding of our origins?
2. What did this lesson teach you about God?
3. What did this lesson teach you about nature?
4. Has this study caused you to think differently about the role of science?
5. When you look and listen to the "voice" of nature, what message does it give? What message does it *not* give?

2
The Way Things Ought to Be
Genesis 2:4–25

The purpose of this chapter is to create in you, dear reader, a feeling of discontentment. Yes, I write hoping to make you unhappy! This has nothing to do with your family, job, health, or finances. No, my intention goes much, much deeper than that. It is to make you aware of a longing, deep inside, a yearning for something that is not there, an absence, a void. Please understand that I am not the one creating this ache! I'm simply making you aware of its presence. You know what I'm talking about; it's the longing you feel when you can't sleep or when you take long walks contemplating the meaning of life. The pain may be triggered by a photograph, a melody, an aroma, or perhaps by something you read—this chapter perhaps. But suddenly, it's there! Though you can't quite describe what it is, the lump in your throat, the tear in your eye, and the ache in your soul remind you that something is not quite right; things are not what they ought to be.

I know of no one who has written more poignantly about this inner ache than C. S. Lewis. In his essay *The Weight of Glory*, Lewis confesses he feels almost like he is committing an indecency to even mention the subject.

> I am trying to rip open the inconsolable secret in each one of you—the secret which hurts so much that you take your revenge on it by calling it names like Nostalgia and Romanticism and Adolescence; the secret also which pierces

with such sweetness that when, in very intimate conversation, the mention of it becomes imminent, we grow awkward and affect to laugh at ourselves; the secret we cannot hide and cannot tell, though we desire to do both. We cannot tell it because it is a desire for something that has never actually appeared in our experience. We cannot hide it because our experience is constantly suggesting it, and we betray ourselves like lovers at the mention of a name. Our commonest expedient is to call it beauty and behave as if that had settled the matter. Wordsworth's expedient was to identify it with certain moments in his own past. But all this is a cheat. If Wordsworth had gone back to those moments in the past, he would not have found the thing itself, but only the reminder of it; what he remembered would turn out to be itself a remembering. The books or the music in which we thought the beauty was located will betray us if we trust to them; it was not *in* them, it only came *through* them, and what came through them was longing. These things—the beauty, the memory of our own past—are good images of what we really desire; but if they are mistaken for the thing itself, they turn into dumb idols, breaking the hearts of their worshippers. For they are not the thing itself; they are only the scent of a flower we have not found, the echo of a tune we have not heard, news from a country we have never yet visited.[1]

Perhaps the best term to describe this inner longing is the word *homesick*. Deep within, we all know it's true: we're not home yet. Even when life is at its best, the inner ache reminds us of our dislocation. We are made for something bigger, better, more lasting, and more perfect than anything we have yet experienced. The author of Ecclesiastes succinctly sums it up by saying that God "has put eternity into man's heart" (Eccl 3:11). This means that nothing in this present world system has the capacity to ultimately satisfy our desires. We are made for eternity; we are made for God.

The second and third chapters of Genesis explain why this is true: paradise has been lost. In the beginning, God created an ideal home for the man and woman he had made. Here they were able to thrive in an environment that was perfectly suited to who they were and what they were made to do. But when sin came, they were expelled from

---

1   Lewis, *The Weight of Glory and Other Addresses*, 28–29.

Paradise. They and their children were forced to live "east of Eden" (Gen 4:16), longing for home but unable to get there. Therefore, the preeminent characteristic of the human condition is perhaps best understood as homesickness. Whether our lives are marked by joy or sorrow, by blessings or curses, by happiness or pain, by abundance or poverty, the ache for home just won't go away. Blaise Pascal called this "wretchedness" and taught that it was the most basic characteristic of the human condition.

> Solomon and Job have known and spoken best about man's wretchedness, one the happiest, the other the unhappiest of men; one knowing by experience the vanity of pleasure, and the other the reality of afflictions.[2]

This chapter aims to explore our original home, the Garden of Eden. Even though you may be unconscious of what you've lost, Genesis 2 can awaken the longing deep within and explain why it just won't go away: you are homesick. So, yes, I sincerely hope that this chapter will make you unhappy! If the ache for Eden is suppressed, then we are truly lost! Malcolm Muggeridge states the issue well:

> The only ultimate disaster that can befall us, I have come to realize, is to feel ourselves to be at home here on earth. As long as we are aliens, we cannot forget our true homeland, which is that other kingdom that Jesus Christ proclaimed.[3]

Genesis 2:4–25 describes the most significant events that occurred on the sixth day of creation, especially those involving the formation of the first human couple. Though some want to see a contradiction between this account and Genesis 1, it is better to see it as complementary. Genesis 2 completes the picture. Here we learn how the Lord formed the first man and placed him in a beautiful garden, where there was only one restriction: a command not to eat of a certain tree. The passage closes with a description of how God created the first woman to provide a corresponding partner for the man.

---

2   Pascal, *Pensées*, 118.
3   Muggeridge, *Jesus Rediscovered*, 47–48.

Though the first man and woman are presented as specific historical figures, their story is meant to be seen as part of everyone's story. Adam (Hebrew, man) and Eve (Hebrew, sounds like the word for life-giver) help us to better understand our own history. The text addresses the most foundational questions of human existence. These are questions of supreme importance not only for the first couple, but also for you and for me.

Who Am I?

It is simply impossible to draw conclusions about our identity without knowing some basic facts about our origin. To answer the question "Who am I?" we must know something about from where and from whom we came. The Genesis account is succinct, yet revolutionary. In the first chapter we learned that human persons are made "in the image of God" (Gen 1:26–27). We are not gods, but we do reflect the image of the One who made us. We are not animals; no animal was created to bear God's image. We are not machines, automatons, or robots. We are not preprogrammed to conform to some predetermined, unchangeable plan. We are human persons. As such, our worth is based not so much in what we do or how we perform. Our value is derived from who we are! Whether young or old, rich or poor, handicapped or whole, mentally deficient or smart, our worth is grounded in the reality of the image we bear. This truth lies at the heart of our culture's traditional belief in the sanctity of human life.

In a day where there is great confusion and debate about gender, it is important to recognize that humans come in two, and only two, varieties: male and female. And this gender distinction is part of God's image! "So God created man in his own image, in the image of God he created him: male and female he created them" (Gen 1:27). The only distinction that Genesis allows us to make among persons, therefore, is not one based on ethnicity, economics, education, or politics, but on gender. And there are only two options: male and female. Just as we do not choose whether to be born, who our parents are, or what our name will be, so we do not get to choose whether we are born male or female. This piece of our identity is assigned to us.

In the second chapter of Genesis, we learn more about man's identity: "then the Lord God formed the man of dust from the ground and breathed into his nostrils the breath of life, and the man became a living creature" (Gen 2:7). Made from dust and animated by God's Spirit, humans are so very like things of earth, and yet at the same time, so very like things of heaven. One could almost call man a hybrid; of mixed origin. Perhaps it would be more appropriate to call him an amphibian. Having a body and a soul, he can operate in two environments: earth and heaven. The fact that we are composed of dirt keeps us humble. The fact that God's breath makes us live gives us dignity. Pascal eloquently expressed this dual reality in man in these words:

> It is dangerous to explain too clearly to man how like he is to the animals without pointing out his greatness. It is also dangerous to make too much of his greatness without his vileness. It is still more dangerous to leave him in ignorance of both, but it is most valuable to represent both to him.[4]

Another indication of the man's identity is found in the single prohibition given to him. He was free to eat from every tree in the garden, "but of the tree of the knowledge of good and evil you shall not eat, for in the day that you eat of it you shall surely die" (Gen 2:17). No other animal was given a command like this! "What is forbidden to man is the power to decide for himself what is in his best interests and what is not. This is a decision God has not delegated to the earthling."[5]

The knowledge of good and evil is part of the image of God in man. God's design is that, in the process of abstaining from eating the forbidden fruit, Adam and Eve gain the ability to discern right from wrong. Later we will see that the serpent makes just the opposite argument: eat the fruit, disobey God's law, experience evil, and *then* you will know good from evil (see Gen 3:1–5). As we will see in the next

---

4   Pascal, *Pensées*, #121, 60.
5   Hamilton, *Genesis*, 1:166.

chapter, Adam and Eve lose the ability to rightly discern good from evil when they take the serpent's suggestion and eat the forbidden fruit.

> You understand sleep when you are awake, not while you are sleeping.... You can understand the nature of drunkenness when you are sober, not when you are drunk. Good people know about both good and evil: bad people do not know about either.[6]

The tree of the knowledge of good and evil is placed in the garden to give man the opportunity to choose. It isn't forbidden because it is evil; it is evil because it is forbidden! Man is a free moral agent who, unlike the animals, will be held accountable for his actions. When a lion kills a gazelle, it is not immoral. But when Cain kills Abel, it is murder. This lone tree in the garden with its single prohibition is all that is necessary to reveal and refine the moral character of man. Adam is no robot; he is a free moral agent. God wants Adam's love, not some scripted, preprogrammed performance. A dog may not be able to act in an "undoggy" manner; but men and women have the freedom to behave in inhuman ways!

Where Do I Belong?

Not only is the Creator intent on helping the man and the woman understand their true identity, he is equally insistent that they recognize and enjoy their true home. The Hebrew word "Eden" indicates a place of delight, pleasure, or bliss—paradise. It is no mystical habitat in some imaginary land (Shangri-La, Nirvana, Utopia[7]). Eden is a real place, watered by four rivers, two of which (the Tigris and the Euphrates), are well known (Gen 2:10–14). Some scholars think the Gihon refers to the Nile. The Pishon, however, remains unknown. Regardless of how one understands these ancient rivers, the global flood that occurred in the days of Noah likely altered the landscape to such a degree that these original rivers became unrecognizable.

---
6   Lewis, *Mere Christianity*. 93.
7   Thomas More (1478–1535) invented the word *utopia* to describe an idealized, imaginary island with a perfect society. His readers, however, will fail to understand his message unless they realize that the word *utopia* literally means *no-place*. It doesn't exist.

Eden is a perfect home for the man and the woman that God has created. It is a place of safety, abundance, and enjoyment. When they are expelled and forbidden re-entry, they and their descendants are forced to live "east of Eden," in the land of Nod (Hebrew, wandering) (see Gen 3:24; 4:16). The human condition, thus, can perhaps be best defined by homesickness. When God calls Abraham and establishes his covenant with him and his descendants, part of the promise he makes is to lead him to a new place, a new home (see Gen 12:1–3). Until the fulfillment of that promise, Abraham and his family are to live as pilgrims, travelers, sojourners.

> *By faith Abraham obeyed when he was called to go out to a place that he was to receive as an inheritance. And he went out, not knowing where he was going. By faith he went to live in the land of promise, as in a foreign land, living in tents with Isaac and Jacob, heirs with him of the same promise. For he was looking forward to the city that has foundations, whose designer and builder is God. (Heb 11:8–10)*

Why Am I Here?

Knowing *who* we are and *where* our home is prepares us for the next great truth revealed in the creation story concerning us: what is our *purpose*? Why are we here? The first chapter of Genesis orients us to two great purposes God has for men and women: to be fruitful and to have dominion over the earth.

> *And God said to them, "Be fruitful and multiply and fill the earth and subdue it, and have dominion over the fish of the sea and over the birds of the heavens and over every living thing that moves on the earth." And God said, "Behold, I have given you every plant yielding seed that is on the face of all the earth, and every tree with seed in its fruit. You shall have them for food. And to every beast of the earth and to every bird of the heavens and to everything that creeps on the earth, everything that has the breath of life, I have given every green plant for food." (Gen 1:28–30)*

The command to be fruitful is an invitation to be a co-laborer with God in the work of creation. The ability to procreate enables us to share in the joy and wonder of bringing into existence that which does not exist. This is the first commandment in history, inviting us to grow not just by addition but by multiplication and to spread out to the very ends of the earth. The parallels between God's first commandment and Jesus' last commandment (see Matt 28:18–20) call for prayerful meditation and discussion.

The second part of God's original command (to subdue the earth and to have dominion over it) sounds harsh to contemporary ears. Many today imagine that such terms carry the connotation of exploitation and abuse of planet earth. This is unfortunate and far from what God was commanding. Adam's mission was not to mistreat the earth and its resources but rather to care for it as a good steward. "The earth is the Lord's and the fullness thereof" (Ps 24:1). According to Genesis, the people of God should be the most ecologically sensitive people in the world. We know that, one day, we will be called to give an account for what we have done with God's creation.

In the second chapter of Genesis, man's purpose becomes even more clear. The Scripture tells us that God put the man in the garden "to work it and keep it" (Gen 2:15). Those who picture the Garden of Eden with a hammock and a glass of iced lemonade, where no one ever lifts a finger to work, simply have not read their Bibles! Work is part of the image of God. God works! In fact, God is a creative, imaginative genius and labors hard in the work he produces. Whether in creation or redemption, God is a master craftsman! And he loves his work. It brings him great joy and fulfillment.

Later in Scripture we will learn that the first person described as being filled with the Spirit of God is not a prophet, priest, or king. He is an artisan (an architect, an interior designer) named Bezalel. His gifts and talents are used not to preach a sermon but to create works of art.

> *The* LORD *said to Moses, "See, I have called by name Bezalel the son of Uri, son of Hur, of the tribe of Judah, and I have filled him with the Spirit of God, with ability and intelligence, with knowledge and all craftsmanship, to devise artistic designs, to work in gold, silver, and bronze, in cutting stones for setting, and in carving wood, to work in every craft. (Exod 31:1–5)*

Part of what it means to be created in the image of God is to work like God works. Adam works in the Garden of Eden and we can imagine that his joy is great in what he accomplishes. Not only does he take care of the vegetation, he names the animals (Gen 2:19–20). This is not some playful game. No, this explains the rise of science! Taxonomy is that branch of science concerned with classification; putting things in their proper category. In his excellent book on Genesis, Leon Kass comments:

> When God brings the animals to the man to see what he would call them, human reason is summoned to activity, to its primordial activity, naming. Indeed, here the man acts for the first time: the prototypical or defining human act is an act of speech, naming. . . . For the ability to name rests on the rational capacity for recognizing otherness and sameness, for separating and combining. . . . The names he gives them—say, "camel" rather than "porcupine"—may be arbitrary, but the distinctions between the creatures that the names recognize and celebrate are not. . . . Human naming, while it does not create the world, creates a linguistic world, a second world, of names, that (partially and interestedly) mirrors the first world, of creatures. As the text indicates, human beings not only practice speech, they create it. Names are the first human inventions.[8]

To be sure, when sin enters the world, human work will be negatively impacted. In the next chapter we will learn how the presence of sin and the expulsion from Eden mean that work is now tragically transformed into "toil" and "sweat," and the fruitful garden is replaced by "thorns and thistles" (see Gen 3:17–19). Man's relationship to his purpose in life has been dramatically altered.

Who Are My People?

A final question that helps us to better understand why the world today is not what it ought to be is the question of community: Who are my people? Where is my tribe? Life will never be what we know deep inside it ought to be until we find where we fit in, not just in terms of a homeland but of a people. Although the Bible will have a lot to

---

8   Kass, *The Beginning of Wisdom*, 74–76.

say about this question as Scripture unfolds, Genesis answers it in the most basic sort of way by introducing us to the concept of family.

Genesis 2:18 surprises us by introducing what sounds to be a discordant note in the creation narrative. "Then the Lord God said, 'It is not good that the man should be alone." Not good? Repeatedly the creation story has underscored the goodness of the created order by saying, "It was good, good, good, very good." How can there be something *not* good in a sinless, perfect paradise? And besides, what is *not* good about solitude, being alone? Adam has God! Isn't God enough?

Apparently, God is not enough. To say those words sounds not only irrational but heretical! If Adam has God and lives in paradise, what can possibly be missing? What's not good about Adam's condition?

I'm so glad you asked!

If we have followed closely the message of these two incredible chapters that introduce the biblical story, we will quickly comprehend that there are two things that are not good about Adam being alone—two things that will be forever impossible if he remains a solitary individual.

First, alone Adam will be unable to reflect the image of the triune God who made him. As we saw in the last chapter, God is one yet three. He is a community of Persons. He is a unity of plurality and a plurality of unity. And *this* is the God who creates humans in his image. Remember the plural pronouns? "Let *us* make man in *our* image" (Gen 1:26). If God had said, "Let *me* make man in *my* image" then perhaps Adam, alone, might have been able to reflect the image of the monistic being who had created him. But no. For Adam to adequately reflect the image of his Creator, he is going to need to be more than one. By himself, alone, he simply can't do it.

Second, alone Adam will never be able to obey the first commandment. "Be fruitful and multiply and fill the earth" (Gen 1:28). Fat chance that commandment is going to be obeyed if Adam remains alone. To be fruitful, to multiply, to reproduce and expand over the earth, demands a marriage partner. When the two become one then the one becomes three . . . and four, five, six, etc. Biblical math is interesting! Neither the first commandment (Be fruitful) nor Jesus' last commandment (Make disciples of all nations) can be fulfilled alone. Relational intimacy makes reproduction possible.

Genesis is underscoring the fact that we are made for relationships. Life was never intended to be lived solo. So God decides to "make a helper fit" for Adam (Gen 2:18). It is obvious that none of the animals fill this role, so God causes a deep sleep to fall upon the man, and while he sleeps, God takes one of Adam's ribs and makes it into a woman and brings her to him (see Gen 2:21–22). When he sees what God has created, Adam suddenly becomes a poet! He has never seen anything so beautiful or so marvelously crafted.

> *This at last is bone of my bones*
> *and flesh of my flesh;*
> *she shall be called Woman,*
> *because she was taken out of Man. (Gen 2:23)*

While perhaps taking poetic license with the facts, Matthew Henry nevertheless captures the truth about this pinnacle moment of the creation week when he says that Eve was made, not out of Adam's

> head to rule over him, nor out of his feet to be trampled upon by him, but out of his side to be equal with him, under his arm to be protected, and near his heart to be loved.[9]

Lest someone think the word *helper* denotes a servant or slave, it is important to note that the Old Testament sometimes uses the term in a military context to refer to God himself (cf. Deut 33:7; Ps 33:20; 124:8; etc.). God creates a helper for Adam because Adam needs help!

To say that Eve is "fit for" Adam means that she corresponds to him. This relates to much more than biological and anatomical correspondence. It denotes the fact that she is equal, yet different. Similar to the triunity found in the Godhead, marriage is, by definition, a union of difference. This means that marriage will be challenging,

---

9 Quoted in Henri Blocher, *In the Beginning,* 99–100.

and at the same time fruitful. Fertility comes out of the difference. Joy comes out of the union. Tim Keller describes what this means.

> When you get married, . . . you always marry somebody who's going to be butting heads with you. . . . Marriage is not designed to bring you so much into confrontation with your spouse; it's actually designed to bring you into confrontation with yourself . . . to show you ways to change that otherwise you never would find.[10]

Human history begins with a wedding. And human history will end with a wedding. In the Garden of Eden, there is no government, not even a church. God shows us his original design for community by beginning human history with a family. The creation story introduces us to the first wedding and the prototype for all future marriages. One man, one woman, in a covenant of love, for life. The two become one. Then one becomes three. Spouses don't lose their identity when they get married; they create a new identity, one that is intimate, fertile, and reflects the image of God.

QUESTIONS FOR DISCUSSION

1. Describe your own image of *home*. What makes you most homesick?
2. The issue of "identity theft" is of great concern today. While this typically refers to financial risk, is it possible that many today suffer from "stolen identity" at a spiritual level? Discuss this.
3. We've all heard the expression "To err is human." After studying Genesis 1–2, do you agree? Would it be more appropriate to say, "To err is inhuman"?
4. The New Testament introduces Jesus as the Second Adam. How is Jesus like Adam? How is he different?
5. Which part of paradise lost speaks most poignantly to you: lost identity? lost home? lost purpose? lost community?
6. What does Genesis 1–2 teach us about marriage and family? Why is this so important today?

---

10 Tim Keller, sermon preached January 4, 2009.

3
There's a Snake in the Garden!
Genesis 3:1–6

Walking in the door of his home after a day at work, a man was greeted by his wife with the words; "Honey, we have a problem with the car." "What kind of problem?" he asked. "I think there's water on the carburetor," she replied. Astounded at his wife's sudden proficiency in auto mechanics, the husband said; "Dear, you don't know the difference between a muffler and a steering wheel. How can you be so sure what the problem is with our car? By the way, where is the car?" "In the swimming pool," she said.

The problem is worse than you think.

Everyone agrees that things on planet earth are not what they ought to be. Whether we are talking about tsunamis, hurricanes, earthquakes, birth defects, pandemics, wars, racism, poverty, abuse, theft, human trafficking, or flat tires, the data is overwhelming: "Houston, we have a problem." While there is widespread agreement that something is wrong, there is broad disagreement on what that something is. But until the problem is accurately diagnosed, the solutions proposed will be inadequate at best, and toxic at worst.

Before a physician can prescribe a plan for wellness, she must first have a clear understanding of those realities in the life of the patient that are hindering health and causing the body to function poorly. Perhaps the environment is toxic. Maybe the patient needs to exercise or change diet. Perhaps there is disease in the body. Wellness comes only when the causes of unwellness are clearly discerned and a viable plan for health is put into place.

In Genesis 3 we have God's authoritative diagnosis concerning what's wrong on planet earth. It would simply be impossible to overemphasize the importance of this chapter. It gives us the basic information we need to both discern why our lives are not what they ought to be and at the same time points us in the right direction to find a cure. The first six verses introduce us to what's wrong. But be forewarned: the problem is worse than you think!

Theologians typically refer to the event described in these verses as "The Fall." However, the metaphor may not be the most suited to describe what is happening. To "fall" tends to imply an unintentional stumble. "Oops! I didn't see that obstacle in my path." The reality depicted in Genesis 3 is hardly a clumsy blunder. What we have is a willful, premeditated, volitional choice to disobey a clear command of God. Perhaps a more appropriate term to describe the event would be "The Rebellion." Emil Brunner captured this understanding of the human condition in the title to his influential book *Man in Revolt* (1937). C. S. Lewis states the matter succinctly when he says: "Fallen man is not simply an imperfect creature who needs improvement: he is a rebel who must lay down his arms."[1]

With divine wisdom and literary artistry of the highest order, the author describes one of the most important events in human history in just six short verses. For over three millennia this short paragraph has been analyzed and studied by the brightest minds of the ages seeking to interpret its meaning.

> *Now the serpent was more crafty than any other beast of the field that the* LORD *God had made. He said to the woman, "Did God actually say, 'You shall not eat of any tree in the garden'?" And the woman said to the serpent, "We may eat of the fruit of the trees in the garden, but God said, 'You shall not eat of the fruit of the tree that is in the midst of the garden, neither shall you touch it, lest you die.'" But the serpent said*

---

1   Lewis, *Mere Christianity*, 56.

> *to the woman, "You will not surely die. For God knows that when you eat of it your eyes will be opened, and you will be like God, knowing good and evil." So when the woman saw that the tree was good for food, and that it was a delight to the eyes, and that the tree was to be desired to make one wise, she took of its fruit and ate, and she also gave some to her husband who was with her, and he ate. (Gen 3:1–6)*

Theologically, the paragraph is brilliant. The author describes the origin of sin without making God sin's author. *Psychologically*, the text is astute. Though innocent and pure, the text shows the steps in the process that made possible the first couple's choice to disobey the God they loved. *Spiritually*, these verses are simply profound. With this foundation for understanding sin's origin, we are now prepared for the rest of the story that will reveal the tragic consequences that follow (Gen 3:7–24).

The Tempter

Classical theology teaches that there are only three possible origins for evil: the world, the flesh and the devil. Because Adam and Eve are innocent and pure, we know that the original source of evil is not in them. And because the Garden of Eden is the perfection of goodness, we know that the origin of evil can't be there. If sin cannot find its origin in the flesh of Adam or in the world of the Garden, it must therefore have its ultimate source in the devil. And this is precisely what Genesis 3 teaches.

But who is this serpent? What is his history? And how did he get in the Garden? The text does not answer these questions. While this may leave some readers frustrated, the Bible apparently intends to bypass the philosophical abstractions and go straight to the pragmatic reality of the human condition. The snake is suddenly *there*! We are left guessing as to who he is, where he came from, how long he has been there, and who let him in the garden!

Though theologians and scholars may wish for more information, the Bible coaches us to not be overly worked up about the origin of evil and the role of the serpent. God knows how such questions can inflame human imagination and capture our attention. Scripture is written in a way to ensure that our focus is on God, not the devil, and that we remain grounded in the things we know, not the things we don't. We do not have to be able to explain evil to be victorious over it!

> *The secret things belong to the* LORD *our God, but the things that are revealed belong to us and to our children forever, that we may do all the words of this law. (Deut 29:29)*

We can perhaps better understand the Bible's reticence to talk about Satan and the origin of sin by recognizing how evil, once introduced, seems to usurp center stage. Notice, for example, how villains often become the "hero" in many popular stories and why many people prefer R–rated movies to those shown on the Hallmark channel. A classic illustration is how in Milton's *Paradise Lost,* Satan is typically seen as the most interesting literary character. The Bible is supremely wise in teaching us that the best way to be victorious in our fight against evil is to keep our focus fixed on the good.

However, the Bible does give important hints concerning the origin of the snake. In fact, there is enough information given in Scripture to enable us to formulate a general understanding of evil's ultimate origin. And as for those questions that remain unanswered, Scripture helps us to at least understand why we don't understand!

Though we won't take the time to examine them here, several texts in both the Old and the New Testaments give important information about Satan's history. Apparently, before the events of Genesis 3 occurred, there was a "war in heaven" (see Rev 12:7–12). What might be called a rogue angel led a rebellion against God. He was defeated and cast out of heaven along with perhaps one-third of the angelic beings who followed him. This wicked creature (Satan, the Devil, the Dragon, the Serpent) came to earth with the objective of deceiving the whole world and tempting others to follow his example and rebel against God (see Isa 14:12–15; Ezek 28:12–17; 2 Pet 2:4; Jude 6).

In one sense, this "explanation" of the origin of evil raises as many questions as it answers. But in a far more important sense, it gives a very logical and coherent rationale for the serpent's presence in the Garden of Eden. Most importantly, this Scriptural background enables us to see beyond the historical circumstances of the original sin, to its deeper, theological meaning—a meaning that has important implications for us today.

1. *God is infinite and good.* There is only one God and he is all-powerful and all-good. And yet, this one God is *not* the author of evil. Evil finds its ultimate origin in the devil; and then later in history, its derivative origin in the flesh and in the world.
2. *Satan is finite and evil.* The serpent is crafty and strong, but his power is limited. He is no god! He is a created being. Rebellious? Yes! But there is no hint of dualism in the Bible. If the serpent is in the garden, it is only because God has permitted him to be there.
3. *Evil is a parasite and a perversion of the good.* There is no such thing as "absolute evil." Only goodness is absolute. Philosophically, this has huge implications for understanding right and wrong, good and evil, justice and wickedness.

THE TEMPTER'S STRATEGY

In telling the story of how sin came into the world, the Bible is doing more than recounting history. It is showing us with crystal clarity how our adversary operates and what are his tactics. In warfare, few things are more important than knowing our enemy's strategy and objectives. In this sense, Genesis 3 is invaluable in preparing us for battle. Speaking of Satan to New Testament believers, Paul says, "we are not ignorant of his designs" (2 Cor 2:11). A close examination of this passage allows us to describe the serpent's action as a three-fold strategy.

First, the serpent seeks to cause the couple to *doubt God's word.* "Did God actually say?" (Gen 3:1). The question drips with diabolical craftiness and is formulated in a manner to engender doubt. This is clearly not an honest question. It is not a question that seeks the truth.

> Rather it intends to *call into question*—authority, opinion, law. It seeks to make simple obedience impossible, in this case by challenging the goodness of the commander. The serpent's question implies that God is a being who is, or might

be, not only arbitrary but also hostile to human beings. . . . Says the serpent, "Is it really true that God has denied you all sustenance?" The serpent's question is a perfect example of mischievous speech.[2]

Temptation starts here! As long as Adam and Eve are firm in their desire to walk in the ways of God and please him in all they do, they are safe from sin's seduction. For sin to take root in their lives, they must first have second thoughts about what they think they heard God say. This is precisely the serpent's purpose: to cause them to be suspicious and confused concerning God's word. One marvels at the nefarious genius of the serpent's tactic. To doubt God's word means that the doubter, at some level, is considering the possibility that he just might be wiser than God.

It is interesting to note that Eve, in her conversation with the serpent, misquotes God's commandment. The prohibition stated simply that they were not to eat the forbidden fruit. However, Eve adds to what God had said: we must not even *touch* it (see Gen 2:17; 3:3). Remember that Eve was not present when God gave the original command to Adam. Therefore, she would have learned of the prohibition only through her husband. Any error she may have had in understanding God's will may, therefore, be due to Adam's spin on what God had said. Some see in the additional prohibition against touching the tree a form of "incipient legalism."[3]

Doubting God's word takes many forms but at its heart is a willful hesitancy to do God's will and a preference to rely on one's own perception of the truth. Lee Strobel offers a wonderful illustration to help us better understand the dynamics involved in doubting the Father's word. He pretends that his daughter, Alison, and her boyfriend are going out on a date one evening. Before walking out the door, he gives her clear instructions: "You must be home before eleven." It sounds straightforward. What's hard to interpret about

---

2   Kass, *The Beginning of Wisdom*, 82.
3   Blocher, *In the Beginning*, 145.

that? He then imagines the couple sitting in a restaurant at 10:45 having the following conversation:

> They say, "What did he really mean when he said, '*You* must be home before eleven'? Did he literally mean us, or was he talking about *you* in a general sense, like people in general? Was he saying, in effect, 'As a general rule, people must be home before eleven'? Or was he just making the observation that, 'Generally, people are in their homes before eleven'? I mean, he wasn't very clear, was he?
>
> And what did he mean by, 'You *must* be home before eleven'? Would a loving father be so adamant and inflexible? He probably means it as a suggestion. I know he loves me, so isn't it implicit that he wants me to have a good time? And if I am having fun, then he wouldn't want me to end the evening so soon.
>
> And what did he mean by, 'You must be *home* before eleven'? He didn't specify *whose* home. It could be anybody's home. Maybe he meant it figuratively. Remember the old saying, 'Home is where the heart is'? My heart is here at the restaurant, so doesn't that mean I'm already home?
>
> And what did he really mean when he said, 'You must be home before *eleven*'? Did he mean that in an exact, literal sense? Besides, he never specified 11:00 PM or 11:00 AM. And he wasn't really clear on whether he was talking about Central Standard Time or Pacific Time. I mean, it's still only a quarter to seven in Honolulu. And as a matter of fact, when you think about it, it's *always* before eleven. Whatever time it is, it's always before the next eleven. So with all these ambiguities, we can't really be sure what he meant at all. If he can't make himself clear, we certainly can't be held responsible.[4]

Doubting God's word is not just a matter of intellectual comprehension of the words that were said. More importantly, it is a matter of the heart. Inner motivation has a huge influence on how we interpret words.

Second, Satan's strategy is to cause the couple to *question God's love*. The serpent insinuates that God prohibited them from eating of the tree because he didn't want them to be like himself (Gen 3:5). In other words, God must have had sinister motives in denying them

---

4   Strobel, *Inside the Mind of Unchurched Harry and Mary*, 115–116.

this right to eat. This means that he doesn't have their best interests at heart and therefore he can't be trusted. He is jealous, selfish, and oppressive. This raises real questions about his goodness in general, and his love in particular.

The point the serpent is seeking to make with Eve is that God can't be trusted because he doesn't really love you. And if God is not watching out for your best interests, who will? You better take matters into your own hands and take charge of your life. Don't passively follow someone else's script; write your own! Become autonomous and decide for yourself what is right and wrong.

Autonomy is viewed by many today as a positive virtue. However, an examination of the word's derivation will shed light on what is really at stake. Composed of the words *auto* (self) and *nomos* (law), to be autonomous is literally to be a law unto yourself. Such persons rely on no outside standards of behavior but look only within themselves for guidance. They do what is right in their own eyes, deciding for themselves what is right and what is wrong. In short, they become their own god. A community composed of people like this is on the road to moral chaos and societal anarchy.

Though it is difficult, if not impossible, to indicate with pinpoint accuracy at what precise moment sin entered Eve's heart, it was perhaps the moment when she concluded that doing *good* (obeying God) was actually a *bad* thing. This made it possible for her to take the next step and conclude that doing *evil* (eating the forbidden fruit) would be a *good* thing. Charles Williams put it in these terms: "The first sin was to know good as evil." Eating of the tree of the knowledge of good and evil had caused the couple to become confused about which was which. When good is seen to be evil and evil is seen to be good, then darkness comes in like a flood and men and women are truly spiritually lost.

> *The eye is the lamp of the body. So, if your eye is healthy, your whole body will be full of light, but if your eye is bad, your whole body will be full of darkness. If then the light in you is darkness, how great is the darkness! (Matt 6:22–23)*

Third, the serpent causes the couple to *deny God's truth*. Emboldened by the way the conversation is going, the serpent blatantly says, "You will not surely die" (Gen 3:4). Moving from subtle innuendos, Satan becomes blunt: "God is a liar. You won't suffer negative consequences when you disobey his will for your life. It's just a piece of fruit. This isn't murder, theft or adultery. No one is going to be hurt by this." Leon Kass summarizes the serpent's strategy in these words: "In one short speech, the serpent manages both to impugn God's veracity and His motives and to provide the inducement for disobeying Him."[5] Satan is a master at minimizing the dangers and maximizing the imagined benefits of sin. Little wonder that Jesus said of the devil that he is "a liar and the father of lies" (John 8:44).

Sin's Allure

We do well to pause and consider that the original sin came through food. The serpent understands that temptation makes its greatest appeal through our appetites. When desire becomes fixated on forbidden fruit, all the ingredients are present for a disaster to happen. This explains why food is one of the great themes in the biblical story. It was an appetite for the milk and honey of Canaan that was intended to propel God's people forward on their journey to spiritual wholeness. But when the desire for the leeks and onions of Egypt became stronger, the nation of Israel wandered aimlessly in the desert for forty years. Manna was given to both nourish the body and cleanse the palate, so that the people's appetites were trained to desire the wholesome nourishment that comes from God.

Jesus came testifying that he was the bread of life. "Unless you eat the flesh of the Son of Man and drink his blood, you have no life in you. . . . For my flesh is true food, and my blood is true drink" (John 6:53, 55). And in his final meal with his disciples, he established a simple ritual that has been the normative act of worship for the Christian Church for two thousand years. "For as often as you eat

---

5   Kass, *The Beginning of Wisdom*, 85.

this bread and drink the cup, you proclaim the Lord's death until he comes" (1 Cor 11:26).

Yes, the Bible is a food-driven book. Ever since the Garden of Eden, human destinies have been determined by whether one's appetite is fixed on the Bread of Heaven or on some forbidden fruit. James K. A. Smith emphasizes that discipleship is more a matter of hungering and thirsting than of knowing and believing.

> We are all familiar, of course, with the truism "You are what you eat." But over the past generation we have learned more and more about the nature of our hungers and how incredibly malleable they are. . . . Our hungers are *learned*. Of course, *that* we get hungry—that we need to eat—is a structural feature of human biology. But the "direction" our hunger takes—what we hunger *for*—is, in important ways, learned. So it's not just that you are what you eat; you are what you *want* to eat, and this is something that is learned.[6]

The Genesis account emphasizes the lush, beautiful, alluring appeal of the fruit they were forbidden to eat. Was it an apple? Perhaps a peach, a pear, a mango? The text does not say; it only describes its seductive attraction: it was "good for food," a "delight to the eyes," and "desired to make one wise" (Gen 3:6). In other words, the fruit was sensually satisfying, aesthetically pleasing, and intellectually stimulating. The apostle John was undoubtedly thinking of this original three-fold description of temptation when he warned early Christians about the dangers of worldliness. "For everything in the world—the lust of the flesh, the lust of the eyes, and the pride of life—comes not from the Father but from the world." (1 John 2:16 NIV).

THE SILENCE OF ADAM

As we move from inward motivation to outward behavior, the precise moment of sin's entry into the world seems to be described in these words: "She took of its fruit and ate, and she gave some to her husband who was with her, and he ate" (Gen 3:6). Note especially the verbs *took* and *ate*. Is it possible that Jesus had these verbs in mind when he instituted the sacrament of Holy Communion by saying,

---

6   Smith, *You Are What You Love*, 58–59.

"*Take, eat*; this is my body" (Matt 26:26). We understand the Gospel correctly when we realize that Jesus came to undo the damage that sin had done.

Because Eve is typically depicted as the primary actor in the original sin, many want to know: but what about Adam? What role did *he* play in sin's coming into the world? He was clearly at Eve's side during the entire conversation with the snake (see Gen 3:6). Present, but passive. Standing beside her, but silent.

Many theologians and preachers have noted how Paul emphasized that "Adam was not deceived, but the woman was deceived and became a transgressor" (1 Tim 2:14). However, we must not forget that Paul also underscores Adam's full culpability when he says, "sin came into the world through one man" (Rom 5:12). The biblical data is clear that Adam and Eve are accomplices in the tragic events in the Garden of Eden; they share in the guilt. And yet, gender distinction seems indeed to play a subtle but important role. Henri Blocher goes so far as to postulate a reversal of the created order. "The woman takes the initiative, contrary to the indications of Genesis 2. . . . But the man shares the responsibility for this reversal since he consented to it."[7]

If one feels inclined to try to determine whether the woman or the man bears the greater blame, I personally feel we should focus attention on the head of the house: Adam. While the word *blame* may be more appropriate for Eve, Adam is clearly "responsible." The Bible is clear in teaching that "the head of every man is Christ" and "the head of a wife is her husband" (1 Cor 11:3). This means that Adam must bear the responsibility for all that occurs in his home. In Eden, we see that his guilt in the first sin comes not so much from what he did but from what he failed to do! His silence and passivity are damnable.

This tragic failure of leadership on the husband's part is a theme that recurs often in the book of Genesis. It seems the Bible wants us to understand that this dysfunctional passivity in men is a tendency that manifests itself often in marriage. In a desperate move to have a child, Sarah pressures Abraham to sleep with the slave woman Hagar

---

7   Blocher, *In the Beginning*, 143.

and he passively complies (Gen 16:2). Lot acquiesces to the demands of his daughters when they cause him to be drunk and then sleep with him so that they can have children (Gen 19:32). Rebekah carries out an audacious act of deception on her husband and her son Jacob agrees to go along with her plan (Gen 27:13). Psychologist Larry Crabb writes insightfully about this age-old tendency in men to silence and passivity:

> Adam, then, was a silent man, a passive man. Like many men in history, he was physically present but emotionally absent. He fades into the background of the story, rather than standing front and center on the stage. . . . His sin began with his silence. He was designed to speak but he said nothing. He listened to the serpent, he listened to his wife, he accepted the fruit, and then he ate. Adam was passive three times before he ate the forbidden fruit. . . . God's speaking brought creation out of chaos; Adam's silence brought chaos back.[8]

Dangerous Freedom

Some may be tempted to blame God for all our troubles because he created the possibility for disobedience. But this would be grossly unfair. God warned Adam concerning the tragic consequences that would come if he disobeyed the commandment. The fault lies squarely with the man and the woman. But once again we discover that the story of what happened to Adam and Eve is much more than ancient history. It serves as a mirror to enable us to see the truth about ourselves.

Suppose God had created robots, rather than humans. Would this have been preferable? What if God had programmed humans so that they were immune to temptation and always chose the right? Would that have made for a better world? No one speaks to this question better than C. S. Lewis:

> If a thing is free to be good it is also free to be bad. And free will is what has made evil possible. Why, then, did God give them free will? Because free will, though it makes evil possible, is also the only thing that makes possible any love or goodness or joy worth having. A world of automata—of creatures that

---

8   Crabb, *The Silence of Adam*, 91.

worked like machines—would hardly be worth creating. The happiness which God designs for his higher creatures is the happiness of being freely, voluntarily united to him and to each other in an ecstasy of love and delight. . . . Of course God knew what would happen if they used their freedom the wrong way: apparently, he thought it worth the risk.[9]

QUESTIONS FOR DISCUSSION

1. Have you ever wished God had created you as a robot? Discuss this.
2. Describe a situation you have known when sin came in because someone doubted God's Word.
3. Why do you think Satan began his work with Eve? Was she somehow more vulnerable than the man?
4. Talk about Adam's silence and passivity; physically present but emotionally absent. Can you describe a time in your life when "the silence of Adam" brought chaos into a situation?
5. Name the most important lesson God taught you from this material and talk about how you intend to apply it in your life.

---

9   Lewis, *Mere Christianity*, 48.

Take and Eat
Stan Key

"Take and eat," the Tempter said, and pointing to the tree,
There hung a luscious piece of fruit, so beautiful to see.
Suspended there so daintily, between the earth and sky,
Its color and allurement stopped my steps as I passed by.

"Forbidden fruit tastes wonderful and it will make you wise,
It proves that you're the one in charge and opens wide your eyes.
You cannot trust this God of yours, he's holding out on you;
Are you convinced his love is real and that his word is true?"

And so I took and ate the food he offered me that day,
And fell into a life of sin and self-absorbed decay.
I lived my life cut off from God and from the tree of life,
And wandered in an alien land of wickedness and strife.

O God, my appetites are such, I fear sin's strong attraction
Will cause me to drift far from you in search of satisfaction.
If only there were stronger food to counteract the yearning,
That gnaws within me constantly and keeps my passions burning.

"Take and eat," the Savior said, and pointing to the tree,
I saw a sight that gripped my heart; transfixed, I stopped to see.
Suspended there so tortuously between the earth and sky,
The Lamb of God was dying in my place: I wondered, "Why?"

"My body is the food you crave, my blood will quench your thirst;
Your hungers will be satisfied when this meal you seek first.
The food is good, the meal is free, so come as you are able;
You'll find that sin has lost its power as you come to the table."

4
The Emperor's New Clothes
Genesis 3:7–13

Hans Christian Andersen tells an amusing story about two dishonest weavers and a vain emperor. The weavers offer to make the emperor an expensive suit of clothes that they claim is visible only to those who are wise, worthy, and culturally sophisticated. For those who are undignified and stupid, the magnificent clothes will be invisible; they will see nothing at all. Immediately hooked, the vain emperor places his order for a new set of clothes. The weavers, of course, make no clothes at all; they only pretend to do the work. When the emperor and his court are "shown" the new clothes, they all with one accord, not wishing to appear unsophisticated in the eyes of their peers, marvel at their colorful texture and exquisite beauty.

Finally, with much fanfare and publicity, the emperor parades through the town before all his subjects in his new suit of "clothes." Though he is clearly naked as a jay bird, no one dares to say so, lest they should appear to be stupid. "Oh, isn't the emperor lovely in his marvelous clothes," they all shout together. But one small child, near the end of the procession, blurts out for all to hear; "But he isn't wearing anything at all!" Though the emperor as well as the crowd realize that the child's statement is true, no one stops the procession, and the charade continues uninterrupted.

Genesis 3:7 tells us that the very first consequence of Adam and Eve's sinful act is the awful realization that they are naked, exposed. Suddenly ashamed of their nudity, the couple begins looking for ways to cover their shame. But who can weave garments that will be able to hide the ugly reality of what they have done? Will fig leaves be sufficient to cover what needs covering? Or will they spend the rest of their lives exposed, pretending to be something they aren't?

In the previous chapter, we learned about the root cause that explains why things are not what they ought to be: sin. The problem is far deeper than an error of judgment or an unfortunate mistake. The original sin was a willful transgression of a known law. We saw how sin is rebellion against God, treason. It is self-assertive autonomy. *My* will be done! Genesis 3:1–6 laid the foundation for understanding what's wrong in the world, in our relationships, and in our own hearts. Now the author of Genesis introduces us to the *consequences* that come when such treacherous wickedness occurs.

A good doctor, in treating an illness, labors to distinguish between the *cause* of a disease (say, infection) and the *symptoms* (say, a fever) and to establish a plan for addressing both. Aspirin may be an important treatment tool for lowering the fever and alleviating the patient's immediate pain and discomfort. But the doctor knows that to reestablish health over the long term, the deeper problem of infection must be addressed. Thus, he may prescribe a round of antibiotics. Health care means more than easing pain by treating symptoms. The real objective is to destroy the infectious disease so that the dangerous symptoms go away, and full health can be restored.

Using a medical model to remind us of the distinction between a disease's cause and its symptoms is a helpful way to understand what the inspired author is doing in the third chapter of Genesis. The first six verses set forth the root cause of what's wrong in the world: sin, rebellion, willful disobedience, self-assertion. This is the soul disease that lies at the foundation of all human dysfunction. But the author wants to give a fuller understanding of the problem by showing not only the root cause but also its nefarious symptoms. He does this in the remainder of the chapter. Just because a fever is *only a symptom* and not the root cause doesn't mean it is something that can be dismissed as unimportant. A high fever can kill a person just as an infection can! The consequences of sin are potentially just as hazardous to our spiritual health as is the root cause.

The remainder of Genesis 3 sets forth the symptoms, or consequences, of sin. In verses 7–13, we are introduced to the *personal and psychological consequences* of sin. We will examine these verses in this chapter. Genesis 3:14–24 directs our attention to the *cosmic and theological consequences* of sin. We will examine these verses in the next chapter.

The Wages of Sin

> *Then the eyes of both were opened, and they knew that they were naked. And they sewed fig leaves together and made themselves loincloths.*
>
> *And they heard the sound of the* Lord *God walking in the garden in the cool of the day, and the man and his wife hid themselves from the presence of the* Lord *God among the trees of the garden. But the* Lord *God called to the man and said to him, "Where are you?" And he said, "I heard the sound of you in the garden, and I was afraid, because I was naked, and I hid myself." He said, "Who told you that you were naked? Have you eaten of the tree of which I commanded you not to eat?" The man said, "The woman whom you gave to be with me, she gave me fruit of the tree, and I ate." Then the* Lord *God said to the woman, "What is this that you have done?" The woman said, "The serpent deceived me, and I ate." (Gen 3:7–13)*

God had warned the couple that if they ate the forbidden fruit, they would die that very day (Gen 2:17). This did not happen, however, at least not in a physical, biological sense. In the Bible, death does not mean so much the cessation of existence as it means to be cut off from the land of the living, to be deprived of life. These verses show how the penalty of death was indeed fulfilled in multiple ways at a spiritual, psychological, and interpersonal level in a succession of disastrous consequences. Physical death also came to both Adam and Eve, but many years later. Genesis makes clear the truth of Paul's statement that "the wages of sin is death" (Rom 6:23). We see the death-working consequences of sin in at least four different areas.

Shame

> *Then the eyes of both were opened, and they knew that they were naked. (Gen 3:7)*

Prior to their sin, Adam and Eve were "naked and not ashamed" (Gen 2:25). Living in moral innocence, they had nothing to hide; either from one another or from God. The absence of shame seems to indicate that the man and woman were not yet self-conscious. In their sinless purity, their orientation was entirely outward, toward the other. Like small children running naked on a public beach, Adam and Eve were blissfully unaware of what sort of image they were projecting. Their lack of shame in being naked was not because their bodies were perfectly shaped and proportioned but rather because their hearts were pure and holy. They lived and loved in joyful self-forgetfulness.

However, the coming of sin changed everything. Suddenly, the man and the woman are painfully aware of their naked, exposed condition. Their disobedience makes them self-conscious. They feel vulnerable, embarrassed, humiliated. For the first time, the man thinks, "It's all about me" and the woman asks, "How do I look?"

Sin makes us blush, and while this is yet another indication of our fallen condition, it is a very good thing! Showing embarrassment when we sin is a sign that our souls are still relatively healthy. We recognize that we have done something wrong. The real problem lies with those who feel no shame for their sinful choices, those who literally act shamelessly. Losing the capacity to blush is a sign that divine judgment may be near. The prophet Jeremiah speaks of such a condition, warning the sinners of his day that they are rapidly approaching the point of no return.

> *"Were they ashamed when they committed abomination?*
> *No, they were not at all ashamed;*

> *They did not know how to blush.*
> *Therefore, they shall fall among those who fall;*
> *At the time that I punish them, they shall be overthrown,"*
> *says the* LORD. *(Jer 6:15)*

Shame is primarily a social reality. It has a huge impact on the way we relate to one another. Not only am I painfully self-conscious of *my* own wickedness, but I can see *your* nakedness as well! Our relationship has taken on the spirit of competition and comparison. Jealousy and rivalry now characterize our interactions. Because I now know that you too are a self-absorbed rebel, I realize that you can't be trusted. This makes you a threat to the kingdom where I have declared myself to be sovereign.

It is highly instructive to notice Adam and Eve's initial reflex when they first experience shame: "they sewed fig leaves together and made themselves loincloths" (Gen 3:7). Leon Kass observes that "the fig leaf, or rather the needle, is the first human invention."[1] It is indeed ironic that man's first efforts in technology are invested in an endeavor aimed at both hiding his own guilt and enhancing his image. There is something comical about trying to cover oneself with leaves sewn together. It takes only a little imagination to realize that this simply doesn't get the job done. If our shame is to be removed, there must be some other way.

GUILT

> *The man and his wife hid themselves from the presence of the* LORD *God. (Gen 3:8)*

Adam and Eve have broken God's law and now they wonder how he will respond. Will he rebuke them? Punish them? Kill them? Expel them from the garden? Whereas before, they had eagerly anticipated moments when they could walk with God in the cool of the day, now the thought of his presence fills them with dread. As shame's primary orientation is horizontal (toward one another), guilt's orientation is primarily vertical (toward God). Their consciences have been

---

1 Kass, *The Beginning of Wisdom*, 90.

awakened and the couple is painfully aware of their culpability. They have willfully and intentionally violated God's instructions and now their guilt is overwhelming; they feel condemned.

Just as the fig leaves were ineffective in concealing their shame, so the trees of the garden are ineffective in hiding from God. Notice that they are seeking to use God's gifts (trees) as a buffer, a shield to protect them from his holy presence. Such efforts are, of course, futile. Trying to hide from the One who is omniscient and omnipresent is not only pointless, it is almost comical.

Through the ages, the children of Adam and Eve have been both creative and industrious in the methods they have employed to try to hide from God. The most sophisticated endeavors have involved using the blessings of God as a shield to protect us from him. Nowhere does this effort take on a more sinister aspect than in worship. Rather than seeing public worship as a means to draw near to God, many use the occasion to actually hide from his penetrating gaze. Whether such a reality is conscious or not, the outcome is the same.

When Jesus cleansed the Temple in Jerusalem, he accused those in attendance of having made it "a den of robbers" (Mark 11:17), a hiding place. Jesus wanted to make it clear that prostitutes, thieves, and murderers are not the only ones trying to hide from God. Sometimes people in church going through the motions of worship are doing the same thing; they are using the words, the prayers, and the songs of worship as a means of running from the truth. Such self-deception, however, will not work. Adam and Eve may run, but they cannot hide from the Holy One. Their sinful past cannot remain hidden forever. Making fig leaves and hiding behind trees will not work for long. The day will come when they must step out of the shadows and face the truth.

Just as shame is a proper and healthy response to sin, so is guilt. A strong, active conscience is a gift from God and those who have one should be very grateful. Like the red light on the dashboard of your car telling you to "Check Engine," so a guilty conscience prompts you to seek help from God in dealing with your sin—now! Stop the car and let

God help you fix what's broken before you face a much bigger problem down the road.

Authentic worship is intended to make us feel worse before making us feel better. This is why the great historic liturgies have always placed confession of sin *before* the promise of forgiveness. God knows that unless our consciences are pricked so that they feel the sting of guilt, we will have little motivation to seek God's grace. *The Book of Common Prayer* gives us a classic illustration. The *Prayer of Confession* makes me squirm as I recite words that remind me of things I'd prefer not to think about in any other setting. Praying these words *causes* me to feel guilty! But that, of course, is just the point. Until we recognize our sin, the gospel of grace will have no practical relevance in our hearts and lives.

> Almighty God, Father of our Lord Jesus Christ, maker of all things, judge of all men: we acknowledge and bewail our manifold sins and wickedness, which we, from time to time, most grievously have committed, by thought, word, and deed, against thy divine majesty, provoking most justly thy wrath and indignation against us. We do earnestly repent and are heartily sorry for these our misdoings; the remembrance of them is grievous unto us; the burden of them is intolerable. Have mercy on us, have mercy on us, most merciful Father.[2]

Fear

> *I heard the sound of you in the garden, and I was afraid. (Gen 3:9)*

Prior to their sin, Adam and Eve delighted in spending time with God. Like Enoch (Gen 5:22–24), Noah (Gen 6:9) and Abraham (Gen 17:1), walking daily with the Holy One seemed to be standard operating procedure. But now, because of unconfessed sin in their lives, they are terrified at the thought of God's presence. How will he respond? What will he do? Because of their evil deeds, the anticipation of God's arrival causes them to scurry like roaches in the basement when the lights are suddenly turned on.

---

2 BCP, 331.

> *And this is the judgment: the light has come into the world, and people loved the darkness rather than the light because their works were evil. For everyone who does wicked things hates the light and does not come to the light, lest his works should be exposed. But whoever does what is true comes to the light, so that it may be clearly seen that his works have been carried out in God. (John 3:19–21)*

Sin is more than breaking a law; it is breaking a relationship. When Adam and Eve ate the forbidden fruit, they betrayed a trust, and this threatened a rupture that would separate friends. As adultery violates the marriage relationship, so sin causes separation from God. One of the words the Bible uses to describe this relational dynamic between a holy God and sinful man is enmity; a condition of hostility now exists where before there had been harmonious peace. Thus, we see that a third consequence of sin is fear. Their disobedience causes Adam and Eve to be afraid of God.

It is important to remember that when the Bible speaks of our attitude toward God, it describes two very different types of fear. One fear is healthy and good; a kind of respect and awe for our Creator and Sovereign King. This kind of fear is indeed "the beginning of wisdom" (Prov 9:10), and we should embrace it and cultivate its healthy expression.

However, the inner terror that suddenly consumes Adam and Eve is fear of another order. They are feeling the pervasive dread that characterizes those who have become aware of their guilt and shame. It is a fear directed primarily at God and manifests itself in a paralysis that affects both one's inner emotions and outward actions. Genesis 3 is suggesting that all human fears have at their root God as their ultimate object. The phobias and anxieties that characterize our lives are ultimately caused by the fact that we are not rightly related to God. We are hiding from the one who created us and loves us, living in dread of what he might do if we dared to come out into the open. Such inner angst causes many to prefer to remain in the shadows where they feel a measure of "safety."

The Lord's simple, searching question—"Where are you?"— is far more than an inquiry into the couple's bodily location. God, of course, knows where they are. His question, rather, is a gracious invitation to come out into the open, to face the truth about what they have done. Indeed, his question is a plea for them to come to him, so that he can not only expose their sin but, more importantly, cover it and ultimately heal it. Victor Hamilton points out that God uses a question rather than a command because he seeks to draw man out of his hiding place rather than drive him out by force.

> He is the good shepherd who seeks the lost sheep. Such a context calls for a display of tenderness rather than toughness. Had God asked "Why are you hiding?" instead of "Where are you?", his question would have drawn attention to the silliness, stupidity, and futility of the couple's attempt to hide from him.[3]

BLAME

> "Have you eaten of the tree of which I commanded you not to eat?" The man said, "The woman whom you gave to be with me, she gave me fruit of the tree, and I ate." Then the LORD God said to the woman, "What is this that you have done?" The woman said, "The serpent deceived me, and I ate." (Gen 3:11–13)

The Genesis account is astounding in the dept of its psychological insight into human nature. God's question is straightforward: "Have you eaten the forbidden fruit?" But rather than responding with a simple yes, Adam becomes defensive and devious. Here we see that one of the effects of sin is denying that we are sinners, making excuses for what we have done. The Bible is teaching us that sin becomes truly damnable when we deny its presence.

When God asks Adam to give an account for what happened, he blames his wife. In so doing, he is actually accusing God who gave her to him. This is amazing! "Through rationalization the criminal becomes the victim, and it is God and the woman who emerge as the

---

3   Hamilton, *Genesis*, 1:193.

real instigators in this scenario."⁴ When God calls the woman to give an account of her actions, she takes a similar strategy to that of her husband. She blames the serpent. In these deceptive responses, we have history's first recorded account of passing the buck, an attempt to avoid taking responsibility for something by shifting the blame to someone else.

We live in a culture where "the blame game" is a national sport. Rather than teaching our children to take responsibility for their choices, we seem to have raised a generation that finds a wide range of creative ways to say, "It's not my fault." Blame my genes, my environment, my parents, my finances, my teachers, my troubled childhood, my racial history, etc., but certainly don't hold *me* accountable. I'm just an unfortunate victim.

An often-told illustration of this culture of victimization occurred years ago in a murder trial in San Francisco. The defense claimed that the perpetrator's violence was, at least in part, caused by too much sugar (he loved Twinkies). Called the "Twinkie Defense," the case became famous in illustrating the absurdity of some attempts to avoid taking responsibility for our actions.

God, however, does not let Adam and Eve off the hook. He holds them fully responsible for their actions. Part of what it means to be created in the image of God is that humans are not captive to their hormones or controlled by their environment. Though mitigating circumstances may need to be considered, men and women will be held ultimately accountable for their actions. This, in fact, is what it means to be a human person.

FIG LEAVES

Like the emperor's new clothes, Adam and Eve's fig leaves only make them look foolish. The leaves simply don't cover what needs covering. And yet such foolishness continues today whenever we try to hide the shameful truth about ourselves. Think of the "fig leaves" we often sew together in a vain attempt to deal with our guilt and shame.

---

4   Ibid., 1:194.

- *Denial.* "Sin? What sin? That behavior may have been considered sinful in a previous age, but not today. I didn't do anything wrong."
- *Justification.* "I had very good reasons for doing what I did. It would have been wrong for me *not* to do what I did. But I doubt you would understand."
- *Rationalization.* "My actions were not perfect but if you knew the full circumstances, you would understand. The pressure was so great, and the issues were so fuzzy, well, if you had been in my place, you would have done the same thing."
- *Blame.* "Actually, it wasn't my fault at all. If my boss had only been clearer about her expectations for my job, this never would have happened."

Such silly efforts are futile. They only aggravate the situation. Worst of all, when we try to defend ourselves and justify our behaviors, we remain stuck in our sinful condition. We continue to hide from the truth by lurking in the shadows of reality. Like the emperor in the fairy tale, we live in an imaginary world of make-believe, pretending that all is fine when the truth is that we are naked as a jay bird.

Just as God came to the guilty couple in Eden asking questions, gently coaxing them to come out of the shadows and face the truth, so he still comes today. The Lord asks questions not because he needs information. He knows what we've done. He knows the truth about who we really are. He asks questions in the hopes that we will step into the light of his holiness and simply confess our sins. No attempts to mitigate, defend or rationalize our behavior—just a humble acknowledgment of the truth.

When we do this, the Lord is willing and ready to forgive our guilt, to cover our shame and to restore us to fellowship. Good News indeed! David knew about the guilt and shame of sin as well as the joy and freedom of God's forgiveness. He wrote about it in Psalm 32.

> *Blessed is the one whose transgression is forgiven,*
> *whose sin is covered.*

> *Blessed is the man against whom the* Lord *counts no iniquity,*
> *and in whose spirit there is no deceit.*
>
> *For when I kept silent, my bones wasted away*
> *through my groaning all day long.*
> *For day and night your hand was heavy upon me;*
> *my strength was dried up as by the heat of summer.*
>
> *I acknowledged my sin to you,*
> *and I did not cover my iniquity;*
> *I said, "I will confess my transgressions to the* Lord*,"*
> *And you forgave the iniquity of my sin. (Ps 32:1–5)*

So, where are you? God wants to know.

Questions for Discussion

1. What is the real meaning of the fairy tale *The Emperor's New Clothes*? How does the fairy tale relate to Genesis 3?
2. Medically, what is the difference between a disease's symptoms and its cause? Why is this distinction important? What is the spiritual application of this truth?
3. Genesis 3:6–13 outlines four different symptoms of sin: shame, guilt, fear and blame. Which of these represents your primary response when you do something wrong?
4. Why is confession so hard? Why do we so often resort to "fig leaves" (denial, justification, blame, etc.) rather than simply acknowledging the truth?
5. Where are you?

I Want a Principle Within
Charles Wesley (1749)

*I want a principle within
Of watchful, godly fear;
A sensibility of sin,
A pain to feel it near.
I want the first approach to feel
Of pride or wrong desire,
To catch the wandering of my will,
And quench the kindling fire.*

*From thee that I no more may stray,
No more thy goodness grieve;
Grant me the filial awe, I pray,
The tender conscience give.
Quick as the apple of an eye,
O God, my conscience make;
Awake my soul when sin is nigh,
And keep it still awake.*

*Almighty God of truth and love,
To me thy power impart;
The mountain from my soul remove,
The hardness from my heart.
O may the least omission pain
My reawakened soul,
And drive me to that blood again,
Which makes the wounded whole.*

5
Spoiler Alert
Genesis 3:14–24

Someone who jumps out of an airplane can enjoy the spine-tingling, breath-taking, heart-pounding free fall *only* if he has a parachute and is confident that it is working properly! Without the assurance that the rapid descent is going to end well, the experience will be sheer terror. Jesus Christ has equipped all his followers with a "parachute"—the gift of faith. This amazing gift assures us that, ultimately, we will land safely, and our stories will have a happy ending. This means, even if the ride gets bumpy and hard, we can enjoy the journey.

On the night before his crucifixion, Jesus reassured his frightened disciples with these words:

> *Let not your hearts be troubled. Believe in God; believe also in me. In my Father's house are many rooms. If it were not so, would I have told you that I go to prepare a place for you? And if I go and prepare a place for you, I will come again and will take you to myself, that where I am you may be also. (John 14:1–3)*

In a sense, Jesus is giving his followers a "spoiler alert." He *wants* them to know how the story is going to end and assures them that, ultimately, everything is going to be OK. Jesus knows how rough the journey ahead will be. He knows that it will at times feel like a terrifying free fall. So, he reassures his disciples by reminding them of their "parachute."

When it comes to entertainment, a "spoiler alert," often contained in a written review of a movie, is something that warns those who have not yet seen a certain film that a vitally important part of the storyline is about to be revealed. This piece of information will "spoil" the movie because it removes the element of suspense and the dramatic thrill of the unknown and the unexpected. The warning is intended to give the movie-goer the opportunity to stop reading the article so as not to detract from the first-time viewing experience.

While this may be entirely appropriate for the make-believe world of movie entertainment, it is *not* the attitude we want to bring to the real-world trauma of human history! Human existence is a white-knuckle experience, filled with conflict, suffering, joy, romance, and unexpected surprises. Participants in the drama of life are often anxious about the future. At times, it feels like a free fall and panic sets in. *What's going on? How will this story end? Will I survive?* This helps us to understand why Jesus came: to equip us for the journey of life by telling us in advance how it's going to end. He *wants* us to know. Genesis 3:14–24 is God's "spoiler alert" for human history. But rather than ruining the story, knowing how it ends actually enriches it and makes it possible to enjoy the journey!

In the last chapter, we saw how Genesis 3:7–13 introduces us to the *personal and psychological consequences* of sin. Genesis 3:14–24 is the focus of this chapter. These verses alert us to sin's *cosmic and theological consequences*. The damage that sin does to a person's inner psyche and moral character is devasting. We saw in the last chapter the tragic results of shame, guilt, and fear, and we learned of the human tendency to make excuses and blame others for the bad things we've done. As terrible as this picture is, the author of Genesis wants us to know that this is only the beginning of sin's ugly devastation. The verses that we will examine in this chapter show us how sin's consequences go much deeper and further than we could have ever imagined. Not only has sin polluted men's and women's personal lives and relationships, it has also had a profound impact on nature, on history, on Satan, and especially on God. It is to these realities that we now turn our attention.

Consequences for the Serpent

> *The* LORD *God said to the serpent,*
> *"Because you have done this,*
> *cursed are you above all livestock*
> *and above all beasts of the field;*
> *on your belly you shall go,*
> *and dust you shall eat*
> *all the days of your life.*
> *I will put enmity between you and the woman,*
> *and between your offspring (seed) and her offspring (seed);*
> *he shall bruise your head,*
> *and you shall bruise his heel." (Gen 3:14–15)*

The severity of the serpent's treatment illustrates how the punishment must fit the crime. Not only was his sin profoundly devious and diabolical, more importantly it was aimed at leading an innocent couple into evil. This brought forth God's curse. Though Adam and Eve are judged and punished for what they've done, they are not cursed. Only the serpent (and the ground, see Gen 3:17) is cursed. The snake is condemned to crawl and "eat dust." Though some believe these words point to a literal change of mobility from walking on legs to crawling on one's belly, the probable intent is to underscore the serpent's permanent humiliation and subjugation to God's sovereign control.

The harshness of the sentence shows how serious God considers the serpent's sin to be. An act of sin is, in and of itself, a terrible thing. But to lead others into sin is damnable wickedness of the highest order. Jesus spoke of the seriousness of causing others to sin when he said, "Whoever causes one of these little ones who believe in me to sin, it would be better for him if a great millstone were hung around his neck and he were thrown into the sea" (Mark 9:42).

The most significant consequence for the serpent, however, is God's prophetic statement concerning the seed of the woman. Although the serpent will bruise the heel of the woman's seed, her seed will one day bruise the serpent's head. This statement is literally pregnant with both theological and historical significance. We will come back at the end of the chapter to examine this important verse in depth.

Consequences for the Woman

> *To the woman he said,*
> *"I will surely multiply your pain in childbearing;*
> *in pain you shall bring forth children.*
> *Your desire shall be contrary to your husband,*
> *but he shall rule over you." (Gen 3:16)*

Sin's devasting repercussions strike the woman in precisely those two areas where, according to Genesis 2, she was created to flourish and thrive the most: childbearing and marriage. It is at first difficult to see the connection between Eve's sin and her punishment. But careful study of the text and prayerful reflection will help us see that God is helping Eve to recognize the twistedness of her heart by causing her to experience pain in two areas of life that touch the very core of her identity as a female person.

While the physical act that makes conception possible is pleasurable, birthing a baby is painful agony! How ironic it is that the consequences of sin for the woman manifest themselves precisely at the place where she was created to find her greatest fulfillment: giving birth to children. The book of Genesis will give at least two dramatic illustrations of the trauma involved in bringing new life into the world. Rebekah, carrying twins in her womb, had such a difficult pregnancy that she finally cried out to the Lord, "Why is this happening to me?" (see Gen 25:22). And Rachel, after "hard labor," died as she gave birth to Benjamin (Gen 35:16–19).

The pain associated with birth, however, is not just related to the physical act of labor and delivery. Perhaps the greatest pains associated with mothering come when children grow up and choose paths in life that are destructive and wicked. When the first birth in history occurred, Eve rejoiced: "I have gotten a man with the help of the Lord" (Gen 4:1). But one can only imagine the depth of her pain when this son, Cain, rose up and murdered his brother! No suffering on earth quite equals that of a mother grieving for her children.

The consequences of sin for Eve are also manifested in her marriage relationship. The words God uses to explain her punishment call for careful and prayerful interpretation. The word "desire" can, at times, carry the idea of a romantic and tender yearning to be with one's beloved. But in the very next chapter, the same word is used to describe sin's attempt to manipulate and control Cain: "sin is crouching at the door. Its *desire* is for you, but you must rule over it." (Gen 4:7)

> The desire of the woman for her husband is akin to the desire of sin that lies poised ready to leap at Cain. It means a desire to break the relationship of equality and turn it into a relationship of servitude and domination. The sinful husband will try to be a tyrant over his wife. Far from being a reign of co-equals over the remainder of God's creation, the relationship now becomes a fierce dispute, with each party trying to rule each other. The two who once reigned as one attempt to rule each other.[1]

Yes, the punishment fits the crime. Eve had led her husband into eating the forbidden fruit. In a sense, she had sought to be the head of the home. She had manipulated the situation in such a way that she got what she wanted. Passively, Adam went along. Now, when the punishments are meted out, God makes sure that Eve gets what her actions deserve. Whereas marriage had been originally created to be a haven of blissful intimacy and shared equality, it now becomes a war zone where two willful sinners fight for dominance. Perhaps the New Living Translation best captures the meaning of the woman's punishment with the words: "And you will desire to control your husband, but he will rule over you."

Many people see Genesis 3:16 as biblical support for the institution of patriarchy, the rule of man over woman. But such a reading of the text is not only unfortunate, it is unnecessary. God is *describing* the human condition, not *prescribing* how humans should act. In the words of Leon Kass, God's speech is "predictive rather than prescriptive . . . it expresses not so much his preference for how things *should* be, but rather . . . his prophecy about how things necessarily

---

[1] Hamilton, *Genesis*, 1:202.

will be."[2] There is no indication that God is giving a command or even an endorsement of either male dominance or female manipulation in marriage. No. Sin may indeed cause the man to abuse his position and try to dominate his wife. The wife may seek to use her charms of persuasion to try to manipulate the husband into doing her will. The climate in the home may often be contentious and adversarial as two strong-headed sinners compete for control. This is *not* the way it should be; it is just the way it is. To claim that Genesis 3:16 sanctions the enslavement of women would necessitate a reading of the text that also condemns anyone who uses pain relievers during childbirth. Both interpretations would be a tragic perversion of the meaning of the text.

CONSEQUENCES FOR THE MAN

> And to Adam he said,
> "Because you have listened to the voice of your wife
> and have eaten of the tree
> of which I commanded you,
> 'You shall not eat of it,'
> cursed is the ground because of you;
> in pain you shall eat of it all the days of your life;
> thorns and thistles it shall bring forth for you;
> and you shall eat the plants of the field.
> By the sweat of your face
> you shall eat bread,
> till you return to the ground,
> for out of it you were taken;
> for you are dust,
> and to dust you shall return." (Gen 3:17–19)

For the woman, the consequences of sin relate primarily to marriage and family. For the man, the negative impact of sin relates mainly to his work. Eve's sin causes a dramatic change in her relationship to her husband. Adam's sin changes his relationship to the earth. Adam's work in the garden had been joyful, energizing, creative and meaningful. God was the original worker; for six days he labored to create the universe. The man, created in God's image, just joined in the fun! Adam was the happy gardener. But with the arrival

---

2   Kass, *The Beginning of Wisdom*, 112–113.

of sin, everything changes. Now work becomes laborious, tedious, monotonous, frustrating, and at times, dangerous.

The consequences of Adam's moral fall take on yet an even darker tone when God announces that the man must die. This should not have been a surprise to Adam. God had clearly warned him not to eat of the tree of the knowledge of good and evil because "in the day that you eat of it you shall surely die" (Gen 2:17). When they ate the forbidden fruit, Adam and Eve died spiritually; their relationship with God was broken and they were expelled from the Garden of Eden. Now, God tells Adam that physical death will also come. "For you are dust, and to dust you shall return" (Gen 3:19). It may not be immediate but don't let the delay make you think that death is any less real: "The soul who sins shall die" (Ezek 18:4).

But Adam's sin also has consequences for nature and the natural order, and this is perhaps the most interesting aspect of what God has to say to the man. The ground is cursed. Thorns and thistles appear. Death becomes a reality. It seems that human sin has provoked a major dysfunction in God's perfect world. The course of nature has been profoundly altered in a very negative way.

Scholars debate whether things like disease, earthquakes, hurricanes, and animal violence existed before sin came into the world. The question is fascinating and indeed, important. Unfortunately, the Bible gives little information to help us. Regardless of how one finally answers such a question, we can certainly recognize that the inspired author of Genesis wants us to know that sin has really messed things up, not only in the life of humans, but also in nature! Like a virus taking up residence in a healthy body, so sin causes the natural order to function abnormally. Sin doesn't belong here. It is toxic. This world will never rediscover its God-ordained perfection until the poison of sin is removed.

In Romans 8, the apostle Paul speaks about the cosmic consequences of sin. But his real point is to fill us with hope. The day of full redemption is coming soon and nature's current "bondage to corruption" will end. This is a solemn promise from God!

Did someone say "spoiler alert"? If ever there was a clear statement about how the story of human history will end, it is here. Tsunamis, tornadoes, disease, and death—these will not have the final word. They are only the groanings of "the pains of childbirth," signaling that the day of full redemption is drawing near. As Sandra Richter says in her book *The Epic of Eden*: "Folks, we are not merely waiting for our personal deliverance, we wait for the day when all of creation will be 'born again.'"[3]

The Bible gives numerous hints of what the redemption of nature will look like but perhaps nowhere is the picture more compelling than in the prophet Isaiah.

> *The wolf shall dwell with the lamb,*
> *and the leopard shall lie down with the young goat,*
> *and the calf and the lion and the fattened calf together;*
> *and a little child shall lead them.*
> *The cow and the bear shall graze;*
> *their young shall lie down together;*
> *and the lion shall eat straw like the ox.*
> *The nursing child shall play over the hole of the cobra,*
> *and the weaned child shall put his hand on the adder's den.*
> *They shall not hurt or destroy*
> *in all my holy mountain;*
> *for the earth shall be full of the knowledge of the* LORD
> *as the waters cover the sea. (Isa 11:6–9)*

CONSEQUENCES FOR GOD

> *And the* LORD *God made for Adam and for his wife garments of skins and clothed them. Then the* LORD *God said, "Behold, the man has become like one of us in knowing good and evil. Now, lest he reach out his hand and take also of the tree of life and eat, and live forever"— therefore the* LORD *God sent him out from the garden of Eden to work the ground from which he was taken. He drove out the man, and at the east of the garden of Eden he placed the cherubim and a flaming sword that turned every way to guard the way to the tree of life. (Gen 3:21–24)*

---

[3] Richter, *The Epic of Eden*, 115.

As we have seen, the coming of sin into the world has huge consequences for the man, the woman, and the serpent. But no one is more impacted by the tragedy in the garden than God himself. He will never again be able to relate to Adam and Eve in quite the same way. Sin has brought a profound change in their relationship. The man and the woman were the pinnacle of creation and God had prepared the garden as a perfect environment for them to inhabit. He delighted to see his creatures freely enjoying all that he had made and found pleasure in walking with them in the cool of the day. But now, the man and the woman have sinned. Brazenly, they have violated a clear command. They have behaved like ungrateful, arrogant, rebellious teenagers! What should God do now? How should he respond?

Here we see the divine dilemma. Justice demands that the couple be punished. "The wages of sin is death" (Rom 6:23). And yet love demands that somehow the offense be remedied. The thought of losing fellowship with his own children breaks God's heart. "How can I give you up, O Ephraim? How can I hand you over, O Israel? . . . My heart recoils within me, my compassion grows warm and tender." (Hos 11:8) If God destroys Adam and Eve, his justice will be vindicated but no one will ever be able to be quite sure of his love. But if he overlooks their sin and in love maintains the relationship, no one will know if he is really a God of justice or not. God seems to be on the horns of an irreconcilable dilemma.

Amazingly God finds a way to respond to the couple's sin that manifests *both* his love *and* his justice. This makes it possible for the Lord to maintain his integrity; he is absolutely just and absolutely loving. But it also makes it possible for him to maintain an on-going relationship with Adam and Eve. Here in the third chapter of Genesis we have the first glimpse of the gospel and begin to see God's plan for the salvation of the whole world!

First, God gives a solemn promise that a champion will one day arrive who will crush the head of the serpent (Gen 3:15). The "seed of the woman" will come and, in defeating the powers of evil, will make possible a redemption that will ultimately restore everything to its original state. John Lennox calls this promise *The Seed Project*.[4] The remainder of the Old Testament will raise the question again and again: *Who* is this seed? *When* will he come? *Where* will he live? *How* will he defeat the forces of evil? *How* will we recognize him? These questions will not be fully answered until the coming of Jesus. To Adam and Eve, God is simply giving the initial promise: Fear not, be at peace; the seed of the woman is coming!

Second, God makes clothing for Adam and Eve (Gen 3:21). Fig leaves are man's attempt to deal with the guilt and shame of sin. But such garments are woefully inadequate to cover what needed covering (Gen 3:7). Now, God steps forward and offers *his* solution, one that works! Note that the initiative for dealing with the couple's sin and shame lies with God, not man. Rather than using fig leaves, God provides "garments of skins" (Gen 3:21). This means that an animal was killed, and blood was shed to make possible an adequate covering for human nakedness.

> God covers sins and its degradation. Here we may recall the biblical picture of justification: the gift of a new robe, rich and pure (Zech 3:4–5; Matt 22:11; Luke 15:22; Gal 3:27; Rev 19:8). History is irreversible, but God is able to do a new thing: we remain sinners, with no merit of our own to show, but where sin has abounded, grace has abounded all the more.[5]

Third, the very act of expelling the couple from Paradise can be seen as an expression of mercy. God is making it impossible for Adam and Eve to eat from the tree of life and thus live forever in their depraved condition. It's one thing to be a sinner. It's another thing to be a sinner *forever*. Such a condition would be—well, it would be hell! The English Standard Version accurately reflects the grammatical reality that the sentence at the end of verse 22 is broken off: "Now, lest he reach out his hand and take also of the tree of life and eat, and live forever—". God can't seem to quite finish what he wants to say. Perhaps he is overcome with emotion as he expels the couple from the

---

4 Lennox, *Joseph*, 23–25.
5 Blocher, *In the Beginning*, 191–192.

Garden of Eden. As they walk toward the east, the drama of human history begins!

Adam and Eve can't return to Eden. The way is blocked. Once innocence has been lost, not even God can bring it back again. He will indeed one day provide a way so that men can be cleansed of their sins and made pure by the blood of the Lamb. Men and women can be pure; but never again can they be innocent.

Now, a new story begins. Human history is a drama that must be lived "east of Eden"—in the land of Nod (wandering; see Gen 4:16). The man and the woman will continue to live with the consequences of sin: shame, guilt, fear, blame, the serpent, troubled marriages, rebellious children, laborious toil, and death. They are lost and homesick; they can't get back to the garden. Adam and Eve must have thought often about *The Seed Project* that God had announced. When will it begin? When will the serpent crusher come to save us?

THE FIRST GOSPEL SERMON

Genesis 3:15 is to the Old Testament what John 3:16 is to the New. As an oak tree is "contained" in a tiny acorn, so this little verse contains the fullness of the blessing of the Good News of salvation that is ours in Jesus Christ. God himself is the preacher and this is the first gospel sermon. Though the words are addressed to the serpent, Adam and Eve are all ears as they seek to grasp the meaning of the message:

> *And I will put enmity*
> *Between you and the woman,*
> *And between your seed and her seed;*
> *He shall bruise [crush] you on the head,*
> *And you shall bruise him on the heel. (Gen 3:15 NASB)*

As in English, the Hebrew word *seed* can have either a singular or plural meaning. This means that "the seed of the woman" could refer to one person (Jesus) or to a collective group (Israel, the church), or conceivably to both. Until Abraham (Gen 12), this single verse was basically all that was known of the "gospel." Though the message was succinct and cryptic, it was enough to guide a few in the way of salvation. Not only Adam and Eve, but Abel (Gen 4:4), Enosh (Gen 4:26), Enoch

(Gen 5:21–24) and Noah (Gen 6:8–9) all understood enough about the way of salvation to have an authentic relationship with God.

In speaking of the enmity between the seed of the woman and the seed of the serpent, God is, at the very beginning, underscoring the reality of spiritual warfare that will characterize human history. God wants Adam and Eve and their descendants to understand that temptations, trials, and suffering are to be expected in this life. Put on your gospel armor and prepare for battle.

Most importantly, this verse promises the world a savior, a champion; one who will come and crush the serpent's head. From these few words, we learn that this coming hero will be fully human. He is to be born of woman; a full member of the human race. And yet, he will have supernatural powers; able to destroy the serpent and the powers of darkness. Of great significance is the announcement that this future victory will be carried out on behalf of sinners! The reason the serpent will be crushed is so that Adam and Eve and their descendants will be liberated forever from Satan's evil power.

However, such a victory will be won at great cost. The coming champion will be wounded in this great conflict, but not ultimately defeated. His heel will be bruised by the serpent. He will suffer, but the wound will be superficial, and he will recover. The serpent's head wound, however, will be a mortal blow! It is interesting to note that the serpent will be crushed by that part of the champion's body (his heel) where he had been wounded.

By this point, it will come as no surprise that the New Testament clearly identifies Jesus Christ as "the seed of the woman" (see Gal 3:16), the Serpent Crusher. He is the ultimate fulfillment of *The Seed Project* announced in Genesis 3:15. In his conflict with evil, Jesus will indeed suffer a wound; but it will only be superficial, and he will fully recover. The serpent, however, will be crushed and destroyed and the power of darkness defeated. Jesus will then reverse the curse and restore his creation to its original purity and glory. His reign on the earth will mean that "the kingdom of the world (will) become the kingdom of our Lord and of his Christ, and he shall reign forever and ever" (Rev 11:15). Perhaps the most amazing part of all this is that Christ invites us to join in this mighty, cosmic conflict and take part in the glorious victory. "The God of peace will soon crush Satan under your feet" (Rom 16:20). So, the next time Satan reminds you of your past, remind him of his future!

QUESTIONS FOR DISCUSSION

1. Why do you think God has arranged things so that pain in childbirth, conflict in marriage, and toil in work are the norm? What is he trying to teach us?
2. Do you find the message of Genesis 3:14–24 to be encouraging or discouraging? Does it cause you to feel hope or despair? Discuss your answer.
3. In what sense is God's punishment for sin also a sign of his mercy and grace?
4. Why is knowing how the story ends so important? Explain why this doesn't "spoil" the story but enhances it.
5. Do you ever feel homesick? How does this chapter help you deal with that feeling?
6. Describe how Genesis 3:15 is the first gospel sermon.

Hark! The Herald Angels Sing
Charles Wesley

Come, Desire of nations, come,
Fix in us thy humble home;
Rise, the woman's conquering seed,
Bruise in us the serpent's head.

Now display thy saving power,
Ruined nature now restore;
Now in mystic union join
Thine to ours, and ours to thine.

Adam's likeness, Lord, efface;
Stamp thine image in its place.
Second Adam from above,
Reinstate us in thy love.

Let us thee, though lost, regain,
Thee, the life, the inner man:
O, to all thyself impart,
Formed in each believing heart.

6
Why Can't We All Just Get Along?
Genesis 4:1–17

In March of 1991, four white police officers in Los Angeles mercilessly beat an African American named Rodney King after he was stopped for a traffic violation. The incident was captured on video and played over and over on national television. When the policemen were acquitted of any criminal behavior, riots erupted throughout the city of Los Angeles, in which fifty-three people died and over 2,000 were injured. During the national furor sparked by these incidents, Rodney King appeared on television and famously asked, "Can't we all just get along?"

Hardly a day passes when we are not confronted with the tragic reality of human conflict. War, theft, racism, divorce, abuse, jealousy, oppression, gossip, and so much more, all testify to the sad fact that human relationships are often adversarial and competitive. Why can't we get along? The question is a good one and Genesis *wants* us to ask it.

The third chapter of Genesis shows how sin brings about a break in man's relationship with God. Though the consequences of sin certainly begin to have a negative effect on how Adam and Eve relate to one another, the focus is primarily vertical. Sin puts man in conflict with God. In Genesis 3, the big question God asks is this: "Where are you?" (Gen 3: 9). But in the fourth chapter of Genesis the emphasis changes. Here we are introduced to the reality that sin brings about a break in man's relationship with his fellow man and the focus is primarily horizontal. In this context, the big question asked by God is this: "Where is your brother?" (Gen 4:9).

The important thing to remember about the conflict between Cain and Abel is that they are brothers. The issue here is sibling rivalry; competition, jealousy and fighting between brothers and sisters. Though Genesis certainly contains examples of tribal conflict and wars between nations, the real emphasis of the book is on brothers and sisters who struggle to get along: Cain and Abel, Isaac and Ishmael, Jacob and Esau, Rachel and Leah, Joseph and his brothers. If we were to expand our study to include conflict between other family members, then we could add to our list Abraham and his nephew, Lot and Jacob and his father-in-law, Laban. And if we were to look beyond Genesis at the rest of Scripture, we would see that this theme of conflict in the family runs throughout the biblical narrative: Moses and Aaron/Miriam, David and his brothers, David and his sons, Mary and Martha, Paul and Barnabas, etc. Yes indeed, conflict between brothers is a major theme in Scripture. Apparently, the Lord wants us to think deeply about Rodney King's question. Why can't we all just get along? Why indeed?

Genesis 4:1–17 is much more than a morality tale that parents and Sunday School teachers can use to urge children to be nice to one another. These seventeen verses introduce us to some of the most fundamental societal and relational dynamics in life. They set the stage for human history and, more importantly, serve as a kind of mirror to enable us to see ourselves.

> *Now Adam knew Eve his wife, and she conceived and bore Cain, saying, "I have gotten a man with the help of the* LORD*." And again, she bore his brother Abel. Now Abel was a keeper of sheep, and Cain a worker of the ground. In the course of time Cain brought to the* LORD *an offering of the fruit of the ground, and Abel also brought of the firstborn of his flock and of their fat portions. And the* LORD *had regard for Abel and his offering, but for Cain and his offering he had no regard. So Cain was very angry, and his face fell. The* LORD *said to*

Cain, "Why are you angry, and why has your face fallen? If you do well, will you not be accepted? And if you do not do well, sin is crouching at the door. Its desire is contrary to you, but you must rule over it."

Cain spoke to Abel his brother. And when they were in the field, Cain rose up against his brother Abel and killed him. Then the LORD *said to Cain, "Where is Abel your brother?" He said, "I do not know; am I my brother's keeper?" And the* LORD *said, "What have you done? The voice of your brother›s blood is crying to me from the ground. And now you are cursed from the ground, which has opened its mouth to receive your brother's blood from your hand. When you work the ground, it shall no longer yield to you its strength. You shall be a fugitive and a wanderer on the earth." Cain said to the* LORD, *"My punishment is greater than I can bear. Behold, you have driven me today away from the ground, and from your face I shall be hidden. I shall be a fugitive and a wanderer on the earth, and whoever finds me will kill me." Then the* LORD *said to him, "Not so! If anyone kills Cain, vengeance shall be taken on him sevenfold." And the* LORD *put a mark on Cain, lest any who found him should attack him. Then Cain went away from the presence of the* LORD *and settled in the land of Nod, east of Eden.*

Cain knew his wife, and she conceived and bore Enoch. When he built a city, he called the name of the city after the name of his son, Enoch. (Gen 4:1–17)

A STORY FULL OF FIRSTS

If a story's beginning is an indication of what comes next, then the story of Cain and Abel, standing at the dawn of human history, gives us an ominous foretaste of what life on planet earth is going to be. Perhaps the first thing to notice is how many first things are here reported.

The first baby. Adam and Eve came into being through a special act of creation by God himself (see Gen 2). But Cain's arrival marked the first "natural" human birth in history. One can only imagine how the parents felt as Eve went through gestation, labor, and delivery. Their questions, their fears, and their hopes would have been far beyond those of couples today who have others to guide them through the birth process, helping them know what to expect. But we can assume that the Lord's promise given in the garden, about how "the seed of the woman" would be the serpent crusher, must have filled them with joyful anticipation. This child, Cain, will be our promised savior. He will reverse the curse and usher in an era of peace. Right? Far from being a child of blessing, Cain brought the curse of sin to a whole new level of tragedy.

The first occupations. Cain was "a worker of the ground;" Abel "a keeper of sheep" (Gen 4:2). It seems that farming and shepherding were the first recognizable professions in history. And just as farmers and shepherds have often struggled to understand one another and live in peace through the centuries, so it was in the beginning. Though the text does not say so directly, it seems that the difference in occupations was an important factor in contributing to the sibling rivalry between the brothers.

The first family. Many social philosophers have tended to describe "primitive" human life as a kind of utopian community, where families lived in happy tranquility, unpolluted by the evils of "civilization." The "noble savage" concept of history, however, simply does not square up with the biblical account of human beginnings. The first family, according to Scripture, was dysfunctional from the start. In fact, virtually all the families portrayed in Genesis are unhealthy in one form or another. Marital conflict, manipulation, abuse, favoritism, secrets, and sibling rivalry are found throughout the book. And rather than hiding these dysfunctions and sins, Genesis highlights them! God apparently wants us to know that the problems in the world find their origin in the family, and so do the solutions!

The first worship service. It is important to notice that the story of Cain and Abel introduces us to the first recorded act of worship in history. In bringing sacrifices and offerings to the Lord, the brothers are participating in a very simple liturgical ceremony whose purpose is to find God's favor and receive his blessing. Ironically, what on the outside appears to be a pious and commendable endeavor turns into an occasion for competition, jealousy, hatred and the first recorded act of violence.

Far from teaching that corporate worship is always something good, the Bible candidly warns us to be very, very careful when we gather together for religious purposes. Public worship can be toxic and often does more harm than good. Though many may be shocked to find such a message in the most famous religious book in the world, even a casual reading of the Bible confronts one with this troubling reality from Genesis to Revelation!

Many today have been wounded by bad church experiences. They know what it feels like to receive the right fist of fellowship. The prophet Zechariah speaks of those with negative religious experiences in these words: "And if one asks him, 'What are these wounds on your back?' he will say, 'The wounds I received in the house of my friends.'" (Zech 13:6)

There are many places in Scripture where we are warned about the potential dangers involved in worship services, but few places state the matter more poignantly than the prophet Isaiah. He describes a time in Israel's history when God was repulsed by the religious actions of those who had gathered to worship him.

What to me is the multitude of your sacrifices?
says the LORD;
I have had enough of burnt offerings of rams
and the fat of well-fed beasts;
I do not delight in the blood of bulls, or of lambs, or of goats.

When you come to appear before me,
who has required of you
this trampling of my courts?
Bring no more vain offerings;
incense is an abomination to me.
New moon and Sabbath and the calling of convocations—
I cannot endure iniquity and solemn assembly.
Your new moons and your appointed feasts
my soul hates;
they have become a burden to me;
I am weary of bearing them.
When you spread out your hands,
I will hide my eyes from you;

> *even though you make many prayers,*
> *I will not listen;*
> *your hands are full of blood. (Isa 1:11–15)*

The first city. Note it well: the first city is built by the first murderer. In what seems to be a flagrant act of defiance, Cain, after killing his brother, builds a city (Gen 4:17). Though God's original command was to "fill the earth" (Gen 1:28), Cain opts to settle down and build a permanent residence. In Genesis, cities are portrayed as wicked settlements of unscattered people. Enoch, Babel, Sodom, and Gomorrah are infamous in the biblical record as centers of wickedness. We will treat this theme in greater detail when we discuss the city of Babel and its famous tower (Gen 11:1–9).

WHY DID GOD ACCEPT ABEL'S OFFERING BUT NOT CAIN'S?

The text is very clear in stating that God is pleased with Abel's offering but not with Cain's (Gen 4:4–5). The text is not clear in explaining *why*. Commentators, theologians, and preachers have wrestled with the question for centuries and basically two types of answers have been proposed.

Some have suggested that God was influenced by the offering itself. For some unexplained reason, God just didn't appreciate Cain's fruit but very much liked Abel's animal. Because the animal offering would, by definition, be a "blood sacrifice," some have claimed that Abel's offering was thus intrinsically better. Support for such a view can be found in the biblical emphasis on blood as an indispensable element in man's salvation. "For the life of the flesh is its blood, and I have given it for you on the altar to make atonement for your souls, for it is the blood that makes atonement by the life." (Lev 17:11). "Without the shedding of blood there is no forgiveness of sins" (Heb 9:22). However, under the law of Moses, God himself establishes "grain offerings" and is apparently pleased when they are used in worship (see Lev 2, etc.). This should make us hesitate before concluding that Cain's offering was displeasing to God because it was fruit.

I believe a better way to understand God's acceptance of Abel's sacrifice and not of Cain's is found not in the offering but in the state of the worshipper's heart. Several indications in the text point in this direction. For one thing, we know that Abel gave to God "the *firstborn* of his flock and their *fat* portions" (Gen 4:4, emphasis added). This is a clear indication that he was giving the best that he had. Abel would very much identify with David who refused to offer God sacrifices "that cost (him) nothing" (2 Sam 24:24). On many occasions the Bible emphasizes that what God is looking for in worship is not perfect liturgical performance but whole-hearted devotion.

- "Has the Lord as great delight in burnt offerings and sacrifices, as in obeying the voice of the Lord? Behold, to obey is better than sacrifice, and to listen than the fat of rams." (1 Sam 15:22)
- "For you will not delight in sacrifice, or I would give it; you will not be pleased with a burnt offering. The sacrifices of God are a broken spirit; a broken and contrite heart, O God, you will not despise." (Ps 51:16–17)
- "This people draw near with their mouth and honor me with their lips, while their hearts are far from me." (Isa 29:13)
- "Let us continually offer up a sacrifice of praise to God, that is, the fruit of lips that acknowledge his name." (Heb 13:15)
- "Go and learn what this means, 'I desire mercy, and not sacrifice.'" (Matt 9:13)

In contrast to Abel's whole-hearted devotion, we get the impression that Cain's act of worship is mediocre, perfunctory, ritualistic, and half-hearted. While the text does not say this explicitly, the remainder of the passage confirms our suspicion that poisonous attitudes lie hidden in Cain's hypocritical heart. As the story unfolds, we discover that Cain has come to worship God while harboring attitudes of bitterness, hatred, and envy. Commenting on why God was pleased with Abel's offering and not with Cain's, Victor Hamilton says:

> Perhaps the silence is the message itself. As outside viewers, we are unable to detect any difference between the two brothers and their offerings. Perhaps the fault is an internal one, an attitude that is known only to God.[1]

---

[1] Hamilton, *Genesis,* 1: 24.

ANALYSIS OF A MURDER

It seems that every detail of this sad story underscores the heinous nature of Cain's murderous act. For one thing, this is no generic homicide; this is fratricide! It is one thing to kill an enemy, a stranger, or even a neighbor. But to murder one's own flesh-and-blood brother is truly evil.

For another thing, Cain murdered a *good* brother. There is no evidence that Abel had ever done anything to provoke Cain in any way. The Bible regards him as an "innocent" man (Matt 23:35), and includes him in the faith hall of fame (Heb 11:4). One might have a measure of understanding for a man who murders a troublemaker; but to brutally take the life of a godly man reveals the depth of depravity in Cain's wicked heart.

The extreme sinfulness of Cain's deed is further seen when we realize that his act of murder is premeditated. This crime is not the result of a sudden loss of temper. There was no verbal dispute that somehow escalated and got out of control. Cain was not suffering from temporary insanity when he killed his brother. No, this act of treachery is cold-blooded, calculated, and planned in advance.

The fact that God warns him and tries to prevent him from the deed shows yet another dimension of Cain's sin. God knew what was going on in Cain's heart and made a personal visit to talk to him about it. Like a good psychologist, God urges Cain to get in touch with his feelings. "Why are you angry, and why has your face fallen?" (Gen 4:6). He then alerts Cain to the horrific consequences he will suffer if he follows through with his plans. "Sin is crouching at the door. Its desire is for you." (Gen 4:7) Cain's willful rejection of God's counsel shows just how hell-bent he is on killing his brother. Satan talked Eve *in* to sin, but not even God could talk Cain *out*!

After the murder, when confronted about what he has done, Cain denies any involvement whatsoever. He callously turns his back on God's mercy and grace. God is not seeking geographical information when he asks, "Where is your brother?" (Gen 4:9). Rather, God is inviting Cain to step into the light, confess his sin and repent. If Cain had done this, the story would have ended very differently. But no, Cain hardens his heart even more and refuses to acknowledge the truth. Though Cain's sin certainly brings suffering to others, the utter folly of his sin is revealed in the fact that his deed brings indescribable misery on himself! Elie Wiesel summarizes the insanity of sin when he writes: "Every murder is a suicide: Cain killed Cain in Abel."[2]

A final indication of the depravity in Cain's heart is seen in the fact that the murder occurs during a worship service. It is one thing to kill someone in a bar or perhaps in a back alley. But at church? Like Thomas Becket, whose murder was more sinister because it happened in Canterbury Cathedral, Cain's treachery is seen in its darkest and most diabolical light when we realize he did it in the context of worship.

So why does Cain kill his brother? What are his motives? For one thing, Cain is angry and depressed. Why? Because God has blessed his brother. Life just isn't fair! Why does my kid brother get more than I do? Sibling rivalry often is rooted in a brother's or sister's inability to rejoice in someone else's blessings.

Jesus told a parable about laborers in a vineyard who worked different amounts of time, but all got the same wages (Matt 20:1–16). The workers who had labored all day and received the fair wage they had agreed upon, were furious that the newcomers got the same wages. They believed this was somehow unjust. This prompted the master to say to them: "Am I not allowed to do what I choose with what belongs to me? Or do you begrudge my generosity?" (Matt 20:15). When you pause to think about it, Cain's problem was not with his brother but with God!

A second factor that motivates Cain to kill his brother is envy. Thomas Aquinas defines envy as "sorrow at another's good." While competition between siblings can be a good thing in healthy families, when it is motivated by envy, it can become ugly and violent.

A third element in Cain's murderous deed is the simple fact that Abel is a righteous man, and this drives Cain crazy! The nature of sin is such that those who do right are despised simply because they do

---

2   Wiesel, *Messengers of God*, 61.

right. Abel's only "crime" is that he is a good man: he walks in integrity, he tells the truth, he refuses to participate in others' wickedness, he loves God with all his heart. And such actions drive Cain to murder. This is the part of the Cain and Abel story that captures the attention of the apostle John many centuries later. Though the text in Genesis mentions anger, depression, and envy as motives for Cain's evil deed, John knows the truth is much simpler:

> *We should not be like Cain, who was of the evil one and murdered his brother. And why did he murder him? Because his own deeds were evil and his brother's righteous. (1 John 3:12)*

We can now understand why the New Testament warns Christians about the dangers of walking in "the way of Cain" (Jude 11). He models a level of wickedness that should make all believers tremble lest they fall into similar kinds of depravity. Allen Ross defines "the way of Cain" as unbelief that manifests itself "in envy of God's dealing with the righteous, in murderous acts, in denial of responsibility for one's brother, and in refusal to accept the punishment."[3]

The Cause and Cure of Conflict

The story of Cain and Abel leaves us feeling depressed and pessimistic about the human condition. Is there no cure for the conflict that accompanies human relationships? What can be done to help us cope with a world of violence and cruelty? Is there no remedy to help us get along with one another? Before closing this chapter, it will be both spiritually edifying and eminently practical to look at a passage in the New Testament that speaks directly to both the cause and the cure of conflict.

> *What causes quarrels and what causes fights among you? Is it not this, that your passions are at war within you? You desire and do not have, so you murder. You covet and cannot obtain, so you fight and quarrel. You do not have, because you do not ask. You ask and do not receive, because you ask wrongly, to spend it on your passions. You adulterous people!*

---

3   Ross, *Creation and Blessing*, 153.

> *Do you not know that friendship with the world is enmity with God? Therefore, whoever wishes to be a friend of the world makes himself an enemy of God. Or do you suppose it is to no purpose that the Scripture says, "He yearns jealously over the spirit that he has made to dwell in us"? But he gives more grace. Therefore it says, "God opposes the proud but gives grace to the humble." Submit yourselves therefore to God. Resist the devil, and he will flee from you. Draw near to God, and he will draw near to you. Cleanse your hands, you sinners, and purify your hearts, you double-minded. Be wretched and mourn and weep. Let your laughter be turned to mourning and your joy to gloom. Humble yourselves before the Lord, and he will exalt you. (Jas 4:1–10)*

Like a skilled physician looking beyond the symptoms of a disease to its root cause, James digs deep, searching for the definitive explanation for why we fight and cause harm to one another. Like peeling away the layers of the proverbial onion, James uncovers, layer by layer, the ever-deepening cause of why we can't get along. He knows that before we can talk meaningfully about curing conflict in the world, we must first understand the spiritual and psychological dynamics of its cause.

On the surface, at the most elementary level, is the problem of unmet desires. What's the cause of conflict? The most obvious answer is simply this: someone didn't get his way.

> *Where do you think all these appalling wars and quarrels come from? Do you think they just happen? Think again. They come about because you want your own way, and fight for it deep inside yourselves. You lust for what you don't have and are willing to kill to get it. (Jas 4:1–2 MSG)*

It doesn't get more basic than this. We want something that we believe will bring us happiness. When that desire is frustrated, then we pick a fight with whomever we perceive to be standing in the way. Whether we are talking about a wife fighting for more covers on her side of the bed or Hitler invading Poland, the cause of conflict is the same: someone is very unhappy because he doesn't have what he so desperately wants. In other words, the Bible is telling us that the conflict on the outside is caused by a conflict on the inside.

Moving to a deeper level, James takes us to a second and more profound understanding of conflict's cause: prayerlessness. Does this surprise you? Think about it. James is saying that we fight because our desires are unmet, but the reason our desires are unmet is because we haven't first talked to God about it. "You do not have, because you do not ask" (Jas 4:2). James' analysis is profound. If we fail to ask God to help us when our desires are unsatisfied is it any wonder that we remain stuck in the muck and mire of our discontent? This is why Jesus repeatedly urges his disciples to "ask."

- "Ask, and it shall be given you; seek, and you will find; knock, and it will be opened to you." (Matt 7:7)
- "Whatever you ask in prayer, believe that you have received it, and it will be yours." (Mk 11:24)
- "If you abide in me, and my words abide in you, ask whatever you wish, and it will be done for you." (John 15:7)
- "Until now you have asked nothing in my name. Ask, and you will receive, that your joy may be full." (John 16:24)

But this leads logically to a third level of reflection. What if I do pray and ask God to give me what I want, but he doesn't answer? What then?

James is blunt as he takes us to yet a deeper level of self-examination: the reason our prayers are unanswered is because we ask wrongly. God will not answer prayers that are driven by pride, carnality, and selfish ambition. When our motives are impure and our will is not aligned with God's will, then our prayers will not rise higher than the ceiling.

> *You ask and do not receive, because you ask wrongly, to spend it on your passions. You adulterous people! Do you not know that friendship with the world is enmity with God? Therefore whoever wishes to be a friend of the world makes himself an enemy of God. (Jas 4:3–4)*

If our prayers are worldly and our desires are selfish, then we make ourselves enemies of God. Does anyone think that God will give his enemies what they ask for? This leaves us with one final question:

Why, oh why, is my heart so worldly and at such cross-purposes with God? Why are my passions so selfish and greedy? Why am I like this?

I thought you'd never ask!

The fourth level of sin takes us to the root cause of all human conflict: double-mindedness and pride. The real problem is not what we *do* or even what we *want*; the root problem is *who we are*! We are arrogant, self-absorbed, egocentric rebels who insist on having our own way. This is not just a behavior problem; this is a perversity of character that goes to the very core of our being. We are double-minded, and this makes us fickle and unstable in all our ways (Jas 1:8; 4:8). This means that we are enemies with God, hostile to his purposes. Our real conflict is not with other people, but with God. Such a reality reflects not only our attitude toward God, but his attitude toward us: "God opposes the proud" (Jas 4:6).

Before we can take on the problem of trying to save the world from violence and war, we must first face the problem of the ugly conflict going on deep within our own tortured souls. In his spiritual autobiography *Surprised by Joy*, C. S. Lewis writes about the moment he came face to face with his inner depravity:

> For the first time I examined myself with a seriously practical purpose. And there I found what appalled me; a zoo of lusts, a bedlam of ambitions, a nursery of fears, a harem of fondled hatreds. My name was legion.[4]

This is not something that can be fixed by a course in behavior modification! What is needed is a new creation, a transformation of the heart.

Now, finally, we are prepared to hear God's amazing solution to the human problem. It is only when we see the depth of sin's pollution that we are able to see the deeper reality of God's amazing grace.

Let's look once more at James' analysis of conflict's cause. It is because you are proud and double-minded that you are at enmity with God. This means your prayers are all wrong and because you pray amiss, your prayers are not answered. When your prayers are

---

4   Lewis, *Surprised by Joy*, 226.

unanswered your desires remain unmet, and that explains why you want to pick a fight with someone!

With this foundation for understanding the *cause* of conflict, we are now soundly positioned to understand its *cure*. In a series of bold, concise commands, James tells us what to do: "Submit to God. . . . Resist the devil. . . . Draw near to God. . . . Cleanse your hands and purify your hearts. . . . Humble yourselves." (Jas 4:7–10) To put this in theological language: the cure for quarreling and fighting is the experience of entire sanctification! It works like this:

- When God sanctifies our hearts, he cures our double-mindedness and purifies our motives.
- When our motives are pure, our prayers will then be aligned with God's will.
- When our prayers are aligned with God's will, then they will be answered.
- When our prayers are answered, then our desires will be met.
- When our desires are met, then we no longer feel the need to quarrel and fight.
- And when we no longer fight but live in peace, love and holiness, then the Kingdom of God has come upon the earth!

Don't you wish someone would share this truth with the United Nations?

QUESTIONS FOR DISCUSSION

1. Have you ever experienced sibling rivalry? What was it like?
2. In your own words, answer the question: Why did Cain kill his brother?
3. In Genesis 3:9 God asks, "Where are you?" In Genesis 4:9 God asks, "Where is your brother?" Explain the relationship between these two questions.
4. Aquinas defined envy as "sorrow at another's good." Discuss this definition. Do you regard envy as one of the "deadly sins"?

5. Describe ways in which worship can be a dangerous place. Why does the Bible emphasize this?
6. Look again at the four levels of sin that cause conflict in James 4:1–10. Which level causes you the most difficulty?

7
Rotten to the Core
Genesis 4:18–6:8

At Yale University in the early 1960s, a psychologist named Stanley Milgram conducted a controversial experiment. He wanted to know how far humans would go in inflicting pain on other people. Paid volunteers were told (falsely) that the purpose of the experiment was to test the effect of punishment on learning. The volunteer's job was to be the teacher who would administer punishment whenever the learner gave an incorrect answer to a series of questions on a test. This was all explained by a scientist dressed in a white lab coat.

The volunteer was taken into a laboratory where he was introduced to another person whom, he was told, was also a volunteer like himself. But this person was in reality an actor, trained and paid by Milgram. The learner/actor was then strapped into a kind of electric chair in the presence of the volunteer as the scientist explained that he would be instructed to give an electric shock to the student for each incorrect answer. The volunteer was then led to an adjoining room where an imposing shock generator was supposedly connected to the student. Labels on the generator read; "Light Shock," "Moderate Shock," "Strong Shock," "Intense Shock," "Danger: Severe Shock," and finally, an ominous "XXX."

Strapped in the chair, the learner/actor had been trained to give many bad answers. For each incorrect response, the scientist instructed the volunteer to administer a shock. With each wrong answer, the voltage was increased to the next level. As the electrical shocks became more and more painful, the moans, cries, and fist poundings on the wall could be heard from the room next door. The man in the chair was, of course, only pretending to be in pain.

When the volunteer began to feel uncomfortable with the experiment because of the groans coming from the adjacent room, the scientist would say firmly, "Please continue," or "It is essential for the success of the experiment that you proceed," or "You *must* go on." The thing that Milgram wanted to know was this: how far will a person go in inflicting pain on someone else simply because he is told to do so by an authority figure in a white coat.

Not every volunteer reacted in the same way, of course. But the results confirmed that many ordinary people can become administrators of torture if the circumstances are right. When it was possible only to hear fists pounding on the wall in the room next door, 65% of the volunteers inflicted the harshest punishment. When the learner was behind a curtain and the volunteer could hear their moans and pleas to stop but could not see them, 62% went all the way. When the subject was in the same room and the volunteer could both hear and see the evidence of the pain he was causing, a disturbing 40% of the volunteers continued to do what they were coached to do.

When asked to explain their behavior, most of the volunteers simply said that they did what they did because they were told to do so. They had volunteered and they were being paid, so they simply were following through with their commitment. It is disturbing to note that this is precisely the explanation given by many Germans at the end of World War II when they were asked why they did such awful things to the Jews in the death camps.

When it comes to the Holocaust or controversial psychological experiments, you may be tempted to point your finger and feel disdain for the evil perpetrators of such wicked cruelty. But the deeper question needs to be asked: what would *you* have done?

WHAT'S SO ORIGINAL ABOUT SIN?

The apostle Paul uses an interesting phrase in talking about sin. He speaks about "the mystery of iniquity" (2 Thess 2:7 KJV). He means that our sinful actions often defy rational explanation. We do bad things because, well, just because. "I don't know why I did it; I just went stupid," is sometimes the best reason we can give. Speaking of his own experience, Paul wrote: "For I do not understand my own actions. For I do not do what I want, but I do the very thing I hate" (Rom 7:15). If we hope to understand the depths of sin and the perversity of human behavior, it will take more than a degree in psychology. We will need the wisdom of God.

Genesis 4:18–6:8 introduces us to the biblical doctrine of total depravity. God doesn't want us to be naïve about the capacity for wickedness that resides in each one of us. He wants to save us from the delusional optimism of those who pretend that humans are basically good. The Bible begins with the bad news about sin not only because this expresses the truth about the human condition, but more importantly because this prepares us for the good news about grace!

The historic Christian faith has consistently affirmed that all humans everywhere are born with an inherent bent toward sinning. And this inward pollution is not partial, it is reflected in our total being; we are *totally* depraved. G. K. Chesterton is purported to have said that though the doctrine of total depravity may be Christianity's most unpopular doctrine, it is the easiest one to prove!

If anyone needs evidence to support this notion, just visit the toddler department of the church nursery! These dear children may be cute, but they often act more like little devils than angelic cherubs. No one needs to teach them how to bully, whine, or demand their own way. For the most part, these tiny versions of Adam and Eve do naughty things automatically. However, when it comes to sharing, being sweet, thinking of others, and saying please and thank you, these dear souls need to be taught. As it is when the wheels on your car are out of alignment, so it is with our human character. Unless we are vigilant at suppressing our inclinations and tendencies, we will end up in a ditch! Goodness, it seems, does not come naturally.

One of the historic expressions of the doctrine of total depravity is found in *The Thirty-Nine Articles of the Church of England*. Article IX is entitled "Of Original or Birth-Sin":

> Original sin ... is the fault and corruption of the nature of every man, that naturally is engendered of the offspring of Adam; whereby man is very far gone from original righteousness, and is of his own nature inclined to evil, so that the flesh lusteth always contrary to the spirit; and therefore in every person born into this world, it deserveth God's wrath and damnation.

Such a doctrine does not mean that we are as sinful as we can possibly be, but rather that every faculty of our humanity has been affected by the stain and corruption of sin: our intellect, our will, our emotions, our desires, etc. Sin is all-pervasive. Like a drop of poison in a glass of water, the water may not be as poisonous as it is capable of being, but the whole glass of water has been contaminated.

The result of this tragic reality is that, apart from grace, all of us are spiritually dead and therefore powerless to either please God or to save ourselves.

> *And you were dead in the trespasses and sins in which you once walked, following the course of this world, following the prince of the power of the air, the spirit that is now at work in the sons of disobedience— among whom we all once lived in the passions of our flesh, carrying out the desires of the body and the mind, and were by nature children of wrath, like the rest of mankind. (Eph 2:1–3)*

In his sermon entitled "Original Sin," based on Genesis 6:5, John Wesley says that the doctrine of total depravity is "the first grand distinguishing point between heathenism and Christianity. . . . All who deny this are but heathens still. . . . Know your disease! Know your cure."[1]

The Cainites

In Genesis 4:18–24 we find the first genealogy in the Bible. Here we meet Cain's descendants. Though many have speculated about

---

[1] Sermon #44.

the origin of Cain's wife, the simplest explanation is that she must be one of the "other daughters" of Adam mentioned in Genesis 5:4. The genealogy names seven generations in the line of Cain, the most famous ancestor being Lamech.

> *And Lamech took two wives. The name of the one was Adah, and the name of the other Zillah. Adah bore Jabal; he was the father of those who dwell in tents and have livestock. His brother's name was Jubal; he was the father of all those who play the lyre and pipe. Zillah also bore Tubal-cain; he was the forger of all instruments of bronze and iron. The sister of Tubal-cain was Naamah.*
>
> *Lamech said to his wives: "Adah and Zillah, hear my voice; you wives of Lamech, listen to what I say: I have killed a man for wounding me, a young man for striking me. If Cain's revenge is sevenfold, then Lamech's is seventy-sevenfold." (Gen 4:19–24)*

In both its depth and its breadth, the pollution of sin seems to be everywhere. With Lamech, we have history's first snapshot of what civilization looks like apart from God. His effort to build up a great culture begins with his redefinition of marriage. He is the first polygamist, proudly taking two wives and fathering four children. It is instructive to realize that sin's dominion over human society begins with a willful decision to ignore the pattern of marriage established by God in Genesis 2. When human society arrogates to itself the right to redefine marriage, the floodwaters of judgment are not far away.

Lamech's three sons become the founding fathers of great advancements in culture. Far from depicting cave men living like brutes, the Bible describes the early generations of human life as surprisingly advanced. Jabal is the father of nomads and farmers. Jubal is the father of music and the arts. And Tubal-Cain is the father of metallurgy, both the making of tools and weapons of war. Genesis seems to be making the point that the world's initial cultural advancements emerged through the wicked and unbelieving Cainites.

Lamech himself is a poet, and seemingly a singer. In Genesis 2:23, Adam had written and perhaps sung the first poetry when he rejoiced in the beauty and companionship of his newly-discovered bride. In contrast, Lamech's poetry is both vicious and arrogant, a type of taunt song, that boasts of killing a man in seventy-sevenfold vengeance for wounding him. Far from being afraid of God or ashamed of his sin, Lamech brings it out into the open to celebrate it! C. John Collins notes that the artistry of Lamech's poem "is as beautiful as its content is repulsive."[2]

Though our information about the world's first civilization and its cultural advancements is minimal, we easily see that the Bible is describing how the dominion of sin means that cultural advancements often go hand in hand with unbelief and rebellion against God. We might say that what we have in Genesis 4 is the first installment of the City of Man, in opposition to the City of God. In Genesis, we will see this worldly approach to culture-building in a much more pronounced degree in the city of Babel with its famous tower (Gen 11:1–9). Ultimately, the City of Man will become Babylon the Great, the Great Prostitute, mentioned in the book of Revelation (see Rev 17–18). There we will learn that only when the City of Man is finally judged and destroyed will the City of God descend in all its glory upon the earth (see Rev 21–22).

The Sethites

Genesis 4:25–5:32 introduces us to another genealogy; this one, the descendants of Seth, Adam and Eve's third son. As in the lineage of Cain, we can assume that Seth's descendants also struggled with temptations to sin and unbelief. However, the author of Genesis is at pains to point out a righteous remnant, a thread of faithfulness, that can be traced through this part of the family tree. It was Seth's descendants who brought about history's first revival. Their godly influence caused people to begin "to call upon the name of the Lord" (Gen 4:26).

Though Adam was created in the likeness of God, his children were born in the likeness of their earthly father (Gen 5:1–3). Though the

---

[2] Collins, *Genesis 1–4*, 212.

divine image was not completely lost in Adam's descendants (see Gen 9:6), it was certainly damaged. From now own, humans will contain a strange mixture of good and evil, the image of God and the image of Adam. The work of redemption that God will soon put into motion will aim at both a full victory over the dominion of sin as well as a full restoration of the divine image.

These genealogies (the descendants of Cain and the descendants of Seth) are important for many reasons, but primarily because of the Seed Project. Biblical history is intent on tracing the seed of the woman who will one day come and crush the head of the serpent and bring salvation to the people of God (see Gen 3:15). The genealogies keep us in suspense, on tiptoe with expectation: Is it Seth? Enoch? Noah?

The most notable character among the Sethites is Enoch (Gen 5:21–24). As Lamech stood out because of his wickedness in the lineage of Cain, so Enoch stands out because of his righteousness in the lineage of Seth. We will give more attention to this amazing spiritual giant at the end of the chapter.

THE POINT OF NO RETURN

As the biblical story moves forward toward the flood, the text labors to make clear that the wickedness on the earth has reached such a level of perversity that the situation is beyond repair. The author of Genesis wants us to understand that the punishment (the flood) will indeed fit the crime. Judgment and death are indeed the wages of sin.

> *When man began to multiply on the face of the land and daughters were born to them, the sons of God saw that the daughters of man were attractive. And they took as their wives any they chose. Then the* LORD *said, "My Spirit shall not abide in man forever, for he is flesh: his days shall be 120 years." The Nephilim were on the earth in those days, and also afterward, when the sons of God came in to the daughters of man and they bore children to them. These were the mighty men who were of old, the men of renown. (Gen 6:1–4)*

The first four verses of the sixth chapter of Genesis are some of the most difficult in the Bible to interpret. Who are these "sons of God" that marry human wives and give birth to a race of "mighty men" (giants?) called the Nephilim? Numerous answers have been proposed.

Some treat this passage as mythological, having no basis in history. Such an approach allows one to put the story of the "sons of God and daughters of man" in the category of make-believe legends along with dragons, centaurs, and leprechauns in the days of old. Others have imagined that the "sons of God" are extraterrestrials or perhaps fallen angels (see Job 1:6) who came to earth and took human wives, producing a race of supermen. Numerous modern scholars believe that the term "sons of God" refers to royalty. In the ancient world, kings were sometimes considered to be semi-divine. This often related to the fact that these rulers dabbled in the occult and thus sometimes possessed demonic powers. This interpretation claims that a royal race of demonically influenced men intermarried with commoners (the "daughters of man") and produced a race of people possessing supernatural powers.

Perhaps the best interpretation is one that avoids the fantastical imaginations of the positions above and fits nicely in the context of the book of Genesis. The "sons of God" refers simply to the Sethites, that part of the family tree maintaining godliness and truth. The "daughters of man" thus refers to ungodly Cainite women. This interpretation underscores a truth that is a prominent theme not only in Genesis but throughout the biblical narrative: the vital importance of marrying within the faith.

The book of Genesis will highlight this theme in the stories of finding a wife for Isaac (Gen 24) and for Jacob (Gen 28:1–5). It is of utmost importance that the people of God marry someone who shares their faith, someone who will help to pass on the covenant promises to the next generation. In the New Testament, the apostle Paul underscores the importance of marrying the right person when he writes to the Corinthians:

> *Do not be unequally yoked with unbelievers. For what partnership has righteousness with lawlessness? Or what fellowship has light with darkness? What accord has Christ with Belial? Or what portion does a believer share with an*

unbeliever? What agreement has the temple of God with idols? For we are the temple of the living God; as God said,

> "I will make my dwelling among them and walk among them,
> and I will be their God,
> and they shall be my people.
> Therefore go out from their midst,
> and be separate from them, says the Lord,
> and touch no unclean thing;
> then I will welcome you,
> and I will be a father to you,
> and you shall be sons and daughters to me,
> says the Lord Almighty." (2 Cor 6:14–18)

Though much may remain unclear about how best to interpret Genesis 6:1–4, one thing is very clear: the sin highlighted here relates to the brazen violation of the boundaries God has set for marriage. The intermarriage between "sons of God" and "daughters of man" is a willful decision to disobey God's plan for marriage and family. When such flagrant rebellion is openly practiced and propagated, God threatens to remove his Spirit (see Gen 6:3). Because it was his Spirit that hovered over the waters at the dawn of creation, working to bring order out of chaos (see Gen 1:1–2), the threat of the Spirit's departure can only mean a return to watery chaos and darkness—a sort of un-creation. This is precisely what happened when God sent the flood!

The human effort to redefine the boundaries of marriage in Genesis 6:1–4 sets the stage for what is perhaps the most sobering description of the human condition anywhere in the Bible:

> *The* LORD *saw that the wickedness of man was great in the earth, and that every intention of the thoughts of his heart was only evil continually. And the* LORD *regretted that he had made man on the earth, and it grieved him to his heart. So the* LORD *said, "I will blot out man whom I have created from the face of the land, man and animals and creeping things and birds of the heavens, for I am sorry that I have made them." But Noah found favor in the eyes of the* LORD. *(Gen 6:5–8)*

Apparently, God sees the situation as beyond repair. Human wickedness has passed the point of no return. Long before God is angry about sin, he is grieved, *deeply* grieved. These factors prepare us for the next great chapter in the story of human history: the flood.

Looking back over the first six chapters of Genesis, we can put together a comprehensive picture of the nature of sin and its pervasive polluting influence in the created order. In its depth as well as its breadth, sin has wrought devastation in the earth. The following seven statements attempt to summarize Genesis' teaching about sin.

1. Sin is defiance; a willful transgression of a known law of God.

Though the Bible recognizes the place of mistakes, errors of judgment, and unintentional harm, that is *not* the way Genesis portrays sin. Adam and Eve make a willful choice to disobey God. Cain refuses to accept God's warning and kills his brother. Lamech boasts of his polygamy and violent behavior. The sons of God willfully intermarry with the daughters of man. These are high-handed sins of brazen defiance. This can only bring God's wrath and judgment.

2. Sin is hereditary.

Though all humans continue to bear the image of God in some qualified way, Adam's descendants look more like Adam than God. Every member of the human race now reflects the image of Adam: skeptical, corrupt, arrogant, greedy, insecure, lustful, frail, mortal, etc.

3. Sin becomes more and more sinful.

Like a metastasizing cancer, sin spreads, and as it spreads, it gains strength. Adam eats forbidden fruit. Cain kills his brother. Lamech boasts of his womanizing and murderous ways and builds a civilization to normalize and perpetuate his behaviors. Left unchecked, sin will pollute and destroy everything!

4. Sin is more than a behavior problem; it is a problem of the heart.

"Every intention of the thoughts of (man's) heart was only evil continually" (Gen 6:5). We are not sinners because we sin; we sin because we are sinners. Sin is not just what we do; sin defines us, it is who we are. The heart of the problem is the problem of the heart. We are rotten to the core.

5. Sin is universal.

Though persons such as Enoch and Noah walk with God, the Bible never says they are without sin. The pollution of sin goes deep in the human heart, but it also goes broad; reaching everyone, everywhere. There are no exceptions.

> *None is righteous, no, not one; no one understands; no one seeks for God. All have turned aside; together they have become worthless; no one does good, not even one. . . . for all have sinned and fall short of the glory of God. (Rom 3:10–12, 23)*

6. Sin provokes God's grief and, finally, his wrath.

God will not ignore sin. His justice demands that wrongs be righted. The flood is God's way of dealing with sin—cleansing the earth of sin's pollution and starting again.

7. Sin need not have the final word.

When God clothed Adam and Eve with garments of skin, covering their guilt and shame (see Gen 3:21), he was announcing that a plan was in place to deal with the sin problem. The Seed Project will one day culminate in the birth of the Serpent Crusher, the Lamb of God who takes away the sin of the world (John 1:29). Though this mighty deliverer has not yet come, the promise of his arrival fills the faithful with the optimism of grace. The shining examples of Enoch and Noah boldly declare that though sinning is probable, it is not inevitable. The dominion of sin can be broken!

WALKING WITH GOD

As a diamond best reveals its beauty when seen against black velvet, so the life of Enoch stands out in stark contrast to the other characters we meet in the opening chapters of Genesis. In four short verses, Enoch's life bears glorious testimony to the fact that sons and daughters of Adam can be set free from the dominion of sin. It is possible to live a holy life in a world of unbelief, temptations, and wickedness. One pauses in wonderment that Enoch alone walks with God. It makes one tremble to realize how narrow is the gate and how hard is the way that leads to life, and only a few find it (Matt 7:13–14). And yet, the example of Enoch is given to fill us with hope that living a godly life in an ungodly world can indeed be the experience of every genuine believer.

> *When Enoch had lived 65 years, he fathered Methuselah. Enoch walked with God after he fathered Methuselah 300 years and had other sons and daughters. Thus all the days of Enoch were 365 years. Enoch walked with God, and he was not, for God took him. (Gen 5:21–24)*

Though Enoch's lifespan was shorter than that of his contemporaries—he lived *only* 365 years—his impact for good was infinitely greater. Every person listed in this genealogy is remembered only for being born, having children, and dying. Hatched, matched, and dispatched. But Enoch stands out from the crowd. His life is different. His godly testimony is such that we still talk about him today! Only one reason is given to explain his uniqueness: Enoch walked with God.

It was a *spiritual walk.* Though God was not physically or visibly present, the relationship between God and Enoch was so very real that it was obvious to everyone.

It was a *distinctive walk.* Just as pagan Egyptians recognized that God was with Joseph (Gen 39:2, 3, 21, 23; 41:38), so people knew that God was present wherever Enoch went. His uniqueness was not to be found in his education, his family, his wealth, his talents, or his connections. Rather, people recognized that Enoch was different for one simple reason: he walked with God.

It was a *sanctifying walk.* One simply cannot walk with God and continue to walk in sin. This explains why Adam and Eve, after they ate the forbidden fruit, hid from God, and refused to walk with him (Gen 3:8). To walk with God is to walk in the light. And one cannot walk in the light and continue to practice the deeds of darkness at the same time.

- "Noah was a righteous man, blameless in his generation. Noah walked with God" (Gen 6:9).
- "The Lord appeared to Abram and said to him, 'I am God Almighty; walk before me and be blameless'" (Gen 17:1).
- "If we walk in the light, as he is in the light, we have fellowship with one another, and the blood of Jesus his Son cleanses us from all sin" (1 John 1:7).

It was an *intimate walk*. To walk together means that two persons are going in the same direction. They have a common goal. "Can two walk together, unless they are agreed?" (Amos 3:3 NKJV). When Jesus said, "Follow me," he was doing more than calling his disciples to begin a journey; he was inviting them into a relationship. The only way to know God is to walk with him.

It was a *significant walk*. All the other persons in Enoch's genealogical tree are either forgettable or memorable for some trivial matter. Methuselah was the oldest man who ever lived. So what? But Enoch lived a life of significance. Why? Because he walked with God.

It was a *homeward walk*. When you walk with God, you are not walking in circles; you are going somewhere. There is a destination. Enoch did not die; God "took" him. Apparently, he was transported out of this life and into the next without suffering death. Perhaps it happened like this: One day as they walked along, God turned to Enoch and said, "Hey, we've walked so long and so far, we're closer now to my house than to yours. Why don't you just come on home with me?" And he did.

QUESTIONS FOR DISCUSSION

1. What are your thoughts and feelings about the doctrine of total depravity?
2. In what sense is human culture an expression of sinfulness and rebellion against God? In what sense is it not?
3. Both Lamech's polygamy and the intermarriages between the sons of God and the daughters of man are bold acts of

defiance against God and his model for the family spelled out in Genesis 2. Do these Scriptures help us to better understand what is happening in our culture today in its attempt to redefine marriage?
4. Do you see similarities between the preflood world of Genesis and our world today? What lessons should we draw from this?
5. The church today tends to ask, "Are you saved?" Genesis tends to ask, "Are you walking with God?" Discuss the difference between these two questions.

8
Deep Waters
Genesis 6:9–8:22

It is said there is a place on the Niagara River called "the point of no return." As the water picks up speed just above the falls, the current becomes so strong and so fast that not even a powerful motorboat can resist. Once caught in these waters, the boat *will* go over the falls and be swept to destruction; there are no exceptions. Having passed the point of no return, the boat's fate is sealed.

In the last chapter, we saw how sin, like a cancer, had spread over the earth during the first generations of human life. In both its depth and its breadth, the stain of wickedness was pervasive, and the downward spiral of moral depravity continued to go from bad to worse. From Cain's murder of his brother, to Lamech's polygamy and arrogant cruelty, to the intermarriage of the sons of God with the daughters of man, human culture became more and more corrupt. At some point in this descent, human society reached the point of no return. "Every intention of the thoughts of (man's) heart was only evil continually" (Gen 6:5). The threshold was crossed, and the tragic outcome became unavoidable. Not even God could save these reprobate sinners.

Although the thought of divine wrath and judgment makes many today uncomfortable, it is a theme emphasized repeatedly in the Bible. When people become hardened in sin and deaf to the voice of God, the floodwaters of destruction are not far away. Like pottery that hardens into a shape the potter never intended, when human hearts become impervious to God's grace, there is nothing left to do but to destroy it.

In the days prior to the flood, men and women had hardened their hearts in willful rebellion for so long that their condition became permanent, their wickedness irredeemable, and their sin unpardonable. The Bible speaks on numerous occasions about the frightful reality of such a state:

- "Thus says the Lord of hosts: So will I break this people and this city, as one breaks a potter's vessel, so that it can never be mended." (Jer 19:11)
- "Truly, I say to you, all sins will be forgiven the children of man, and whatever blasphemies they utter, but whoever blasphemes against the Holy Spirit never has forgiveness, but is guilty of an eternal sin." (Mark 3:28–29)
- "If anyone sees his brother committing a sin not leading to death, he shall ask, and God will give him life—to those who commit sins that do not lead to death. There is sin that leads to death; I do not say that one should pray for that." (1 John 5:16)

The book of Genesis tells us that when human wickedness reached the point of intransigent insubordination and willful unbelief, God responded in kind. Realizing the futility of any further gracious appeals for men to repent and come back to him, God withdrew his Spirit (see Gen 6:3). Though invisible and often unrecognized, God's Spirit is that gracious medium that enables sinners to hear his voice, to discern his will, and to feel the conviction of sin. Creation began when the Spirit of God hovered over the formless void of a watery darkness, working with the divine Word to create a universe out of chaotic nothingness (see Gen 1:1–2). But now, the announcement that God's Spirit would no longer abide in man indicates that the world is about to revert once again to a watery chaos. The flood threatens to uncreate all that God has created.

Though it brings him great grief, the Lord God decides to put an end to the cruelty and suffering on earth caused by sin. His plan is to destroy everything and start over.

> *And the* Lord *regretted that he had made man on the earth, and it grieved him to his heart. So the* Lord *said, "I will blot*

out man whom I have created from the face of the land, man and animals and creeping things and birds of the heavens, for I am sorry that I have made them." . . .

Now the earth was corrupt in God's sight, and the earth was filled with violence. And God saw the earth, and behold, it was corrupt, for all flesh had corrupted their way on the earth. And God said to Noah, "I have determined to make an end of all flesh, for the earth is filled with violence through them. Behold, I will destroy them with the earth. (Gen 6:6–7, 11–13)

A Happy Floating Zoo?

Most children's books and many songs learned in Sunday School depict the story of "Noah and the Flood" as a delightful tale of smiling animals on a cruise ship. It creates the impression of a happy floating zoo. Often it sounds more like a cute fairy tale than an historical event. When you pause to think about it, this can have tragic consequences in the minds and hearts of children. It blinds them to the factuality of an important event in history and camouflages the horrifying reality of divine judgment on sin. A plague in an exhibit called "Fairy Tale Ark" at the *Ark Encounter* in Williamstown, Kentucky says it well:

> By treating Noah's Ark and the Flood as fairy tales rather than sobering reminders of divine judgment on a sin-filled world, these storybooks frequently trivialize the Lord's righteous and holy character.

For a true understanding of what the story of Noah and the Flood is about, all one needs to do is read the account in Genesis. Even a cursory acquaintance with the text makes it clear that the story is written to anchor us in three foundational realities. Coming at the dawn of history, apparently God intends that these truths will form the bedrock of all human life and thought.

First, the story emphasizes *the depths of human sin*. The men and women of Noah's generation are wicked, cruel, and perverse. They are greatly fallen from their original design. Every thought they have is only evil all the time (see Gen 6:5). And yet, at least one man,

Noah, stands out from the crowd. It is possible to live a holy life in an unholy world.

Second, the story dramatizes *the intensity of divine wrath*. Floods are horrifying realities. The rising waters, the powerful currents, the widespread devastation, and the anticipation of death by drowning comprise some of our greatest nightmares. Though God is longsuffering and patient, there is a tipping point when his wrath against sin and rebellion spills out in judgment.

Third, the story illustrates *the lavishness of God's grace*. When all is said and done, the story really is about how God saved Noah and his family from a global cataclysm. Even in the worst conditions of human sinfulness and the greatest devastation of divine judgment, God is there to reach out in grace to redeem those who belong to him. The ark is perhaps the greatest symbol of salvation in the Old Testament.

Matters of Secondary Importance

While the Biblical emphasis on sin, wrath, and grace is clear to anyone who reads Genesis 6–9, many who study this portion of Scripture seem to get side-tracked into matters of secondary importance. It is the purpose of this study to be true to Scripture and ensure that the main thing remains the main thing. However, as with perhaps no other passage in all the Bible, the story of Noah and the Flood is loaded with ancillary information that, though it may be of secondary importance, is extremely interesting.

For example, the story of the flood has great implications for how we think about *human history*. Many today picture ancient man as barbaric, unintelligent brutes, living in caves. But the biblical record indicates that primitive man had an advanced civilization where metallurgy, musical instruments, and boat building were surprisingly advanced.

Bringing further historical validity to the biblical record is the fact that over two hundred legends of an ancient flood have been discovered in a wide range of cultures from around the world. Though there is great variation in these accounts, certain themes recur:

- The gods are upset and decide to send a flood on the earth.

- A hero builds a "boat" and saves himself, his family, and some animals.
- Birds are sent out from the boat to see if the land is dry.
- After the flood, the survivors make a sacrifice of thanksgiving.

After looking at the evidence from so many different cultures and so many different places, it is hard to escape the conclusion that a single universal flood lies at the origin of them all.

Those who are interested in *geology* should also be intrigued by what the Bible has to say about a global flood. The biblical account describes the antediluvian world as having no rain (see Gen 2:5). Apparently, a vaporous canopy of water encircled the earth (see Gen 1:6–8). This could have provided a uniform tropical climate, a type of "greenhouse effect," and may help to explain the long lifespans of people before the flood. When the flood came, two sources of water are mentioned: "on that day all the fountains of the great deep burst forth, and the windows of the heavens were opened" (Gen 7:11). These waters were sufficient to cover the entire earth. The Bible seems clear in depicting the flood as a global phenomenon, not a local catastrophe. The text makes note of the fact that the highest mountains were covered by water to a depth of twenty feet (see Gen 7:19–20).

These enormous amounts of water coursing over the earth would have had power to change the direction of rivers, rearrange landscapes, level forests, carve out canyons, and reshape continents. Layers of rock and sediment would have been formed rather suddenly, not gradually over the course of millions of years as is often claimed.

Yet another secondary subject of great interest is the whole issue of *boat building*. Scientists and engineers agree that Noah's "ark" is a very impressive piece of engineering. The text explains that the ark was designed for stability, safety, strength, and seaworthiness. It was not designed for speed (there was no sail or oars) or navigation (there was no rudder). It was basically a floating box, roughly the length of one-and-a-half football fields and four stories tall. Its dimensions (510 feet long, 51 feet tall, and 85 feet wide) correspond amazingly well with modern ocean-going ships. This is in dramatic contrast to the vessels described in other cultural legends of the flood where the hero built either a canoe, raft, coracle, or cube-shaped container. The capacity of Noah's ark was approximately 1.88 million cubic feet, large enough to contain nearly 450 semi-truck trailers.

The subject of *zoology* will be of great interest those who want to know more about the animals on the ark and whether there was room for them all. God specified the animals were to be gathered according to their "kinds" (Gen 6:20). This probably refers to a broader category than what scientists mean today by the word "species." Thus, a "kind" could include many species. If one thinks in terms of a pair of "dog kind," "cattle kind," "alligator kind," etc. one begins to see the possibility of including "all" the animals of the world on the ark. Some have estimated that the world contains roughly 1,400 known living and extinct "kinds" of animals (birds, insects, mammals, etc.). After the flood, the kinds would have proliferated into a wider variety of species.

Yet another ancillary area of interest is *the fossil record*. Popular thought claims that fossils are formed over long periods of time. An animal dies and is slowly buried by sediment so that the bones eventually are fossilized. A global flood, however, looks at things differently. Millions of animals would have drowned in a very short period and then been buried rapidly under layers of sediment stirred up by the floodwaters. This creates an entirely different paradigm for how to understand the fossil record.

Our survey of secondary areas of interest must make mention of the *Ice Age*. A global flood would have had a huge impact on climate all over the earth. Perhaps the explanation for the Ice Age is found here.

Finally, a global flood causes us to imagine *the origin of tribes and languages* in a way quite different from what one is typically taught. The Bible claims that every person alive today is a direct descendant of one of Noah's three sons (see Gen 9:18–19). This means there is only one "race." It is interesting to note that Mount Ararat, where the ark landed, is roughly in the geographic center of three continents:

Asia, Africa, and Europe. This makes the repopulation of the earth strategically possible.

Those with a specific interest in any of these areas of study are encouraged to pursue the matter in books devoted to a much deeper examination of that subject than the present volume can do. Here, our interest is to simply let the text define what is important and focus our attention there.

MATTERS OF FIRST IMPORTANCE

We have already noted how the story of Noah and the Flood emphasizes the depth of human sin, the intensity of divine wrath, and the lavishness of God's grace. The New Testament gives further guidance in helping us understand what this story is all about. Jesus and Peter speak about the flood and use it to both encourage and admonish believers.

Jesus speaks about the days of Noah to exhort his listeners to prepare for the Day of the Lord that is soon coming on the earth.

> *But concerning that day and hour no one knows, not even the angels of heaven, nor the Son, but the Father only. For as were the days of Noah, so will be the coming of the Son of Man. For as in those days before the flood they were eating and drinking, marrying and giving in marriage, until the day when Noah entered the ark, and they were unaware until the flood came and swept them all away, so will be the coming of the Son of Man. Then two men will be in the field; one will be taken and one left. Two women will be grinding at the mill; one will be taken and one left. Therefore, stay awake, for you do not know on what day your Lord is coming. (Matt 24:36–42)*

Jesus is comparing "the days of Noah" to what life on earth will be like just prior to the return of the Son of Man and the final judgment. We have learned from our study of Genesis what the days of Noah were like: advances in technology (Gen 4:22), disregard for God's plan for marriage (Gen 4:19; 6:2), passion for the arts and entertainment (Gen 4:21), widespread violence (Gen 6:11, 13), and moral corruption (Gen 6:5, 12). But the primary characteristic of the days of Noah that Jesus mentions is man's total unpreparedness and shock when the flood comes. They are "eating and drinking" and "marrying" as if everything was normal. When the flood suddenly comes, it is too late to reform their ways, and the waters sweep them all away (Matt 24:38–39).

The apostle Peter also talks about "the days of Noah" and makes a surprising analogy. He uses the waters of the flood as a metaphor to explain the meaning of baptism.

> *When God's patience waited in the days of Noah, while the ark was being prepared, in which a few, that is, eight persons, were brought safely through water. Baptism, which corresponds to this, now saves you, not as a removal of dirt from the body but as an appeal to God for a good conscience, through the resurrection of Jesus Christ. (1 Pet 3:20–21)*

The waters of the flood not only punish sin, they also symbolically wash away moral filth and make it possible to start over again. In other words, the floodwaters bring about a new creation. The same waters that inflict judgment on sinners buoy Noah and his family to safety as they find shelter in the ark. They are saved *from* water, *by* water!

The flood, and baptism to which it points, represents an essential step in salvation. Being washed clean from the guilt of sinful behaviors and saved from divine wrath are no small victories. And yet, something is still lacking. After the flood, we are surprised to discover that the intentions of man's heart continue to be evil (see Gen 8:21). Even more shocking is the fact that righteous Noah himself experiences moral failure when he becomes drunk and lies naked in his tent (see Gen 9:18–29). And the arrogant presumption of human sinfulness in building the tower of Babel illustrates yet again that the cleansing waters of the flood have failed to defeat the dominion of sin in the human heart (see Gen 11:1–9).

Whether talking about the Genesis flood or the gospel ordinance of water baptism, it seems that the washing of water deals primarily with outward behaviors. There is forgiveness for bad things we do. This is glorious. But it seems that the sinful heart of man remains unchanged. At this point in the book of Genesis, we have assurance that God's gracious work of salvation deals with the fruit of sin, but we don't yet know whether he offers a cure for the root. We know he stands ready to forgive a sinful action, but can he cleanse a sinful nature? The story of the flood helps us to realize that it will take more than water baptism to fix the sin problem. Though we can be profoundly grateful for the divine grace that saves us from wrath, the story of Noah leaves us inwardly groaning for more.

Going Deep

"Superficiality is the curse of our age. . . . The desperate need today is not for a greater number of intelligent people, or gifted people, but for deep people."[1] Read rightly, the story of Noah moves us from shallow thinking and practice into the depths of spiritual authenticity. As we close this chapter, let me invite you to think deeply about the great truths taught in the story of Noah and the Flood: deep sin, deep wrath, deep grace.

Deep Sin

One will never understand the depth of God's grace until one comes to grips with the depths of our sin. A superficial understanding of the problem will produce a superficial understanding of the solution. The opening chapters of Genesis introduce us to a world where sin is the defining reality in human conduct and interpersonal relationships. The Bible labors to teach us that sin is not just something we do; it defines who we are. The problem is not just in our hands; the real issue is in our hearts. "Every intention of the thoughts of (our) heart (is) only evil continually" (Gen 6:5). Perhaps the greatest surprise of the Noah story is that the flood does *not* solve the sin problem that had provoked it! Man's sinful state remains unchanged (see Gen 8:21).

Genesis tells us that the antediluvian world was "corrupt" (Gen 6:11–12). The word describes something good that has become spoiled, blemished, and polluted. In other words, the world was already ruined *before* the flood came. As Victor Hamilton says, "God's decision is to destroy what is virtually self-destroyed and self-destroying already."[2]

---

1 Foster, *Celebration of Discipline*, 1.
2 Hamilton, *Genesis*, 1:278.

Not only does the sin problem go deep, it goes broad. Everyone—male and female, old and young, educated and ignorant, white and black, religious and irreligious—is tainted by sin. God sends the flood because "all flesh" has corrupted their way on the earth (see Gen 6:12). There are no exceptions. "None is righteous, no, not one" (Rom 3:10).

No one gets far in Christian discipleship without a lucid understanding of the depth and breadth of sin. The problem goes far deeper than our actions; it goes to our motives and inner desires. The heart of the problem is the problem of the heart. "The whole head is sick, and the whole heart faint. From the sole of the foot even to the head, there is no soundness in it, but bruises and sores and raw wounds." (Isa 1:5–6)

The doctrines of Total Depravity and Original Sin summarize the biblical teaching by orienting us to sin's pervasive and destructive influence:

- *Our hearts are deceived.* "The heart is deceitful above all things, and desperately sick; who can understand it?" (Jer 17:9). One is deceived when one believes something that isn't true. This means that deceived people, by definition, don't know they are deceived! No one can be delivered from sin's power until they first become humble enough to ask if perhaps, they are mistaken about their own goodness.
- *Our wills are enslaved.* Though many live with the assumption that they can change anytime they choose, this is an illusion. Our human nature is twisted in such a way that, without the help of God's grace, we will always choose the bad. We are "slaves" to our passions and pleasures (see Titus 3:3). Without the enabling power of grace, we cannot choose what is right. "No one can come to me unless the Father who sent me draws him" (John 6:44). "You did not choose me, but I chose you" (John 15:16).
- *Our affections are perverted.* Our desires and appetites are by nature fixed on forbidden fruit. We seem to prefer the leeks and onions of this world to the milk and honey of Canaan. We love darkness rather than light (see John 3:19).

- *Our minds are darkened.* Perhaps the most disturbing characteristic of sin is the way it taints our rational capacities so that relying on human reason becomes a pathway to hell. "Whoever trusts in his own mind is a fool" (Prov 28:26). "Every man is stupid and without knowledge" (Jer 10:14).

Yes, the problem is worse than you think!

Deep Wrath

If anyone wants to know what God thinks about human sinfulness, the story of Noah and the Flood gives a definitive answer! Here we have a dramatic and unforgettable statement concerning God's fixed attitude toward sin. His eyes are too pure to look on evil (see Hab 1:13). "He is angry with the wicked every day" (Ps 7:11. NLT).

But the flood is no temper tantrum. Before he got angry, God was grieved in his heart (Gen 6:6). God's wrath reflects his love. He takes no pleasure in the death of the wicked (Ezek 18:32). Sending judgment on sinners is God's "alien work" (Isa 28:21).

Scripture reminds us that Noah was a "preacher of righteousness" (2 Pet 2:5). We can imagine that during the many decades it took Noah to build the ark, the world had the chance to hear God's Word proclaimed by this righteous man. They had the opportunity to turn from their wicked ways and seek God's favor. But they hardened their hearts in willful unbelief. God is slow to anger (see Exod 34:6). He longs for everyone to be saved (see 1 Tim 2:4). He is not willing that any should perish, but that all should reach repentance (see 2 Pet 3:9). But there is a tipping point when the day of grace comes to an end and judgment comes like a flood.

The story of the flood reveals several deep truths about God's judgment:

- God's judgment is *sudden*. Despite Noah's preaching, the flood caught everyone by surprise (see Matt 24:38–39). The reason believers are exhorted to live in constant readiness for the Lord's return is because his coming will be "like a thief in the night. While people are saying, 'There is peace and security,' then sudden destruction will come upon them as labor pains

come upon a pregnant woman, and they will not escape" (1 Thess 5:2–3).
- God's judgment is *final*. When God shut the door of the ark, the opportunity for sinners to repent and reform their ways was closed forever (see Gen 7:16; Matt 25:10). No more chances. No more appeals. No more time. Not even God could turn back the clock. When the curtain falls, the play is over. "It is appointed for man to die once, and after that, the judgment" (Heb 9:27).
- God's judgment is *horrific*. For the people who lived in Noah's day, one can only imagine the terror of the rising waters, the raging destruction, and the realization that the ark's door was permanently shut. We love to sing *The Battle Hymn of the Republic* (by Julia Ward Howe) but we tend to forget the frightful imagery of the words: "He is trampling out the vintage where the grapes of wrath are stored / He hath loosed the fateful lightning of his terrible swift sword / His truth is marching on."
- God's judgment is *fair*. Regardless of how we may feel about the flood, the Scriptures are clear that the punishment fits the crime. Before the rains began to fall, God came and "saw" for himself what was happening, verifying that the flood was justified (see Gen 6:5, 11–12). No one was able to accuse the Just One of acting unjustly.

DEEP GRACE

Noah "found grace" in the eyes of the Lord (Gen 6:8). In a corrupt and violent world, Noah experienced the unmerited favor of God. "Where sin increased, grace abounded all the more" (Rom 5:20). Sin goes deep, but grace goes deeper still.

The ark itself is perhaps the most beautiful illustration of grace in the entire Old Testament. It gives a dramatic and unforgettable picture of how grace can work in a sinful world. Numerous scholars have pointed out that the word "pitch" (Hebrew *kopher*), used to make the ark waterproof (see Gen 6:14), is equivalent to the Hebrew *kaphar* ("to cover"). This latter term, in its noun form, is the regular Hebrew word for "atonement" (see Lev 17:11; etc.).

> In essence, therefore, this is the first mention of "atonement" in the Bible. Whatever the exact nature of this "pitch" may have been (probably a resinous substance of some kind), it sufficed as a perfect covering for the ark, to keep out the waters of judgment, just as the blood of the Lamb provides a perfect atonement for the soul.[3]

The salvation of Noah and his family is all of grace, from start to finish. The initiative is God's. "By grace you have been saved through faith. And this is not your own doing, it is the gift of God" (Eph 2:8). And yet human participation is involved. Noah believed God and then simply did all that he was told to do (Gen 6:22; 7:5). "By faith Noah, being warned by God concerning events as yet unseen, in reverent fear constructed an ark, for the saving of his household" (Heb 11:7). Inside the ark, everyone is safe and secure. It is interesting to note that Noah, though one of the greatest heroes in the Bible, almost never speaks. He only believes and obeys.

There may be theological significance in the fact that the ark is said to "rest" on the mountains of Ararat (see Gen 8:4). For many months it had labored in accomplishing the work of salvation for Noah and his family. Now, its work is done. As God "rested" after his work of creation (see Gen 2:2–3), so the ark "rests" after its work of salvation. When seen as a type of Christ, the ark at "rest" reminds us of Jesus' words on the cross, "It is finished" (John 19:30). "As God 'finished' his work of creation and the ark 'finished' its mission, so Christ 'finished' his work of salvation."[4]

---

3   Morris, *The Genesis Record*, 182.
4   Ibid., 209.

QUESTIONS FOR DISCUSSION

1. What happens when we tell the story of Noah and the Flood as if it were a cute fairy tale of a happy floating zoo?
2. Of all the items mentioned of "secondary interest" (history, geology, zoology, boat building, etc.), which one interests you the most? Why?
3. How does the story of the flood help you to better understand your baptism?
4. Can wrath coexist with love? Discuss this.
5. Do you think most Christians today are superficial and shallow in their understanding of sin, wrath, and grace? Why is it important to go deep?
6. Do you think we are living in the Last Days? Do you think our nation has passed "the point of no return"? How has this study impacted your thinking about these things?

I Asked the Lord that I Might Grow
John Newton

I asked the Lord that I might grow
In faith and love and ev'ry grace,
Might more of His salvation know,
And seek more earnestly His face.

'Twas He who taught me thus to pray,
And He, I trust, has answered prayer,
But it has been in such a way
As almost drove me to despair.

I hoped that in some favored hour
At once He'd answer my request
And, by His love's constraining pow'r,
Subdue my sins and give me rest.

Instead of this, He made me feel
The hidden evils of my heart
And let the angry pow'rs of hell
Assault my soul in ev'ry part.

Yea, more with His own hand He seemed
Intent to aggravate my woe,
Crossed all the fair designs I schemed,
Humbled my heart and laid me low.

"Lord, why is this," I trembling cried;
"Wilt Thou pursue Thy worm to death?"
"'Tis in this way," the Lord replied,
"I answer prayer for grace and faith."

"These inward trials I employ
From self and pride to set thee free
And break thy schemes of earthly joy
That thou may'st find thy all in Me."

9
Daddy's Drunk!
Genesis 9:1–29

As the earth dries out after the flood, Noah and his family seek to re-establish a measure of normalcy. Though we know little about their thoughts or feelings, we can imagine how challenging it must have been. The questions were many and the answers were not obvious. Where to live? What to eat? How to raise a family? Are the animals OK? However, for the eight members of Noah's family, the overwhelming emotion must have been sheer awe and amazement that they had survived the greatest cataclysm in history! The ark had shielded them from the storm and carried them to safety. Little wonder that their first act after disembarking from the ark was to offer a sacrifice of thanksgiving (Gen 8:20–22).

Now, as they begin to turn the focus of their attention from the horrors of the past to the prospects of the future, their hearts must have been humbled at the realization that human history was about to begin again—with them! Perhaps feeling some of what Adam and Eve may have felt in the beginning, the family of Noah must have been filled with wonder and anticipation as they looked at the newly washed world that lay open before them. God was giving humanity another chance. Creation was being renewed. A new world order was about to begin. Though similar in some respects to the situation with Adam and Eve, this time, there were important differences. Innocence, once lost, can never be regained.

Noah and his family are sinners saved by grace. Not only have they been delivered from wrath and judgment, but at least Noah has also experienced a genuine measure of righteousness and blamelessness (see Gen 6:8–9). But after the flood, neither God nor man are naïve concerning the twisted perversity that resides in the human heart, even of those who have experienced saving grace. In contrast to how God began with Adam and Eve, Part Two of human history begins with the frank acknowledgement that "the intention of man's heart is evil from his youth" (Gen 8:21). This causes us to wonder what this new world will be like. Will it be an improvement on the old world order, or will it be more of the same? Can redeemed sinners build a righteous society? We are soon to find out.

The Rule of Law

The Lord begins Part Two of human history by establishing what might be called the founding document of the new world order. Genesis 9:1–17 sets down the most basic conditions God has established for civil society. These foundational instructions are comprised of two parts: the law (Gen 9:1–7) and the covenant (Gen 9:8–17). Note well that this original charter for human conduct is given to all mankind. One must not read these verses as applicable to Jews only. Instituted a full ten generations before the call of Abraham (the first "Jew"), this document is universal in its application.

> *And God blessed Noah and his sons and said to them, "Be fruitful and multiply and fill the earth. The fear of you and the dread of you shall be upon every beast of the earth and upon every bird of the heavens, upon everything that creeps on the ground and all the fish of the sea. Into your hand they are delivered. Every moving thing that lives shall be food for you. And as I gave you the green plants, I give you everything. But you shall not eat flesh with its life, that is, its blood. And for your lifeblood I will require a reckoning: from every beast I will require it and from man. From his fellow man I will require a reckoning for the life of man.*

> *"Whoever sheds the blood of man,*
> *by man shall his blood be shed,*
> *for God made man in his own image.*
>
> *And you, be fruitful and multiply, increase greatly on the earth and multiply in it." (Gen 9:1–7)*

Essentially, the original law given by God to man relates to two prohibitions concerning blood:

- Do not eat the blood of animals (Gen 9:4).
- Do not shed the blood of humans (Gen 9:5–6).

The Mosaic law will explain that "the life of every creature is its blood: its blood is its life." (Lev 17:14). The emphasis on blood underscores the emphatic value God places on life, especially human life. This universal mandate, coming at the dawn of the new world order, establishes the foundational importance of the sanctity of life. Cultures that disregard this most basic of all civic duties are building on a foundation that is sure to crumble.

Note especially how this first law is presented in the context of blessing. The divine blessing of fertility and fruitfulness frame the entire legislation (see Gen 9: 1, 7). The law is literally wrapped in a blessing. The author of Genesis obviously wants us to remember the identical blessing given in the beginning to Adam and Eve (Gen 1:28). Both the blessing of fruitfulness and the law against eating or shedding blood show God's passionate purpose in promoting the sanctity of life.

Though many have tried to see this earliest legal prohibition as part of the so-called "Natural Law" (the rule of conscience), the biblical text underscores the fact that this law comes directly from God. Noah does not think it up himself. He does not invent it. It is revealed by God.

As with many legal codes, the law is stated in the form of a prohibition: *Do not* eat the blood of animals; *do not* shed the blood of humans. For those who may be troubled by such negativism, we should remember that every "no" automatically implies a "yes." The warning about doing something wrong awakens the soul to the possibility of doing something right! In prohibiting the eating of blood and the taking of human life, God is encouraging humans, in the strongest language possible, to show deep respect for animals and to regard all human life as sacred!

The first law is focused on man's relationship to animals. "Every moving thing that lives shall be food for you. . . . But you shall not eat flesh with its life, that is, its blood" (Gen 9:3–4). The new world order does not envision a vegetarian diet for humans. In contrast to the instructions given to Adam and Eve, Noah's family is specifically told that they are free to eat of "every moving thing that lives." The prohibition relates not to meat, but to *living* flesh, or blood. The Levitical law cited above gives the reason for this prohibition. Blood is not to be eaten because it *is* the animal's life (see Lev 17:14). One is to avoid eating blood simply out of awe and respect for animal life. Leon Kass summarizes the law this way: "The shepherd will now tend his flock with at least part of his mind on lamb chops. Yet the shepherd is not—and must not become—a wolf."[1]

Showing respect for the dignity of animals by not eating their blood may be more important than one first thinks. God sees a connection between the treatment of animals and the way we treat one another. The first law prohibits the eating of animal blood. The second prohibits the shedding of human blood. When a culture begins to show disrespect for animals, beware. It is only a short step to moving to crimes much more serious.

The second law prohibits murder. Here at the dawn of the new world order, God is making it clear that the first and foremost responsibility of a civil society is to both protect and preserve human life. And when this law is broken, God demands that the offender be punished severely.

> *And I will require the blood of anyone who takes another person's life. If a wild animal kills a person, it must die. And anyone who murders a fellow human must die. If anyone takes a human life, that person's life will also be taken by human hands. For God made human beings in his own image. (Gen 9:5–6 NLT)*

---

[1] Kass, *The Beginning of Wisdom*, 178.

Though some will be troubled by the insistence on capital punishment, one must remember that such a law was, in fact, a way to *restrain* violence, not make it greater. In a world ignorant of God's justice, the tendency has always been to seek revenge for a crime by raising the level of harshness.

- You slander my reputation, then I will steal your cow.
- You steal my cow, then I will kill your son.
- You kill my son, then we will burn your village.
- You burn my village, then our nation will declare war on your nation.
- You attack my nation with tanks and guns, we will attack your nation with weapons of mass destruction.

In a world where escalating vengeance is the norm, God's standard of "life for life, eye for eye, tooth for tooth, hand for hand, foot for foot, burn for burn, wound for wound, stripe for stripe" (Exod 21:23–25) is a welcome standard indeed!

> The temptation of righteous indignation to excessive vengeance, with spiraling violence begetting more violence, is strongly curtailed. Anger and force are brought under rational rule and measured proportion, which is to say, are brought into line with an idea of justice. The murderer's life for the life he murdered in fact exemplifies the first principle of strict and equal justice: the violator gets exactly what he deserves.[2]

In prohibiting murder, God could have simply said, "Because I say so, that's why!" Or he could have hoped that the threat of capital punishment would scare people into compliance. But neither of these possible explanations for why murder is wrong gets at the heart of the matter. The law clearly states that the real reason taking another person's life is strictly forbidden in the new world order is because "God made man in his own image" (Gen 9:6). The life of *every* person must be respected and treated with dignity because man is more than an animal. Even in his fallen state, each human being still reflects the image of God. Whether we are talking about someone who is old or young, rich or poor, white or black, neighbor or foreigner, healthy or

---

2   Ibid., 182.

infirm, religious or irreligious, educated or ignorant, born or unborn, the image of God that is intrinsically tied to every human life makes the preservation and protection of that life civil society's top priority.

The Promise of the Covenant

The new world order is founded not only on law, but also on a covenant promise from God himself that his intention toward the world is good; he will never again destroy all flesh with water.

> *Then God said to Noah and to his sons with him, "Behold, I establish my covenant with you and your offspring after you, and with every living creature that is with you, the birds, the livestock, and every beast of the earth with you, as many as came out of the ark; it is for every beast of the earth. I establish my covenant with you, that never again shall all flesh be cut off by the waters of the flood, and never again shall there be a flood to destroy the earth." And God said, "This is the sign of the covenant that I make between me and you and every living creature that is with you, for all future generations: I have set my bow in the cloud, and it shall be a sign of the covenant between me and the earth. (Gen 9:8–13)*

The word *covenant* (Hebrew, *berith*) points to one of the most important concepts in all the Bible. It refers to an agreement established between two parties, in which one or both make solemn promises. More personal than a contract, a covenant binds two parties together who would remain separate without it and clarifies the nature of that relationship. In his covenant with Noah, God reestablishes his most basic relationship with fallen humanity. Note especially that this covenant is made with all people everywhere, not just the Hebrews. In fact, it includes the animals as well!

Not only is this covenant with Noah universal; it is unilateral, one-sided. Noah is a passive participant. He says nothing and promises nothing. God takes the initiative and makes an unconditional promise to never again judge the world with water. He asks for nothing in return. The covenant doesn't even depend on man's obedience to the law that God has just given. God just shows up and makes a solemn vow to never again destroy all flesh by sending a flood.

Earlier, when Noah and his family first came out of the ark, God stated the reason for his decision to never again destroy the earth: "for the intention of man's heart is evil from his youth" (Gen 8:21). According to Genesis 6:5–7, the reason God sent the flood in the first place was because every intention of man's heart was evil. But now we learn that God will *not* send another flood because the intention of man's heart is evil. In other words, God destroys humans because they are sinful and then promises not to destroy them because they are sinful. What?

Some have interpreted this to mean that God is frustrated because the flood hadn't done what it was supposed to do. It destroyed humans but did not reform human nature. So, in promising Noah he will never do *that* again, perhaps God is admitting that he made a mistake.

Victor Hamilton offers a much better explanation. Now, after the flood, as sinners continue in their willful rejection of righteousness, God would be fully justified in destroying them yet again. However, now he "chooses not to exercise that option. No longer will man be treated as under a curse."[3] In the new world order, God's initial response to all human behaviors is going to be gracious and tender. The covenant with Noah is a clear and unambiguous signal that God loves the world so much that he desperately hopes he will never have to give them what their sins deserve.

The rainbow is the sign of the covenant. It reminds both God in heaven and humans on earth of the divine promise being made. The Hebrew word *bow*, as in English, can also refer to a weapon of war (bow and arrows). Thus, the rainbow in the sky is an everlasting picture of God hanging up his weapons. He wants the whole world to know of his desire for peace and goodwill toward all his creatures.

Belief in the covenant is of crucial importance for the new world order. Humans have often been haunted by the recurring fear that nature and the cosmos are arrayed against them. The rainbow is a permanent reminder that God's intention for human beings

---

[3] Hamilton, *Genesis*, 1:309.

everywhere is good, not evil. "What then shall we say to these things? If God is for us, who can be against us?" (Rom 8:31).

WHEN SAINTS ACT LIKE IDIOTS

The story of Noah's naked drunkenness is certainly one of the strangest and most difficult to interpret passages in all the Bible. Almost everything about this brief incident is either offensive, disturbing, or difficult to understand. But such a reality must not deter us from making the effort to listen to its message. The rewards are rich for those who have the will and the courage to make the endeavor.

> *Noah began to be a man of the soil, and he planted a vineyard. He drank of the wine and became drunk and lay uncovered in his tent. And Ham, the father of Canaan, saw the nakedness of his father and told his two brothers outside. Then Shem and Japheth took a garment, laid it on both their shoulders, and walked backward and covered the nakedness of their father. Their faces were turned backward, and they did not see their father's nakedness. When Noah awoke from his wine and knew what his youngest son had done to him, he said,*
>
> *"Cursed be Canaan; a servant of servants*
> *shall he be to his brothers."*
>
> *He also said, "Blessed be the LORD, the God of Shem;*
> *and let Canaan be his servant.*
> *May God enlarge Japheth,*
> *and let him dwell in the tents of Shem,*
> *and let Canaan be his servant."*
>
> *After the flood Noah lived 350 years. All the days of Noah were 950 years, and he died. (Gen 9:20–29)*

This bizarre story is of great importance for several reasons. For one thing, it is the Bible's first description of fatherhood (and sonship). It describes sin's tragic influence on one of life's more significant relationships; that of a father and his children. Secondly, this story reminds us that even heroes of the faith are susceptible to moral failure. Though it is disturbing to see one of history's greatest saints lying naked in a drunken stupor in his tent, the Bible recognizes that such things sometimes happen. If this makes the reader uncomfortable, well, get over it! The Bible simply refuses to put a spiritual spin on the tragic reality that saints sometimes fail us. The way this story underscores the significance of shame is yet a third reason why this passage is important. Though we in the West tend to understand guilt, we have a much more difficult time grasping the profound importance of shame. By covering their father's nakedness, Shem and Japheth were seeking to protect him from shame, not to absolve him of guilt. A final reason that this story is worthy of our attention is that it helps to answer the question: "How should I respond when a God-ordained authority (father, husband, pastor, boss, president, etc.) behaves like an idiot?" Unfortunately, many will have to admit that such a question has practical relevance for their life situation today.

Noah's sin is recounted in the briefest manner: he "became drunk and lay uncovered in his tent" (Gen 9:21). What a contrast this is to the earlier Noah who found grace in the eyes of the Lord and was called righteous and blameless. He walked with God and did everything the Lord commanded him to do (see Gen 6:8–9, 22). His godly character placed him among the greatest heroes of the Old Testament (see Ezek 14:14). The New Testament calls him a "herald of righteousness" (2 Pet 2:5) and includes him in the faith hall of fame (see Heb 11:7). To think that such a godly man, after centuries of such faithful living, would end up like *this*, sends shock waves into the depths of our souls.

It seems that once the crisis of the flood had passed, Noah let down his guard and carelessly became vulnerable to temptation and sin. Peace and prosperity proved to be a greater danger to Noah's soul than the violent wickedness and arrogant unbelief of the world before the flood. One of the lessons of this tragic story is simply this: a good start does not guarantee a good finish.

This is the first recorded instance of substance abuse in history. The biblical injunctions against drunkenness are numerous (see for example, Prov 20:1; 23:29–35; Luke 21:34; Rom 13:13–14; Gal 5:19–21; Eph 5:18; etc.). Far from enjoying a "social drink" with his family, Noah drinks to the point that he passes out! His self-inflicted drunken and naked condition means that he has lost both his dignity and his honor.

Noah's inebriated state is connected to his foolish behavior of lying naked in his tent. Alcohol lowers one's inhibitions and drunkards often do things they would never think of doing while sober. As with Adam and Eve's original sin in the garden, nakedness brings shame (see Gen 3:7). Unless someone covers him, Noah may never recover from the loss of face he has experienced. Preserving a father's honor is a matter of great importance, even if his embarrassment is caused by his own idiocy and folly.

But what are we to make of Ham's sin? Indeed, it is even more difficult to understand than Noah's. The textual account is brief and to the point: Ham "saw the nakedness of his father and told his two brothers outside" (Gen 9:22). The verbs *saw* and *told* seem to summarize his sinful deed.

Some scholars have claimed that Ham's sin was some form of perverted sexual behavior. Making much of Noah's statement that Ham "had done" something "to him" (Gen 9:24), these interpretations suggest that his sin was an act, not just something he saw. "Seeing someone's nakedness" is treated as a euphemism for immoral conduct. Thus, some have pretended that Ham's sin was sodomy; that he raped his drunken father. Indeed, Leviticus 18 uses the idiom "uncovering the nakedness of" for describing a wide variety of types of incest.

Others have taken a very different angle and claimed that Ham raped not his father, but his mother, who perhaps became pregnant with Canaan as a result. This interpretation is built on the assumption that the phrase "his father's nakedness" refers to Noah's wife, not to himself.

As interesting and creative as these interpretations may be, they see more in the text than is actually there. The best way to understand Ham's sin is the most obvious one. He *saw* his father lying naked. By looking, he inadvertently brought shame to the father he was supposed to honor. But it is what happens next that makes Ham's deed truly wicked. Rather than shielding his eyes and seeking a means to cover his father so that no further shame would come to him, Ham went outside the tent and *told* his brothers. Perhaps he said something like this: "Hey guys, wanna see something funny? Daddy's drunk and lying naked in the tent. Come on, have a look!" In other words, Ham's sin was showing disrespect for his father. Though the Mosaic Law had not yet been given, he broke what would be later called the fifth commandment: "Honor your father and your mother" (Exod 20:12). When one thinks through all the dynamics of what is happening here, one begins to realize that gravity of Ham's sin:

- He does nothing to protect his father's dignity.
- He seems to find enjoyment in shaming his father by telling others.
- He does not honor his father.
- He exploits his father's moral failure for his own personal advantage.

The behavior of Shem and Japheth confirms this interpretation by showing what Ham *should* have done! By taking a garment, walking backward, refusing to look on their naked father, and then covering him, they honor their father and preserve his dignity. They are not blind to the fact that their father has dishonored himself and acted like a drunken fool, but this does not keep them from showing their father the honor he deserves simply because he is their father.

Perhaps the part of the story that is most difficult to understand comes next. When Noah wakes from his drunken stupor and realizes how his son Ham has dishonored him, he curses his grandson Canaan, who had nothing to do with it (see Gen 9:24–25)! We could understand perhaps if Noah had directed his anger at Ham. But at Canaan? This feels very unfair. How are we to understand this?

The most compelling explanation for Noah's unexpected behavior is that his words are intended to be prophetic rather than imprecatory. His intent, it seems, is not really to place a curse on his grandson but rather to announce what Ham's family (including Canaan) is going to experience in the future. With a father like Ham for a model, just imagine what his children and grandchildren are going to be like. If they follow the example of their founding father, the Hamites will become a tribe of rebels who have no respect for authority and take delight in shaming others! They will create a world where no one's "nakedness" is off limits to their passions and desires. Genesis 10 tells us that Ham's descendants became Egyptians, Babylonians, Assyrians, Canaanites, etc. These nations were known for violence, moral impurity and especially for hostility toward the Jews (See Gen 10:6–20).

Make It Personal

Though contemporary LGBT activists may have seized the rainbow as a logo for their political movement, we must never forget its original symbolic meaning. Spanning the heavens in brilliant colors, seen best when skies are grey and storm clouds threaten, the rainbow is God's bold and eternal promise that he is for us. It is the sign of God's love and good will toward all men everywhere. God states this truth with poetic beauty through Isaiah the prophet:

> *"This is like the days of Noah to me:*
> *as I swore that the waters of Noah*
> *should no more go over the earth,*
> *so I have sworn that I will not be angry with you,*
> *and will not rebuke you.*
> *For the mountains may depart*
> *and the hills be removed,*
> *but my steadfast love shall not depart from you,*
> *and my covenant of peace shall not be removed,"*
> says the LORD, *who has compassion on you.* (Isa 54:9–10)

But it takes more than a promise from God to ensure that men and women will behave in ways that are morally good and relationally healthy. Noah's drunkenness and Ham's dishonoring of his father remind us that walking with God in righteousness and moral integrity may be harder than we first imagined. As we close this chapter, two great moral lessons help us both summarize what we have learned and apply it to our own lives today.

Noah's drunken folly reminds us that godliness in the past does not necessarily make godliness in the future a certain thing. A good start does not guarantee a successful finish. Though he had walked with God for 600 years, the final 350 years of Noah's life are tainted by his moral compromise and substance abuse. The fact that the Bible includes this sad story about one of history's greatest spiritual giants is God's way of warning us of the need for constant vigilance in our own spiritual walk. No one, regardless of his or her spiritual victories in the past, is immune from doing something stupid and tarnishing their life's testimony. Just as a race is determined at the finish line, so we are called to go the distance and finish strong. Jesus stated the matter succinctly when he said, "The one who endures to the end will be saved" (Matt 24:13).

Ham's disrespect toward his father points us to the second great moral lesson taught in this passage. Though Noah's foolish and sinful behavior certainly make the matter more difficult, Ham's failure to honor his father is nevertheless a great and grievous sin. Human society can only work properly when people in God-ordained positions of authority (parents, civil leaders, pastors, bosses, etc.) are treated with respect and honor, even if they behave like idiots. The Scriptures will later teach the proper parameters of submission and even indicate when resistance to evil authority is called for. But here in Genesis 9, at the dawn of the new world order, God simply wants to emphasize the fundamental importance of giving honor to parents, and by implication, other God-ordained authorities, even when they behave badly.

QUESTIONS FOR DISCUSSION

1. Why does God have such an interest in blood? Whether eating the blood of animals or shedding the blood of humans, what's the big deal about blood?
2. State in your own words what God is saying to the world through the rainbow.
3. Have you ever known a godly person who experienced a moral failure? How did you respond? What did you feel? What lessons did you learn?

4. A foot race is determined at the finish line. Discuss this statement in terms of your own spiritual walk.
5. Apparently, God expects us to show honor to those in God-ordained positions of authority even when they behave like idiots. Talk about this.

10
The City of Man
Genesis 11:1–9

In 1516, Thomas Moore published his influential book *Utopia*. Written originally in Latin, the work depicts a fictional island and its culture, habits, government, and religion. Moore's book is a sociopolitical satire, describing an idealized world, a society where all are cared for equally and no one acts unjustly. However, it is the title that perhaps best conveys the real message of Moore's book. While today we use the word *utopia* to describe a place of ideal perfection and sublime happiness, the word's actual meaning is quite different. Derived from the Greek prefix *ou*, meaning, *not* or *no*, and the root word *topos*, meaning *place*, the word literally means *nowhere* or *no place*. One could easily draw the conclusion that Moore's real message is that an ideal society of happiness and peace simply does not exist!

The city of Babel is perhaps the earliest attempt in history at building a perfect society. We might say that its builders are the first utopians. They are certainly not the last. Though Cain gets the credit for being the first city-builder (see Gen 4:17), Babel is the most important city in Genesis, her significance going far beyond her size or military strength. Her importance relates to two events that happened there: 1) the building of the tower, and 2) the origin of human languages. Furthermore, as Babel eventually morphs into Babylon, the quintessential embodiment of politicized evil in the Bible, we see yet again the enormous significance of the events recorded in Genesis 11:1–9.

Now the whole earth had one language and the same words. And as people migrated from the east, they found a plain in the land of Shinar and settled there. And they said to one another, "Come, let us make bricks, and burn them thoroughly." And they had brick for stone, and bitumen for mortar. Then they said, "Come, let us build ourselves a city and a tower with its top in the heavens, and let us make a name for ourselves, lest we be dispersed over the face of the whole earth." And the Lord came down to see the city and the tower, which the children of man had built. And the Lord said, "Behold, they are one people, and they have all one language, and this is only the beginning of what they will do. And nothing that they propose to do will now be impossible for them. Come, let us go down and there confuse their language, so that they may not understand one another's speech." So the Lord dispersed them from there over the face of all the earth, and they left off building the city. Therefore its name was called Babel, because there the Lord confused the language of all the earth. And from there the Lord dispersed them over the face of all the earth. (Gen 11:1–9)

Unscattered People

After the flood, God gave a clear and unambiguous command to Noah and his descendants: "Be fruitful and multiply and fill the earth" (Gen 9:1). This mandate was essentially a repetition of the original command given to Adam and Eve at the very beginning of human history (see Gen 1:28). The Genesis narrative makes it clear that God wants his creatures to disperse, to scatter over the earth. His intent is missional; he wants the world to be filled with men and women devoted to doing his will and enjoying his blessings. When you pause to think about it, the similarities are great between God's first commandment and Jesus' last commandment, what we often call The Great Commission (see Matt 28:19, Mark 16:15, etc.).

But Genesis 11:1–9 underscores the fact that the inhabitants of Babel had made a conscious and willful choice to do just the opposite of what God had commanded. The tower they built was a flagrant symbol of their rebellious spirit. The real sin at Babel was not so much the building of the tower but rather the heart attitudes that lay behind their construction project. God said, "Scatter, fill the earth," and the citizens of Babel said, "Nope, that's not going to happen!" This is more than generic misbehavior or sins of ignorance. This is *willful disobedience*. This is highhanded rebellion. "Come, let us build ourselves a city and a tower, . . . *lest we be dispersed over the face of the whole earth*" (Gen 11:4). The judgment God sent upon these sinners (the confusion of languages) forced them to do what they had stubbornly refused to do: to scatter over the earth. "So the Lord dispersed them from there over the face of all the earth" (Gen 11:8–9).

A second sin clearly visible in the events at Babel is *human pride*. Their arrogant ethnocentrism is easily discernible in the words they use to promote their great building project. "Come, let us build ourselves a city and a tower with its top in the heavens, and let us make a name for ourselves" (Gen 11:4). Far from wanting to exalt God, these citizens of Babel wanted to exalt themselves and be remembered forever. Ironically, they succeeded! Four thousand years later we are still talking about these men and women, but not because of some great cultural achievement. We remember them because of their grandiose and spectacular failure! Perhaps Jesus was thinking of Babel when he said:

> *For which of you, desiring to build a tower, does not first sit down and count the cost, whether he has enough to complete it? Otherwise, when he has laid a foundation and is not able to finish, all who see it begin to mock him, saying, "This man began to build and was not able to finish." (Luke 14:28–30)*

A third sin at work in the lives of these builders of Babel is *unbelief*. Perhaps the tower was built to be a place of refuge and safety in case another global flood should ever come upon the earth. But it is at the city's founding that we see the most obvious evidence of Babel's willful unbelief. Genesis 10:8–10 tells us that the city was founded by Nimrod. In Hebrew, the word *Nimrod* means *rebel*. This undoubtedly describes the character of the founder of history's most important city. According to some ancient traditions, Nimrod personally led the construction project to build the tower. As "the first on earth to be a mighty man" (Gen 10:8), Nimrod was apparently greedy and ambitious for conquest and power. Being a descendant of Noah through the cursed line of Ham (see Gen 9:18–25), Nimrod's wickedness contributed in a profound way to the spiritual DNA of the city of Babel and its successor, Babylon, making her proverbial for her rebellion against God.

The tower itself is far more than a massive civic building project. This pyramidal, spiral-shaped ziggurat is a defiant symbol of arrogant unbelief. Its purpose is to exalt human achievement and glorify the City of Man. Ziggurats in the ancient world typically had a stairway either running up one side of the structure or circling upward in a rising spiral. At Babel, the tower's purpose was to reach the very gate of heaven. It is important to remember that the word *Babel* is derived from a Sumerian phrase meaning "gate of god." Whether literally or metaphorically, these builders, using human ingenuity and state-of-the-art technology, aimed to reach "the heavens" (Gen 11:4). In effect, they were trying to find their way back to the gate to the Garden of Eden that God had decisively shut (see Gen 3:24). They hoped that by human effort they could once again gain access to God and the tree of life. The tower was intended to be a stairway to heaven, establishing a link between man and God. Babel was aspiring to be what her name implied: the gate of God.

The tower of Babel is the first real human attempt to find God. The story reminds us, in no uncertain terms, of the utter futility and folly of all such efforts. The chasm between God's holiness and human sinfulness is so great that the most noble attempts of men and women to bridge the gap fall woefully short. The story of what happened at Babel teaches us that if this great chasm separating God and man is to be bridged, it will have to be initiated from God's side, not man's! Looking forward in the Genesis narrative, we discover that this is precisely what happened when God revealed himself to Jacob. Amazingly, Jacob was not even looking for God. But God was looking for Jacob! And in setting up a "ladder" between heaven and earth, God was taking the initiative to make it possible for sinners to have a relationship with him.

> *Jacob left Beersheba and went toward Haran. And he came to a certain place and stayed there that night, because the sun had set. Taking one of the stones of the place, he put it under his head and lay down in that place to sleep. And he dreamed, and behold, there was a ladder (or, a flight of steps) set up on the earth, and the top of it reached to heaven. And behold, the angels of God were ascending and descending on it! And behold, the LORD stood above it (or, beside him) and said, "I am the LORD, the God of Abraham your father and the God of Isaac. . . . Then Jacob awoke from his sleep and said, "Surely the LORD is in this place. . . . This is none other than the house of God, and this is the gate of heaven." (Gen 28:10–13, 16–17)*

It would not be an exaggeration to say that the entire message of the Bible begins to come into focus in this amazing comparison between Babel's tower and Jacob's stairway. Both structures are intended to bridge the chasm between heaven and earth, making it possible to have access to heaven's gate. But here the similarities end. Babel's tower is a human endeavor representing man's search for God. Jacob's ladder is a divine endeavor representing God's search for man. But the primary difference between the two structures is seen in the fact that only one of them actually works! While Babel's tower is a complete fiasco, Jacob's ladder reaches all the way from earth to the gate of heaven. The connection is such that both God and angels can freely travel back and forth from one world to the other. God himself has established a link to bridge the chasm between earth and heaven. Now, it is finally possible for human sinners to have a relationship with a holy God. Little wonder that Jesus, as he sought to explain his identity and mission, described himself in terms of Jacob's ladder (see John 1:51). He is the ultimate bridge, the mediator, between God and man.

A Tale of Two Cities

Babel (soon to become Babylon) is the quintessential City of Man; a place of human wickedness and rebellion against God. As the biblical narrative unfolds, we learn that Babylon becomes the city where God's people are sent into exile and ultimately, she will become the Great Prostitute mentioned in the book of Revelation. Her final destiny is to be judged, condemned, and destroyed. Her demise ushers in that climactic moment at the end of human history when the new Jerusalem, the City of God, descends from heaven "prepared as a bride adorned for her husband" (Rev 21:2). Charles Dickens' novel, *A Tale of Two Cities* (1859), recounts the dramatic contrast between life in two very different locations: Paris and London. On a much greater scale, the Bible recounts the cosmic saga, stretching from Genesis to Revelation, of the reality of two—and only two— cities that define human history: the City of God and the City of Man, Jerusalem and Babylon.

Numerous thinkers and writers have seized upon the reality of "the city" to define the meaning of human existence. For example, Neil Postman, in his influential book *Amusing Ourselves to Death* (1985), describes how cities have defined American culture throughout its history. In the 18th century, *Boston* was the focal point of the American spirit. Her promotion of patriotism, political idealism, and revolution were the defining realities for the first century after America's birth. But in the middle of the 19th century, a new city set the standard for what it meant to be an American: *New York*. Ellis Island defined how the nation saw herself as a melting pot for cultures from all over the world. Moving west, the 20th century revealed that *Chicago* had become the great symbol of the American reality. With her industry, railroads, and entrepreneurship, she seemed to capture the spirit of America. Today, however, according to Postman, the city that best serves as a metaphor of our national character is *Las Vegas*. For she is

> a city entirely devoted to the idea of entertainment, and as such proclaims the spirit of a culture in which all public discourse increasingly takes the form of entertainment. . . . The result is that we are a people on the verge of amusing ourselves to death.[1]

Perhaps the earliest Christian thinker outside the Bible to see the importance of cities was Augustine (354–430). When the city of Rome was overrun by barbarians and destroyed, he wrote his monumental theology of history, *The City of God* (426). His purpose was to show

---

[1] Postman, *Amusing Ourselves to Death*, 3–4.

that these two cities (the City of Man and the City of God) are entangled together in this world so that we must make a choice concerning our identity by defining our true citizenship and then living in accordance with our choice. His point was to emphasize that the City of Man is all about the love of power while the City of God is all about the power of love.

John Bunyan (1628–1688) is yet another Christian thinker who thought deeply about the theological significance of "the city." In his classic *Pilgrim's Progress*, three cities punctuate the journey of Christian as he travels the path of discipleship. He begins his pilgrimage in the City of Destruction, travels through Vanity Fair and eventually reaches his destination: the Celestial City. Bunyan's amazing allegory of the Christian life illustrates how cities can be both sources of great danger as well as great blessing.

French philosopher, sociologist, and theologian Jacques Ellul (1912–1994) made a great contribution to the theological significance of cities in his groundbreaking book *The Meaning of the City* (1970). His goal was simple: to explore what the Bible says about "the city." Ellul concluded that the city, in the Biblical narrative, represents man's ultimate rejection of God. But rather than history culminating in some idyllic return to the Garden of Eden, Ellul shows how redemption will find its final and absolute expression in the coming City of God (see Rev 21–22).

Ellul recognizes that the biblical depiction of Babel/Babylon is thus the story of man's attempt to create a home for himself apart from God. God had responded to Adam's solitude by giving him a family (see Gen 2:18–25). But once sin entered the human condition, man's response to his loneliness was to build a city (see Gen 4:17). Though Aristotle and others have claimed that the city is man's highest achievement, the Bible tells a very different story. Babylon (the City of Man) eventually becomes the Great Prostitute, ruled over by God's enemy, Satan. In her wicked rebellion, she has become irredeemable and must ultimately be destroyed.

> Babylon is not a city. She is *the* city. . . . All the cities of the world are brought together in her, she is the synthesis of them all (Dan 3–4; Rev 14, 18). She is the head of, and the standard for the other cities. . . . Babylon, Venice, Paris, New York—they are all the same city, only one Babel always reappearing.[2]

The Meaning of the City

Yes, the Bible has much to say about "the city." Whether we are talking about cities of long ago or cities of today, the Bible alerts us to the spiritual reality that is present in the places where we choose to live. A quick survey of the Bible will make this truth abundantly clear.

Genesis introduces us to the spiritual DNA of cities when it tells us that the first city in history was built by the first murderer, Cain (see Gen 4:16–17). To help him cope with the terrible consequences of the sin of killing his own brother, Cain built a city and named it *Enoch*. Apparently, he believed this would satisfy his inner yearning for security, stability, and meaningful relationships. Alas, he never found what he was looking for in this original City of Man. Ellul points out that all future city-builders are "sons of Cain" who "act with his purpose."[3]

After Enoch (Gen 4:16–17) and Babel (Gen 11:1–9), the next city we meet in the book of Genesis is *Sodom*, a city proverbial for great wickedness. In fact, Sodom's sinfulness is such that God decides to destroy her (along with Gomorrah) with fire and brimstone (see Gen 19). Though sexual perversity is her most obvious sin, Sodom's wickedness includes a wide range of profane attitudes and depraved behaviors.

> *Behold, this was the guilt of your sister Sodom: she and her daughters had pride, excess of food, and prosperous ease, but did not aid the poor and needy. They were haughty and did an abomination before me. So I removed them, when I saw it. (Ezek 16:49–50)*

---

2   Ellul, *The Meaning of the City*, 20–21.
3   Ibid., 10.

Later in the Old Testament we are introduced to the city of *Jerusalem*. Once in possession of the land of Canaan, the people of God capture and then build up this great city which is destined to play such a vital role in the history of the world. Although Jerusalem is the City of God, the Bible is candid in recognizing what a strange mixture of good and evil she is. On the one hand, Jerusalem is holy because the Temple of God is there (see Ps 87, etc.). But on the other hand, she is often no different from other cities in the ancient world. Ezekiel goes so far as to say that in comparison to Jerusalem, Sodom appears righteous (Ezek 16:52)! Isaiah voices the lament: "How the faithful city has become a whore" (Isa 1:21). As a result of her continued sin and rebellion, God finally sends his people living in Jerusalem into exile. The place he chooses to send them is not accidental: Babylon.

As we have seen, *Babylon* (originally called Babel) is the quintessential City of Man in the biblical story. More than any other city, Babylon represents human life apart from God; men and women in revolt against their Creator. For God's people to be exiled in Babylon is perhaps the picture that best describes the human condition as understood from a biblical worldview. It is here, in Babylon, that believers must learn how to live out their Christian discipleship. Surprisingly, God does not tell his exiled children to rise in revolt, to reform the government, or to try to escape. His words, conveyed through Jeremiah the prophet, are startling and should be the subject of deep meditation for every genuine believer:

> *Thus says the* LORD *of hosts, the God of Israel, to all the exiles whom I have sent into exile from Jerusalem to Babylon: Build houses and live in them; plant gardens and eat their produce. Take wives and have sons and daughters; take wives for your sons, and give your daughters in marriage, that they may bear sons and daughters; multiply there, and do not decrease. But seek the welfare (shalom) of the city where I have sent you into exile, and pray to the* LORD *on its behalf, for in its welfare you will find your welfare. . . . For thus says the* LORD*: When seventy years are completed for Babylon, I will visit you, and I will fulfill to you my promise and bring you back to this place. For I know the plans I have for you,*

declares the LORD, *plans for welfare (shalom) and not for evil, to give you a future and a hope. (Jer 29:4–7, 10–11)*

These amazing words describe the attitude every child of God should adopt as he tries to live out his faith in a hostile environment. Though living in the City of Man, we have our citizenship in Jerusalem, the City of God. In other words, though called to live in Babylon, we must not become Babylonians! Our identity is to be defined by our true home, Jerusalem, where our citizenship belongs. After 70 years (the span of a human life), we will finally move to our true country and enjoy forever the City of God, the New Jerusalem. But in the meantime, our Lord urges us to settle down in Babylon. We are to build houses, get married, and raise our families here. Surprisingly perhaps, we are commanded to have compassion for our Babylonian neighbors and seek their well-being (*shalom*). God wants us to know that he loves the Babylonians and longs for them also to become part of his great global family. His primary way of reaching them is through us!

As the Biblical story reaches its conclusion in the book of Revelation, we discover that the City of God is far more wonderful than we ever imagined. The earthly Jerusalem in Israel is only a faint hint of the *New Jerusalem* that is yet to be revealed. Although human history began in a garden, it will not end there. A city beyond your wildest imagination awaits those who have put their trust in the Lord. This is a city whose designer and builder is God (Heb 11:10)!

> *Then I saw a new heaven and a new earth, for the first heaven and the first earth had passed away, and the sea was no more. And I saw the holy city, new Jerusalem, coming down out of heaven from God, prepared as a bride adorned for her husband. And I heard a loud voice from the throne saying, "Behold, the dwelling place of God is with man. He will dwell with them, and they will be his people, and God himself will be with them as their God. He will wipe away every tear from their eyes, and death shall be no more, neither shall there be mourning, nor crying, nor pain anymore, for the former things have passed away."*

Then came one of the seven angels who had the seven bowls full of the seven last plagues and spoke to me, saying, "Come, I will show you the Bride, the wife of the Lamb." And he carried me away in the Spirit to a great, high mountain, and showed me the holy city Jerusalem coming down out of heaven from God, having the glory of God, its radiance like a most rare jewel, like a jasper, clear as crystal. It had a great, high wall, with twelve gates, and at the gates twelve angels, and on the gates the names of the twelve tribes of the sons of Israel were inscribed. (Rev 21:1–4; 9–12)

In summary, the overarching message of the Bible can be understood as a Tale of Two Cities. Every human being must make a choice as to which city will be his/her home. A simple chart outlines the difference:

The City of Man—Babylon	The City of God—New Jerusalem
Designed and built by man	Designed and built by God
Made of bricks (human technology)	Made of precious stones
Reveals the glory of man	Reveals the glory of God
Man protects himself	God is our refuge, a mighty fortress
Man strives to reach up to God	God strives to reach down to man
The Great Prostitute	The spotless Bride of Christ
Confusion and division/many tongues	Unity/understanding (Pentecost)
The love of power	The power of love
We live as aliens, exiles	This is our home, we are citizens
Will be destroyed	Will endure forever

THE MESSAGE OF THE CITY

Genesis 11:1–9 invites us to think theologically about the city. It encourages us to become missional in our mindset and strategic in our vision concerning the place where we live. Read properly, this amazing text is a call to radical obedience to the Great Commission Jesus gave us to make disciples everywhere. We can summarize our calling in the following manner:

Live as exiles and pilgrims. Although we are called to live in Babylon, we must resist the temptation to become Babylonian! This world is not our home. Our citizenship is in heaven. Therefore, be good neighbors; but keep your bags packed!

> *Beloved, I urge you as sojourners and exiles to abstain from the passions of the flesh, which wage war against your soul. Keep your conduct among the Gentiles honorable, so that when they speak against you as evildoers, they may see your good deeds and glorify God on the day of visitation. (1 Pet 2:11–12)*

Seek the wellbeing (shalom) or your pagan neighbors. Though the wicked city is ultimately destined for destruction, in the meantime, love your Babylonian neighbors and minister to their needs. God loves the Babylonians and sent his Son to die for them just as much as he loves you! He has given you the privilege of making known his love to them.

> *You have heard that it was said, "You shall love your neighbor and hate your enemy." But I say to you, love your enemies and pray for those who persecute you, so that you may be sons of your Father who is in heaven. For he makes his sun rise on the evil and on the good, and sends rain on the just and on the unjust. (Matt 5:43–45)*

Pray fervently "Thy kingdom come." Don't be surprised if the world hates you. Persecution may come and the cost of discipleship will be great. So, taking your cue from the prayer Jesus taught us, long earnestly and pray fervently for the return of the King when the kingdoms of this world will become the Kingdom of our Lord and of his Christ and he shall reign forever and ever (see Rev 11:15).

Walk as Abraham walked. In the book of Genesis, the story of Abraham follows the story of Babel. It is only as we absorb the reality of the failure of the City of Man that we become ready for the next step in the journey to spiritual wholeness.

> *By faith Abraham obeyed when he was called to go out to a place that he was to receive as an inheritance. And he went out, not knowing where he was going. By faith he went to live in the land of promise, as in a foreign land, living in tents with Isaac and Jacob, heirs with him of the same promise. For he was looking forward to the city that has foundations, whose*

designer and builder is God. . . . These all died in faith, not having received the things promised, but having seen them and greeted them from afar, and having acknowledged that they were strangers and exiles on the earth. For people who speak thus make it clear that they are seeking a homeland. If they had been thinking of that land from which they had gone out, they would have had opportunity to return. But as it is, they desire a better country, that is, a heavenly one. Therefore God is not ashamed to be called their God, for he has prepared for them a city. (Heb 11:8–10, 13–16)

QUESTIONS FOR DISCUSSION

1. If you were to preach a sermon comparing Babel's tower to Jacob's ladder, what would be the main points of your message?
2. Have you ever experienced a city as a "spiritual presence"? Talk about this.
3. How has this study affected the way that you think about cities? Specifically, how has it affected the way you think about the city where you live?
4. Why does the author treat Genesis 11:1–9 as a missionary text?
5. The Bible seems to say that Babylon (though not the Babylonians!) is irredeemable. What implications does this have for Christian involvement in politics?
6. The earthly Jerusalem was (and is) a strange mixture of good and evil. What lessons should we learn from this?

11
The Call
Genesis 12:1–9

The call of Abraham marks a dramatic change in the Genesis narrative. The first eleven chapters have focused on global events, a type of universal history. The creation, the Garden of Eden, the flood, and the multinational building project at Babel—all describe human history without great attention paid to a specific location or a particular people group. However, beginning with Genesis 12, we are suddenly introduced to a specific family and a particular place. From this point forward, the storyline of Genesis will focus on one chosen people (the Hebrews) and one favored location (Canaan).

Genesis 1–11 describes a world of wickedness and sin, one which is the recipient of God's wrath and judgment. But Genesis 12 reveals that God is putting together a plan of redemption that has the potential to save all men and women everywhere from the condemnation that sin always brings. The covenant that God establishes with Abraham and his family is the means through which God will work out his saving purposes not only for the Hebrews but, through them, to the ends of the earth.

When God chooses Abraham and calls him to a life of faithful obedience, he is putting in place a salvation project that will stretch across the centuries and reach around the world. By calling Abraham, God is boldly announcing that sin will not have the last word. The serpent's strategy of deception and temptation will ultimately be unsuccessful. And though Babel's tower has failed to link earth to heaven, God himself will establish a "ladder" that will gloriously get the job done! Through Abraham's lineage the seed of the woman will one day be born who will crush the serpent's head (see Gen 3:15). The tragedy of Babel's City of Man (see Gen 11:1–9) will be ultimately remedied when God's Messiah comes to establish the City of God. And it all begins when one man hears God's call and responds in faithful obedience.

A True Hero

We live in a day when heroes are in short supply. Trendy political movements and fanatical devotion to political correctness have resulted in some of our nation's most celebrated heroes being pulled from their pedestals—sometimes, literally! It takes little more than a rumored hint of past sexual impropriety to ruin the career of a politician, pastor, corporate leader, celebrity, or Supreme Court nominee. And the fact that someone long ago may have used language or engaged in practices that are considered "racist" by today's standards is all that it takes to legitimize the defacing of public monuments erected in their honor.

It is interesting to note that Abraham, a hero for Jews, Christians, and Muslims, is guilty of the two offenses that are highest on the "hit list" of today's vigilantes: sexual harassment and racism. More than once he mistreated both his wife and his concubine, so that charges of "sexual harassment" would not be unfounded. Furthermore, he owned slaves and could easily be accused of some of the racist behaviors so typical of his age. And yet, the Bible elevates Abraham as one of the greatest heroes of history.

It is important to recognize that not only does scripture tell us of Abraham's greatness, it candidly tells us his flaws, shortcomings, blind spots, and sins. Far from hiding his feet of clay, the Bible highlights them! As we study Abraham's life, we will discover how Genesis insists that we see this giant of history for who he truly was! There is no need to remove his statue from its pedestal or deface the plaque celebrating his life and legacy. Scripture gives us all the data we need to remember accurately and honestly his flaws in the hopes that we will not make the same mistakes!

Having recognized that Abraham's flawed humanity is similar to our own, we are now prepared to examine the remarkable greatness of this unlikely hero of the faith. It would be difficult to overestimate the significance of his legacy. This is why Scripture actually *commands us* to study his life:

> *Listen to me, you who pursue righteousness,*
> *you who seek the* Lord*:*
> *look to the rock from which you were hewn,*
> *and to the quarry from which you were dug.*
> *Look to Abraham your father*
> *and to Sarah who bore you;*
> *for he was but one when I called him,*
> *that I might bless him and multiply him. (Isa 51:1–2)*

The significance of Abraham's life is seen in multiple ways. *First*, we are struck by the fact that he is the biological father of approximately fourteen million Jews and hundreds of millions of Muslims. Beyond that, he is the *spiritual* father of all who call themselves Christian. The apostle Paul urged Gentile believers to consider themselves as part of Abraham's spiritual family: "If you are Christ's, then you are Abraham's offspring, heirs according to the promise." (Gal 3:29). Little wonder that we speak of *Father* Abraham.

Secondly, Abraham is worthy of study because his life introduces us to the concept of the covenant. One could argue that this is the dominant theme in the entire Biblical narrative. The division of Scripture into the Old and New Testaments (or Covenants) attests to the foundational reality of its importance. We first encountered the covenant idea in the story of Noah (see Gen 8:20–9:17) but it is only with Abraham that we begin to discover its redemptive potency. Though there will be future covenants with Moses and David, it is the Abrahamic covenant that is the most essential for understanding the foundational ingredients necessary for an authentic relationship between God and man. With Abraham, we are also introduced to the sacramental sign of this covenant relationship: circumcision. One can never fully understand what Jesus meant by the New Covenant without first understanding the original covenant with Abraham. More like a marriage than a business contract, the covenant with Abraham sets the framework for a lifelong personal relationship with God. It is built on trust and fidelity.

A *third* reason Abraham's life is of significance is because of how he introduces us to the concept of salvation as journey. The story begins when God calls Abraham to *leave* his home and *go* to the land that he would show him. From Ur to Haran to Canaan to Egypt and then back to Canaan; Abraham lives as a pilgrim all his life. The symbol of his life is a tent.

> *By faith Abraham obeyed when he was called to go out to a place that he was to receive as an inheritance. And he went out, not knowing where he was going. By faith he went to live in the land of promise, as in a foreign land, living in tents with Isaac and Jacob, heirs with him of the same promise. For he was looking forward to the city that has foundations, whose designer and builder is God. . . .*
>
> *These all died in faith, not having received the things promised, but having seen them and greeted them from afar, and having acknowledged that they were strangers and exiles on the earth. For people who speak thus make it clear that they are seeking a homeland. (Heb 11:8–10, 13–14)*

Long before Paul envisioned salvation in judicial terms of pardon, the story of Abraham anchors us in the more foundational concept of salvation as journey. Abraham's fundamental problem was not that he had broken God's law, but rather that he was homesick and lost. As he walked with God and faithfully followed the call, he illustrates what it means to put our faith in the One who says, "Follow me" (see Mk 1:17; etc.).

Learning about the true nature of worship is yet a *fourth* reason to study the life of Abraham. Converted out of idolatrous paganism (see Josh 24:2–3), Abraham exhibited the zeal and passion of a first-generation believer. Thus, almost everywhere he went, he built an altar: at Shechem (Gen 12:6–7), at Bethel (Gen 12:8; 13:2–4), at Hebron (Gen 13:18), and at Moriah (Gen 22:9–19). Abraham's journey could be traced by the altars he made. What is an altar? It is a place of encounter with God; a place of praise, thanksgiving, sacrifice, and public testimony. Abraham simply could not express strongly enough or often enough how grateful he was for the rescue operation God had performed on his soul.

A *fifth* reason Abraham's life has such importance in the Biblical narrative is because of what he teaches us about the family. Although there is much that is worthy of imitation about the way Abraham serves as a husband, father, and uncle, there is also much that that is deeply troubling. In fact, the life of Abraham could be considered the original case study for family dysfunction! Twice he claimed that Sarah was his sister to protect himself (Gen 12:10–19; 20:1–18), once he slept with a family servant (Gen 16), and, after Sarah's death, he married Keturah and had other concubines and children (Gen 25:1–6). God apparently wants us to know that before Abraham can be the leader of a great nation, he must first learn to be a great husband and a great father. In this respect, his record is somewhat mixed.

Finally, and most significantly of all, it is important to study the life of Abraham because of what he can teach us about faith. Indeed, this is the primary theme of his life. Centuries later, when Paul speaks of the indispensable role of faith in being made right with God, he chooses Abraham as Exhibit A (see Rom 4 and Gal 3). The Bible is crystal clear in stating that Abraham's intimate relationship with God is based solely on faith; he believed God's promises and God counted that as righteousness (see Gen 15:6). In other words, Abraham was justified by faith alone! This is the reason he has the distinction of being called God's friend (see Isa 41:8; Jas 2:23). Long before there was a priesthood or a temple, long before the law had been given on Mount Sinai, and long before there was even something that might be called "true religion," Abraham enjoyed a right relationship with God based on *faith alone*!

As we study Abraham's life in the coming chapters, we will discover that his faith is tested again and again. At times he wavers and sometimes he doubts, but ultimately, he manifests the Old Testament's most dramatic illustration of faith when he builds an altar to sacrifice his son Isaac. In fact, his victory of faith is of such magnitude, that God, speaking to him through an angel, says: "Now I know that you fear God, seeing you have not withheld your son, your only son, from me." (Gen 22:12).

It is Abraham's *first* step, however, that gives us the best picture of what faith really looks like. When he left his home in Ur of the Chaldeans in response to God's call, Abraham gave the world an unforgettable illustration of what God wants from each of us. Though there would be many other occasions when Abraham would be called to exercise faith, this first step laid the foundation for all that followed.

The Obedience of Faith

God's call and Abraham's response are recorded for us in sacred Scripture. It is not an exaggeration to say that this moment is one of the most important events in the history of the world.

> *Now the* Lord *said to Abram, "Go from your country and your kindred and your father's house to the land that I will show you. And I will make of you a great nation, and I will bless you and make your name great, so that you will be a blessing. I will bless those who bless you, and him who dishonors you I will curse, and in you all the families of the earth shall be blessed." So Abram went, as the* Lord *had told him, and Lot went with him. Abram was seventy-five years old when he departed from Haran. (Gen 12:1–4)*

At its core, God's call to Abraham is a two-fold command: *go from* your homeland and *go to* the land I will show you. In other words, God is inviting Abraham to break out of his comfort zone, reject the status quo, and courageously obey the voice that calls him to something more. For Abraham, as for everyone after him who hears the call of God, the journey to spiritual wholeness begins with a first step.

We can imagine that Abraham had only a vague idea of who was calling him and where the journey would go. As he took that first step, there was surely much that he did not understand. But the authority in the voice of the one who called him, and the inner certainty that there must be more to life than he currently knew, compelled Abraham to step out in faith and follow the call. Though he had freedom to resist, the voice was so insistent he felt he had no choice. He *must* go. So, Abraham took the first step. The journey had begun!

The two-fold nature of the command (go from/go to) points to the foundational necessity of the two most important actions a person can ever make: repent and believe. To leave his home country involved more than a change of geography. God was calling Abraham to make a clean break with his idolatrous past. Though repentance also involves putting away sinful behaviors and attitudes, at its core it is a conscious choice to stop trusting in false gods. The Lord has prepared a future filled with promise for Abraham, but he must first let go of the past in order to receive all that God has promised. This two-fold rhythm (go from/go to, repent/believe) sets the pattern for all that follows.

It is important to recognize that God's call to Abraham came in a verbal form. God used words conveying a rational and coherent message to beckon Abraham to set out on the journey. His faith, therefore, was not based on mystical feelings, a restless inner urge, or some yearning for adventure. He was not guided by wishful thinking and his was no sentimental journey. No. Abraham's walk of faith was grounded in a rational response to a coherent word. It all began with a clear, inescapable, word from God: "The Lord said to Abram . . . ."

"In the beginning was the Word" (John 1:1). In the first chapter of Genesis we saw how God created the universe by *speaking* it into existence: "'Let there be light,' and there was light" (Gen 1:3; etc.). In a similar manner, Jesus created his first band of disciples by *speaking* them into existence: "Follow me," he said (Mark 1:17). And they did. So it was with Abraham. It all began when he heard God's Word. Abraham's faith was not a generic optimism for a better future nor a belief in "progress." Abraham's faith was a response to the Word of God. The journey to spiritual wholeness starts here. "Faith comes from hearing, and hearing through the word of Christ" (Rom 10:17).

A closer look at Genesis 12:1–3 reveals that there is more involved in Abraham's call than a divine command. Just as importantly, God's word contains a promise; a manifold promise! It is only as he boldly steps out in the obedience of faith, leaving the idolatrous past and walking into the unknown future, that these promises begin to come true in his life. God's promises to Abraham are revealed in the multiple times he says, "I will."

> *"Go from your country and your kindred and your father's house to the land that I will show you. And I will make of you a great nation, and I will bless you and make your name great, so that you will be a blessing. I will bless those who bless you, and him who dishonors you I will curse, and in you all the families of the earth shall be blessed." (Gen 12:1–3)*

As Abraham puts into practice the obedience of faith, note the promises that God assures him will come true in his life.

- *The promise of guidance.* "I will show you (the way)." God assures Abraham that as he walks the walk of faith, he will never be lost. Far better than a map, God promises to be Abraham's personal guide during every step of the journey.
- *The promise of children.* "I will make of you a great nation." Though Abraham is seventy-five years old and his wife Sarah is sixty-five and barren (see Gen 11:30), God makes a solemn promise that he will have many descendants.
- *The promise of blessing.* "I will bless you." Without specifying the exact form his blessing will take, God assures Abraham of his favor as they walk together on the journey of life. As the story unfolds, we discover that God's blessing does not spare Abraham from suffering, but it does guarantee that his journey will ultimately end in an abundance of joy.
- *The promise of significance.* "I will make your name great." The builders of the Tower of Babel had hoped to make a name for themselves but succeeded only in leaving a legacy of folly (see Gen 11:4). Abraham's life teaches us that true greatness and significance come as a gift from God, not as a result of human achievement.
- *The promise to be a blessing to others.* "I will bless those who bless you . . . and in you all the families of the earth shall be blessed." The reason God chose, called, and blessed Abraham was *not* because he liked him more than others! No. God chose

Abraham because he wants to reach the world *through* him.

Abraham is blessed so that he can be a blessing to others.

As Abraham follows God's call in the obedience of faith, he receives yet another divine promise when God tells him that he will give the land of Canaan to him and his descendants.

> *When they came to the land of Canaan, Abram passed through the land to the place at Shechem, to the oak of Moreh. At that time the Canaanites were in the land. Then the* LORD *appeared to Abram and said, "To your offspring I will give this land." So he built there an altar to the* LORD, *who had appeared to him. (Gen 12:5–7)*

It is noteworthy that with two of God's promises there is an immediate and obvious problem. The promise of children must confront the reality that Sarah is old and barren. And here, the promise of Canaan must face the fact that "the Canaanites (are) in the land." To complicate the issue even more, this land of promise is currently experiencing a famine (Gen 12:10)! God is testing Abraham's faith. Will he believe the promise that he will have children even when his wife is barren? Will he believe that he will receive the land of Canaan even when it is already inhabited by others? Even when it seems worthless because of the famine? Believing the promises of God may be harder than you think!

HAVE YOU HEARD THE CALL?

The mountaineer John Muir (1838–1914), one of the fathers of the U. S. National Park system, famously said, "The mountains are calling, and I must go." Those who hear the call simply can't resist the urge to travel to the Smokies, the Adirondacks, or the Rockies to drive the roads, smell the aromas, gaze on the panoramas, and climb the peaks. However, not everyone has ears to hear. Most people, it seems, are unaware of the invitation urging them to imagine something beyond their experience.

In a similar way, not everyone hears the call of God. Though his call goes out to everyone everywhere, most seem deaf to the Voice that invites them to begin the journey to spiritual wholeness. The problem is not that God is not calling. The problem is that people are not listening! Oswald Chambers says it well:

> The call of God is like the call of the sea, or of the mountains; no one hears these calls but the one who has the nature of the sea or of the mountains; and no one hears the call of God who has not the nature of God in him.[1]

The story of Abraham helps us to recognize what a genuine call from God looks and sounds like. The ingredients that constituted Abraham's call so many centuries ago continue to be the defining characteristics of every authentic call from God.

First, we must not be blind to that which is most obvious: the call is initiated by God. In other words, there is no calling without a Caller. Abraham did not *choose* to go on this journey, he was *chosen*! Though freewill obviously plays an important part, the overwhelming message of Genesis 12:1–3 is not that Abraham decided to put his trust in God, but that God decided to put his trust in Abraham! As a famous couplet puts it: "How odd of God / To choose the Jews."[2]

American evangelicals tend to emphasize "making a decision" and "choosing" to become a follower of Jesus Christ. While the importance of this is self-evident, we must remember that the Bible's focus is not so much on our choice of God, but his choice of us! No one stated the issue more clearly than Jesus: "You did not choose me, but I chose you." (John 15:16). The story of Abraham's call anchors us in the Gospel truth that no one begins the journey to spiritual wholeness without being awestruck and humbled by the awareness of God's sovereign grace in choosing someone like me.

> *Oh, to grace how great a debtor*
> *Daily I'm constrained to be!*
> *Let thy goodness, like a fetter,*
> *Bind my wandering heart to thee.*
> —Robert Robinson (1758)

---

[1] Chambers, *Not Knowing Whither*, 1934.
[2] Authorship has been debated, but most think the original source for this couplet is British journalist William N. Ewer (1885–1976).

A *second* truth we must remember is that God's call is to a journey as much as it is to a destination. Many believers today have the notion that a divine call is all about the final landing place. New believers are told they are called to heaven when they die. A missionary may feel called to China. Such thinking causes many to conclude that the important element in God's call is *where* we end up. While the destination is obviously important, the story of Abraham introduces us to the reality that the journey itself is equally important. When Jesus said, "I am the way" (John 14:6), he was referring to much more than the end of the road. When the Lord calls us to follow him, he promises not only to meet us at the end of the journey but to walk with us each step of the way.

Like Enoch and Noah before him, Abraham walked with God (Gen 5:22; 6:9; 17:1). His faith was focused not so much on some future destination as on a present relationship. When Abraham first obeyed God's call, he went out "not knowing where he was going" (Heb 11:8). He lived in tents as he followed the path God laid out before him. The message of Abraham's life is seen not so much in *where* he went but in *how* he walked. Though God had promised to give him the land of Canaan, it is noteworthy that the only piece of real estate Abraham ever personally owned was the cave of Machpelah; a burial plot (see Gen 23).

I'm intrigued by the fact that when Jesus called his first disciples by saying "Follow me," not one of them paused to ask: "Master, before we sign up, *where* we are going?" The moral of the story seems to be that if the Second Person of the Trinity steps in your path, putting his finger in your chest and inviting you to follow, it really doesn't matter where you go. As long you are walking side by side with the King of the Universe and the Lord of Glory, you could not possibly be in a better location!

A *third* truth about God's call is that it relates more to a relationship than it does to a task. We have just seen how many people mistakenly think of a divine calling in terms of a destination rather than a journey. In a similar manner, many think of God's call in terms of some ministry or occupation and miss completely the invitation to a divine relationship. The English word we sometimes use to describe a person's professional life, *vocation* (from the Latin *vocare*, "to call"), tends to orient us to this way of thinking. Thus, we may hear someone say, "I'm called to medicine," "I'm called to education," or "I'm called to the ministry."

But the story of Abraham reminds us that long before Abraham was called to *do* something, he was called to *be* something. The call on his life was first and foremost an invitation to know God, intimately and personally, to be God's friend. This understanding of Abraham's call was made even more clear years after his initial step of obedience when God said to him, "Walk before me and be blameless" (Gen 17:1). Abraham is the preeminent model of faith because he clearly understood that his call was first and foremost to *be* holy by *being* in a right relationship with God. Only then was he rightly able to *do* the work of ministry.

Once again, it is Jesus who best illustrates this powerful truth. When he called his disciples, his intention went much deeper than plans for their future employment in ministry.

> *And he went up on the mountain and called to him those whom he desired, and they came to him. And he appointed twelve (whom he also named apostles) so that they might be with him and he might send them out to preach and have authority to cast out demons. (Mark 3:13–15)*

Priority number one for someone called to be a disciple of Jesus was *to be with him* (Mark 3:14). Once that part of their calling was mastered, then and only then were they ready to be sent out to preach and cast out demons. In the Gospel call, who we are is more important than what we do!

A fourth characteristic of God's call is this: it will cost you everything. Though salvation is free, it is not cheap. God's promised blessings to Abraham can only be received when he leaves his home, and all that he holds dear, and ventures forth in obedience to the call. The biblical narrative of Abraham's life culminates in that climactic moment when he literally puts his all on the altar at Mount Moriah (see Gen 22). Though the promises of God are all free, they can only be received when we have first emptied our arms of all the earthly treasures to which we so tightly cling. Jesus stated the matter succinctly: "Any one of you who does not renounce all that he has cannot be my disciple" (Luke 14:33). Like a trapeze artist wanting to leap to the next trapeze, the deed can only be accomplished when we let go!

Perhaps no one in the twentieth century better understood the cost involved in following the call than Dietrich Bonhoeffer. He recognized that there are two crosses in the Gospel. The most important one, of course, belongs to Jesus. But each of his disciples has a cross as well. The cost is typically first experienced in the call to abandon those worldly attachments that hinder obedience to God. Because Bonhoeffer practiced what he preached, his words are backed up by the integrity of his life.

> Thus it begins; the cross is not the terrible end to an otherwise God-fearing and happy life, but it meets us at the beginning of our communion with Christ. When Christ calls a man, he bids him come and die.... Jesus' summons to the rich young man was calling him to die, because only the man who is dead to his own will can follow Christ. In fact, every command of Jesus is a call to die.[3]

Fifth, and finally, a divine call will always be outwardly focused. It is possible that, at first, Abraham imagined he was chosen and called because God liked him better than others. Perhaps he thought that he was elected by God because of his intelligence, good works, and pleasant disposition. But as Abraham walked with God, it didn't take long to discover what every genuine disciple must learn: it's not about me! God chose Abraham because he wanted to reach the nations through him. He blessed Abraham so that he could be a blessing to others.

The doctrine of election has nothing to do with favoritism! God calls us not because of anything worthy of merit in us. No. He calls us out of the sheer goodness and graciousness of his own heart. And

---

3   Bonhoeffer, *The Cost of Discipleship*, 89–90.

more than that, he calls us because he loves the world and desperately wants Canaanites, Egyptians, Babylonians, Greeks, and Romans to also hear the call of God and step out in faith to begin their own journey to spiritual wholeness. God wants to reach the world, whether across the street or across the ocean, through people like us.

God is calling. Can you hear his voice?

QUESTIONS FOR DISCUSSION

1. How does "the call of the mountains" help you to better understand the call of God?
2. Describe a time in your life when you heard God's call. How did you respond?
3. "You did not choose me, but I chose you" (John 15:16). Discuss this verse.
4. What is the difference between being called to a task (occupation, ministry) and called to a relationship?
5. If salvation is free, why is the cost of following so great?
6. If it's not about me, then who is it about?

12
A Lot to Remember
Genesis 13:1–14:16; 19:1–38

In the last chapter, we learned that God himself has commanded us, through Isaiah the prophet, to study the life of Abraham and learn from his example (see Isa 51:1–2). Jesus also commands us to examine Abraham's life by looking carefully at his nephew; specifically, at his nephew's wife. "Remember Lot's wife" (Luke 17:32). In the Greek, Jesus' command is in the present imperative tense, meaning; "Keep on remembering Lot's wife." Jesus never told us to remember Gideon, Ruth, or Daniel. But he pleads with us to never, ever forget this nameless woman. Why? What was it Jesus feared we would not remember?

God knows that some forms of spiritual amnesia are deadly. Thus, we are warned of the mortal danger that comes when we forget to remember.

- *Remember* the Sabbath day to keep it holy (Exod 20:8).
- *Remember* the whole way that the Lord your God has led you these forty years in the wilderness (Deut 8:2).
- *Remember* from where you have fallen and repent (Rev 2:5).
- Do this in *remembrance* of me (Luke 22:19).

The biblical concept of remembering involves more than a cognitive recall of certain facts. When my wife asks if I remembered her birthday, she is talking about more than a mental awareness of a date on the calendar. She wonders if I bought her a present! To remember, means literally to reassemble the members of a past event, to reexperience the reality. When Jesus commands us to remember Lot's wife, he is urging us to know the stories of her life so well that we are motivated to develop a lifestyle that protects us from descending into the spiritual darkness that she experienced.

When God called Abraham to leave Ur of the Chaldeans, his nephew Lot went with him (see Gen 11:27–32). This would mean, of course, that Lot's wife was there too, accompanying Father Abraham as he ventured forth on one of the greatest spiritual journeys in human history. Because Lot's father, Haran, Abraham's brother, had died, Abraham became a type of surrogate father to his nephew (see Gen 11:27–32). This seemed like an ideal relationship: Lot had no father and Abraham had no son. As the story begins, it appears that Lot is the heir apparent to Abraham's legacy. It is easy to imagine that Abraham and Sarah must have often wondered if Lot was the promised child God had foretold. Perhaps he was the coming liberator who would finally crush the serpent's head (see Gen 3:15).

In these early years, Lot's most distinctive characteristic, his defining quality, was simply that he accompanied his uncle everywhere he went. Repeatedly, the text emphasizes this point. "So Abram went, as the Lord had told him, and *Lot went with him*" (Gen 12:4, emphasis added). "So Abram went up from Egypt . . . and *Lot with him*" (Gen 13:1, emphasis added). "And Lot, *who went with Abram*, also had flocks and herds and tents" (Gen 13:5, emphasis added). This gives an early hint concerning Lot's true spiritual condition. Abraham walked with God. Lot walked with Abraham. As long as Lot and his wife were near his godly uncle, things went well.

But what will happen if this bond breaks and Mr. and Mrs. Lot find themselves separated from Uncle Abraham? Will their faith survive? Is their walk with God authentic and personal, or is it vicarious and second-hand? Can Lot live a life of truth and godliness when he is no longer in the company of his saintly uncle? The tragic story of Lot and his family reminds us that godly character cannot be obtained by osmosis. Spiritual maturity can never be achieved by merely hanging out with saints! Each of us must develop his own personal walk with

God. This is something that Lot and his wife never quite learned how to do. And this is why Jesus insisted that we must remember their story!

Lot's Choice

The Bible gives a surprising amount of information concerning Lot and his family. As we examine the narrative, we discover important details that help us to better understand the true character of Mr. and Mrs. Lot.

The story begins when competition for pastureland causes interpersonal conflict between Lot and his uncle (see Gen 13:5–13). Both men have become extremely wealthy as a result of Abraham's ill-advised trip to Egypt (see Gen 12:16; 13:2). They now own such a vast number of flocks and herds that the land cannot "support both of them dwelling together" (Gen 13:6). This creates contention and strife between the two camps. The conflict becomes so great that Abraham and Lot finally agree to choose different grazing lands and separate.

In a gracious gesture of good will, Abraham gives first choice to his junior partner. As big doors swing on tiny hinges, so the decision Lot made that day played a decisive role in determining his future destiny as well as that of his wife and children. This turns out to be the most important decision he ever made. Standing together in an elevated location, the two men survey the landscape. The text is incredibly precise in describing the details of Lot's famous choice.

> *And Lot lifted up his eyes and saw that the Jordan Valley was well watered everywhere like the garden of the* Lord, *like the land of Egypt, in the direction of Zoar. (This was before the* Lord *destroyed Sodom and Gomorrah.) So Lot chose for himself all the Jordan Valley, and Lot journeyed east. Thus they separated from each other. Abram settled in the land of Canaan, while Lot settled among the cities of the valley and moved his tent as far as Sodom. Now the men of Sodom were wicked, great sinners against the* Lord. *(Gen 13:10–13)*

In the Garden of Eden, we discovered how sin entered the world because Eve's eyes became focused on something that God had forbidden. She *saw* that the tree was good for food and that it was *a delight to the eyes* (see Gen 3:6). In a similar manner, Lot's problems began when he "lifted up his eyes and saw" the lush Jordan Valley and the wicked cities that were there (Gen 13:10). The fatal error for both Eve and Lot was to trust their own eyes to discern the difference between good and evil. In gazing at the forbidden fruit, Eve concluded that God's *good* command to abstain from eating was really an *evil* command. Lot's mistake was to believe that the *evil* city of Sodom would be a *good* place to live. Isaiah's words give a cogent description of what is happening: "Woe to those who call evil good and good evil" (Isa 5:20).

Lot's choice was further influenced by the fact that the Jordan Valley reminded him of Egypt (see Gen 13:10). Not only was the area lush and green like the Nile valley, but it triggered his memory of the worldly pleasures he had seen in Egypt during his excursion there with his uncle some years earlier. In the Bible, Egypt, as well as Babylon, is often used as a metaphor for sin and worldliness. Though Lot loved the Lord, he also loved the things of this world.

When the Bible commands us not to love this world (see 1 John 2:15–17; Jas 4:4), it is not forbidding us to love the people of the world. The warning, rather, is against worldliness, loving material pleasures and sensual delights, and trusting in their ability to satisfy our souls. Jesus alerts us to the danger of worldliness when he categorically states the impossibility of serving two masters: "You cannot serve God and mammon" (Matt 6:24). Lot, however, had not yet learned this truth. Trying to live for God while at the same time living for worldly pleasures, Lot became a double-minded man, and thus unstable in all his ways (see Jas 1:8).

The text describes Lot's decision with the words, he "chose for himself" (Gen 13:11). There is no indication that he prayed or sought counsel. Was he aware that God had a plan for his life? Did he even care? Apparently, he simply opted for what seemed to be in his own best interests. Lot's decision was precisely that—*Lot's* decision! As will soon become obvious, the choice Lot made was *not* God's will. Thus, we should not be surprised at the catastrophic consequences that come to both Lot and his entire family.

Once his choice was made, Lot "moved his tent as far as Sodom" (Gen 13:12). *The New International Version* translates the verse as saying, he "pitched his tent near Sodom." Because of its notorious reputation, Lot seems to know better than to buy a house and move inside the city. But his love for this world and the things of this world causes him to be so enamored with this early version of Las Vegas that he wants to live as close to it as he can.

Lot illustrates an early form of spiritual bipolar disorder. He has a love/hate relationship with Sodom. He is enticed by its worldly pleasures and yet has just enough religion to keep the city at arm's length. Lot flirts with disaster by following a code of behavior that tries to live as close as possible to sin and worldliness without becoming a child of hell himself! It is easy to see that this is a story that is not going to have a happy ending.

Lot's Rescue

Having analyzed the motivation that caused Lot to make his fateful choice, we should not be surprised to learn that his flirtation with evil quickly leads to another bad decision. Dissatisfied with living in a tent *near* Sodom, Lot and his family decide to move into a house *in* the city itself (see Gen 14:12). One dumb decision often leads to another. This sets the stage for what happens next.

Sodom and a coalition of neighboring cities find themselves allied together in a war against an invading army that is spreading terror and destruction throughout the region. During the conflict, the city of Sodom is defeated and plundered.

> *So the enemy took all the possessions of Sodom and Gomorrah, and all their provisions, and went their way. They also took Lot, the son of Abram's brother, who was dwelling in Sodom, and his possessions, and went their way. Then one who had escaped came and told Abram the Hebrew, who was living by the oaks of Mamre. . . . When Abram heard that his kinsman had been taken captive, he led forth his trained men, born in his house, 318 of them, and went in pursuit as far as Dan. And he divided his forces against them by night, he and his servants, and defeated them and pursued them to Hobah, north of Damascus. Then he brought back all the*

possessions, and also brought back his kinsman Lot with his possessions, and the women and the people. (Gen 14:11–16)

How easy it would have been for Abraham to have said: "Not my problem. My foolish nephew got himself into this fix. He made his bed; let him lie in it!" Amazingly, in an act of magnanimous graciousness, not to mention courage, Abraham forms a militia and, in a daring night raid, rescues Lot and the other hostages. What a beautiful story of grace and redemption! This merciful rescue seems to be a moment of divine opportunity for Lot to confess his sins, acknowledge his foolish choices, and get his life back on track. God is giving him the chance to reverse the downward direction his life has taken.

Looking back on Lot's life, it is easy to recognize the lessons that he and his family *should* have learned from this incident. For one thing, Lot should have realized that God still loved him and had a plan for his life. His bad choices did not necessarily have to be the defining reality of his story. If he would only recognize his errors, confess his sins, and change his ways, he could once again become a recipient of the Abrahamic blessings.

Additionally, this episode should have taught Lot and his family the utter folly of Sodomite ways. The pleasures of life in this wicked city were short-lived. After his experience as a hostage, wasn't it obvious that the consequences of sin were going to be disastrous? And even if Lot felt that he himself was strong enough to withstand the temptations of the wicked city, what about his wife and children? What effect was life in Sodom going to have on them? Isn't it time to move back to Canaan and restore fellowship with Uncle Abraham?

As we will learn from the rest of the story, Lot's rescue from captivity seems to have had no significant impact on his spiritual life. Once the crisis was over, he and his family moved back to their home in Sodom and resumed their lives as before.

Lot's Legacy

Our next encounter with Lot finds him "sitting in the gate of Sodom" (Gen 19:1). Note the progression: from living in a tent *near*

Sodom (Gen 13:12), he moved to a house *in* Sodom (Gen 14:12), and now he sits in *the city gate*. In the Ancient Near East, "the gate" was the place where the elders of a city sat to conduct business and important civic affairs. By this point in the story, Lot has so integrated himself into Sodomite culture and adapted himself to Sodomite ways that he has become part of the leadership of the city. He calls the men of Sodom his "brothers" (see Gen 19:7).

But God is not blind to the city's great wickedness and has sent two angel messengers to verify whether or not the situation is irreversible. It takes only a short time for the angels to discover how deep and permanent Sodom's sin really is. They explain their mission to Lot in these words: "We are about to destroy this place, because the outcry against its people has become great before the Lord, and the Lord has sent us to destroy it" (Gen 19:13).

It is important to remember that Sodom's wickedness was not the garden variety type of sin. The citizens of this city were not people who occasionally did naughty things or foolishly wandered into inappropriate behavior. No! These men and women had adopted a lifestyle of flagrant, willful, and continual rebellion against God. They shook their fists at heaven in brazen rejection of God and his plan for their lives. The Scripture uses strong language in describing the gravity of the situation. These men were "great sinners against the Lord" (Gen 13:13). Their wickedness was so "very grave" (Gen 18:20) that it provoked an "outcry" against the city that was heard even in heaven (Gen 18:20–21; 19:13). The prophet Ezekiel, referring apparently to one particular sin, calls their behavior "an abomination" (Ezek 16:49–50).

The context of Genesis makes plain what was the specific nature of Sodom's most grievous sin. The provocation for God's wrath and judgment was specifically tied to the city's sexual perversity in general and homosexual rape in particular. The men of Sodom not only practiced these wicked behaviors, they identified themselves with them! Their sin was more than an outward action (this is what *we do*). It had become their very identity (this is who *we are*!). The apostle Peter zeroes in on the despicable character of Sodom's sin when he describes how God's fiercest punishment is reserved for those who "indulge in the lust of defiling passion and despise authority" (2 Pet 2:10).

While sexual perversity may be the sin for which Sodom is most famous, her wickedness was much broader than this. The prophet Ezekiel reminds us that the city was guilty of other sins as well.

> *Behold, this was the guilt of your sister Sodom: she and her daughters had pride, excess of food, and prosperous ease, but did not aid the poor and needy. They were haughty and did an abomination before me. So I removed them, when I saw it. (Ezek 16:49–50)*

A cursory reading of Genesis 19 may cause some to rejoice in the fact that at least Lot was rescued from the wrath and destruction that rained down on Sodom and Gomorrah. Yes, it's true; in answer to the intercessory prayer of his uncle (see Gen 18:22–33; 19:29), Lot's life was miraculously spared in an amazing display of divine mercy. But a closer reading of the narrative reveals that Lot's deliverance is hardly a story of spiritual triumph. He is saved, yes; but barely. Perhaps Paul was thinking of Lot when he spoke of those who are saved "but only as through fire" (1 Cor 3:15).

When Lot told his future sons-in-law about God's wrath soon to fall on the city and invited them to flee with him and his family to safety, they laughed at him, thinking he was joking (see Gen 19:14). Apparently, the testimony of his life was so negligible that members of his own family didn't take him seriously when he finally tried to tell them the truth. The story of what happened next is sobering indeed.

> *As morning dawned, the angels urged Lot, saying, "Up! Take your wife and your two daughters who are here, lest you be swept away in the punishment of the city." But he lingered. So the men seized him and his wife and his two daughters by the hand, the* LORD *being merciful to him, and they brought him out and set him outside the city. And as they brought them out, one said, "Escape for your life. Do not look back or stop anywhere in the valley. Escape to the hills, lest you be swept away."... Then the* LORD *rained on Sodom and*

> Gomorrah sulfur and fire from the LORD out of heaven. And he overthrew those cities, and all the valley, and all the inhabitants of the cities, and what grew on the ground. But Lot's wife, behind him, looked back, and she became a pillar of salt. (Gen 19:15–17, 24–26)

The text is graphic in its description. Lot's deliverance is nothing short of an act of sovereign grace. The fact that he lingered and had to be forced out of the city reveals the depth of Lot's love for the worldly pleasures of Sodom. His heart had been seduced and captured by the City of Man.

But perhaps the saddest part of the drama is that, though Lot himself was saved, he lost his entire family. His sons-in-law refused to come with him and were destroyed in the conflagration. His wife, yearning for all that was lost in Sodom's destruction, was struck dead and turned into a pillar of salt. This was the event that was particularly in Jesus' mind when he commanded us to remember Lot's wife. And Lot also lost his two daughters. Though by God's grace, they survived the destruction, their lives were a spiritual disaster as we learn from the sequel to the story. Their actions prove that it is possible to take a bad situation and make it even worse!

> Now Lot . . . lived in a cave with his two daughters. And the firstborn said to the younger, "Our father is old, and there is not a man on earth to come in to us after the manner of all the earth. Come, let us make our father drink wine, and we will lie with him, that we may preserve offspring from our father." So they made their father drink wine that night. And the firstborn went in and lay with her father. He did not know when she lay down or when she arose. The next day, the firstborn said to the younger, "Behold, I lay last night with my father. Let us make him drink wine tonight also. Then you go in and lie with him, that we may preserve offspring from our father." So they made their father drink wine that night also. And the younger arose and lay with him, and he did not know when she lay down or when she arose. Thus both the daughters of Lot became pregnant by their father. The firstborn bore a son and called his name Moab. He is the father of the Moabites to this day. The younger also bore a son and called his name Ben-ammi. He is the father of the Ammonites to this day. (Gen 19:30–38)

Sodom had been destroyed but, in that cave, the Sodomite culture was reborn. It would be difficult to decide which sin was worse: sodomy or incest?

Thus, we see the tragic consequences of Lot's choice to move his family into the Jordan Valley continue to produce disastrous results. Not only are these consequences apparent in Lot's lifetime, but, through the future conflicts that will come to Israel through the Moabites and the Ammonites, the damage will be felt for centuries to come.

And all this happened through the life of a man who professed to be a believer in God and a member of Abraham's family. Lot's problem was simply this: he had a divided heart. He loved God but he loved this world as well. The Bible wants us to know that doublemindedness produces a life filled with regrets! It is one thing to get Lot out of Sodom, it is another thing to get Sodom out of Lot!

The Worldly Christian

Almost no one preaches against the sin of worldliness today. This seems to be one of those transgressions that has dropped off the radar screen of the contemporary church. In a previous generation, preachers and evangelists warned their congregations of the spiritual danger of loving this world. Unfortunately, many fell into the legalistic trap of equating worldliness with specific, litmus test types of behavior: skirt lengths, jewelry, hair styles, smoking, movies, dancing, etc. This has resulted in a generation of Christians who smile condescendingly at the naiveté of their parents and grandparents. "We're beyond that now," they boast. "We're wiser than they were and have grown out of such legalism."

And yet the Biblical warnings will not go away! It is important to note that when the Bible speaks against worldliness, the emphasis is nearly always on the inner motivation and desire rather than on some specific outward behavior. Worldliness, according to the Bible, will be recognized not so much by how we act, but by what we love. This makes the issue both simpler to deal with and harder to conquer! The heart of the matter is the matter of the heart.

- "If the world hates you, know that it has hated me before it hated you. If you were of the world, the world would love you as its own; but because you are not of the world, but I chose you out of the world, therefore the world hates you." (John 15:18–19)
- "Do not be conformed to this world but be transformed by the renewal of your mind." (Rom 12:2)
- "If then you have been raised with Christ, seek the things that are above, where Christ is, seated at the right hand of God. Set your minds on things that are above, not on things that are on earth." (Col 3:1–2)
- "Do not love the world or the things in the world. If anyone loves the world, the love of the Father is not in him. For all that is in the world—the desires of the flesh and the desires of the eyes and pride of life—is not from the Father but is from the world. And the world is passing away along with its desires, but whoever does the will of God abides forever." (1 John 2:15–17)
- "You adulterous people! Do you not know that friendship with the world is enmity with God? Therefore whoever wishes to be a friend of the world makes himself an enemy of God. . . . Cleanse your hands, you sinners, and purify your hearts, you double-minded." (Jas 4:4, 8)

Remembering the story of Lot and his wife is a powerful way to learn about the sin of worldliness: what it is, how it works, and what are its consequences. For example, from Lot we learn that a worldly Christian is someone who has *second-hand faith*. Lot had faith, but it was derived primarily from proximity to his uncle Abraham. If Lot was in a godly environment, he loved and worshiped God and desired to do what was right. But when he found himself in a spiritually hostile setting, separated from his spiritual roots, it became evident how shallow and mercurial his faith really was.

The story of Lot also teaches us that a worldly Christian is someone who *trusts in his own understanding*. Lot's problem was his wandering eyes. His troubles began when he *saw* the Jordan Valley and ogled the pleasures that he believed could be found there. Worldliness begins with the imagination. Lot lusted and fantasized about what it would be like to live in Sodom. But worse than that, he *trusted* his instincts and did what his heart told him to do. He believed that obeying his desires would bring happiness. What a fool. If only he had learned to follow the wisdom taught in a Sunday School chorus:

> *Oh, be careful little eyes what you see,*
> *Oh, be careful little eyes what you see;*
> *For the Father up above is looking down in love,*
> *Oh, be careful little eyes what you see.*

The main thing, however, that we learn from Lot about the sin of worldliness is the toxic nature of *doublemindedness*. Lot loved the Lord and wanted to do what was right. But he also loved this world and wanted to fit in. He had a divided heart, and this caused him to waffle between the City of God and the City of Man. Such spiritual schizophrenia leads to misery, instability, hypocrisy, and a wasted life. If only he had learned to pray the prayer of David, his life could have been dramatically different: "Give me an undivided heart, that I may fear your name" (Ps 86:11 NIV)

Knowing what we know about Lot, it is surprising to learn that the New Testament calls him a "righteous" man (2 Pet 2:7). In comparison to the Sodomites, I suppose it is true. His behavior was radically different than theirs. But God will not let his children off the hook by comparing their behavior to the reprobate sinners who live next door. No, he has a much higher standard than that!

Although Lot was the recipient of God's saving grace, his legacy and testimony are greatly compromised by his worldly ways. His tragic example is a dramatic reminder of the folly of trying to follow the call of God with a divided heart. The walk of faith is possible only when we trust in the Lord with *all* our hearts. "You will seek me and find me, when you seek me with all your heart" (Jer 29:13).

Don't Forget to Remember Lot's Wife

Perhaps now we can understand why Jesus insists that we remember Lot's wife (Luke 17:32). He fears what will happen if we forget the story of how Lot's family disintegrated when they became enamored with the glitz and seduced by the pleasures of this world. Specifically, we can summarize Jesus' command by saying there are three things we should remember about Mrs. Lot.

First, we should remember *her opportunities*. Think about it: Lot's wife was essentially the daughter-in-law of one of the greatest saints in the history of the world. What must it have been like to live in a tent next door to Abraham and Sarah? Imagine the conversations at the dinner table. And yet, despite such an incredible opportunity, Mrs. Lot turned her back and chose a Sodomite lifestyle instead! How terrible will be her fate at the final judgment when her destiny is determined by the opportunities she willfully chose to reject! "When someone has been given much, much will be required in return; and when someone has been entrusted with much, even more will be required." (Luke 12:48 NLT)

Secondly, Jesus wants us to remember *her sin*. There is no indication that Lot's wife participated in Sodomite perversity or was guilty of reprobate behavior. The horrible judgment she experienced was provoked by the seemingly innocuous fact that she "looked back" (Gen 19:26). Her sin was not some outward debauchery but rather an inward desire. She loved Sodom and yearned for its pleasures. She couldn't bear the thought of losing her worldly possessions. Being a friend of this world made her an enemy of God (see Jas 4:4). As philosopher James K. A. Smith has famously said, "You are what you love."[1]

Finally, Jesus exhorts us to remember *her judgment*. Perhaps only in the book of Revelation do we have a picture of God's wrath and judgment that is more terrifying than when "the Lord rained on Sodom and Gomorrah sulfur and fire out of heaven" (Gen 19:24). Lot's wife was killed in the conflagration and her body was turned into a pillar of salt (Gen 19:26). Her judgment was painful, horrific, and permanent. Jesus wants us to not forget this tragic incident because "the fear of the Lord is the beginning of wisdom" (Prov 9:10).

---

[1] Smith, *You Are What You Love*, 7.

Questions for Discussion

1. Why did Jesus insist that we remember Lot's wife?
2. Early in life, Lot made a choice that influenced everything that happened after that. Can you remember a decision you made that had such long-lasting consequences?
3. Lot felt he could live in Sodom without becoming a Sodomite. Jesus calls us to be in the world but not of the world. Discuss this.
4. How do you define worldliness? How is it recognized?
5. Are Sodom's sins worse than other sins? In what way?
6. James K. A. Smith says that we are what we love. Discuss this.

13
The Obedience of Faith
Genesis 15:1–21

Many people think of faith as a mental, perhaps psychological, expression of confidence in God. They consider it to be a *spiritual* activity that has little or nothing to do with outward behavior. Believing is something we do in our hearts, a private matter that others cannot see. Faith may be born in a moment of prayer, experienced as a sense of inner peace, and expressed by feelings of love and worship. To say that good works are involved is, for many Protestant Christians, not only confusing, but heretical!

It is, therefore, somewhat shocking to learn that Paul, in his epistle to the Romans, a book famous for its clear proclamation of justification by faith alone, both begins and ends his letter by referencing "the obedience of faith" (Rom 1:5; 16:26). Indeed, this is the very purpose that motivates him to write his most famous book. The goal of his apostolic ministry is "to bring about the obedience of faith for the sake of his name among all the nations, including you who are called to belong to Jesus Christ." (Rom 1:5–6).

Paul knows that authentic faith is more than a spiritual feeling of trust in the Lord's grace and goodness. It is an active, volitional, walk of obedience to the revealed will of God. Leaning more on his Jewish roots than his Greek education, Paul regards faith as something one *does* more than something one has. It is an action more than a possession. Dietrich Bonhoeffer states the matter succinctly when he says, "Only he who believes is obedient, and only he who is obedient believes."[1] For the apostle Paul, no one better illustrates this truth than Abraham. In the fourth chapter of Romans, he boldly declares that Abraham is "the father of all who believe" (Rom 4:11). Consequently, if our faith is to be authentic, it must be modeled after Abraham's.

Even a cursory examination of the New Testament reveals the supreme importance of faith[2] in Christian discipleship. Without faith we cannot please God (Heb 11:6) or do his work (John 6:28–29). Without faith we have no shield of protection (Eph 6:16) and are unable to do anything but sin (Rom 14:23). We simply cannot be saved without faith (Acts 16:30–31) and those who die in unbelief will be lost in hell forever (John 3:18). On the other hand, those who have faith are promised great and amazing blessings. Nothing is impossible for those who believe (Matt 17:20). When they pray, they will receive whatever they ask (Matt 21:22). Those who have faith will overcome the world (1 John 5:4)! This helps to explain why, from the very beginning, followers of Jesus were called "believers" (Acts 2:44; 5:14; etc.) and the Christian religion was called "The Faith" (1 Tim 4:6; 2 Tim 4:7; Jude 3; etc.).

Paul's choice of Abraham as the supreme example of faith is amazing. He lived centuries before the Law was given at Sinai or the Tabernacle was constructed with its sacrifices and ceremonies. Yet Abraham was in a right relationship with God. Even before he was circumcised, he was declared to be righteous. How? By faith alone!

The primary Scripture Paul uses to support his case is Genesis 15:6: "(Abraham) believed the Lord, and (the Lord) counted it to him as righteousness". Quoted three times in the New Testament (Rom 4:3; Gal 3:6; Jas 2:23), this short verse is foundational for understanding how one can have a right relationship with God. The example of Abraham anchors us in the gospel truth that the only way to be right with God is through faith! Moral behavior, doctrinal orthodoxy, and sincere piety will not suffice. Righteousness is possible through faith alone!

---

1 Bonhoeffer, *The Cost of Discipleship*, 63.
2 *Faith* is the noun, *to believe* is the verb. Though the terms in English are different, in Greek the root form is the same.

Defining Faith

When I first became a Christian, I remember my surprise at how easy it was. "You mean all I have to do is believe? Is that all? Piece of cake." It wasn't long, however, until I realized that living a life of faith was a lot harder than I anticipated. In fact, it was impossible without divine help. I soon learned that faith is not a human endeavor, a psychological effort to think positive thoughts. The ability to believe God and his promises is a gift of God (see Eph 2:8–9).

There is much fuzzy thinking today about what faith actually is and what it looks like in a person's life. Some confuse faith with optimism. Doesn't a cheery, positive outlook on life indicate the presence of faith? But some people are simply born with a personality trait that causes them to see the glass as half-full rather than half-empty. Optimism is certainly not a synonym for biblical faith.

Others think of faith in terms of sincerity. The important thing is not *what* you believe, but *that* you believe and that you believe whole-heartedly. Such a position, however, is faith in faith, not faith in God! There are many in the world who are sincere about what they believe (Buddhists, Atheists, Scientologists, Marxists, etc.), but they are sincerely wrong. To believe whole-heartedly in something that is not true exemplifies not great faith but great foolishness.

A third mistake is to think of faith in terms of mental assent to certain truths or agreement with certain facts. When people with this view of faith say, "I believe in God," they only mean "I believe there is a God; I believe he exists." Though it is certainly important to believe in the historic, orthodox creeds of the Church, it must be frankly stated that such "faith" is insufficient to establish a right relationship with God. Many, even in the church, don't seem to know this. James reminds us that even demons "believe" in God—and tremble (Jas 2:19)! A mental acknowledgment of certain doctrines is *not* what the Bible means by faith. Such a position is nothing more than a passive awareness of certain facts.

Do you believe in bungee jumping? Someone may claim they believe because they have an intellectual awareness that bungee jumping exists and is a relatively safe and enjoyable activity for many people. However, the Bible would call such a person an unbeliever! Why? Because true faith in bungee jumping is demonstrated only by putting on the harness and jumping off a bridge! "Faith apart from works is dead" (Jas 2:26).

Finally, many mistakenly think of faith as a leap in the dark. What's important for these people is a person's commitment to what he thinks is true. It's the jump that matters, not where one lands. While biblical faith is certainly a leap, it is never a leap in the dark. Rather, we are invited to jump into the promises of God! Does this take courage? To be sure. But no one is asked to take a step of faith without first understanding *who* is calling and *what* is promised. When our daughters were small, I would sometimes stand them on the kitchen table, step back, open my arms and say, "Jump to Daddy!" They soon learned, without hesitation, to leap forward in sheer delight knowing that daddy had given them a wonderful promise. I never dropped my girls, not even once! Biblical faith is not a leap in the dark, but rather a courageous step into the promises of God! "Some trust in chariots and some in horses, but we trust in the name of the Lord our God" (Ps 20:7).

What is faith? Faith is putting one's complete trust in the Lord; that what he promises, he is able to perform. Faith itself does not save us. The Lord Jesus is the only one who can do that! But faith connects us to him; he does the rest, working both in us and through us to accomplish his divine purposes. An electrical extension cord has no power in and of itself. But when it is plugged into the electrical socket—suddenly we see its amazing purpose. Faith is the link that connects us to God. Once his divine power begins to flow in our mortal bodies, we are then enabled to walk with God, obey his commandments, and live a life that matters. In other words, we are able to practice "the obedience of faith."

> *For* by grace you have been saved through *faith. And this is not your own doing; it is the gift of God, not a result of works, so that no one may boast. For we are his workmanship, created in Christ Jesus* for *good works, which God prepared*

beforehand, that we should walk in them. (Eph 2:8–10, emphasis added)

It's all in the prepositions: salvation is *by* grace, *through* faith, *for* good works.

THE TEST OF FAITH

The book of Genesis makes clear that "the obedience of faith" is the dominant theme of Abraham's life. From the moment he heard God's call and left Ur of the Chaldeans, to when he stood on Mount Moriah, ready to offer his only son as a sacrifice to God, Abraham's life is a journey composed of steps of faith. For the most part, he performed nobly, in an exemplary manner. But he sometimes stumbled in unbelief and failed miserably. The overall message of his life, however, is crystal clear: God can be trusted, and those who walk in faith will never be disappointed. Little wonder that Hebrews 11 describes him as one of history's greatest heroes of faith:

> *By faith Abraham obeyed when he was called to go out to a place that he was to receive as an inheritance. And he went out, not knowing where he was going. By faith he went to live in the land of promise, as in a foreign land, living in tents with Isaac and Jacob, heirs with him of the same promise. For he was looking forward to the city that has foundations, whose designer and builder is God. By faith Sarah herself received power to conceive, even when she was past the age, since she considered him faithful who had promised. Therefore from one man, and him as good as dead, were born descendants as many as the stars of heaven and as many as the innumerable grains of sand by the seashore. (Heb 11:8–10)*

This passage summarizes Abraham's life by reminding us of the two primary promises that defined his journey: 1) the promise that God would give him many children, and 2) the promise that he and his descendants would inherit the land of Canaan forever. Genesis tells the story of how Abraham's belief that these promises would be fulfilled was tested again and again. Can God make a 90-year-old post-menopausal woman pregnant? Can God give the land of Canaan to an old man with a small family even when the Canaanites are well established and claim ownership to the territory? Is the Lord able to make such incredible promises come true?

The story of Abraham teaches us that untested faith is no faith at all! God arranged a series of tests to verify that Abraham's faith was sound. He wanted to leave no doubt in anyone's mind that this man was a true believer! The climactic moment came when God "tested" Abraham on Mount Moriah by asking him to sacrifice his only son, Isaac (see Gen 22:1–2). In this dramatic, final exam, Abraham gave an unforgettable illustration of what "the obedience of faith" looks like. The angel's response reveals what had been God's purpose all along in orchestrating the events of Abraham's journey: "Now I know that you fear God" (Gen 22:12).

When I was in high school, I well remember the tests Mrs. Johnson used to give us in 10th grade geometry class. What painful moments! From where we sat, it appeared that Mrs. Johnson gave those tests because she was a cruel woman with sadistic tendencies. But as I now think back on her class, I realize the purpose of those tests was not to hurt us, but to reveal whether we had been learning our lessons or not. She was testing us to prepare us for the final exam. None of us wanted to come back next year and repeat this course! In a similar manner, Abraham's journey was composed of a series of tests. Though these experiences were painful, God's purposes were always good. These tests were teaching him to walk by faith. This was the only way he could be in a right relationship with God.

For example, when Abraham first left Ur of the Chaldeans and came to Canaan, he perhaps imagined that this wonderful land of promise would resemble the Garden of Eden. But on arrival, he discovered that Canaan was in the midst of a terrible famine (see Gen 12: 7, 10). "I left Ur for this?" But this was a test. God wanted to know if the faith that brought Abraham to Canaan was strong enough to keep him there, even when the situation got tough. Unfortunately, Abraham failed this test. Rather than trusting God to help him face the famine, he packed his bags and moved to Egypt.

Next, we read about the test that came in Egypt when Pharaoh wanted to make Sarah one of his wives (see Gen 12:11–20). Once again, Abraham failed this test of faith. Rather than turning to God in trust, he lied by claiming Sarah was his sister. This not only put his wife in mortal danger but, because she was to be the mother of the child of promise, his actions jeopardized the entire plan of God for the redemption of the world! Abraham's motives were brazenly selfish as he coached Sarah to deny their marriage, so that "it may go well with me because of you" (Gen 12:13). When will Abraham learn to trust God?

Upon his return to Canaan after the debacle in Egypt, Abraham went immediately to Bethel, "to the place where he had made an altar at the first" (Gen 13:4; see Gen 12:8). Sobered by his failure to trust God, Abraham went back to where he knew he could reset his compass and get back on track. Here at Bethel's altar, he found grace to make a fresh start.

The next story assures us that Abraham had indeed learned from his mistakes and was growing in his faith. Finding himself in conflict with his nephew because the land was not adequate to support them both, he showed great trust in God by allowing Lot to have first choice (see Gen 13:1–18). Going back to Bethel had made a difference! Abraham didn't have to scheme and manipulate the situation to ensure that it turned out the way he wanted. No, he simply trusted God to do what God had promised. On this test, Abraham did very well.

Ground Zero

It is in the fifteenth chapter of Genesis, however, that we see the classic expression of Abraham's belief in God. When it comes to the subject of faith, perhaps no passage in all the Bible is more important than this.

> *After these things the word of the* Lord *came to Abram in a vision: "Fear not, Abram, I am your shield; your reward shall be very great." But Abram said, "O* Lord *God, what will you give me, for I continue childless, and the heir of my house is Eliezer of Damascus?" And Abram said, "Behold, you have given me no offspring, and a member of my household will*

> be my heir." And behold, the word of the Lord came to him: "This man shall not be your heir; your very own son shall be your heir." And he brought him outside and said, "Look toward heaven, and number the stars, if you are able to number them." Then he said to him, "So shall your offspring be." And he believed the Lord, and he counted it to him as righteousness. And he said to him, "I am the Lord who brought you out from Ur of the Chaldeans to give you this land to possess." (Gen 15:1–7)

Once again, we see that God's promise to Abraham focuses on two things: descendants (vv 4–5) and the land of Canaan (v 7). Once again, we see Abraham express his faith and confidence in God. He believes the Lord. And once again, we see that Abraham's faith is tested. At this point, Abraham is approximately 80 years of age and Sarah is 70. They have already waited what must have seemed like a long time (five years) for God to give them a miracle baby. Little do they know they will have to wait another twenty years before Isaac is born! Will Abraham and Sarah believe that God will keep his promise and give them a baby even though they are old and have to wait a quarter of a century for the miracle to occur? Will they believe that God will give them this land even though they own no property and the territory is currently occupied by the Kenites, Kenizzites, Kadmonites, Hittites, Perizzites, Rephaim, Amorites, Canaanites, Girgashites and Jebusites (see Gen 15:18–21)? Yes, believing the Lord may be harder than you think!

Like the father in the New Testament who said to Jesus, "I believe; help my unbelief!" (Mark 9:24), Abraham trusted God's promise, and yet at the same time needed divine reassurance. "O Lord God, how am I to know that I shall inherit it?" (Gen 15:8). Though Abraham's question related specifically to God's promise of the land, his candid request for further evidence reveals how challenging faith can be. Abraham is asking the Lord to help him conquer his doubts and give him the gift of faith. This is a request the Lord is always ready to answer! "Bring me a heifer," God said (Gen 15:9).

God does not respond to Abraham's question by rebuking him for his slowness to believe or scolding him for his request for further evidence. Even as Jesus graciously responded to Thomas' doubts about the resurrection (see John 20:24–29), so God responded to Abraham's question with tender compassion. He did not decide to shore up Abraham's shaky faith by performing signs and wonders or by giving the patriarch a course in apologetics. In asking for a heifer, God's response was to come personally to Abraham in a solemn covenant-making ceremony, where he would reveal both the depth of his love and the lengths to which he was willing to go to guarantee that his promises would indeed be fulfilled. In other words, God answers Abraham's question not by removing the obstacles to faith nor by a quick fulfillment of the promises. His response to Abraham's struggle with faith is to reveal to him the true character and nature of the God he worships.

> *He said to him, "Bring me a heifer three years old, a female goat three years old, a ram three years old, a turtledove, and a young pigeon." And he brought him all these, cut them in half, and laid each half over against the other. . . . As the sun was going down, a deep sleep fell on Abram. And behold, dreadful and great darkness fell upon him. . . . When the sun had gone down and it was dark, behold, a smoking fire pot and a flaming torch passed between these pieces. On that day the* Lord *made a covenant with Abram, saying, "To your offspring I give this land, from the river of Egypt to the great river, the river Euphrates, the land of the Kenites, the Kenizzites, the Kadmonites, the Hittites, the Perizzites, the Rephaim, the Amorites, the Canaanites, the Girgashites and the Jebusites." (Gen 15:9–10, 12, 17–21)*

God responds to Abraham's need for reassurance by establishing (literally, *cutting*) a covenant with him and his descendants. In the Ancient Near East, a covenant was a binding agreement that defined how two parties were to relate to one another. A covenant-making ceremony was dramatic and solemn. Typically, it included oaths and promises. Often blessings were promised when the covenant was kept, and curses threatened if it should be violated. The concept of "cutting" a covenant came from the fact that sacrificial animals were literally cut in half, laying their bloody, divided carcasses on the ground in two parallel rows. The climax of the ceremony occurred when the two parties making the covenant walked between the divided carcasses.

This was a symbolic way of saying, "May I be ripped apart like these animals if I fail to keep my end of this covenant agreement." The prophet Jeremiah gives a vivid description of the drama involved in such a ceremony.

> *Because you have broken the terms of our covenant, I will cut you apart just as you cut apart the calf when you walked between its halves to solemnize your vows. Yes, I will cut you apart, whether you are officials of Judah or Jerusalem, court officials, priests, or common people—for you have broken your oath. (Jer 34:18–19 NLT)*

But notice that in *this* ceremony the Lord is making with Abraham, only God passes between the sacrificial animals! Abraham is a spectator to what God is doing. The smoking pot and flaming torch symbolize that God is making a unilateral, unconditional covenant with Abraham. In the most solemn manner possible, God is saying, "Abraham, if I fail to keep my promises to you, may I be dismembered, and my body ripped apart!" Abraham's response was to humbly say, "I can trust a God like that!"

RIGHTEOUSNESS

Perhaps the most astonishing truth from this amazing chapter has not yet been stated. While Abraham's trust in God is certainly remarkable, the biggest surprise is the Lord's response to Abraham's faith: he "counted it to him as righteousness" (Gen 15:6). The word *counted* (reckoned, credited) has the idea of evaluating the worth of something, establishing its value. God esteemed Abraham's faith as equivalent to righteousness. In other words, Abraham was right with God not because of something he did but because he believed God's word and trusted God's promise. Though he had left everything in order to follow God's call, built altars so he could worship, and treated his nephew with grace and kindness, none of this made Abraham a righteous man. Neither his good deeds nor his acts of piety put him in a right relationship with God. Abraham's righteousness was the result of faith alone.

Not only is it surprising to realize that faith makes a man or woman right with God, but it is equally astounding to discover what this righteousness actually looks like. Most people have a vague idea that "righteousness" has to do with moral behavior, good works, and pious deeds. But Abraham's life causes us to think about righteousness in an entirely new way. Long before Moses gave the moral law or built the Tabernacle, Abraham was living a life of righteousness. How? By faith alone. As Paul explains in Romans 4, the essence of righteousness is faith in God. Being righteous is not so much a matter of what one does as what one believes.

> *For what does the Scripture say? "Abraham believed God, and it was counted to him as righteousness." Now to the one who works, his wages are not counted as a gift but as his due. And to the one who does not work but believes in him who justifies the ungodly, his faith is counted as righteousness. . . . But the words "it was counted to him" were not written for his sake alone, but for ours also. It will be counted to us who believe in him who raised from the dead Jesus our Lord. (Rom 4:3–5, 23–24)*

God measures righteousness not so much in terms of outward behaviors, but in terms of where we put our trust. It is faith that makes us rightly related to God, and because of that right relationship, we are considered by God himself to be righteous! In his commentary on Genesis, Victor Hamilton quotes scholar Brevard Childs as saying, "Righteousness is not an ideal, absolute norm, but a right relationship."[3]

This is revolutionary! Paul's discovery that Abraham was made righteous by faith transformed both his life and his theology! And when he began to preach the good news of justification by faith alone, the message ignited a revival across the Mediterranean world of the first century.

> *For I am not ashamed of this Good News about Christ. It is the power of God at work, saving everyone who believes—the Jew first and also the Gentile. This Good News tells us how God makes us right in his sight. This is accomplished from*

---

3   Hamilton, *Genesis,* 1:427.

start to finish by faith. As the Scriptures say, "It is through faith that a righteous person has life." (Rom 1:16–17 NLT)

Similarly, in the 16th century, Martin Luther rediscovered this world-shaking reality. Not only did this truth cause a transformation in his own soul, but as he preached the righteousness of faith, the Church experienced a re-formation.

What God wants more than anything else is that we believe his Word and trust his promises; that we practice "the obedience of faith." This puts us in a right relationship with God and makes us righteous. Abraham is the father of all who believe. His story is not just history, it is written so that his example will inspire us to walk as he walked.

QUESTIONS FOR DISCUSSION

1. What is faith?
2. Where is faith most difficult for you? Where do you struggle most with doubt?
3. Why did God "test" Abraham's faith? Has he ever tested yours? Did you pass the test?
4. What is righteousness? Have you ever known someone who was genuinely righteous? What were they like?
5. Describe the importance of God's covenant with Abraham.

14
How to Birth a Donkey
Genesis 16:1–16

According to anecdotal evidence, the most dangerous year on the job for a fire fighter is year ten. Statistically, this is when the greatest number of injuries and deaths occur. Though at first, this may seem surprising, pause, and think about it. After a decade on the force, a fire fighter may feel that he has experienced every possible situation and, because he has survived, he can therefore handle anything. Such overconfidence is the very thing that sets him up for tragedy. When it comes to fighting fires, the only way to be sure one never makes a stupid mistake is to be constantly vigilant.

It is interesting to note that Abraham's greatest failure occurred roughly ten years after his conversion. Genesis 16 tells the sad story. Abraham and Sarah, now aged eighty-six and seventy-six respectively, have grown tired of waiting on God to fulfill his promise to give them a child. In frustration, they come up with their own plan for accomplishing God's will. Abraham's decision to father a child with Hagar the Egyptian is the greatest mistake of his life. In no other single event is the folly of unbelief more prominently displayed. Ishmael's birth is the origin of the Arab-Israeli conflict that has troubled international politics for over 3,000 years!

WHEN GOD'S WORK IS DONE MAN'S WAY

Genesis 12 introduced us to a seventy-five-year-old Abraham as he left Ur of the Chaldeans in obedience to God's call. This first step of faith put him in a right relationship with God. Genesis 15, which we examined in the last chapter, told of how God made a covenant with Abraham, confirming his status as a "righteous" man. We saw how the New Testament calls this the first illustration in history of the doctrine of justification by faith alone.

In the next chapter, we will examine Genesis 17 when Abraham will be ninety-nine years of age. In this amazing chapter, God will visit the elderly patriarch and perform a deeper work of grace in his heart, giving him a new commandment be blameless, or perfect (see Gen 17:1). In recognition of the transformation that has occurred in his character, God will change his name from Abram to Abraham (see Gen 17:5).

Let's pause to put these pieces together. In Genesis 15, God does a great work *for* Abraham by declaring him righteous and making a covenant with him. Abraham's *status* is changed. In Genesis 17, God does an even greater work *in* Abraham, transforming his heart and empowering him to walk blamelessly. In other words, Abraham's *character* is changed. It seems that Genesis 15 is giving us an Old Testament description of justification and Genesis 17 a picture of sanctification.

It is only when we put Genesis 16 in this broader context that we interpret it correctly. The story of Abraham's greatest failure is strategically placed *after* his justification (Gen 15) and *before* his sanctification (Gen 17). The narrative is thus introducing us to the subject of sin in the believer's life. It is one thing to think about the reality of sin in the life of an unbelieving pagan. But it is another thing entirely to think about sin's presence in the life of a believer. In Genesis 16, Abraham is clearly in a right relationship with God, so it is disturbing to see this Old Testament saint seeking to live the life of the Spirit in the power of the flesh. It is troubling to see Father Abraham using worldly wisdom and fleshly resources in a foolish effort to do God's will man's way. The results are disastrous.

In New Testament terms, Genesis 16 is a picture of carnal Christianity. Paul addresses this nagging issue on numerous occasions in his letters. He is deeply concerned for Christians who live beneath their calling, who continue to think and behave as they did before they were converted. How can those who are called to be holy continue to live in sin? In writing to the believers in Galatia, Paul addresses this issue by using the story of Abraham's sin to drive home his message.

> *Abraham had two sons, one by a slave woman and one by a free woman. But the son of the slave was born according to the flesh, while the son of the free woman was born through promise. Now this may be interpreted allegorically: these women are two covenants. One is from Mount Sinai, bearing children for slavery; she is Hagar. Now Hagar is Mount Sinai in Arabia; she corresponds to the present Jerusalem, for she is in slavery with her children. But the Jerusalem above is free, and she is our mother. (Gal 4:22–26)*

Paul makes no secret of the fact that he is interpreting the story "allegorically" (Gal 4:24). With spiritual insight as well as hermeneutical skill, Paul uses Abraham's two sons to illustrate two very different spiritual realities. Ishmael was born "according to the flesh" (Gal 4:23, 29). In other words, there was nothing supernatural about him. He came into the world in the normal, human manner. Isaac, on the other hand, was born "through promise" (Gal 4:23), "according to the Spirit" (Gal 4:29). His birth was truly a miracle. God did it! Paul is saying that those who model their lives after Isaac, by living according to the Spirit and trusting in the promises of God, experience freedom and the blessed assurance of being rightly related to God. But those who model their lives after Ishmael, the child of the flesh, are enslaved to a recurring cycle of sin and doubt.

Paul's point is not to draw a contrast between Christians and Jews, but rather between those who walk in the Spirit and those who walk in the flesh, those who live under grace and those who live under law. Paul is warning New Testament believers not to make the mistake that Abraham did by seeking to accomplish God's will man's way. He uses Genesis 16 to warn the Galatian Christians about the danger of trying to live the life of the Spirit in the power of the flesh. "O foolish Galatians! Who has bewitched you? . . . Are you so foolish?

Having begun by the Spirit, are you now being perfected by the flesh?" (Gal 3:1, 3).

In his book *He Came Down from Heaven*, Charles Williams says there are three degrees on the journey of salvation:

1. The old self on the old way.
2. The old self on the new way.
3. The new self on the new way.[1]

This simple outline provides a helpful model for understanding Abraham's story. As a pagan living in Ur of the Chaldeans, he clearly illustrates the old self in the old way. But when he heard God's call and stepped out in faith, he was gloriously converted and began to walk in the new way. However, as we have seen from the Genesis story, though Abraham was on a new path, he still manifested many of the worldly, carnal traits of his old self. He had a new status, but he did not yet have a new nature. In the next chapter, we will discover how God can take an old man, transform his character, and give him a brand-new start!

The language used in Genesis 16 is shocking and somewhat crude in describing Ishmael's birth. Though God loved him and blessed him, the Scripture is unambiguous in its caustic evaluation of what was happening. The message the angel brought to Hagar concerning her son must have troubled her mother's heart:

> *He shall be a wild donkey of a man, his hand against everyone and everyone's hand against him, and he shall dwell over against all his kinsmen. (Gen 16:12)*

By walking in the flesh and trying to do God's will man's way, Abraham had succeeded in giving birth to a donkey!

SARAH'S BRIGHT IDEA

The Bible highlights the fact that the original idea for having a child with Hagar came from Sarah, not Abraham. Though Abraham, as the head of his home, is fully responsible for what happened, the blame first falls on Sarah.

---

[1] Williams, *He Came Down from Heaven*, 85.

> *Now Sarai, Abram's wife, had borne him no children. She had a female Egyptian servant whose name was Hagar. And Sarai said to Abram, "Behold now, the* Lord *has prevented me from bearing children. Go in to my servant; it may be that I shall obtain children by her." And Abram listened to the voice of Sarai. (Gen 16:1–2)*

The aging couple must have felt desperate. Time was running out. Ten years is a long time to wait for God to act. After seeing fertility specialists and undergoing hormone therapy, Sarah, blaming her barren condition on God, decides to take matters into her own hands. God helps those who help themselves, right?

It is interesting to note that Sarah and Abraham neglect the most obvious path they could have taken to find help. Not once do they turn to the Lord for guidance! Years later, when Isaac faced a similar situation, he "prayed to the Lord for his wife, because she was barren, and Rebekah his wife conceived" (Gen 25:21). Oh, how different history could have been if only Abraham had followed a similar path.

Today, surrogate pregnancies can be accomplished without sexual relations. Not so in Abraham's day. Yet there is nothing intrinsically immoral about Abraham's relations with his servant concubine. This was a culturally acceptable way for a barren couple to have a child and then adopt him as their own. But the text makes it clear that this was *not* God's original plan. Everything about this birth is troubling. Not only does the narrative underscore the fact that Hagar is not Abraham's wife, it pointedly reminds us that she is an Egyptian! We can easily anticipate that a child born of such a union will not only challenge marital harmony, it will also complicate the biological lineage of God's covenant family.

In subtle, and sometimes not-so-subtle, ways, the narrative reveals the dysfunction that exists in the marriage of Abraham and Sarah. We gain the impression that there was trouble in this home long before the events recorded in this chapter. For one thing, Sarah is manipulative. Her desperation to have a child makes her willing to do almost anything to get what she wants. Reminiscent of Eve in the Garden of Eden (see Gen 3), Sarah comes up with a plan and then gently coerces her husband to go along. The plan, however, leads to disaster and many regrets. In speaking about what happened in the Garden, Paul makes the point that, though Adam was certainly responsible for what happened, it was "the woman (who) was deceived" (1 Tim 2:14). Genesis 16 tells a similar story.

Abraham's passivity is a diabolical match for Sarah's manipulation. Silent and emotionally detached, Abraham wimpishly acquiesces to his wife's plan. Never raising a question or pausing to pray, he simply submits to her leadership. "Whatever you say, dear." Like Adam, who took the role of a silent spectator while Eve conversed with the snake and led the way into sin, Abraham did nothing to protect his home from danger. Perhaps he was afraid to disagree with his wife. Perhaps he was unable to come up with an alternative plan. Perhaps he liked the idea of spending the night with young, beautiful Hagar. Whatever his reasons may have been, Abraham, at a critical moment in time, failed to take charge of the situation and be the head of his family. He passively watched as chaos and turmoil engulfed his home.

It would be a terrible mistake, however, to conclude that Scripture is teaching that women are less intelligent than men and therefore a man should never listen to his wife's counsel. Reality is much more complex than that! It is important to see how other Scriptures shed light on this volatile subject. For example, while it is true that Adam and Abraham should *not* have taken the advice of their wives, Pilate *should* have! During Jesus' trial, his wife sent him a message: "Leave that innocent man alone. I suffered through a terrible nightmare about him last night" (Matt 27:19 NLT). When he pulled rank and refused to listen to his wife's counsel, Pilate may have imagined himself a strong leader; in reality, he was only a pompous idiot! Nabal is another man who should have listened to his wife. In refusing Abigail's counsel to show kindness to David's servants, he only proved to everyone what a fool he really was (see 1 Sam 25).

It is interesting to note how the story of Abraham and Hagar is, in many ways, a mirror image of what had happened earlier in Egypt with Sarah and Pharaoh (Gen 12:10–20). There, Abraham encouraged Sarah to deny their marriage by pretending to be his sister. Consequently, she "was taken into Pharaoh's house" and apparently was, for a short time at least, a part of his harem (see Gen 12:15). In Genesis 16, the tables are turned and now it is Sarah who encourages Abraham to "deny their marriage" by sleeping with Hagar. Perhaps, there is more going on in this dysfunctional home than just a desire for a baby. Sarah may have wanted to even the score! Tit for tat. All is fair in love and war.

God's Love for Hagar and Ishmael

A superficial reading of Genesis may give the impression that God is somehow punishing Hagar and her son Ishmael for what happened. Through no fault of their own, they seem to be unfairly excluded from God's plan and perhaps from his love. Nothing could be further from the truth. Though it is certainly clear that God's covenant purposes have an exclusive focus on Isaac and his descendants, the Genesis narrative tells us that he has good things in store for Ishmael as well. God wants us to know that he can redeem bad choices and transform sinful mistakes into something good.

It is no surprise that Hagar's pregnancy provoked tension in the family. Sarah treated her so harshly that she fled into the desert for safety. Amazingly, "the angel of the Lord" himself came to meet her there. This is the first mention of this heavenly personage in the Bible. More than an ordinary angel, many scholars believe "the angel of the Lord" is some sort of physical manifestation of God himself. Perhaps Hagar's visitor in the desert was none other than a preincarnate manifestation of the Second Person of the Trinity! It is remarkable that such an unprecedented event would be visited upon someone like Hagar: an Egyptian, a slave, and a woman.

Encouraged by the Lord, Hagar agreed to return and submit to Abraham and Sarah. But before he left, the angel of the Lord assured her that he knew of the injustice she had experienced. Specifically, he told her of wonderful plans in store for her and the child in her womb: "I will surely multiply your offspring so that they cannot be numbered for multitude" (Gen 16:10). Later in the narrative, God again promises blessings and many descendants: "As for Ishmael . . . I have blessed him and will make him fruitful and multiply him greatly. He shall father twelve princes, and I will make him into a great nation." (Gen 17:20; see also Gen 21:8–21)

But the strongest evidence of God's love for Hagar and her descendants is seen in the specially chosen names that are the climax to the whole story. In the Old Testament, names carry great significance and often bear witness to the work that God is doing. That is certainly true here.

> *And the angel of the* Lord *said to her, "Behold, you are pregnant and shall bear a son. You shall call his name Ishmael (God hears), because the* Lord *has listened to your affliction. . . . So she called the name of the* Lord *who spoke to her, "You are a God of seeing (El Roi, God sees)," for she said, "Truly here I have seen him who looks after me." Therefore the well was called Beer-lahai-roi (the well of the Living One who sees me); it lies between Kadesh and Bered. (Gen 16:11, 13–14)*

God himself chose the name for Hagar's son. *Ishmael* means "God hears." This child will be a constant reminder that God is listening to the hopes and prayers of those who, like Hagar, find themselves trapped in bondage and victims of injustice. Yes, God hears; and he cares! One day he will come and dry our tears and make things right.

This spiritual encounter is so transformative for Hagar that she decides to give a new name to God. She calls him *El Roi*; the God who sees. She already knew that God heard her; the name of her son assured her of that. But now she knows that God sees her as well. He has seen the injustice she has experienced. And now he has come to do something about it. We can find examples of people giving names to other people, to animals, and to places. But nowhere in the Bible do we read of someone giving a name to God. As far as we know, this Egyptian slave woman is the only one in history with the spiritual boldness to do this!

Finally, the entire encounter between the Lord and Hagar is memorialized by giving a special name to the well in the desert where these events took place. It was called *Beer Lahai Roi*, which means "the well of the Living One who sees me."

These names bear witness to the God who is working in and through all the tortured events of this amazing chapter. They also reveal what a remarkable woman Hagar is. She too has a special relationship with God. But more than this, these names serve as a rebuke to the unbelief and impatience of Abraham and Sarah. If only they had believed that God heard their prayers and saw their circumstances, how different the story might have been.

HEE HAW!

The story of Abraham, Sarah, and Hagar gives us an unforgettable picture of what happens when Christians seek to do God's will man's way, when believers try to live the life of the Spirit in the power of the flesh. God wants us to know that carnal methods will never produce godly results. Such human striving can only give birth to a donkey!

In seeking to summarize this amazing passage of Scripture and make application for our lives today, let's look once more at the decision Sarah and Abraham made to have a child through Hagar. Though it is easy, from a personal and cultural point of view, to understand why they made such a choice, the Bible is clear that what they did was not in alignment with God's original plan. The tragic consequences of their decision serve as a warning to all future believers to be vigilant lest they make a similar mistake. We might say that Genesis 16 offers a sure-fire, bona-fide, money-back-guaranteed formula for birthing a donkey. If I, for some ungodly reason, should ever actually *want* to do such a stupid thing, then all I need to do is follow the example of Sarah and Abraham. Here's how.

First, *do God's work my way*. Abraham and Sarah had a clear understanding of what God had promised them: children. Not only did they understand the promise, they believed it would come true. This is no small accomplishment! Abraham and Sarah were quite advanced in their spiritual development. They were believers. They were justified by faith. However, they did not yet understand *how* God was going to fulfill such a promise. After a decade of waiting, perhaps they concluded that God must need help. Perhaps they reasoned that what mattered was having a baby; *how* that baby was born was inconsequential. In other words, in a matter as important as this, perhaps they felt that the end would justify the means!

So, Sarah came up with her own idea for how to have a baby and she got Abraham to go along with her plan. They would employ a surrogate mother and then adopt the child as their own. Their plan was logical, efficient, practical, and culturally acceptable. They would do God's will man's way. It all made perfect sense.

Abraham and Sarah had not yet learned that trusting God has an important corollary: doubting yourself. Even Socrates understood that the beginning of wisdom is the recognition of one's own ignorance. How much more should Abraham's faith in God have led him to be wise concerning his own lack of wisdom, to know how much he still did not know, to be reasonable about the limits of human reasoning. How different the story would have been if Abraham and Sarah had been smart enough to recognize their capacity to make a dumb decision. They had not yet learned the truth of Proverbs 3:5–6: "Trust in the Lord with all your heart and *do not lean on your own understanding. In all your ways acknowledge him, and he will make your paths straight* (NASB, emphasis added)." The Bible has a special term to describe those who rely on their own instincts and trust in their own intelligence: "Whoever trusts in his own mind is a fool" (Prov 28:26).

If there is any singing in hell, perhaps the only music that will seem appropriate is that blasphemous song made popular by Frank Sinatra, "I Did It My Way." Yes, in a place specially prepared for those who insist on having their own way, this song may well be the National Anthem of Hell.

> *Yes, there were times, I'm sure you knew*
> *When I bit off more than I could chew*
> *But through it all, when there was doubt*
> *I ate it up and spit it out*
> *I faced it all and I stood tall*
> *And did it my way.—Paul Anka*

Second, *do God's work in my time*. Abraham and Sarah were already old when God first called them. Making a difficult situation even worse, Sarah was barren. Thus, the promise that they would have children was challenging even from the start. Their decision to use Hagar as a surrogate mother came only after waiting ten long years for God to act. Little did they know that God would require them to wait an additional fifteen *more* years for Isaac's miraculous birth. Thus, from the first announcement of God's promise to its fulfilment, they waited twenty-five years. Abraham was one hundred years old and Sarah was ninety when Isaac was finally born. That's a long time to wait! Though getting on God's timetable and waiting for him to act may be hard, this story reminds us that the alternative is much worse. Those who try to do God's work according to their own timetable will birth a donkey every time!

In the Bible, "to wait" on the Lord and "to believe" in the Lord are two ways of saying the same thing. In fact, English Bible translations oscillate between the two terms. To say that Abraham and Sarah failed to *wait* on God to fulfill his promise is synonymous with saying they did not trust him, they did not believe. In the Bible, unbelief is a serious sin. "Without faith it is impossible to please God" (Heb 11:6). Repeatedly the Bible calls us to trust in the Lord by waiting on him.

- "Wait for the Lord; be strong, and let your heart take courage; wait for the Lord!" (Ps 27:14)
- "The Lord is good to those who wait for him, to the soul who seeks him. It is good that one should wait quietly for the salvation of the Lord." (Lam 3:25–26)
- "They who wait for the Lord shall renew their strength; they shall mount up with wings like eagles; they shall run and not be weary; they shall walk and not faint." (Isa 40:31)
- "For still the vision awaits its appointed time; it hastens to the end—it will not lie. If it seems slow, wait for it; it will surely come; it will not delay." (Hab 2:3)
- "And let us not grow weary of doing good, for in due season we will reap, if we do not give up." (Gal 6:9)

- "The Lord is not slow to fulfill his promise as some count slowness, but is patient toward you, not wishing that any should perish, but that all should reach repentance." (2 Pet 3:9)

Just as God's ways are different than man's ways, so is his timing. From a human perspective, it may seem that God is slow, even late. But such "delays" are divine opportunities to learn to trust him more.

Third, *do God's work with my resources*. Abraham birthed a donkey not only because he tried to do God's work in man's way and in man's time, but also because he operated in man's strength. In relying on Hagar, he opted for human resources rather than divine. He sought to do the work of the Spirit in the power of the flesh. As Jesus said so succinctly, "That which is born of the flesh is flesh" (John 3:6). Ishmael was the child of flesh. He was the product of human ingenuity, worldly wisdom, and carnal strength. This meant that he would be part of the problem on planet earth, not part of the solution!

Abraham and Sarah finally succeeded in getting what they had always wanted: a baby boy. Everyone should have been happy, right? Ironically, almost immediately, their dream became a nightmare. They had birthed a donkey! God "gave them what they asked for, but he sent a plague along with it" (Ps 106:15 NLT). They had climbed to the top of the ladder of success only to discover that it was leaning against the wrong wall! The worst thing that can happen to those who labor in the flesh is that they might just achieve their goal. A fate far worse than failure is that of succeeding in doing the wrong thing.

QUESTIONS FOR DISCUSSION

1. Does this lesson shed any light on current tensions in the Middle East? Does it influence the way Christians should think about Muslims? Discuss this.
2. What did you learn from this lesson about dysfunctional marriages—notably manipulative wives and passive husbands?
3. Describe a time in your own life when you tried to do God's will man's way, when you sought to do the work of the Spirit in the power of the flesh. What happened?
4. What is your reaction to the song *I Did It My Way*?

5. Do you agree with the idea that "waiting on God" and "believing in God" are two ways of saying the same thing? Why is this important?
6. Have you ever succeeded in doing the wrong thing? Has God ever given you what you asked for in prayer but "sent a plague along with it"?

15
An Old Man Gets a New Start
Genesis 17:1–27

G. K. Chesterton, in his book *Orthodoxy*, contends that we learn our most important theology from the story books read to us as children. In a marvelous chapter entitled "The Ethics of Elfland," he tells how the fairy tales he heard as a child laid the foundation for his eventual conversion to Christianity as an adult.

> My first and last philosophy, that which I believe in with unbroken certainty, I learnt in the nursery. . . . The things I believed most then, the things I believe most now, are the things called fairy tales. They seem to me to be the entirely reasonable things. They are not fantasies. . . . Fairyland is nothing but the sunny country of common sense. It is not earth that judges heaven, but heaven that judges earth; so for me at least it was not earth that criticized elfland, but elfland that criticized the earth.[1]

Chesterton's point is that children's books introduce us to a different kind of reality, a new way of seeing things, a completely different way to think. Life is not what it seems. There is more going on than is going on. And only the young at heart can see clearly. Jesus expressed the same truth this way: "Unless you turn and become like children, you will never enter the kingdom of heaven" (Matt 18:3).

---

1   Chesterton, *Orthodoxy*, 252.

This introduction will help you to understand why I want to begin this chapter with an extended quotation taken from a book written by one of my favorite "theologians," Dr. Seuss. I have no idea whether *On Beyond Zebra* was written to entertain, to amuse, or to stimulate theological debate. All I know is that this whimsical story serves as an excellent introduction to Genesis 17. So, gather round children, I have a story to read to you.

> *Said Conrad Cornelius o'Donald o'Dell,*
> *My very young friend who is learning to spell:*
> *"The A is for Ape. The B is for Bear.*
> *The C is for Camel. The H is for Hare.*
> *The M is for Mouse. And the R is for Rat.*
> *I know all the twenty-six letters like that . . .*
> *. . .through to Z is for Zebra. I know them all well."*
> *Said Conrad Cornelius o'Donald o'Dell.*
> *"So now I know everything anyone knows*
> *From beginning to end. From the start to the close.*
> *Because Z is as far as the alphabet does."*
>
> *Then he almost fell flat on his face on the floor*
> *When I picked up the chalk and drew one letter more!*
> *A letter he never had dreamed of before!*
> *And I said, "You can stop, if you want, with the Z*
> *Because most people stop with the Z*
> *But not me!*
>
> *In the places I go there are things that I see*
> *That I never could spell if I stopped with the Z.*
> *I'm telling you this 'cause you're one of my friends.*
> *My alphabet starts where your alphabet ends!*
>
> *My alphabet starts with this letter called YUZZ.*
> *It's the letter I use to spell Yuzz-a-ma-Tuzz.*
> *You'll be sort of surprised what there is to be found*
> *Once you go beyond Z and start poking around!"*

The narrator continues the delightful rhyme by introducing Conrad to a whole series of amazing letters that exist on beyond Z; letters that make possible a new world inhabited by creatures that he had never even imagined. For example, the letter WUM is for Wumbus, a whale who lives on a hill. And FUDDLE is needed to spell Miss Fuddle-dee-Duddle, an exotic bird with a very, very long tail. And way past Z is a letter called ITCH. You simply cannot imagine what a swarm of Itch-a-pods is like without this letter.

Written in a style that only a child can understand, the book boldly proclaims that there is a whole new dimension of reality just waiting to be discovered, *if* one has the courage to go 'on beyond Zebra.' Our twenty-six-letter alphabet is a great place to begin, but it can take us only so far. We need new letters and a new vocabulary to see and experience the greater reality of which most people are simply ignorant.

After a lengthy journey taking Conrad through a universe populated by Glickers, Sneedles, Quandaries, Thnadners, and Floob-Boober-Bab-Boober-Bubs, the narrator finally concludes the story by saying:

> *The places I took him!*
> *I tried hard to tell*
> *Young Conrad Cornelius o'Donald o'Dell*
> *A few brand-new wonderful words he might spell.*
> *I led him around and I tried hard to show*
> *There are things beyond Z that most people don't know.*
> *I took him past Zebra. As far as I could.*
> *And I think, perhaps, maybe I did him some good . . .*
> *Because, finally, he said:*
> *"This is really great stuff!*
> *And I guess the old alphabet isn't enough!"*

In order to understand what happens in the life of Abraham in Genesis 17, we are going to need a new alphabet and a new vocabulary. God's alphabet of grace begins precisely at the place where our human alphabet ends. "You'll be sort of surprised what there is to be found once you go beyond Z and start poking around!"

Is That All There Is?

Genesis 17 begins with a candid acknowledgment of Abraham's age; he is ninety-nine years old. This reminds us that it has been twenty-five long years since he first heard God's call and stepped out in the obedience of faith. For a quarter of a century, he has been walking with God, waiting for the promises to be fulfilled.

Abraham is the Bible's primary illustration of justification by faith. In the last chapter, we learned that although God had done a great work *for* Abraham, he has not yet done a great work *in* him. Being rightly related to God through faith did not change his carnal nature. The birth of Ishmael illustrated the sad fact that Abraham was still trying to do the work of the Spirit in the power of the flesh. And though he had repeatedly learned that doing God's will man's way always leads to tragic results, Abraham didn't know how to change this discouraging reality. For all he knew, his carnal nature and sinful patterns of behavior would be with him forever. Perhaps this was all there is to salvation. Perhaps this is as good as it gets.

Making a difficult situation even worse is the sober fact that, after twenty-five years of waiting, the promises of God remain unfulfilled. Though Abraham has continued to believe that God will do what he said, nothing has come of it. Although God has promised him the land of Canaan, the territory continues to be inhabited by the Canaanites. And although God has promised him multitudes of children, so far, only one child has been born, Ishmael, "a wild donkey of a man." And God made it clear that this was *not* the child of promise. Abraham must have wondered what faith can really mean if the promises are not fulfilled. Must we wait until heaven to see the evidence of God's faithfulness?

The truth is that Abraham's spiritual condition in Genesis 17 is like that of many Christians today. They too have put their faith in God and walked with him for many years. They too have assurance of their covenant relationship with the Lord. And yet, deep inside they are frustrated. Although walking on the new path of faith, it seems their old nature continues to define their steps. Their lives bear little or no spiritual fruit. And many of God's promises remain unfilled. Is this all there is? Is this as good as it gets? Identifying with the aging patriarch, perhaps these believers would describe their situation in these terms:

- *I'm tired.* I've been walking with you, Lord, for decades; going to church, doing ministry, giving my tithe, having daily devotions, and obeying the commandments. Sometimes it just feels like I'm going through motions, doing my duty, fulfilling an obligation.

- *I'm stuck.* Lord, even when I get a glimpse of what you want for my life, I can't get there. I've tried to pray more, serve more, give more; but the harder I try, the more I realize how stuck I am. This is a situation that I can't fix.

- *I'm defeated.* Lord, I keep battling the same sins I've struggled with for years. It seems I'm walking in circles. I stumble and then ask for your help. I stumble again, and ask again for your help. Is this what salvation looks like?

- *I'm bored.* I hate to admit it, Lord, but the routines of obedience have become just that; routine. The song has gone from my heart and skip from my step. I go through the motions, but my heart is not in it. I'm on autopilot.

- *I'm barren.* You promised, Lord, that if I followed you, I would be fruitful; my life would make a difference. I continue to sow seeds, but nothing seems to happen. My labors are fleshly efforts that produce fleshly results. Where is your power? Is this all there is? Is this as good as it gets?

If we are operating with the old alphabet, then Abraham's condition represents the normal Christian life. This is all we can hope for in this world. Romans 7, and its description of the recurring cycle of sin and forgiveness, is as good as it gets. The promises of God may be true, but we'll have to wait till we get to heaven to see their fulfillment.

But what if working harder with the old alphabet actually makes our condition worse? What if there really is an alphabet of grace that makes it possible to imagine the unimaginable, to think the unthinkable, and to experience real victory, fruitfulness, and rest here and now? What if God's grace really can take us on beyond Zebra into a new dimension of spiritual reality that we never thought possible? What if God's alphabet starts where our alphabet ends?

The Alphabet of Grace

The 17th chapter of Genesis is literally pregnant with new beginnings! But to experience the new dimensions of grace that God has prepared, Abraham must first move boldly beyond the limitations of his old ways of thinking and step into the reality made possible by the new alphabet of grace. In this amazing chapter, Abraham discovers five new realities that transform his heart and life.

First, Abraham gains a new understanding of God.

It is difficult to know exactly how much Abraham understood about the nature and character of the One he worshipped. Living centuries before God's much fuller revelation of himself at Mount Sinai, Abraham's knowledge would have been elementary. Did he understand monotheism? The moral law? Proper worship? He certainly knew that the deity who had called him was powerful, personal, moral, loving, and worthy of trust. And his knowledge was sufficient to make possible a covenant relationship with this God and to experience the righteousness that comes through faith. But Abraham's knowledge jumped to a whole new level when God visited him and revealed his personal name. "I am *El Shaddai*" (Gen 17:1). Up until this point, Abraham had basically worshipped "God." This is a title, not a name. It describes God's role and function. But now God comes to the aging patriarch and says, "Abraham, let's get personal. I'd like our relationship to be on a first-name basis."

Although the term *El Shaddai* (the Almighty; the All-Sufficient One) sounds somewhat like another title, the context makes clear that it also serves as a personal name. According to his old alphabet, Abraham worshiped a somewhat generic deity who performed certain functions. But now that he knows God's name, Abraham moves on beyond Zebra into a more intimate, face-to-face relationship. God and Abraham have become "friends" (see Isa 41:8; Jas 2:23). Knowing God up close and personal takes Abraham's faith to a whole new level.

Centuries later at the burning bush, God revealed to Moses a name that is even more personal and intimate: *Yahweh* (see Ex 3:13–15). Though Genesis indicates that the patriarchs seemed to be aware of this name (translated in English as "the LORD"), they certainly did not understand its full significance as the personal, covenant name of the deity they worshipped. God explained the history of his name to Moses this way:

> *God spoke to Moses and said to him, "I am the* LORD *(Yahweh), I appeared to Abraham, to Isaac, and to Jacob, as God Almighty (El Shaddai), but by my name the* LORD *(Yahweh) I did not make myself known to them." (Exod 6:2–3)*

When I served as senior pastor of a rather large congregation, most people called me "Pastor." The term was a label that reminded me of my function and role as the leader of the church. By using my title, the one speaking to me assumed a corresponding role of "parishioner." But if someone came up at church and said, "Good morning, Stan", the situation was immediately different. Intuitively, we both knew that this conversation was more than a pastor talking with a parishioner. More was happening here than job performance. This was a friendship!

The story of Abraham alerts us to the fact that it is possible to have a functional relationship with God that focuses on roles and responsibilities. The relationship may be authentic so that the worshipper is justified by faith and becomes part of God's covenant family. Yet such a situation, meaningful as it may be, falls short of the face-to-face intimacy that God desires. Genesis 17 introduces us to the fact that God wants to get to know us on a first-name basis. In New Testament terms, this means knowing God as Jesus. "There is no other name under heaven given among men by which we must be saved" (Acts 4:12).

One of the reasons that Abraham was tired, stuck, defeated, bored and barren is the simple fact that his relationship with God was predicated on roles and responsibilities. When he stepped into the new alphabet of grace and began to relate to God on a first-name basis, his life was transformed. As J. I. Packer famously said, "A little knowledge *of* God is worth more than a great deal of knowledge *about* him."[2]

Second, Abraham gains *a* new identity.

At ninety-nine years of age, God gives the aging patriarch a new name, dramatically signifying that something momentous is taking

---

2   Packer, *Knowing God*, 21.

place. "No longer shall your name be called Abram, but your name shall be Abraham, for I have made you the father of a multitude of nations" (Gen 17:5). The difference between Abram (exalted father) and Abraham (father of a multitude) is slight. The significance of the name change is seen not so much in the nuance of meaning between the two words, but rather in the act of renaming itself. God is dramatizing the fact that he is giving this old man a brand-new start!

The sequence of events here is important. It is only *after* Abraham gains a new understanding of God that he gains a new understanding of himself. In other words, as Abraham lost himself in the knowledge of *El Shaddai*, he found himself. Does that seem odd? Did not Jesus say something similar when he said, "For whoever would save his life will lose it, but whoever loses his life for my sake will find it" (Matt 16:25)?

The Bible insists that the only way to know myself is to know the One who created me. I find myself only when I find him. Knowing God precedes knowing self. The question "Who am I?" can only be answered when I first answer the question "Who is God?" This explains why those who set off on some noble quest to "find themselves" never reach their goal. C. S. Lewis writes eloquently about this:

> Christ will indeed give you a real personality: but you must not go to Him for the sake of that. As long as your own personality is what you are bothering about, you are not going to Him at all. The very first step is to try to forget about the self altogether. Your real, new self . . . will not come as long as you are looking for it. It will come when you are looking for Him. Does that sound strange? The same principle holds, you know, for more everyday matters. Even in social life, you will never make a good impression on other people until you stop thinking about what sort of impression you are making. Even in literature and art, no man who bothers about originality will ever be original: whereas if you simply try to tell the truth . . . you will, nine times out of ten, become original without ever having noticed it. The principle runs through all life from top to bottom. Give up yourself, and you will find your real self. Lose your life and you will save it.[3]

---

3   Lewis, *Mere Christianity*, 226–227.

One of the reasons Abraham needed a deeper work of grace was because, even at ninety-nine years of age, he was still confused about his own identity. Who am I? Sanctification describes what happens when we lose ourselves in God, and in the process, discover our true selves!

Third, Abraham gets a new sense of humor.

When God visited Abraham and revealed to him deeper dimensions of grace, he "fell on his face" in worship (Gen 17:3). But when God told Abraham that his 90-year-old wife was going to have a baby, he "fell on his face and laughed and said to himself, 'Shall a child be born to a man who is a hundred years old? Shall Sarah, who is ninety years old, bear a child?'" (Gen 17:17). Apparently, the mental image of Sarah going to the mall to buy maternity clothes was just too much, and the old geezer fell to the floor laughing. I think he laughed so hard that his dentures fell out.

Try to imagine what is happening here. Life has been hard for Abraham and Sarah. Since they started this journey of faith, they have experienced famine, war, kidnappings, family conflict, and marital troubles. We can easily imagine they have also had their share of problems that typically come with old age: arthritis, back aches, osteoporosis, high blood pressure, prostate issues, hearing loss, trips to the pharmacy, and doctor appointments. Perhaps it's been twenty-five years since they've had a good laugh. So when God tells Abraham that Sarah is going to get pregnant, he simply can't control himself. This is hilarious!

Use your sanctified imagination and try to envision the humor of it all:

- Sarah squinting through her bifocals as she tries to do a Google search on her phone while shouting to her deaf husband; "Hey Abe! How do you spell gynecology?"
- Abraham pushing his walker through the aisles at the grocery story asking the clerk where he can find a jar of pickles.
- Abraham and Sarah attending childbirth classes.

- Sarah hobbling to the nursery after church to pick up baby Isaac only to be asked by the lady in charge, "Oh, are you his great-grandmother?"
- Abraham depositing his Social Security check so he can pay his maternity bill.

But Abraham is not the only one laughing. Perhaps the best part of the story is the discovery that God is laughing too! In fact, the situation is so funny that God decides to give the baby a name that will memorialize forever the holy hilarity of what is happening (see Gen 17:19). The name Isaac means "laughter" or "he laughs."

God's sense of humor must not be confused with the cheap substitutes of comedy offered by this world. The hilarity of grace is best seen in the surprising incongruity of God's lavish goodness poured out where it is least expected. God's holy humor is on display when a donkey talks, an axe-head floats, ravens show up with supper, a lame man dances, a dead man lives, thousands of people are fed with one Happy Meal, and taxes are paid with money found in the mouth of a fish. Now *that's* funny! An even greater display of God's humor is seen when he takes a self-righteous, pompous, little Pharisee named Paul and turns him into a saint. But best of all, if you really want to experience sanctified humor, just go look in the mirror and gaze in wonder at the lengths to which God will go to reveal the hilarity of what his grace can do!

Before leaving this subject, we need to remember that not all laughter is the same. Discernment is needed. When Sarah learned of God's plan for her pregnancy, she too laughed. But how different was her humor from that of her husband. Hers was the cynical laugh of unbelief.

> *The* LORD *said, "I will surely return to you about this time next year, and Sarah your wife shall have a son." And Sarah was listening at the tent door behind him. Now Abraham and Sarah were old, advanced in years. The way of women had ceased to be with Sarah. So Sarah laughed to herself, saying, "After I am worn out, and my* LORD *is old, shall I have pleasure?" The* LORD *said to Abraham, "Why did Sarah laugh and say, 'Shall I indeed bear a child, now that I am old?' Is*

> *anything too hard for the* LORD? *At the appointed time I will return to you, about this time next year, and Sarah shall have a son." But Sarah denied it, saying, "I did not laugh," for she was afraid. He said, "No, but you did laugh." (Gen 18:10–15)*

What about you? How long has it been since you experienced holy humor and sanctified laughter? If you are tired, stuck, defeated, bored and barren, God wants to take you on beyond Zebra so that, like Abraham, you too can experience the hilarity of grace.

Fourth, Abraham receives a new sacramental understanding of the covenant.

Just as the rainbow was the sign of the covenant God made with Noah (see Gen 9:13–17), so circumcision is the sign of the covenant God made with Abraham. Abraham may have wondered why the rite was necessary when he had already experienced the reality without it (see Gen 15). God did not give circumcision to create the covenant; rather its purpose was to confirm and bear witness to what he had already done. As a wedding ring symbolizes marriage and signifies that vows have been taken, so circumcision is an outward physical symbol of an inward spiritual reality. In giving this sacred rite to Abraham and his family, God is teaching us how symbols, rituals and sacraments can deepen our faith and offer meaningful channels through which sanctifying grace can continue to nourish our hearts through corporate worship.

> *And God said to Abraham, "As for you, you shall keep my covenant, you and your offspring after you throughout their generations. This is my covenant, which you shall keep, between me and you and your offspring after you: Every male among you shall be circumcised. You shall be circumcised in the flesh of your foreskins, and it shall be a sign of the covenant between me and you. He who is eight days old among you shall be circumcised. Every male throughout your generations, whether born in your house or bought with your money from any foreigner who is not of your offspring, both he who is born in your house and he who is bought with your money, shall surely be circumcised. So shall my covenant be in your flesh an everlasting covenant. Any uncircumcised male who is not circumcised in the flesh*

of his foreskin shall be cut off from his people; he has broken my covenant." (Gen 17:9–14)

Although the *what? who? when?* and *where?* of circumcision are important questions worthy of prayerful reflection, answering them goes beyond the scope of this chapter. Our purposes here are served by the profoundly simple recognition that circumcision is a *physical* act that represents a *spiritual* reality. This sacred ceremony both confirms and deepens Abraham's covenant relationship with God. In learning the sacramental nature of worship and the role of sacred symbols that help to convey God's grace, Abraham experiences yet another dimension of the new alphabet of grace. Much like water baptism in the New Testament, circumcision is an outward sign of an inward grace. It both symbolizes and promises a deeper work that God longs to do in the heart.

Fifth, Abraham receives a new commandment.

As Abraham moves on beyond Zebra and steps into the new dimensions of faith made possible by the alphabet of grace, God gives him an astonishing command: "Walk before me and be blameless" (Gen 17:1). There was nothing really new in the mandate to *walk* with God. Abraham had been doing that for years. But the sequence of the two imperatives implies that he is to walk with God *in order that* he may be blameless. The one is a prerequisite for the other. The new reality for Abraham is the call to be *blameless*.

Though God had given numerous directives through the years, never had Abraham been given a command like this! The English word "blameless" translates the Hebrew *tamim*. It means whole, entire, complete, undivided. The *King James Version* renders it as *perfect*. A person who is blameless, or perfect, is one who is completely devoted to God, entirely consecrated, wholly committed. His heart is undivided in its allegiance to God. The word focuses more on inward motivation than on outward behavior. God is not commanding Abraham to be *faultless*, but *blameless*. The distinction is important. A blameless person may stumble and make mistakes yet remain pure in his intentions. God's call is to a perfection of love, *not* a perfection of performance. Flawless behavior is an unachievable standard this side of heaven. But purity of intention is apparently something that is not only possible in this life, it is demanded by God.

God's command is not so much to *do* something, as to *be* something. Who we are is so much more important than what we do! Lest God's great purpose for men and women be forgotten, he enshrined it forever in the words of the Greatest Commandment: "You shall love the Lord your God with *all* your heart and with *all* your soul and with *all* your might." (Deut 6:5, emphasis added). The whole point of salvation, what God wants more than anything else, is perfect love flowing from pure hearts.

Coming to grips with God's new commandment and the realization that what he wants is not a perfection of performance but a perfection of love, typically produces two very opposite reactions. At first, one may experience a sense of great relief. "Oh, so it's not really about my behavior; it's about my heart, my motives. Whew, that's good news!" But then, a feeling of terror sets in as one imagines what it will be like for God to search the heart.

> Oh, so it's about my inner motives and desires. He wants to know whether I love him with *all* my heart. Wouldn't he be satisfied if I just loved him with *most* of it? Maybe even 99%? Does he have any idea how polluted, divided, and egocentric my heart really is? God wants an undivided heart: the one thing he is demanding is the one thing I am incapable of doing!

It would be a tragic mistake to imagine that Abraham's blameless heart was the result of good works, devoted service, or pious practices. It would be equally wrong to think that it came about gradually through growth. No, just as his justification was by grace through faith, so was his sanctification. How was Abraham's heart made perfect in love? God did it!

> *And the* Lord *your God will circumcise your heart and the heart of your offspring, so that you will love the* Lord *your God with all your heart and with all your soul, that you may live. (Deut 30:6)*

QUESTIONS FOR DISCUSSION

1. Summarize in your own words how Dr. Seuss's book *On Beyond Zebra* relates to the doctrine and the experience of sanctification.
2. Can you relate to feeling tired? Stuck? Defeated? Bored? Barren? The author says that sanctification is the answer. Do you agree?
3. What is the difference between knowing *about* God and knowing God?
4. What did you learn from this study about humor? Define "the hilarity of grace" and describe how sanctified humor should characterize the lives of the saints.
5. Describe how your church practices rites, ceremonies, symbols, and sacraments. What has this lesson taught you about such matters?
6. Describe what a blameless (perfect) heart is like and how such a heart can be obtained.

16
Is Anything Too Hard for the Lord?
Genesis 18:1–33

Perhaps you heard the story of the man who wanted to write a book on parenting. Although this had been a life goal, at age eighty the task remained undone. A friend asked him why. "I can't decide on a title," he responded. "When I was in my twenties and unmarried, I wanted to name the book *Twenty Proven Practices for Raising Spectacular Kids*. But in my thirties, after I got married and we had a few children, I decided a better title would be *Fourteen Wise Principles*. But as our children grew, and I entered my forties, the title would have been *Ten Foundational Ideas*. When our kids hit adolescence and began moving out of the house, in my fifties the book would have been called *Eight Inspiring Goals*. Then, when I was in my sixties, watching my kids become adults and have their own families, the title would have been *Five Things to Pray For*. And now that I am eighty years of age, I suppose if I ever write a book on parenting, I'll just call it *A Few Tentative Suggestions*."

When it comes to the subject of intercessory prayer, I easily identify with that man. When I was a young Christian, praying for others seemed so straightforward and obvious. You ask God to do something, and then you trust him to do it. Right? "Whatever you ask in prayer, you will receive, if you believe" (Matt 21:22). "Ask, and it will be given you" (Matt 7:7). What could be more self-evident than *that*? But after several decades of reading Scripture and trying to live the Christian life, I must confess that I'm not sure I understand intercession at all. And yet, like the old man who kept wanting to figure out a formula for good parenting, the desire to intercede and stand in the gap for others has never been stronger!

The dictionary defines intercession as the act of intervening for the sake of another. To intercede is to interpose oneself on behalf of someone in difficulty or trouble. It often involves pleading their case or making a petition on their behalf. Intercession often involves an attempt to reconcile differences between two people or groups, a form of mediation.

It would be a mistake to think of intercession only in terms of bowing our heads and closing our eyes in times of prayer. The Bible encourages us to think of the ministry of intercession as a lifestyle—the on-going practice of stepping into the gap, that yawning chasm between human need and divine resources, and seeking to bring them together. Intercessors talk to God about those who are in need, and then they talk to those who are in need about God. It is a form of shuttle diplomacy, moving back and forth from man to God and from God to man. No form of ministry is more demanding or costly than this. And no form of ministry has more potential to change the world!

Like parenting, the ministry of intercession is hard to understand and difficult to do well. The fact that parents may not fully understand what they are doing and may often do it poorly does not discourage them from wanting to raise good kids. In a similar manner, the challenges of intercession should never be a deterrent for followers of Jesus Christ.

Intercessory prayer is not so much a riddle to solve or a technique to master. It is a mystery to embrace. And the greatest part of this mystery is trying to fathom how God's sovereignty interacts with man's free will. Ah, there's the crux of the matter. The ministry of intercession invites us into that turbulent place where these two seemingly contradictory realities collide.

On the one hand, the Bible tells us that God is sovereign and all-powerful. He does whatever he pleases. He knows the end from the beginning. His purposes are immutable, and nothing can thwart the accomplishment of his will. To plead in prayer with such a God, asking that he not do what he is doing or do what he is not doing, seems absurd, even blasphemous. We might as well pray that the sun not rise as to ask God to change his plans. Isn't our role, rather to submit to God's predetermined plan? Shouldn't prayer focus on asking God to grant us the serenity to accept the things we cannot change? Who would be audacious enough to step into the gap and ask the Lord God Almighty to change his mind, to ask the Sovereign One to be less than sovereign?

But on the other hand, the Bible is emphatic that men and women are free moral agents, fully responsible for their choices. Created in God's own image, human persons are not robots, programmed to follow a predetermined script. No, men and women have been granted a great measure of freedom to make their own choices. Astoundingly, this freedom makes it possible to disobey their Creator! "My will be done" seems capable of trumping "Thy will be done." Though God has a foreordained purpose for every life, men and women have the terrifying capability of rejecting God's plan and going their own way instead.

So, what happens when divine sovereignty and human freedom are at cross purposes, when God's will is contradictory to man's? This question takes us to the very core of what human history is all about. If God pulls rank and imposes his will, then human freedom is violated. If God does nothing while men and women live in willful, continual disobedience, then his sovereign purposes are frustrated. Confronting the mystery of this perplexing reality is what the ministry of intercession is all about! And no one gives us a better illustration of what this looks like than Father Abraham. When he stepped into the gap and audaciously pleaded with God Almighty not to destroy the wicked cities of Sodom and Gomorrah, he gave the first recorded example in history of intercessory prayer.

A Rhetorical Question?

Before we examine Abraham's ministry of intercession, however, we need to look at the broader context of Genesis 18. In the first half of the chapter, God announces to ninety-year-old Sarah that, within a year, she will give birth to a son (Gen 18:1–15). In all the Bible, we would be hard-pressed to find a clearer example of God's sovereign power and foreordained purpose than this. *El Shaddai* is indeed God Almighty!

But it is in the second half of the chapter where the plot really thickens (Gen 18:16–33). Here, God tells Abraham that he is about to visit the cities of Sodom and Gomorrah "to see whether they have done altogether according to the outcry that has come to me" (Gen 18:21). Amazingly, Abraham responds to this divine declaration by literally stepping into the gap. Physically placing himself between a holy God and a perverse humanity, Abraham intercedes for the wicked cities, boldly asking the sovereign Lord not to do what he is planning to do.

At first glance, it may not be obvious how these two stories go together. What is the relationship between Sarah's miracle pregnancy (vv 1–15) and the announced destruction of Sodom and Gomorrah (vv 16–33)? The verse that holds these two stories together and establishes the overarching theme for the entire chapter is Genesis 18:14: "Is anything too hard for the Lord?" Readers of Genesis, who know how the story ends, know that making an old, post-menopausal woman pregnant is *not* too hard for God. Such miracles are a piece of cake for *El Shaddai*. The drama comes when we remember what happens next. We know God can make an old woman pregnant, but can he save Sodom and Gomorrah? Can divine omnipotence deliver those who have chosen to turn their back on God in willful unbelief and sin? With all his mighty power, can God save Sodom? *Is anything too hard for the Lord?*

Prior to studying this chapter, I had always assumed Genesis 18:14 was asking a rhetorical question. In other words, I assumed that the answer was obvious. *Is anything too hard for the Lord?* Every child in Sunday School knows the answer immediately: No! Nothing is too hard for God! His name is *El Shaddai* (God Almighty) and he can do anything: create the universe, send a global flood, divide the Red Sea, make the sun stand still, heal a leper, and raise the dead. It's obvious, isn't it? *Nothing* is too hard for our God!

But deeper reflection on this matter has caused me to conclude that this question is *not* rhetorical. The answer is *not* obvious! Sure, God can make Sarah pregnant. But can he save Sodom and Gomorrah? Can he? With all his sovereign power is *El Shaddai* able to save unrepentant sinners? Frankly, just asking the question takes my breath away and makes me wonder if I'm flirting with heresy.

I'm struck by the fact that this question is not asked by curious theologians enjoying a moment of philosophical speculation. No, God himself is the one asking the question! Speaking of himself in the third person, God *wants* Abraham to think deeply about this: *Is anything too hard for the Lord?* He *wants* Abraham, and us, to answer the question. Responding with a simple "yes" or "no" will only reveal how superficial our thoughts about God really are. God is encouraging us to think deeply both about what he *can* do—and what he *can't*!

Entertaining Angels

You have to admit that the language used in the opening verses of Genesis 18 is profoundly intriguing. It's hard to avoid seeing what seems to be a veiled allusion to the Trinity mysteriously woven into the text.

> *And the* LORD *appeared to (Abraham) by the oaks of Mamre, as he sat at the door of his tent in the heat of the day. He lifted up his eyes and looked, and behold, three men were standing in front of him. (Gen 18:1–2)*

"The Lord appeared to Abraham . . . and behold, three men." What can this mean? How can one God appear in the form of three men? As the story unfolds, the three visitors seem to speak with one divine voice. Arriving in Sodom, the sacred company is identified as "two angels" (see Gen 19:1). This is all very interesting, and frankly, full of mystery.

So, who exactly came to visit Abraham? Is it God plus two angels? Or is it perhaps a three-personned manifestation of the one true God? Attempts by scholars and theologians to explain this divine visitation often raise more questions than they answer. Admittedly, the textual data leaves open the possibility of different interpretations. But regardless of how one chooses to understand the text, it is striking how the description of God's visit to Abraham is consistent with the historic orthodox Christian teaching about the Trinity: one God eternally existent in three Persons.

Abraham and Sarah welcome their special guests by extending a lavish display of Middle Eastern hospitality. The Scripture gives a surprising amount of details about the preparation and service of the meal (see Gen 18:3–8). Centuries later, when Christians wanted to underscore the importance of showing kindness to strangers and foreigners, they often referred to Genesis 18 as the prototypical example. "Do not neglect to show hospitality to strangers, for thereby some have entertained angels unawares" (Heb 13:2). Christian hospitality is much more than benevolent charity to the needy. It is predicated on the assumption that in welcoming the stranger into our home, we are welcoming Christ himself! "I was hungry and you gave me food, I was thirsty and you gave me drink, I was a stranger and you welcomed me. . . . As you did it to one of the least of these my brothers, you did it to me" (Matt 25:35, 40).

Abraham soon realizes that these visitors have an agenda. They are not here by accident. They are on a mission and have a twofold message for Abraham. First, the Lord announces that in twelve months' time, Sarah will have a son. Though she is gently rebuked for her cynical laugh, the Lord graciously insists that this amazing miracle will indeed come true (see Gen 18:9–15). These words, of course, refer to the birth of Isaac, the son through whom all the covenant blessings promised to Abraham will flow.

The second message the Lord has for Abraham relates to Sodom and Gomorrah. It becomes apparent that, in stopping at Abraham's tent, he is looking for more than refreshment and rest. The Lord is looking for an intercessor!

> *Then the men set out from there, and they looked down toward Sodom. And Abraham went with them to set them on their way. The* LORD *said, "Shall I hide from Abraham what I am about to do . . . ?" Then the* LORD *said, "Because the outcry against Sodom and Gomorrah is great and their sin is very grave, I will go down to see whether they have done altogether according to the outcry that has come to me. And if not, I will know." (Gen 18:16–17, 20–21)*

When God asks, "Shall I hide from Abraham what I am about to do?" he is talking to himself! Although it may be surprising to learn that God talks to himself, it is even more surprising to realize that he wants to make Abraham privy to his innermost thoughts. God wants his friend Abraham to be aware of the dilemma he faces: what to do about Sodom and Gomorrah. Should he show wrath or mercy? With a little creative imagination, we might envision God's internal dialogue as taking place among the three Persons of the Trinity. Perhaps the conversation went something like this:

The Father: "What are we going to do about Sodom and Gomorrah? Things are so bad that something must be done."

The Son: "I think we should give them more time. Perhaps we could send them a prophet who could show them the error of their ways. Perhaps they will repent."

The Spirit: "I think their hearts are so hard that they are now guilty of an unpardonable sin. To delay judgment only means more people will be hurt. The most merciful thing we can do is to destroy them."

The Father: "Ok, these are excellent points, but let's bring Abraham into this conversation. I'd like to know what he thinks!"

While such a conversation is obviously imaginary, it helps to capture the mind-boggling reality of our trinitarian faith. Even more to the point, it reminds us that the ministry of intercession for Sodom and Gomorrah begins *not* with Abraham, but with God himself. True intercession always has its origin in the heart of God!

The remainder of Abraham's conversation with the Lord only underscores and deepens the mystery of intercession.

> *So the men turned from there and went toward Sodom, but Abraham still stood before the* Lord. *Then Abraham drew near and said, "Will you indeed sweep away the righteous with the wicked? Suppose there are fifty righteous within the city. Will you then sweep away the place and not spare it for the fifty righteous who are in it? Far be it from you to do such a thing, to put the righteous to death with the wicked, so that the righteous fare as the wicked! Far be that from you! Shall not the Judge of all the earth do what is just?" And the* Lord *said, "If I find at Sodom fifty righteous in the city, I will spare the whole place for their sake." Abraham answered and said, "Behold, I have undertaken to speak to the* Lord, *I who am but dust and ashes. Suppose five of the fifty righteous are lacking. Will you destroy the whole city for lack of five?" And he said, "I will not destroy it if I find forty-five there." Again he spoke to him and said, "Suppose forty are found there." He answered, "For the sake of forty I will not do it." Then he said, "Oh let not the* Lord *be angry, and I will speak. Suppose thirty are found there." He answered, "I will not do it, if I find thirty there." He said, "Behold, I have undertaken to speak to the* Lord. *Suppose twenty are found there." He answered, "For the sake of twenty I will not destroy it." Then he said, "Oh let not the* Lord *be angry, and I will speak again but this once. Suppose ten are found there." He answered, "For the sake of ten I will not destroy it." And the* Lord *went his way, when he had finished speaking to Abraham, and Abraham returned to his place. (Gen 18:22–33)*

The conversation between Abraham and God is passionate, bold, confrontational, and full of mystery. For Abraham to tell the Judge of all the earth to behave justly must have required a large measure of audacity (see v 25). And craftily bargaining with God moving the number of righteous persons in Sodom from fifty to ten, looks like brazen manipulation. But the audacity is reciprocated when God makes Abraham his partner in determining the fate of Sodom and Gomorrah. It's as if God is saying, "Abraham, I need your input to help me know what to do with these wicked cities!" God is making Abraham share in the responsibility for determining the destiny of these two cities. Yes, the candor and brashness of the conversation is almost breath-taking. Real intercession gets up close and personal; it is noisy, and messy. Only close friends would dare to talk so frankly to one another.

As Abraham worked the numbers from fifty, to thirty, and finally to ten, one wonders why he stopped there. This question has tantalized scholars and preachers for centuries and I suppose will always remain one of the greatest mysteries in the history of intercessory prayer. Though numerous suggestions have been offered, the best answer seems to be the most obvious. Abraham stopped at ten because God indicated that the conversation was over. Verse 33 tells us that *God*, not Abraham, ended the dialogue. If Abraham wanted to take the number lower, we'll never know. Just as God had initiated the conversation, so he chose where it would end. There is a limit beyond which even the most fervent intercessor dares not go.

FIVE CHARACTERISTICS OF INTERCESSORY PRAYER

Abraham's prayer for the cities of Sodom and Gomorrah may be the Bible's first example of intercession, but it is certainly not the last. The Scriptures tell of a host of others who stood in the gap and interceded in desperate situations: Samuel (1 Sam 7:5–9; 12:19–25), Elijah (1 Kgs 17:17–23), Elisha (2 Kgs 4:33; 6:15–20), Job (Job 42:7–9), Amos (Amos 7:1–6) and especially Moses (Exod 32:11–13, 31–34; Num 12:11–13; 14:13–19). The ultimate illustration of intercession is, of course, Jesus. Lifted up in his death on the cross, he literally hung suspended in the gap between God in his holiness and earth in its sinfulness. There on the cross, Jesus bridged the chasm that separates God and man. His work of mediation and shuttle diplomacy is the ultimate illustration of the ministry of intercession.

To summarize what the Bible teaches, let's close this chapter by highlighting five characteristics of intercessory prayer.

1. The *origin* of intercessory prayer

Although Abraham certainly had a burden for Lot and his family who lived in Sodom, his compassion was *not* the origin of his bold intercession. The Bible makes clear that *God* was the one who carried the real burden. Long before Abraham opened his mouth in prayer, God was wrestling with the dilemma of what should be done. It is only after God shared his burden with Abraham, that Abraham had the courage to intercede for the wicked cities.

We misunderstand intercessory prayer when we think of it in terms of begging a reluctant deity to do what he doesn't want to do, or to not do what he does want to do. Intercession begins in the heart of God, not man. In Abraham, God has found a friend with whom he can share his innermost thoughts. He invites Abraham to join in the conversation he is having within himself and help him come to a decision. It's almost as if God is using Abraham as a sounding board, as if he needs Abraham's heart to be the place where he works out his feelings and decides what to do.

Intercessory prayer occurs when the Spirit of God inspires and encourages the intercessor to petition God the Father about a certain situation. The prayer God is listening to is thus a prayer that he himself has generated! It is God talking to himself through the medium of a willing human heart. In the eighth chapter of Romans, Paul explains how this works:

> *Likewise the Spirit helps us in our weakness. For we do not know what to pray for as we ought, but the Spirit himself intercedes for us with groanings too deep for words. And he who searches hearts knows what is the mind of the Spirit, because the Spirit intercedes for the saints according to the will of God. (Rom 8:26–27)*

2. The *nature* of intercessory prayer

Most translations say that "Abraham still stood before the Lord" (Gen 18:22). However, some manuscripts suggest *God* was the one standing before Abraham. Was Abraham blocking God's journey toward Sodom, pleading with him to slow down? Or was God the one blocking Abraham's path, as if to say, "Aren't you going to stop me?"? Regardless of who was blocking whom, the message is the same: intercession is God and man getting up close and personal, in each other's face; it is confrontational, messy, and at times, downright argumentative.

Perhaps the most startling example of the in-your-face nature of intercession is seen in Moses' prayer for the people of Israel after their sin with the golden calf (see Exod 32:7–14). When God announces his intention to destroy the rebellious sinners, Moses steps into the gap and boldly tells God to "repent of this evil" (Exod 32:12 KJV). I've been to many prayer meetings in my life, but I've never yet heard anyone tell God to repent! At times the conversation between Moses and God sounds more like a shouting match than a prayer meeting.

Muslims tend to see prayer as submission to the will of Allah. Since everything has already been predetermined, to argue with Allah or challenge his purposes would be the height of impiety. How differently the Bible presents these matters! Here we are taught that the very nature of intercessory prayer is wrestling with God. We hear it in the prayer of Rachel, "Give me children, or I die" (Gen 30:1), of Jacob, "I will not let you go unless you bless me" (Gen 32:26), and of Abraham, "Suppose there are fifty righteous within the city? Thirty? Ten?" (Gen 18:22–33). In the Garden of Gethsemane, even Jesus struggled with God in prayer. His threefold "Let this cup pass" reveals the depth of his wrestling match with his Father (see Matt 26:36–46). Submission to the will of God comes *at the end* of intercession, not the beginning. Oswald Chambers says it well: "It is an insult to sink before God and say, 'Thy will be done' when there has been no intercession."[1]

3. The *power* of intercessory prayer

When God announced his intention to destroy Sodom and Gomorrah, Abraham could have said; "Well, since you have revealed your will, my role is to accept it and submit to your sovereign plan." Amazingly, he did no such thing. Rather, he pleaded with God to reconsider what he was planning to do. In other words, Abraham asked God to change his mind!

The Bible tells us plainly that God does not "change his mind" (Lev 23:19). The Hebrew word can also be translated "repent." When used

---
[1] Chambers, *Not Knowing Whither*, 887.

in reference to God, it does not imply evil, but simply the act of turning, changing one's mind. And yet, on numerous occasions, we read how God does indeed "change his mind/repent." We have already seen how Moses told the Lord to "repent" at the incident with the golden calf. Amazingly, God changed his mind and did not carry out his original intention to destroy the nation (see Exod 32:12, 14). We read also in the Bible of how the Lord changed his mind concerning Saul. Though chosen by God as Israel's first king, Saul's unbelief and sin caused the Lord to "repent" of what he had done (see 1 Sam 15:11, 29, 35). Perhaps the most amusing illustration of God's repentance is found in the book of Jonah. Though he had told Jonah that he was going to destroy Nineveh, God changed his mind when the Ninevites turned from their sin and cried out to God for mercy (see Jonah 3:9–10).

These Bible stories describe God in very personal terms. He feels things deeply. Though he is infinite in justice, he is equally infinite in mercy. This often creates a divine dilemma. How will he respond? As we have seen, his actions are often predicated on the choices and attitudes of men and women. His response hinges on theirs. But he is not capricious, and he does not make mistakes. His character *never* changes; he is always holy, righteous, loving, and merciful. But his actions may change.

> *If at any time I declare concerning a nation or a kingdom, that I will pluck up and break down and destroy it, and if that nation, concerning which I have spoken, turns from its evil, I will relent (repent) of the disaster that I intended to do to it. And if at any time I declare concerning a nation or a kingdom that I will build and plant it, and if it does evil in my sight, not listening to my voice, then I will relent (repent) of the good that I had intended to do to it. (Jer 18:7–10)*

The power of intercessory prayer is the power to move the heart of God and cause him to change his mind, to not do what he was planning to do or to do what he was not planning to do. One staggers at the magnitude of such a thought, and yet, the biblical evidence for such a position is overwhelming. Intercessory prayer has the capacity to change history! As Pascal stated so succinctly; "God instituted prayer to impart to his creatures the dignity of causality."[2]

4. The *content* of intercessory prayer

"Shall not the Judge of all the earth do what is just?" (Gen 18:25). Abraham's question reveals that his intercession involves so much more than a personal concern for his nephew Lot. God's reputation is at stake in what happens to Sodom and Gomorrah, and Abraham's prayer is a plea that God will be glorified in what happens there. True intercession is never merely about the personal petitions of the one praying. The focus of prayer goes far beyond the desire to relieve some pain or provide some need. What is really at stake is the glory of God!

We see this vividly displayed in Moses' prayer after the incident with the golden calf. Moses reminds God that, if he annihilates the Hebrew nation, his reputation as a great and holy God will be destroyed among the Egyptians. Further, if God kills all the Jews, many will conclude that he can't be trusted because he doesn't keep his promises. Moses' intercession is effective precisely because he focuses his prayer on these matters.

> *"Why should the Egyptians say, 'With evil intent did he bring them out, to kill them in the mountains and to consume them from the face of the earth'? Turn from your burning anger and relent (repent) from this disaster against your people. Remember Abraham, Isaac, and Israel, your servants, to whom you swore by your own self, and said to them, 'I will multiply your offspring as the stars of heaven, and all this land that I have promised I will give to your offspring, and they shall inherit it forever.'" (Exod 32:12–13)*

5. The *cost* of intercessory prayer

In seeking to lower the number of righteous individuals found in Sodom from fifty to ten, Abraham was taking a risk. He was jeopardizing his own relationship with God by such a bold plea for sinners. It was almost as if Abraham was linking his future destiny to that of Sodom! Thus, we learn that the cost of intercession goes far beyond the time

---

2   Pascal, *Pensées*, #930, 320.

and energy involved in prayer. Identifying so openly and completely with sinners has the potential of threatening one's relationship with God. What will the Holy One think of me when I urge him to turn from his righteous wrath and show mercy to sinners instead? How will God respond when I link my destiny to that of sinners? Moses, Paul, and Jesus were effective intercessors precisely because they were ready to pay the price.

- "But now, if you will forgive their sin—but if not, please blot me out of your book that you have written." (Exod 32:32)
- "I have great sorrow and unceasing anguish in my heart. For I could wish that I myself were accursed and cut off from Christ for the sake of my brothers, my kinsmen according to the flesh." (Rom 9:2–3)
- "For our sake he made him to be sin who knew no sin, so that in him we might become the righteousness of God." (2 Cor 5:21)

Conclusion

Is anything too hard for the Lord? This is the question that lies at the heart of intercessory prayer and this is the question that makes it such a mystery. Abraham's prayer for Sodom and Gomorrah introduces us to the origin, nature, power, content, and cost involved in standing in the gap. His example enables us to better understand why there are so few intercessors and why this kind of praying is so rare.

And yet, God is looking, intently looking, for men and women who will intercede for the desperate situations to be found all over the world. If he can find one intercessor, just one, human history can be different. "And I sought for a man among them who should build up the wall and stand in the breach before me for the land, that I should not destroy it, but I found none." (Ezek 22:30)

Questions for Discussion

1. The author calls intercessory prayer a form of "shuttle diplomacy." What does he mean by this?
2. Is anything too hard for the Lord?

3. What do you think about the notion that God talks to himself? Is it possible to live close enough to God that one can overhear what he is saying?
4. What is the difference between Muslim prayer and Christian prayer?
5. Describe the difference in praying that God will alleviate pain or provide a need and praying that he will be glorified in and through a certain situation.
6. Where is God asking you to be an intercessor? What are you going to do about it?

Too Hard for God?
Stan Key

Is anything too hard for God?
Perhaps you think my question odd,
But listen and I think you'll see
The cause of my perplexity.

I do not doubt that God alone
Can speak a word, and from his throne
The universe is set in place,
And stars are hung in empty space.

'Twas easy to create the sun:
He spoke the word—and it was done!
Miracles, signs, and wonders too
It seems there's nothing God can't do!

But saving souls like you and me
Reveals a deeper mystery:
For all the powers in heaven above
Can never force a heart to love.

Deep within my soul I see
A kingdom that belongs to me,
Where I am sovereign, I decide,
And even God can't come inside!

If I was destined by decree
Created so I'd bow the knee,
Then like a robot I'd obey . . . .
No! God must find another way!

To melt my selfish heart of stone
The Mighty One gave up his throne
And came to die upon a tree
In hopes that love would conquer me.

For even God will never force
A sinful man to change his course
Until he opens wide his heart
And lets God's grace fill every part.

Is there nothing God can't do?
I leave the answer up to you.
Your response, this very hour,
Will demonstrate his sovereign power.

17
Abraham Had Two Sons
Genesis 21:1–21

When it comes to God's salvation plan for the world, no one can accuse the Bible of being ambiguous. From among all the peoples of the earth, God chose *one man* through whom he would accomplish his redemptive purposes for all humanity: Abraham the Hebrew. Then, from among Abraham's descendants, God was even more clear about which ones would be part of his covenant family and which ones would not: Isaac, *not* Ishmael; Jacob, *not* Esau. This theme of God's choosing one person rather than another (theologians call it the doctrine of election) is a major motif that runs throughout the book of Genesis. Whether we are talking about Cain and Abel, the three sons of Noah, Isaac and Ishmael, Jacob and Esau, Leah and Rachel, or Joseph and his brothers, we see God's sovereign choice at work in almost every chapter. The narrative of Genesis describes time and again how the characters in the story struggle to understand how to live in a world where God's sovereign will has the final verdict. A famous epigram composed by British journalist William Norman Ewer expresses this sobering reality in a pithy rhyme:

> *How odd of God*
> *To choose the Jews.*

No other religion makes such a bold and frankly, offensive, declaration. That God would choose one man and his family to be the single channel through whom he would reveal his plan of salvation for all the earth is, well, hard to swallow. The particularity and specificity of such a claim almost takes one's breath away.

As one reads through the chapters of Genesis, one begins to realize that this book is about more than ancient history. The reader may squirm as he begins to recognize that the narrative is confronting *him* with a choice. Gently but firmly, the text is forcing him to decide: Is this story true? Did God really call Abraham and reveal his plan for the world through this one Middle Eastern Hebrew? The question demands a yes or no answer. Neutrality is impossible. Either God chose Abraham, or he didn't. Either Abraham is the father of all who believe, or he isn't. No reader of Genesis can avoid answering this question!

If the Genesis story is nothing more than a compilation of myths and legends written to support the cause of Jewish nationalism, then readers are free to dismiss it as the fanciful fabrication of ethnocentric arrogance. The stories may teach a moral lesson, but like other ancient folklore they have no real relevance for us today. Like Aesop's fables, these stories are quaint and perhaps inspiring, but they certainly are not to be considered as historically accurate or true. However, if the Genesis narrative accurately recounts events that happened in time and space, as the text claims to do, then reading these ancient stories suddenly becomes very real, relevant, and personal! Regardless of how one may *feel* about God's choice of Abraham, Isaac, and Jacob, there is only one question that really matters: *is it true?* Few questions in life are more important than this one! Discerning the truth is a matter of life and death.

Perhaps no one in the twentieth century better illustrates the importance of discerning truth from error than the Russian Orthodox Christian and Nobel laureate Alexander Solzhenitsyn (1918–2008). He was undoubtedly the most famous anti-communist dissident in the 20th century. His book *The Gulag Archipelago* (1973) exposed the terrifying truth about Soviet totalitarianism and made Solzhenitsyn an international hero. He believed that the core problem in Russia, the foundational explanation for all the evil and injustice of the communist system, was spiritual, not political: men and women had turned their back on the truth and put their faith in lies.

When Moscow forcibly expelled him to the West in 1974, Solzhenitsyn published a final, short farewell message to the Russian people entitled "Live Not by Lies!" In this pamphlet, he explained that to "live by lies" was to accept, without protest, all the propaganda and politically correct ideology that the state was compelling its citizens to affirm (or at least, not to oppose). His point was that totalitarianism can only exist when its citizens live by the lies they have been told to believe. Those who out of weakness, fear, or willful blindness refuse to challenge the lies, became complicit in the evil system. It is only when one stands up to expose the lies and live in truth that one can be truly free.

It is interesting to note that during his years of exile while living in the West, Solzhenitsyn discovered that millions of people in the "free" world live under a different kind of oppression because they too have chosen to live by lies. Solzhenitsyn's passionate plea was for all people everywhere, whether in Russia or America, to reject lies and live in truth. He loved to quote an old Russian proverb: "One word of truth outweighs the whole world!" But rejecting lies and walking in truth may be harder than you think!

ISHMAEL AND ISAAC

In the New Testament, Paul casually makes the innocuous-sounding statement that "Abraham had two sons" (Gal 4:22). At first glance, these words seem to do nothing more than to state the obvious. Yet, on closer examination we discover that Paul is confronting people in the New Testament era with the same choice that had been thrust upon Abraham and his family in the Old Testament era. Which son, Ishmael or Isaac, is the child of the covenant? Through which son will God's redemptive purposes for the world be accomplished? The two sons have the same father, share the same culture, and were both circumcised into the same basic belief system. And yet God chose only one of these boys to be the child of promise. Which one is it? This is one of the most important questions in all the Bible. When one remembers that today roughly one billion Muslims believe that Ishmael, not Isaac, is the son on whom the divine favor rests, one is reminded of the profound significance of this question.

The story of Ishmael and Isaac reminds us of how difficult it can be to discern who is truly a member of God's covenant family and who is not. If one relies on pedigree, outward behaviors, and religious practices, one may be fooled. Not only among the different religions of the world, but also in the Church, there have always been those who claimed to be members of the covenant family of God who were gravely mistaken!

Perhaps the most important lesson we should learn from this story of Ishmael and Isaac is a personal one. What about *me*? What about *my* relationship with God? How can *I* be sure that *I* am a child of God? Is it possible that I could be mistaken concerning my own spiritual identity? Apparently, Paul believed this was a terrifying possibility. He pleaded with the members of the church in Corinth:

> *Examine yourselves to see if your faith is really genuine. Test yourselves. If you cannot tell that Jesus Christ is among you, it means you have failed the test. (2 Cor 13:5 NLT)*

For the discerning reader, the study of Genesis 21 and Paul's application of this passage in Galatians 4:21–31, is much more than interesting history. It is the means for helping to discern those who are God's true children from those who are not.

Though the story is told in a straightforward manner, we can feel the joy and elation in the hearts of Abraham and Sarah when Isaac is finally born. Sarah is ninety years old and Abraham is a hundred. It has been twenty-five long years since God first promised them a child. Finally, the day has come and God's promise is fulfilled.

> *The* LORD *visited Sarah as he had said, and the* LORD *did to Sarah as he had promised. And Sarah conceived and bore Abraham a son in his old age at the time of which God had spoken to him. Abraham called the name of his son who was born to him, whom Sarah bore him, Isaac. And Abraham circumcised his son Isaac when he was eight days old, as God had commanded him. Abraham was a hundred years old*

when his son Isaac was born to him. And Sarah said, "God has made laughter for me; everyone who hears will laugh over me." (Gen 21:1–6)

It wasn't long, however, until the joy of Isaac's birth became the occasion for renewed rivalry between Sarah and Hagar. Things came to an ugly impasse when Ishmael was a young teenager and Isaac was still a small boy.

And the child grew and was weaned. And Abraham made a great feast on the day that Isaac was weaned. But Sarah saw the son of Hagar the Egyptian, whom she had borne to Abraham, laughing. So she said to Abraham, "Cast out this slave woman with her son, for the son of this slave woman shall not be heir with my son Isaac." And the thing was very displeasing to Abraham on account of his son. But God said to Abraham, "Be not displeased because of the boy and because of your slave woman. Whatever Sarah says to you, do as she tells you, for through Isaac shall your offspring be named. And I will make a nation of the son of the slave woman also, because he is your offspring." So Abraham rose early in the morning and took bread and a skin of water and gave it to Hagar, putting it on her shoulder, along with the child, and sent her away. And she departed and wandered in the wilderness of Beersheba. (Gen 21:8–14)

What was Ishmael doing that caused such a strong reaction from Sarah? Verse 9 simply says that he was "laughing" (ESV), perhaps "mocking" (NIV), or "making fun of Isaac" (NLT). The ambiguity of the text forces us to fill in the gaps concerning what was really going on. If Ishmael's treatment of his kid brother was just innocent joking around, it is hard to explain Sarah's anger and harsh demand that Hagar and her son be disinherited. It seems that something more sinister must have been involved in the boys' "play." Many interpreters believe that Ishmael was bullying his younger brother, perhaps abusing him in some inappropriate way. Paul seems to see the situation this way when he interprets Ishmael's behavior toward Isaac as a form of "persecution" (see Gal 4:29).

Regardless of how we understand the provocation, Sarah's response was immediate and strong. She demands that Hagar and

Ishmael be "cast out" (Gen 21:10). Although her motives may have been wrong (jealousy, hatred, vindictiveness, etc.), her instincts were right: Ishmael's presence was a threat to God's work in Abraham's family. If Hagar and her son were permitted to stay in the home, it would be difficult, if not impossible, to discern not only who God's covenant family is, but what that family is called to do. God affirmed Sarah's actions and told Abraham to listen to his wife. Though God loved Ishmael and had a good plan for his life, he had determined that Isaac alone was to be Abraham's rightful heir.

The trauma of getting rid of his first-born son was "very displeasing" to Abraham (Gen 21:11). It "upset (him) very much" (NLT). Indeed, sending Ishmael away into the wilderness was a sort of "sacrifice" made in obedience to God. It is important to see that before Abraham was ready to sacrifice the child of promise in his great and final test (see Gen 22), he first had to cast out the child of flesh! Commenting on this episode in Abraham's life, Oswald Chambers astutely says: "If we do not resolutely cast out the natural, the supernatural can never become natural in us.... Remember, Abraham had to offer up Ishmael before he offered up Isaac."[1]

A New Testament Sermon from an Old Testament Story

In Galatians 4:21–31, Paul, under the inspiration of the Holy Spirit, preaches a gospel sermon based on this event recorded in Genesis 21. He explains that he is using the story "allegorically" or "figuratively" (Gal 4:24). That is, he is using an historical event to illustrate a spiritual truth. In other words, Paul believes that what happened to Sarah and Hagar long ago in Canaan is similar to what was happening to Galatian Christians many centuries later. Indeed, the story in Genesis 21 has relevance for us in our spiritual lives today! The two women, Hagar and Sarah, are symbols of two very different types of people.

> *Tell me, you who desire to be under the law, do you not listen to the law? For it is written that Abraham had two sons, one by a slave woman and one by a free woman. But the son of*

---

[1] Chambers, *Not Knowing Whither*, 896–897.

> the slave was born according to the flesh, while the son of the free woman was born through promise. Now this may be interpreted allegorically: these women are two covenants. One is from Mount Sinai, bearing children for slavery; she is Hagar. Now Hagar is Mount Sinai in Arabia; she corresponds to the present Jerusalem, for she is in slavery with her children. But the Jerusalem above is free, and she is our mother. For it is written,
>
> "Rejoice, O barren one who does not bear; break forth and cry aloud, you who are not in labor! For the children of the desolate one will be more than those of the one who has a husband."
>
> Now you, brothers, like Isaac, are children of promise. But just as at that time he who was born according to the flesh persecuted him who was born according to the Spirit, so also it is now. But what does the Scripture say? "Cast out the slave woman and her son, for the son of the slave woman shall not inherit with the son of the free woman." So, brothers, we are not children of the slave but of the free woman. (Gal 4:21–31)

This is a remarkable way to interpret the Old Testament, but it is not the only such example in the New Testament. In 1 Corinthians 10:1–13, Paul uses a similar interpretive approach. Taking the journey from Egypt to Canaan as his text, Paul tells Christians in Corinth that this Old Testament story is written as an "example" (Greek, *tupos*) for them (vv 6, 11). And in John 3:14 Jesus told Nicodemus that his coming death on the cross could be better understood by examining the Old Testament story of Moses lifting up the bronze serpent in the wilderness (see Num 21:4–9). Other examples could be cited. Christians today miss a huge blessing when they do not learn to read the Old Testament as Paul did! "For whatever was written in former days was written for our instruction, that through endurance and through the encouragement of the Scriptures we might have hope" (Rom 15:4).

As a theologically trained Pharisee, Paul had been rigorously taught the Bible, what Christians call the "Old Testament." His education taught him to begin at Mount Sinai and the giving of the law (see Exod

19ff.). If one is going to be right with God (justified), one must keep God's law. It's that simple. As a Pharisee, Paul devoted his life to strict obedience, believing that if he kept the law well enough, he would earn God's favor. But at his conversion to Jesus Christ on the road to Damascus, Paul experienced not only a spiritual transformation, but an intellectual one as well. He began to think differently! And this affected how he read the Old Testament. He began to read the Scriptures in a way he had never read them before. He saw things that had always been there in the text, yet until his conversion, they had somehow remained hidden from his eyes.

Paul began to realize, for example, that the book of Genesis (the story of Abraham) comes *before* the book of Exodus (the story of Moses and Mount Sinai). How did he miss *that*? Though he had read the story perhaps hundreds of times, Paul now saw that Abraham was right with God (justified) 430 years *before* the law was even given at Mount Sinai (see Gal 3:16–18). Further, he now saw clearly in the text that Abraham was justified by faith, *not* by the keeping of the law (see Gen 15:6). There it was, right in his own Bible, plain as day. Paul was shocked to realize that the pharisaical notion that justification comes through obedience to the law was simply not what the Bible teaches! The just shall live by faith (see Hab 2:4; Rom 1:17).

Paul had made the revolutionary discovery that the gospel of Jesus Christ is not opposed to the Old Testament. No, the gospel is its fulfillment. It is the pharisaical interpretation of the Old Testament that is the problem, not the Old Testament itself! Tragically, the Galatian Christians had been influenced by a pharisaical interpretation of the Bible. They had the idea that faith alone was not enough. To be right with God (justified), they needed to keep the law, do good works, earn their way into God's favor. Paul knew that this was not only impossible; it was not what the Bible said!

This helps us to understand why Paul decided to preach a sermon to the Galatian Christians using Genesis 21 as his text. Drawing on the contrast between Hagar and Sarah, Paul's point was that many in the Galatian church were acting like children of Hagar rather than children of Sarah. These two women represent two very different ways of understanding how to be in a right relationship with God. One is by works of the law, the other is by grace through faith.

We might chart the contrast between these two women this way:

Hagar—the slave	Sarah—the wife
Ishmael	Isaac
Under the law	Under grace
Born according to the flesh	Born according to the Spirit
Natural life	Spiritual life
Sinai—present Jerusalem	The Jerusalem above
Bondage	Freedom
Walks in the flesh	Walks in the Spirit
Works	Faith
Persecutor	Persecuted
Will be cast out	Will receive the inheritance
Old Covenant	New Covenant
The Law	The Promise

IMAGINING WHAT PAUL'S SERMON WAS LIKE

I want to invite you to use your sanctified imagination and try to picture a contemporary Pastor Paul stepping into the pulpit of Galatia Community Church, taking his Bible, and inviting the congregation to turn with him to Genesis 21. After reading the text, he says, "The name of my sermon this morning is 'Who's Your Mother?'" Looking at the congregation of Christian believers sitting before him, Pastor Paul continues: "My message has four basic points."[2]

First, are you reading the Bible correctly?

It is obvious to me that you really love God's Word. You especially like those first five books of the Bible we Jews call the Torah, the Law. Here we discover God's Ten Commandments and other regulations

---

[2] I make no claim that these four points give an exhaustive explication of Galatians 4:21–31 but only that they help to highlight the warning Paul is giving here to Christians. The sermon contained in these "four basic points" is my own, based on the book of Galatians. But I present it as if it were Paul's. The references inserted into the text in parentheses point to the verses in Galatians that further elucidate the points Paul is making.

he gave to us at Mount Sinai. I know you consider yourselves to be Christ followers, but you seem to believe that his death on the cross will be of no benefit to you unless you obey all these laws. That's why you love Bible study so much. You want to know God's Word so you can obey him and thus be pleasing to him. Believe me when I say, I fully understand where you are coming from. I was trained as a Pharisee. I get it.

So, tell me this: if you love God's law so much, why aren't you listening to what it says (Gal 4:21)? I'm not just talking about the book of Exodus. I'm talking about the book that comes *before* Exodus: Genesis. This is also part of God's Torah; in fact, Genesis lays the foundation for all that follows. In Genesis 15:6 we learn that Abraham was right with God by faith. Now remember, this was 430 years *before* the law was even given (Gal 3:16–18)! Yes, long before anyone knew anything about laws, sacrifices, and rituals, Abraham was in a right relationship with God—by faith alone!

So, dear friends, is it possible that in our zeal to study the Bible, we have misunderstood what it says? That's why I want us to look at Genesis 21 this morning. Yes, it's true that Abraham is the father of all who believe. But remember this: he had *two* sons! One was a child of flesh, the other was a child of the Spirit. Yes, Ishmael was a child of Abraham and thus, a sort of believer. But Ishmael was not the chosen heir of the covenant. In other words, not all of Abraham's children are members of the covenant family of God. I'm not making this up. It says so right here in the Book!

Second, have you fallen back into slavery?

This morning, if you think that you are in a right relationship with God because you conform to a set of behavioral standards that make you worthy, then you are clearly a child of Hagar, the slave woman. Ishmael was a member of Abraham's family by human efforts; there was nothing supernatural about it. He was a child of the flesh; the Spirit had nothing to do with it. Yes, I fear that many of you sitting here this morning are like Ishmael. You are trying to live the life of the

Spirit in the power of the flesh. Do I need to explain to you that such an attempt is futile, crazy, foolish? It just won't work.

Think back to your conversion, when you first put your faith in Jesus and his atoning blood. How did your new life begin? By working hard to please God? By obeying the law? No! Birth into God's family was a gift of grace, a work of the Spirit. You understood that—then. Have you lost your memory? Do you now think that you can complete by human effort what was begun by God's Spirit (Gal 3:1–3)? How can you turn back to those legalistic formulas and ritualistic obligations that never worked in the first place? Do you really want to be a slave again? (Gal 4:9). Sometimes it feels like my ministry here has been a complete failure (Gal 4:11).

Listen to me: Christ has set you free from all that! So, stand firm and don't fall back into slavery again (Gal 5:1). Jesus will be of no benefit to you if you try to please God by keeping those laws. Yes, your salvation will be then based on your work rather than his grace (Gal 5:2–4). Good luck with that!

Third, be who you are!

I have good news for you: you are *not* children of Hagar; you are children of Sarah. You are *not* children of the flesh; you are children of the Spirit. You are *not* under law; you are under grace. You are *not* slaves; you are free! Yes, you are children of promise (Gal 4:28). So, my message to you this morning is simply this: be who you are!

It's not about keeping a bunch of rules and regulations. It's about a walk; a walk with God. When you walk in the Spirit you won't feel the need to gratify the desires of the flesh (Gal 5:16). Those who let the Spirit lead them are, by definition, freed from the tyranny of the law (Gal 5:18). This is true liberty. Such Spirit-filled living means that God is producing wonderful "fruit" in your lives: love, joy, peace, patience, kindness, goodness, faithfulness, gentleness, and self-control. You can be sure that there is no law against those things (Gal 5:22–23).

Fourth, deal radically with any indwelling sin.

So, dear brothers and sisters, if this morning you discover that you have slipped back into the bondage of legalism and works righteousness, if you find that your life resembles Ishmael more than Isaac, I want to boldly ask you to do what Sarah did: "Cast out the slave woman and her son" (Gal 4:30). Yes, deal radically with sin! There is no other way. That part of your old self that wants to do wrong and rebel against God (the flesh), must be dealt with severely. The sinful flesh within you can't be educated, civilized, or reformed. It must be killed, cast out, destroyed. Those who belong to Christ Jesus have crucified the flesh with its passions and desires (Gal 5:24). There is no compromising or negotiating with the flesh. This wickedness that dwells within you must be dealt a death blow.

Let me share my own story. I, Paul, can testify to the fact that I never found the freedom that Christ came to make possible until I dealt radically with the dwelling-in-me sin. But I could only do it with God's help. You see, I have been crucified with Christ. It is no longer I who live, but Christ lives in me. And the life I now live in the flesh I live by faith in the Son of God, who loved me and gave himself for me (Gal 2:20).

My fellow Galatians, has the Spirit of God been talking to you this morning about the state of your own heart? Is it possible, that even in a good congregation like Galatia Community Church, among good people like you, there is someone that realizes their mother is not who they thought she was? If you are living like a child of Hagar, I want to ask you to pray this prayer:

> Dear Lord, I am ready to stop pretending that I am in a right relationship with you when it is obvious that I'm living in bondage, legalism, and works righteousness. Forgive me, Lord. I've settled for being Abraham's child through Hagar! I once knew your grace and walked in your Spirit, but somehow, I've fallen from the joyous freedom I once knew. Restore to me the joy of my salvation. Fill me with your Spirit so that I can crucify the flesh with its passions and desires. Help me to cast out the slave woman and her son once and for all. Enable me to be who I am in Jesus Christ. Amen.

QUESTIONS FOR DISCUSSION

1. Tell a story from your own life experience when it was difficult to discern the true children of God from the false. What did you learn?
2. Has this lesson made you think differently about the Old Testament? Explain.
3. Have you ever known of a Christian situation (church, ministry, small group, etc.) that fell back to being "under law" when it had once been "under grace"? What happened?
4. Did this lesson help you to discern areas in your own life where perhaps you resemble Ishmael more than Isaac? What do you intend to do about this?

18
Abraham's Final Exam
Genesis 22:1–19

Looking back over the life of Abraham, we see a long series of tests. Like exams given in school, these tests were intended to motivate and encourage Abraham to learn those lessons that God most wanted to teach him. Though scholastic tests can be frightening and even painful, the teacher's purpose is not malevolent (though it may feel that way to the student!). Rather, the professor wants the student to acquire certain knowledge and skills so that she can advance to the next level. It is simply a reality of the educational process that no one progresses far in life without being tested.

In Abraham's case, God's goal was to teach him to walk by faith and not by sight. If Abraham was to be "the father of all who believe" (see Rom 4:16), then it was of mandatory importance that his faith be tested. Did he *really* trust in the promises of God? The tests would reveal the truth. Only in this way could everyone know whether Abraham's faith was genuine or not.

God began Abraham's education by calling him to leave his home and family and promising him a bright future. "And he went out, not knowing where he was going" (Heb 11:8). Other tests soon followed. Would Abraham trust in the promises of God when there was famine in the land of Canaan and conflict with his nephew Lot? Would he believe God's promises when his wife Sarah remained barren for twenty-five long years? Would he trust in the goodness of God when divine wrath was poured out on the cities of Sodom and Gomorrah? The Bible makes no secret of the fact that Abraham was not a straight-A student. He did better on some tests than on others. However, the overall picture was positive. Abraham was learning to walk by faith and these tests were of vital importance in that process. His education was making a difference. Abraham was becoming a true man of faith.

We could call Genesis 22 Abraham's final exam. The chapter begins with these words: "After these things God tested Abraham" (Gen 22:1). Though he had been tested many times before, Abraham had never been tested like this! Neither would he experience any future tests of similar intensity. Once this test was behind him, it was obvious that Abraham had learned his lessons well. The angel of the Lord summed it all up by saying, "Now I know that you fear God" (Gen 22:12).

Abraham's Finest Hour

Few chapters in the Bible can match Genesis 22 for enthralling drama, emotional intensity, and theological profundity. For agnostics and critics, the story told here confirms their worst fears: God is cruel, capricious, and promotes child abuse. But for those who have eyes to see, this chapter is one of the clearest presentations of the gospel ever written. As the story unfolds, readers catch their breath as they try to absorb what is happening. They want to take off their shoes; this is holy ground.

The *place* is holy. In Abraham's day it appears that Mount Moriah, and the region around it, is uninhabited. But centuries later, this area will become Jerusalem and this mountain the site of Solomon's Temple (see 2 Chr 3:1). Even more than Mount Sinai, *this* mountain will be considered by the people of God to be the holiest of all holy places. Long before God revealed his commandments on Mount Sinai, he revealed his heart on Mount Moriah!

The *persons* are holy. The main characters in this drama are the original patriarchs of the covenant people of God: Abraham and Isaac. But more than that, they are father and son. Their united, harmonious actions of *making* a sacrifice and *being* a sacrifice take us to the very core of the divine mystery buried deep in the heart of the triune God. It is not just Abraham's act of offering a sacrifice that makes Mount

Moriah so significant; it is Isaac's consent to his father's will that seals the deal. Seen in this light, the reader of Genesis gets a hint of the ultimate drama that will be played out in this very same location centuries later when God the Father and God the Son will work together to accomplish another, and much greater, sacrifice.

The *action* is holy. Long before the Bible attempts to define abstract theological concepts like faith, sacrifice, substitution, fatherhood, and sonship, it introduces us to these realities through an historical story. If a picture paints a thousand words, then Genesis 22 is a masterpiece! The truths conveyed in this story are simple enough for a child to understand yet so profound that theologians are still plumbing the depths of its full significance.

The drama begins when, unbeknownst to Abraham, the reader is told God's purpose for what is about to happen. This is a "test" (Gen 22:1); specifically, it is a test of Abraham's faith. Does he really believe the promises of God? Will he trust God enough to obey him even when the command he is given makes no sense? Will he continue to walk in faith even when God takes away his blessings?

It is important to distinguish between a "test" and a "temptation." Unlike a test, the purpose of a temptation is sinister. Its goal is to cause someone to stumble and fall. Satan is the tempter, not God (see Rev 12:9; Jas 1:13). God never wants his children to fall. That is precisely why he tests them; so that they won't! Thus, we see many occasions in Scripture when God tests his children (e.g., Ex 15:25; 16:4; 20:20; Jdgs 3:1–4; 2 Chr 32:31; 1 Cor 10:13; Jas 1:2–4; 1 Pet 1:6–7; etc.). God arranges these tests not because he is sadistic and cruel, but to strengthen and prepare his children for what lies ahead, to burn away what is impure, and to reveal the true character of his followers. As we saw earlier, God has a very good purpose in testing Abraham. He is teaching him, training him, building him up, and preparing him to be a godly influence for all human history.

The instructions Abraham received from God were simple and clear. Yet, every word must have cut like a knife: "Take your son, your only son Isaac, whom you love, and go to the land of Moriah, and offer him there as a burnt offering." (Gen 22:2). Victor Hamilton writes: "The intensity of the test is magnified by the three direct objects of the imperative: 'your son', 'your precious son whom you love', 'Isaac.' Each of the objects hits a little closer to home, as the list moves from the general to the more intimate."[1]

Now we can perhaps better understand the events of the previous chapter (Gen 21). There, Abraham reluctantly agreed to cast out his other son, Ishmael, and his mother, Hagar. Though he loved them and though God promised to take care of them, Abraham had to disinherit Ishmael so that there would be no confusion about which son was the true heir. Before he could make the kind of sacrifice that was really pleasing to God, Abraham had to first put away the son that was the result of his own human efforts, the child of flesh. Sacrifices that please God can only be made when all works of the flesh have been definitively put away, once and for all.

God tells Abraham to offer Isaac as a "burnt offering." The Hebrew term *olah* is the root from which our English word *holocaust* is derived. The book of Leviticus will later explain that a "burnt offering" is a sacrifice that is *totally* consumed by flames on the altar (e.g., Lev 1:3ff.). The animal being sacrificed was literally turned into smoke and ashes. While other offerings allowed the priest or the worshipper to eat part of the meat, not so with the holocaust. This was an offering wholly, completely, and entirely devoted to God alone. Allen P. Ross notes that while Abraham may have been the first person to realize that God demanded complete devotion and full surrender from his worshipers, he was certainly not the last. In fact, it is what Jesus expects of all believers today!

> Jesus' requirement of forsaking one's family, leaving all, and following him (Luke 14:26–27) is similar to the test of obedience that was taught in Genesis 22. If anyone is inclined to be a true worshiper of the Lord, it will involve the willingness to sacrifice whatever is dearest and most treasured, even if such should be considered a gift from God.[2]

---

1 Hamilton, *Genesis,* 1:102.
2 Ross, *Creation and Blessing,* 398.

This test on Mount Moriah would reveal once and for all whether Abraham loved God more than he loved his son; whether he loved the gift more than the Giver. A. B. Simpson, the founder of The Christian and Missionary Alliance, wrote a hymn in 1891 entitled *Himself* that expresses this spiritual reality in words intended to become the singer's own testimony.

> *Once it was the blessing,*
> *Now it is the Lord;*
> *Once it was the feeling,*
> *Now it is His Word;*
> *Once His gift I wanted,*
> *Now, the Giver own;*
> *Once I sought for healing,*
> *Now Himself alone.*
>
> *Once it was my working,*
> *His it hence shall be;*
> *Once I tried to use Him,*
> *Now He uses me;*
> *Once the pow'r I wanted,*
> *Now the Mighty One;*
> *Once for self I labored,*
> *Now for Him alone.*

FAITH IS THE VICTORY

The Bible tells us what happened next:

So Abraham rose early in the morning, saddled his donkey, and took two of his young men with him, and his son Isaac. And he cut the wood for the burnt offering and arose and went to the place of which God had told him. On the third day Abraham lifted up his eyes and saw the place from afar. Then Abraham said to his young men, "Stay here with the donkey; I and the boy will go over there and worship and come again to you." (Gen 22:3–5)

Years earlier, when God announced his plan to destroy Sodom and Gomorrah, Abraham pleaded with God to reconsider (see Gen 18:16–33). However, this time, Abraham says nothing. Rather than begging God to change his plans, he rises early, saddles his donkey, and promptly obeys. It seems that the patriarch knew God well enough to realize that, this time, there was to be no discussion on the matter. Silent obedience was the only appropriate response to the divine command. Hebrews 11:17–19 hints at what Abraham may have been thinking: he "considered that God was able even to raise (Isaac) from the dead." Perhaps on the morning he began that journey, Abraham prayed an early version of The Serenity Prayer: "God, grant me the serenity to accept the things I cannot change, the courage to change the things I can, and the wisdom to know the difference."

> *And Abraham took the wood of the burnt offering and laid it on Isaac his son. And he took in his hand the fire and the knife. So they went both of them together. And Isaac said to his father Abraham, "My father!" And he said, "Here I am, my son." He said, "Behold, the fire and the wood, but where is the lamb for a burnt offering?" Abraham said, "God will provide for himself the lamb for a burnt offering, my son." So they went both of them together. When they came to the place of which God had told him, Abraham built the altar there and laid the wood in order and bound Isaac his son and laid him on the altar, on top of the wood. Then Abraham reached out his hand and took the knife to slaughter his son. But the angel of the* LORD *called to him from heaven and said, "Abraham, Abraham!" And he said, "Here I am." He said, "Do not lay your hand on the boy or do anything to him, for now I know that you fear God, seeing you have not withheld your son, your only son, from me." (Gen 22:6–12)*

When I was a boy and my mother called my name twice, "Stanley, Stanley!" I knew something of great significance was happening. By the tone of her voice, I could easily tell whether I was being warned, rebuked, or affirmed. So it is in this text. The tone in God's voice must have immediately let Abraham know what had always been in the heart of God: "Abraham, Abraham! . . . Do not lay your hand on the boy . . . now I know that you fear God." Although later Scriptures would reveal that God was adamantly opposed to child sacrifice (Lev 20:1–5; Jer 7:30–31; etc.), this may not have been clear to Abraham at the time. Other religions encouraged such horrid practices, why should his God be any different? It is interesting to note that God lets the drama play out to the last second before he intervenes. Thankfully, he stops the horror and provides another plan.

> *And Abraham lifted up his eyes and looked, and behold, behind him was a ram, caught in a thicket by his horns. And Abraham went and took the ram and offered it up as a burnt offering instead of his son. So Abraham called the name of that place, "The* Lord *will provide"; as it is said to this day, "On the mount of the* Lord *it shall be provided." (Gen 22:13–14)*

God never budged on his demand that a sacrifice was indeed required. But what relief Abraham must have felt when he learned that God would accept a substitute; a *suitable* substitute, one that he himself would provide. In the place of Isaac, God provided a lamb. To be precise, he provided a ram—the *father* of a lamb. The technicality should not be missed! The roles of fathers and sons in this divine drama are perhaps the most important part of the story. Apparently, the ram had been there all along, but Abraham was able to see God's amazing provision only *after* he had come to a point of full and complete surrender to the divine plan.

Once Abraham passes the test, God renews the covenant with him, repeating some of its many, amazing promises (see Gen 22:15–19). Similar to what he had promised on earlier occasions, God assures Abraham that he will bless him, give him innumerable descendants, and make him a blessing to all nations. But this time, God adds something new! He confirms these covenant promises with an oath! "Buy myself I have sworn . . ." God says to Abraham (Gen 22:16). Though it would be easy to miss the significance of what appears to be a minor addition, the author of Hebrews points out that these little words are of momentous importance:

> *For when God made a promise to Abraham, since he had no one greater by whom to swear, he swore by himself, saying, "Surely I will bless you and multiply you." And thus Abraham, having patiently waited, obtained the promise. For people swear by something greater than themselves, and in all their disputes an oath is final for confirmation. So when God desired to show more convincingly to the heirs*

of the promise the unchangeable character of his purpose, he guaranteed it with an oath, so that by two unchangeable things, in which it is impossible for God to lie, we who have fled for refuge might have strong encouragement to hold fast to the hope set before us. (Heb 6:13–18)

As if a divine promise were not enough, God swears an oath to keep the promise he has just made. These "two unchangeable things" (a promise and an oath) underscore the absolute reliability of what God is saying to Abraham and to his descendants. In the strongest way possible, God is saying, "You can count on me; I am a promise-keeping God!" This fact, says the author of Hebrews, serves as "a sure and steadfast anchor of the soul" for everyone who puts their trust in God (Heb 6:19).

MAKING IT PERSONAL

It is tempting to close a chapter like this with a hard-hitting exhortation that calls the reader to full surrender and total consecration by asking the convicting question, "Is your all on the altar?" Although there is certainly a place for such calls to surrender, the tone of Genesis 22 seems to invite a more contemplative approach. Let's look at the story again, but this time sequentially through the eyes of the three main characters: Abraham, Isaac, and the Lord God. Use your sanctified imagination and try to feel what they each must have felt as the dramatic events of this amazing chapter played themselves out.

Abraham

Put yourself in Abraham's sandals and try to imagine what must have been going through his mind when God commanded him to make an offering of his son.

- Lord, ever since I first heard your call, I've been building altars where I could offer you sacrifices of praise and thanksgiving: at Shechem, at Bethel, and at Hebron. Why are you asking me to build yet another altar at Moriah?
- O God, I've already sacrificed my home and family to follow your call. I've turned my back on possessions and reputation,

- and even let go of Ishmael so I could obey your voice. Isn't that enough? What more do you want?
- Lord, this doesn't make sense! For twenty-five years I waited in faith for you to give me a child as you promised you would. Isaac came as a gift from you. He's a miracle of grace. So, why are you asking me to give him back?
- Lord, if I sacrifice Isaac then what will happen to your work in the world? He is the channel through whom your covenant blessings will flow to the nations, remember? If he dies, your promises will all fail.

Abraham's obedience to the will of God is certainly one of the greatest examples of faith in all Scripture. In this act of devotion on Mount Moriah, Abraham set the standard for what it means to have faith in God. Søren Kierkegaard wrote an entire book about Abraham's sacrifice called *Fear and Trembling*, where he says that Abraham was great with that power whose strength is powerlessness, great in that wisdom whose secret is folly, great in that hope whose outward form is insanity, great in that love which is hatred of self. . . . I cannot understand Abraham, I can only admire him.[3]

Isaac

Most treatments of Genesis 22 focus on Abraham and what a hero of the faith he was. That's fair, but only up to a certain point. We must never forget the role that Isaac played in this sacred drama. As we look more closely, we realize that Isaac's part in the story is perhaps as important as Abraham's; being a son can be just as challenging as being a father. Put yourself in Isaac's sandals and try to imagine what the events of this story must have been like for him.

First, we need to remember that Isaac was no small child when these events took place. Many depictions of Genesis 22 imagine Isaac as a young boy being directed by a strong, authoritarian faither—helpless, clueless, and passive. But this is simply not the case! Isaac was at least an older teen and was perhaps as old as thirty years of age. Abraham would have been around one hundred and thirty. It

---

3 Kierkegaard, *Fear and Trembling*, 50, 136.

takes only a little imagination to realize that Isaac could have easily run away and escaped his elderly father. And when Abraham began to bind him with ropes, he could have resisted and overpowered the old man. The story takes on a whole new meaning when we begin to realize that Isaac was no victim; he was a *willing* sacrifice!

Those who pretend that Genesis 22 is an early example of child abuse simply do not know what they are talking about. Isaac's role at Mount Moriah was just as free and deliberate as was that of his father. Abraham was not the only one counting the cost. Isaac made a solemn decision to submit to the will of his father even as Abraham had made a solemn decision to submit to God. Abraham came to Mount Moriah to *make* a sacrifice. Isaac came to *be* one!

Perhaps this was the image Paul had in mind when he urged the Christians in Rome to offer their bodies as a "living sacrifice" to God (see Rom 12:1). More importantly, perhaps Jesus meditated deeply on this event and all the relational dynamics between a father and a son. He too would be called on to submit to the will of his Father when in Gethsemane he prayed, "Not what I will, but what you will" (Mark 14:36).

Although there are numerous similarities between Jesus and Isaac, the primary likeness is the way that each man freely chose to submit to the will of his father and embrace the sacrifice that was demanded of him. Neither one was a victim. Both were willing participants in what happened.

Many portrayals of Jesus' crucifixion imagine him as trapped and victimized by evil men who forced him to do what he didn't want to do. His life was *taken* from him. "Poor Jesus, it's too bad those bullies won; it wasn't supposed to end like this" is how the story is often told. And then we gather around the cross and feel pity for the helpless victim. But this interpretation is simply *not* how the gospels tell the story! To understand the death of Jesus in these terms is to misunderstand the death of Jesus. Yes, he was betrayed by a friend, given an unfair trail, and brutally murdered. But make no mistake about it; Jesus was no victim. No one *took* his life; he freely *gave* it!

> *For this reason the Father loves me, because I lay down my life that I may take it up again. No one takes it from me, but I lay it down of my own accord. I have authority to lay it down, and I have authority to take it up again. This charge I have received from my Father. (John 10:17–18)*

Genesis 22 is not just about what it means to be a father. It is equally about what it means to be a son! Isaac is just as much a hero in this story as is Abraham. The father and the son are solemnly working together, acting in unison. One is offering a sacrifice to God, the other is being that sacrifice. It is as the father and the son cooperate in this most holy work that the redemption of the world becomes possible!

If Abraham is the preeminent model of what it means to be a father, Isaac is the preeminent model of what it means to be a son. The ceremony of circumcision, performed on Isaac when he was eight days old (cf. Gen 21:4) was that moment when Abraham dedicated his son to God and confirmed this commitment by marking his son's flesh with the sign of the covenant. Did Abraham fully understand the significance of what he was doing? Isaac, as a son of the covenant, now belonged to God. Whether or not Abraham was fully alert to what was happening, God was! The sacrifice on Mount Moriah was, in one sense, nothing more than the logical outworking of the infant dedication ceremony that had taken place so many years before. Parents, be alert! When you dedicate your child to God, make sure you understand what you are doing.

It is interesting to note that the only recorded words of Isaac in the entire drama relate to his question about the sacrifice. "My father.... Behold, the fire, and the wood, but where is the lamb for a burnt offering?" (Gen 22:7). Abraham's response must have filled his son with wonder and awe when he replied, "God will provide for himself the lamb for a burnt offering, my son." (Gen 22:8). Isaac would always remember that this father had taught him to put his trust in the Lord who will provide all that is needed when we need it!

The Lord God

What kind of God would give a test like this; telling a father to sacrifice his only son? *That* is a really good question! To conclude that such a deity would be cruel, capricious, and irrational would be to give a very bad answer to a very good question.

As we have already seen, the dramatic events of Genesis 22 in some mysterious way foreshadow the crucifixion of Jesus many centuries later. Mount Moriah and Mount Calvary were adjacent summits. Abraham and Isaac were not the only father and son implicated in what was happening. The similarities between the two events are worth noting:

- Isaac carried the wood to the place of sacrifice even as Jesus did (Gen 22: 6 and John 19:17).
- Abraham's statement that God would himself provide a lamb for sacrifice (cf. Gen 22:8) may well have been in the mind of John the Baptist when he introduced Jesus as the "Lamb of God" (John 1:29).
- The father/son relationship is the central focus in both stories. It is only as the father and son work together, one sacrificing and the other being sacrificed, that God's redemptive power can be displayed in all its glory.

In New Testament terms, we learn that the atonement is not simply the work of the Father's will, nor is it simply the work of the Son's willing sacrifice. It is only as the Father and the Son work together that salvation for others becomes possible. Jewish survivor of the Holocaust and Nobel laureate Elie Wiesel writes:

> And so the father and the son walked away together—the one to bind and the other to be bound, the one to slaughter and the other to be slaughtered—sharing the same allegiance to the same God, responding to the same call. The sacrifice was to be their joint offering; father and son had never before been so close.[4]

---

4 Wiesel, *Messengers of God*, 88.

Genesis 22 provides the foundation for understanding the gospel of Jesus Christ. "For God so loved the world, that he gave his only Son." (John 3:16). "He who did not spare his own Son but gave him up for us all, how will he not also with him graciously give us all things?" (Rom 8:32).

Dennis Kinlaw recalls a sermon that he heard Henry Clay Morrison (1857–1942) preach many years ago in which the evangelist gave a poignant description of what was really going on in the events of Genesis 22.

> The Triune God was looking on at the sacrifice of Isaac. One member of the Godhead said to another one, "This is not the last time we're going to be on this mountain, is it?" And the First Person of the blessed Trinity said, "No, it will be about two thousand years and we will be back, right here." And the Second Person of the blessed Trinity said to the First Person, "And when we come back next time, it's not going to be one of them on that altar, is it?" And the First Person of the blessed Trinity said, "No, when we come back the next time it won't be one of them—it will be one of Us." And then the Second Person of the blessed Trinity said to the First, "And when they put me on that altar of sacrifice, are you going to say, 'Stop, don't touch the lad?'" And the Father said, "No. We never ask them to do in symbol what we haven't been willing to do in reality."[5]

QUESTIONS FOR DISCUSSION

1. Has God ever "tested" you like he tested Abraham? Would you be willing to share this story with others?
2. For which of the three characters in the story was the sacrifice of Isaac the most difficult: for Abraham? for Isaac? or for God?
3. With which character in the story do you most identify: the father or the son?

---

[5] Kinlaw, *Lectures in Old Testament Theology*, 190.

4. Is God asking you to make a sacrifice to him that is costly? Or perhaps is God asking you to be sacrificed? How does Genesis 22 help you to better understand what God may be doing?
5. Has this lesson caused you to have a deeper appreciation for the ceremony of Infant Dedication? (or Infant Baptism?).

19
Hatched, Matched, and Dispatched
Genesis 23–24

From a mundane and purely biological perspective, human existence often seems to be nothing more than birth, marriage, children, and death. From one generation to the next, the cycle is repeated again and again. Hatched, matched, and dispatched. The question must be asked: Is that all there is? Is there no more significance than *that* to human life? Perhaps Macbeth was right when he said:

> Life's but a walking shadow, a poor player, that struts and frets his hour upon the stage, and then is heard no more. It is a tale told by an idiot, full of sound and fury, signifying nothing.[1]

It is interesting to note that the genealogies of Genesis sometimes actually reinforce this impression. Human life seems just another form of animal existence: we are born, we produce children, and we die. Our children produce children and then they die; and so it goes. For example:

> *When Seth had lived 105 years, he fathered Enosh. Seth lived after he fathered Enosh 807 years and had other sons and daughters. Thus all the days of Seth were 912 years, and he died. When Enosh had lived 90 years, he fathered Kenan. Enosh lived after he fathered Kenan 815 years and had other sons and daughters. Thus all the days of Enosh were*

---

[1] Shakespeare, *Macbeth*, Act V, Scene 5.

> 905 years, and he died. When Kenan had lived 70 years, he fathered Mahalalel. (Gen 5:6–12)

> When Shem was 100 years old, he fathered Arpachshad two years after the flood. And Shem lived after he fathered Arpachshad 500 years and had other sons and daughters. When Arpachshad had lived 35 years, he fathered Shelah. And Arpachshad lived after he fathered Shelah 403 years and had other sons and daughters. When Shelah had lived 30 years, he fathered Eber. (Gen 11:10–14)

> These are the names of Esau's sons: Eliphaz the son of Adah the wife of Esau, Reuel the son of Basemath the wife of Esau. The sons of Eliphaz were Teman, Omar, Zepho, Gatam, and Kenaz. (Timna was a concubine of Eliphaz, Esau's son; she bore Amalek to Eliphaz.) These are the sons of Adah, Esau's wife. These are the sons of Reuel: Nahath, Zerah, Shammah, and Mizzah. . . . (Gen 36:10–13)

You get the idea. We live, we propagate, we die. That pretty much sums it up, right?

In the 1960s, vocalist Peggy Lee became famous for her hit song "Is That All There Is?" The lyrics are a kind of depressing testimonial of someone who discovers that there really is nothing of great significance to human life. It is just a series of meaningless events, then we die and drop into oblivion. Trying to make the best out of a tragic reality, she bravely smiles and sings:

> Is that all there is, is that all there is?
> If that's all there is my friends, then let's keep dancing.
> Let's break out the booze and have a ball;
> If that's all there is.

Thankfully, Peggy Lee and Macbeth are wrong. Life *does* have significance! The book of Genesis loudly proclaims that when men and women are rightly related to their creator, they can then discover the purpose for which they were born. When we walk with God, trusting his word and believing his promises, our lives have meaning. Mark Twain spoke wisely when he said, "The two most important days in your life are the day you are born and the day you find out why."

Abraham's story (Gen 12–25) is about to come to an end. He is old and death is near. But before his final exit, he devotes his attention to two matters of vital importance: a burial plot for his wife and a suitable bride for his son. Sarah must be buried. Isaac must be married.

A Piece of Canaan Land

We know that the death of Sarah, at the age of 127, was a wrenching experience for both Abraham and Isaac. The Bible tells us that Abraham both "mourned" and "wept" for her (see Gen 23:2). The use of two verbs to describe his emotions may underscore the depth of Abraham's grief. In the next chapter, Genesis tells us that Isaac grieved his mother's death for many months, if not years (see Gen 24:67). Sarah's death was undoubtedly a traumatic event that required a new step of faith for both Abraham and Isaac.

On a more practical level, Sarah's death presented Abraham with two immediate questions. The first related to burial customs: *What should be done with the body?* In the Ancient Near East, there were multiple options for answering a question like this. While Genesis 23 is obviously a *description* of what Abraham chose to do and not a *prescription* for what others should do, his actions are nevertheless instructive for those who think deeply about such matters. Especially, we should notice what he chose *not* to do. Abraham did not mummify Sarah's body, cremate it, or toss it unceremoniously in a common grave. Neither did he build a mausoleum and deify his dead wife. Rather, he showed respect for the body by ceremoniously placing it in the ground; specifically, in a cave. The location of her grave would help him to remember her and preserve her legacy. As he covered his wife's dead body with dirt, perhaps Abraham recalled the words God had spoken to Adam centuries earlier:

> *By the sweat of your face you shall eat bread, till you return to the ground, for out of it you were taken; for you are dust, and to dust you shall return. (Gen 3:19)*

These simple gestures taken by Abraham showed respect for the body and acknowledged the finality of death. Seen in contrast to the burial customs of others, Abraham's actions made a powerful statement to the watching world. The way he treated his wife's dead body had a profound influence on how his descendants, both biological and spiritual, would bury their dead. In fact, the burial customs of Jews and Christians throughout the centuries have been one of the primary ways in which they bore witness of their faith before a watching world. Today, in a post-Christian environment, believers need to think deeply once again about these matters and work to establish burial customs that reflect their true faith.

The second question related to a burial place: *Where should Sarah's body be buried?* Although it may not at first be obvious, this question had more theological implications than the first one!

As one reads the rather tedious account of the business transaction between Abraham and Ephron the Hittite recorded in Genesis 23, one may wonder if there is any spiritual significance to what is happening. Sitting in the gate surrounded by the elders of the city, a price is negotiated, and the transaction is formalized. Perhaps real estate brokers may enjoy a chapter like this; but the rest of us? What's going on here?

But Genesis 23 can be regarded as one of the most important chapters in the Bible because here, for the *first* time, the covenant people of God gain possession of a piece of real estate in Canaan, the Land of Promise. This has huge implications, not only for the Jews but for the entire world. In fact, we still are dealing with these implications today! With the purchase of the Cave of Machpelah, the conquest of Canaan had begun! Until this moment, Abraham had owned no land. As he says so clearly to his Hittite neighbors, "I am a sojourner and foreigner among you" (Gen 23:4). In buying a burial place for his wife, he was doing much more than making funeral arrangements. He was establishing a beachhead! This was his first claim on the entire property that the Lord God himself had promised to give him and his descendants forever.

It would be a gross misjudgment to interpret Abraham's purchase of land as an act of imperialism or an attempt to establish racial dominance. No! Abraham's desire to possess the land of Canaan was based solely on one unshakeable conviction: God had promised to give it to him. In fact, God made this promise to Abraham not once, but many times. Along with the promise of children, the promise of land was at the heart of the covenant agreement.

- "Then the Lord appeared to Abram and said, 'To your offspring I will give this land.'" (Gen 12:7)
- "The Lord said to Abram . . . 'Lift up your eyes and look from the place where you are, northward and southward and eastward and westward, for all the land that you see I will give to you and to your offspring forever.'" (Gen 13:14–15)
- "On that day the Lord made a covenant with Abram, saying, 'To your offspring I give this land, from the river of Egypt to the great river, the river Euphrates, the land of the Kenites, the Kenizzites, the Kadmonites, the Hittites, the Perizzites, the Rephaim, the Amorites, the Canaanites, the Girgashites and the Jebusites.'" (Gen 15:18–21)
- "And I will give to you and to your offspring after you the land of your sojournings, all the land of Canaan, for an everlasting possession, and I will be their God." (Gen 17:8)

God makes promises and he keeps them! But be warned; rarely does the fulfillment of God's promise come as we expect it. When God is at work, you can be sure that the accomplishment of his plan will come only with testing, waiting, and pain. Just as Jesus had to die before he could be raised in power and glory, so every promise of God contains a "cross." In fact, it is safe to say that if there is no "cross" in the promises you hope for, they are not from God.

When God promised children to Abraham and Sarah, they may have assumed a series of quick pregnancies and deliveries. God had another plan in mind. The aging couple had to wait twenty-five long years for God to do what he had said he would. They anticipated many children born in a natural way, but God gave them only one, born in a supernatural way. Then he demanded that this son be put to death on an altar of sacrifice! Yes, God kept his promise, but in a way they could never have imagined.

In a similar manner, God's promise to give the land of Canaan to Abraham came true; but not at all as he envisioned it. Abraham, perhaps, imagined a spacious, beautiful territory, freely given to him where his descendants could thrive and prosper in peace and security. But what God gave him was a burial plot, a cave; and he paid top dollar to get it! Yes, God was keeping his promise but in a way that Abraham could never have imagined. The conquest of Canaan had begun with a place to die! A burial plot was to be the first piece of real estate Abraham owned in the Promised Land.

Once again, we see the greatness of Abraham's faith. Through it all, he kept on believing in the promises of God and, more importantly, in the God of the promises. As he put Sarah's body in the ground, he was doing more than burying a corpse; he was planting a seed! God's promises stretch far beyond the grave. His purposes are stronger than death! Is it possible that Jesus was thinking of the Cave of Machpelah, Sarah's grave, when on the eve of his crucifixion, he said: "Truly, truly, I say to you, unless a grain of wheat falls into the earth and dies, it remains alone; but if it dies, it bears much fruit" (John 12:24).

A Marriage Made in Heaven

In this chapter, we are looking at those final two priorities that Abraham needed to take care of before he died. The first was making funeral arrangements for Sarah. The second was making wedding arrangements for Isaac. Getting his wife buried and his son married were Abraham's final decisions, and, in some ways, the most consequential actions he ever took. Genesis 23 told us the story of Sarah's funeral. Genesis 24 will tell us the story of Isaac's marriage. It is interesting to note that Genesis 24, one of the greatest love stories in the Bible, is the longest chapter in the book of Genesis. More space is devoted to how Isaac met Rebekah than to the creation of the universe!

The unsung hero of this story is Abraham's servant. Though he is not named, most scholars assume it was Eliezer of Damascus (see Gen 15:2). Abraham gave him an assignment of top priority and made him swear an oath in the name of God himself that he would keep it. He was to travel to the land of Mesopotamia, Abraham's home country, and find a wife for Isaac from among his own kinsmen. Specifically, he was warned "not to take a wife for (Isaac) from the daughters of the Canaanites" (see Gen 24:3–4). Abraham knew that the choice of a wife for his son was a matter of monumental importance. In a sense, the future of the world was hanging in the balance on how this issue was settled. To make a mistake concerning marriage is to endanger the entire human race!

This story is the first of three stories in the Pentateuch about a man meeting a woman at a well: Isaac and Rebekah (Gen 24), Jacob and Rachel (Gen 29:1–14), and Moses and Zipporah (Exod 2:15–22). Each story is distinct, yet one cannot fail to recognize the common themes found in each one:

- A man visits a foreign land and meets a woman at a well.
- The woman runs home and tells her family and friends about the amazing man she has met.
- The encounter at the well leads to a marriage and a family that changes history!

These stories are literally pregnant with significance! We have seen on several occasions how a story in Genesis sheds new light on events in the New Testament. These stories about romance at a well are no exception. One is struck by how they resemble the story of Jesus meeting the Samaritan woman at a well, told in the fourth chapter of John. Jesus is a foreigner in Samaria. After meeting him, the woman runs back to her village to share her excitement about the man she has met. The fact that this encounter happened to take place at *Jacob's* well only heightens the connection with Genesis. Could it be that John wrote the story knowing that readers would be reminded of its Old Testament counterparts? Is it possible that this was John's way of saying that Jesus is looking for his bride? If so, the message of John 4 is that Jesus may have found his "bride," but the wedding day is still in the future!

Genesis 24 is full of details that are of great interest to both scholars and historians alike. Some of these details relate to customs in the ancient Near East and others to theology and the spiritual walk. For example:

- Oath taking. "Put your hand under my thigh, that I may make you swear." (vv 2–3).
- Travel. A ten-camel caravan traveling hundreds of miles must have been an impressive means of transportation (v 10).
- How much water does a camel drink? Rebekah's offer to draw water for ten camels must have been a herculean task (v 20).[2]
- Bride price. How were brides chosen? What did marriage cost? For Rebekah, it took a caravan of ten camels to carry the rings, bracelets, jewelry, garments, and costly ornaments to make the transaction (vv 10, 22, 53),
- Discerning the will of God. Although the servant used some unconventional methods for discerning God's will, he achieved his goal of finding "the one" (v 14). In fact, he did his job so well that everyone, even the duplicitous and deceitful Laban, was compelled to say, "this thing has come from the Lord" (v 50).
- When did women wear veils? And for what purpose? (v 65).
- Grief. Isaac is mourning the loss of his mother many months, perhaps years, after her death. Is this normal? (v 67).

It would be easy to get sidetracked into matters of secondary importance and miss the primary message of Genesis 24. As we close this chapter, let's focus on keeping the main thing the main thing.

Marriage Matters

Using the story of Isaac and Rebekah as a starting point, let's look at the big picture of what Genesis, and indeed the whole Bible, has to say about marriage.

Today, in the post-Christian and post-modern West, questions about gender, marriage, birth, and family have surfaced as perhaps the most troubling and contentious issues of this generation. Whether

---

[2] Typical estimates suggest that a thirsty camel can drink 25 gallons of water. Ten camels would therefore need 250 gallons!

we are talking about gender identity, same-sex marriage, divorce, abortion, or in vitro fertilization, passions run hot as people debate the issues. There is no cultural consensus on how to move forward. One of the motivations for writing this book has been the desire to encourage people to look at Genesis once again as a helpful place to begin in trying to understand the Creator's intention for marriage and the family.

Definition: What Marriage Is

For most of human history, there has been almost universal agreement on the definition of marriage. Not just Christians, but the great majority of Jews, Muslims, Hindus, Buddhists, and even humanists and secularists have all believed basically the same thing: marriage is the legal union of one man and one woman. Though there have been times when some cultures promoted polygamy, the basic definition remained unchanged: a legal union of male and female. All of us are now aware that this historic definition is being fiercely challenged. In 2015, for example, the U.S. Supreme Court tampered with the dictionary and redefined marriage to include same-sex unions.

When we examined the creation of the world as recorded in Genesis 1–2, we learned that human persons come in two, and only two, varieties: male and female. With God's blessing upon them and the divine mandate to be fruitful and multiply, Adam and Eve established the normative standard for human life. History began, not with a government, or even a church. It all began with a marriage: one man and one woman in a union of love, for life. This was God's plan for the foundation of human civilization.

Conforming to God's plan, Adam and Eve became one. Their marriage was a union of two persons, one male and one female. Without losing their individual identity, something new had been created: the marriage couple. The two became one. And then, the one became three! Then four, five, and so on. It was in their union of persons that Adam and Eve *together* best reflected the image of the triune God who had created them in his image. Their unity was the prerequisite for their fertility. Though they were not able to create *ex nihilo* as God had created, they were able to procreate!

Genesis 1–2 introduces us to ground zero for the human experience. When the home is right, then the world runs the way God intends it to run. When the home is wrong . . . well, things fall apart—as happened with Sodom and Gomorrah (see Gen 19).

Yes, our culture may be confused about marriage, but the Bible is crystal clear! It tells us that not only did human history *begin* with a marriage, but it will *end* with one as well (see Rev 19–22). The book of Revelation tells of that future day when the Great Prostitute, Babylon, will be destroyed and the New Jerusalem will appear "prepared as a bride adorned for her husband" (Rev 21:2). Christ, the groom, will marry the Church, his bride, and they will live happily ever after. Those who try to change the definition of marriage are tampering with the eternal plan of God. One day, they will be called to give an account for such brazen audacity!

Purpose: What Marriage Is For

Surveying what the Bible has to say about marriage, we might summarize its purpose in three great statements:

Sanctification. Marriage is, by definition, a union of differences. Male and female living together and striving for unity is a guaranteed recipe for conflict. We might say that incompatibility goes with the territory! Those who seek a life of tranquility and peace should not get married. But it is in this abrasive friction that something wonderful begins to happen. Like sandpaper, one spouse begins to rub away the bumps and imperfections of the other. It may hurt, but the outcome is very good. Both husband and wife, separately and corporately, begin to reflect more accurately the image of the triune God who created them and brought them together. God is more concerned about the holiness of the man and woman than he is about their happiness. Marriage thus becomes God's primary laboratory for producing saints!

Multiplication. God's first commandment to Adam and Eve helped them understand why they had been brought together: "Be fruitful, multiply, and fill the earth" (Gen 1:28). Not only was God encouraging the couple to express romantic love to one another, he was revealing his intention to propagate the species. But God was interested in much more than the number of children they would have. Adam and Eve were not rabbits. More than just a large family, God wanted them to have a godly family. He was concerned about the quality, not just the quantity of their children. Later in the book of Genesis, God will explain specifically why he chose Abraham from among all the peoples of the earth: "I have chosen him, that he may command his children and his household after him to keep the way of the Lord by doing righteousness and justice" (Gen 18:19). In the book of Malachi, God laments that the marriages in Israel have failed to do the one thing they were supposed to do; produce "godly offspring" (see Mal 2:14–15).

Illustration. "Let *us* make man in *our* image," God said (Gen 1:26 emphasis added). One of the primary reasons it was "not good" for Adam to be alone (see Gen 2:18), was because by himself he could not reflect the image of the tri-personned God who had created him. God is three, yet one. In his perfect union of three divine Persons, God illustrates the kind of corporate life he wants to see replicated in marriage. When the two become one they do not cease to be two persons; rather they create a new corporate identity, where one coinheres with the other. This union is both creative and fertile. It reflects God's image. The apostle Paul could not think about marriage without thinking about the nature of God; and he could not think about the nature of God without thinking about how a husband and wife live together as one. After writing to the Ephesians about marriage (Eph 5:22–33), he surprisingly says, "but I'm talking about Christ and the church" (Eph 5:32 NIV). For Paul, marriage was the ultimate illustration of the nature of God.

Function: How Marriage Works

One might think that having a clear understanding of the definition of marriage and its purpose would be all that a couple needed to make their marriage work. Unfortunately, life is more complicated than that.

Although knowing the "What?" and the "Why?" are extremely helpful, most husbands and wives continue to need help with the "How?".

The book of Genesis gives a surprising amount of information about the inner workings of several different marriages: Adam and Eve, Abraham and Sarah, Isaac and Rebekah, and Jacob and Rachel/Leah. Rather than hiding the flaws and sins of these husbands and wives, the Scripture highlights them! Each marriage, though ordained and blessed by God, has dysfunctional elements in it! We close this chapter with the prayer that the marriages of Genesis will be a source of great encouragement to you. The journey may be long and hard, but it's worth it!

Be careful whom you marry. Perhaps the best thing one can do to increase the possibility that one will have a good marriage is to think long and pray hard *before* you get married! Although some have tried to find a proven formula in the Bible for finding the perfect mate, it simply isn't there. Different cultures and different ages have used a wide variety of methods in selecting a spouse: arranged marriages, courtship, dating, online websites, etc. We see some of this variety in the Bible itself, where sometimes parents choose a wife for their son (Gen 21:21; 38:6) and sometimes they choose a husband for their daughter (Ruth 3:1–2; 1 Sam 18:21). Sometimes a man chooses his own wife and then seeks parental approval (Gen 34:4–8; Judg 14:2). Sometimes a woman seems to have the final decision in the matter (Gen 24:58). And sometimes children deliberately marry against their parents' wishes (Gen 26:34–35; 28:6–9). So while the Bible describes a wide variety of practices, it stops short of mandating one particular method as God's universal plan. However, one principle is stated clearly, strongly, and often. It is a transcultural absolute: do not marry outside the faith. This is what motivated Abraham to say to his servant, "You will not take a wife for my son from the Canaanites" (Gen 24:3). In the New Testament, Paul states the principle in these words: "Do not be unequally yoked with unbelievers" (2 Cor 6:14).

Love the one you're with. Which comes first? Love or marriage? In Western culture, the answer for most people seems obvious.

First, you fall in love and then you get married. Right? This is the pattern portrayed in countless movies and books. While there is certainly a measure of truth in this position, the Bible brings a much deeper perspective to the equation. The love story that we have been considering in this chapter tells us that Isaac "took Rebekah and she became his wife, and he loved her" (Gen 24:67). Wait a minute! Hasn't the text gotten it backwards? Rather than saying he loved the one he married, shouldn't it have said that he married the one he loved? Regardless of the level of emotional chemistry (*eros*) that may have been present before their wedding, true love (*agape*) between Isaac and Rebekah came *after* the vows had been said. Marriage, as God intends it to be, requires more than romantic feelings and sexual chemistry. It demands covenant faithfulness where the partners learn patience, forgiveness, and grace. It involves learning how to handle imperfections, annoying habits, and sins. This is how God showed covenant love to us. And this is how we are called to show covenant love to the one we married.

Be realistic and get help when you need it. In the coming chapters, we will learn that though the marriage of Isaac and Rebekah was clearly "made in heaven," it was filled with competition, secrecy, lies, and conflict. In fact, *every* marriage in Genesis is dysfunctional at one level or another. But rather than hiding this troubling fact, the author of Genesis seems to highlight it! The moral of the story is this: just because God leads two people together and blesses their union doesn't mean they won't struggle to make the marriage work.

So be encouraged. If your marriage is limping along and sometimes you wonder if it will survive—welcome to biblical reality! God's pattern for marriage takes into account real people, living in a real world, facing real problems. He wants to enter your brokenness, dysfunction, and sin so that he can do something beautiful and good; something that only the grace of God can do.

QUESTIONS FOR DISCUSSION

1. Do you believe secular burial practices have crept into the church? What burial practices can Christians use that bear witness to their faith before a watching world?
2. If you are married, how did you meet your wife? At what point did you know that she was "the one"? Would you consider your romance to be exemplary and a model that others should follow? Why or why not?
3. Why do you believe our culture is so confused about gender and marriage? What should Christians do to confront this issue?
4. Do you agree with the author that God's purpose in marriage is our holiness more than our happiness? Discuss this.
5. Which comes first, love or marriage?
6. Discuss the author's claim that marriages "made in heaven" can still be dysfunctional. What should we learn from this?

20
The Man in the Middle
Genesis 26:1–35

When it comes to relay races at track and field competitions, the 4 X 100-meter event is nearly always the most popular. Four athletes form *one* team, and together they run *one* race. But they don't run at the same time. They run in sequence, one after the other. The most critical moments are those when the baton is passed from one runner to the next. To fail in this endeavor is an error of the most serious magnitude. The goal, of course, is that the four runners, competing as a united team, will together win the race.

The last runner, called the anchor, is usually the fastest, while the first runner is typically the second fastest. People in the crowd often know their names and rise to cheer when they run their segments of the race. But runners #2 and #3 don't typically generate much excitement. As they run, spectators use the occasion to talk to their neighbors, check their phones, or order a hot dog. And yet, though their runs may be lackluster and forgettable in comparison, these two runners in the middle are just as important to the successful completion of the race as runners #1 and #4.

It is helpful to think of the four major characters in Genesis 12–50 as members of a relay team running the most important race in human history. When the gun fires, signaling the beginning of the race, Abraham sets out with such speed and determination that everyone in the watching crowd gasps in awe and amazement. It takes fourteen chapters to tell the amazing story of his legendary run (Gen

12–25). And then, running fourth, in the anchor position, is Joseph. Oh, how that boy could fly! Genesis devotes another fourteen chapters to describing one of the most perfect races ever run (Gen 37–50). After centuries of analysis, scholars still seem unable to find a single flaw in the way he ran his race. When he crossed the finish line it seemed that the eyes of the whole world were watching, cheering him on to victory.

It is interesting to note that in Genesis, the third runner, Jacob, attracts a surprising amount of attention. It takes eleven chapters to tell the story (Gen 25–35). Watching him run, we soon realize why: he dropped the baton! Though the handoff from his predecessor had been successful, he lost focus and the baton slipped out of his hand. For a few heart-pounding moments, it seemed that the race would be lost. The crowd held its breath as Jacob found the ability to pick up the baton and run again. Amazingly, he finished his leg of the race surprisingly well.

But that second runner in the relay; what was his name again? Oh, yeah, Isaac. According to Genesis, the most important events of his life may have been both before and after he had the baton. While he carried it, the entirety of his run can be told in one short chapter (Gen 26). We might say that his race was remarkable for being unremarkable! There were no major blunders, but neither were there any major triumphs. His run produced more yawns than cheers. Isaac teaches us the significance of being insignificant.

Perhaps you wonder why you have been called to run in a race where others on the team are so much faster and stronger than you. Perhaps you feel that, in comparison to others, your life is bland, boring, forgettable. Perhaps it appears that no one is even watching or caring about how you run your race. If this describes how you feel, then this chapter is for you! Like Isaac, God may have called you to be "the man in the middle." It just may be the case that the very ordinariness of your life is the thing that makes you so extraordinary!

Sonship

In studying Abraham's life, we saw his struggles to become a father. With God's help, not only did he become a father; he became a *great* father, the quintessential father; *Father* Abraham, the father of all who believe (cf. Rom 4:16). But now, as the narrative of Genesis transitions from Abraham to Isaac, the emphasis changes. No longer is the focus on fatherhood; it is now on sonship. As Abraham modeled what it means to be a father, so Isaac models what it means to be a son. Sonship shaped Isaac's identity and became the defining characteristic of his life.[1] Of course, Isaac too must one day also become a father. But in Genesis, the Isaac narrative puts the focus on the way in which he, perhaps more than any other person in history, exemplifies what sonship is all about. Isaac is the quintessential son.

At first, one might envy the perks and advantages that Isaac had as a son. Being born into the family of a great man who would be the founder of a nation and shaper of human history was undoubtedly a great privilege. From the outside, Isaac's life seems almost idyllic. But being a son is harder than it first appears. Just as Genesis reveals how Abraham struggled to be a good father, so it reveals how Isaac struggled to be a good son.

Every son, simply by being a son, is defined in relation to his parents. His ethnicity, language, culture and even his name have all been predetermined. No one even asked him if he wanted to be born! To be a son is to be given life and identity by someone else—to be dependent, derivative, and subordinate. To be the son of a great father, a spiritual giant, accentuates these realities many times over. From the very moment of his birth, before we know any details of his life, we easily imagine that Isaac will be permanently overshadowed by his famous father. Even as an adult he will always be "Abraham's boy." Leon Kass writes insightfully:

> Precisely to reveal the problem of sonship, especially within the covenant and the new way, the script calls for a man weaker and paler than Abraham who nevertheless will not in the end reject his father's example. The text does not disappoint expectations. Compared to Abraham, Isaac

---

1   In emphasizing the role of a "son" rather than the grammatically more cumbersome "son or daughter," the author means no disrespect to women. He is simply following the example of Scripture. Obviously, what the Bible has to say about "sons" is applicable as well for "daughters."

appears drab, passive, and gullible, more victim than hero, a man of few words and prosaic deeds. . . . Yet despite—or is it because of?—the absence of large natural virtues, Isaac finally succeeds his father as a conveyer of the covenant. If such a son can inherit from his superior father and grow into his father's replacement, perhaps anyone can.[2]

Where fathers are proactive, decisive, and strong, sons, precisely because of their relationship to their father, are more passive, responsive, and submissive. This reality helps us to better understand the difficult race that Isaac was called on to run.

Fathers give life	Sons receive life
Fathers forge their own identity	Sons are given an identity
Fathers dedicate their children to God	Sons are dedicated to God
Fathers provide	Sons are provided for
Fathers protect	Sons are protected
Fathers bless	Sons are blessed
Fathers lead	Sons are led
Fathers teach	Sons are taught
Fathers make things happen	Sons respond to what happens
Fathers are proactive	Sons are reactive
Fathers sometimes make mistakes	Sons live with the consequences

Now, perhaps, we are better prepared to understand Isaac's unique and indispensable role as "the man in the middle." Running second in the relay race, Isaac's run is noteworthy precisely because it is so unnoteworthy. The fact that his race was unheroic made Isaac a true hero!

Isaac's identity as a son began when his ninety-year-old mother, Sarah, conceived and then gave him birth. Everyone understood that his birth was a miracle gift of God's grace. When Ishmael, his older half-brother, mocked and bullied him, Isaac's mother came to the rescue. One gets the impression that young Isaac was coddled, pampered, and spoiled by his doting, elderly mother.

---

2   Kass, *The Beginning of Wisdom*, 353.

Isaac must have often wondered about the meaning of his name: "He laughs." What kind of a name is *that*? Undoubtedly, his parents had told him the story of his miracle birth and how God himself had chosen the name (Gen 17:19). But why "Laughter"? In a world where names were very significant, Isaac must have scratched his head about such a strange name. His father's name (Abraham) had deep spiritual significance ("father of a multitude"—see Gen 17:5) as did the name of his son (Israel means "he struggles with God"—see Gen 32:28). But "Laughter"? Perhaps Isaac wondered: "Does that mean I'm a joke? Or perhaps that I'm not to be taken seriously?"

Repeatedly the narrative tells of how Isaac had to passively receive what was chosen for him by others. For example, his circumcision and dedication to God; no one asked *his* opinion on the matter! His father simply made the decision for him and informed him that he was now a member of God's covenant community (see Gen 21:4).

In no other single event was Isaac's sonship put to the test as it was on Mount Moriah where his father almost killed his son (see Gen 22). As we saw in Chapter Eighteen, Isaac was old enough and strong enough to resist his father's actions but instead, he freely chose to cooperate. In no other single event was Isaac's sonship more magnificent than when he freely surrendered to the will of his father. But even here on Mount Moriah, Isaac's heroic actions are overshadowed by those of his father. Whenever this story is told down through the centuries, it is typically Abraham, not Isaac, who is celebrated and remembered as the main character in the drama.

The next event recorded in Isaac's life is the death of his mother (see Gen 23). He is thirty-seven years old and still single, apparently living with his parents. His mother's death must have been very difficult in that Isaac grieved her passing for several years (see Gen 24:67).

Perhaps the most intriguing snapshot we have of Isaac's passivity is his marriage to Rebekah when he is forty years old (see Gen 25:20). Is his slowness to marry yet another hint of his hesitancy to lead and make decisions? Is this another indication that Isaac prefers to let things happen rather than make things happen? In this case, his father once again steps up and takes the initiative and proactively finds a wife for his son (see Gen 24).

THE DEPARTMENT OF REDUNDANCY DEPARTMENT

In telling the story of Isaac, the second patriarch of Israel, the Scriptures depict a man who is passive, silent, and at times, impotent—a reactor more than an actor. On occasion, he seems almost to take the role of a victim. While other men and women in Genesis *make* things happen, Isaac seems to prefer to *watch* things happen. He spends most of his life responding to the actions of others. Like Adam centuries earlier, Isaac is a classic portrayal of the silent male.

Although his life spans many chapters (Gen 21–35), in only one do we see him acting like a leader, a patriarch. Genesis 26 describes that season of Isaac's life when he took the baton and ran his portion of the race. This is the single chapter where we see his proactive contribution to the patriarchal legacy. The son has become a man.

Though the three stories told in Genesis 26 are all about Isaac, one cannot miss the similarities to Abraham's story. In fact, the text emphasizes Abraham, now dead and buried, almost as much as Isaac. The son, it seems, is an echo of his father. Even as an adult, running his own race, Isaac cannot escape the ever-present shadow of his father's influence.

> *Now there was a famine in the land, besides the former famine that was in the days of Abraham. And Isaac went to Gerar to Abimelech king of the Philistines. And the* LORD *appeared to him and said, "Do not go down to Egypt; dwell in the land of which I shall tell you. Sojourn in this land, and I will be with you and will bless you, for to you and to your offspring I will give all these lands, and I will establish the oath that I swore to Abraham your father. I will multiply your offspring as the stars of heaven and will give to your offspring all these lands. And in your offspring all the nations of the earth shall be blessed, because Abraham obeyed my voice and kept my charge, my commandments, my statutes, and my laws." (Gen 26:1–5)*

It is interesting to note that Abraham's story began with the command, "Go" (Gen 12:1), but Isaac's story begins with the command,

"Stay" (Gen 26:3 NIV). This distinction sets the tone for how Isaac's life will be so very different from that of his father. Called to forsake everything and leave his home in Ur of the Chaldeans to follow God's call, Abraham's life was an exciting journey of adventure, danger, and discovery. In comparison, Isaac's call to stay home seems bland, dull, and boring. His task is to preserve and maintain the victories that his father has won. Abraham was called to go forth and conquer. Isaac was told to stay home and keep shop; be still and know that God is God.

Just as Abraham had to deal with famine in the land of Canaan (Gen 12:10), so did his son (Gen 26:1). Warned by God, however, Isaac was able to avert the mistake his father had made by going down to Egypt.

The most important way that Isaac's life echoes his father's is in the renewal of the covenant. When "the Lord appeared" to Isaac (Gen 26:2), repeating the same promises he had made to Abraham, we have the assurance that the covenant has been passed on to the next generation. In no other single event was the transition from father to son more important than this. Genesis 26 reassures us that Isaac is now not just a son of Abraham, he is a true son of the covenant. No longer is his faith merely a mechanical repetition of a creed he learned from his father. Isaac now has a faith of his own.

> *So Isaac settled in Gerar. When the men of the place asked him about his wife, he said, "She is my sister," for he feared to say, "My wife," thinking, "lest the men of the place should kill me because of Rebekah," because she was attractive in appearance. When he had been there a long time, Abimelech king of the Philistines looked out of a window and saw Isaac laughing with Rebekah his wife. So Abimelech called Isaac and said, "Behold, she is your wife. How then could you say, 'She is my sister'?" (Gen 26:6–9)*

Sound familiar? In Genesis 12:10–20 we saw how Abraham lied to Pharaoh during his visit to Egypt, claiming that Sarah was his sister. Then in Genesis 20 Abraham visited the land of Gerar and again pretended that Sarah was his sister to save his own skin. The king's name was Abimelech.[3] What are we to make of the fact that now, decades later, Isaac is pulling a similar stunt with a king who has the same name? What is going on here?

These stories remind us of the maxim: like father, like son. It is obvious where Isaac learned the wicked idea of protecting himself by putting his wife in mortal danger. He learned it from his daddy! This does not excuse Isaac's sin, but it does make it understandable. Not only is Abraham's influence a source of blessing, this story reminds us that fathers can leave a bad legacy for their children as well as a good one.

A third story told in Genesis 26 describes how Isaac became a businessman and prospered.

> *And Isaac sowed in that land and reaped in the same year a hundredfold. The* LORD *blessed him, and the man became rich, and gained more and more until he became very wealthy. He had possessions of flocks and herds and many servants, so that the Philistines envied him. (Now the Philistines had stopped and filled with earth all the wells that his father's servants had dug in the days of Abraham his father.) And Abimelech said to Isaac, "Go away from us, for you are much mightier than we." So Isaac departed from there and encamped in the Valley of Gerar and settled there. And Isaac dug again the wells of water that had been dug in the days of Abraham his father, which the Philistines had stopped after the death of Abraham. And he gave them the names that his father had given them. (Gen 26:12–18)*

The Scriptures recognize that Isaac is a good businessman but credit his wealth not so much to his savvy and skill as to the legacy of his father's blessing. It is the wells that Abraham dug that enable Isaac to become so prosperous. This fills his pagan neighbors with jealousy. They are not strong enough to force Isaac to leave, so they sabotage his wells, filling them with dirt. Isaac refuses to retaliate and simply re-digs the wells his father had dug, giving them the same names his

---

[3] The time interval between Genesis 20 (Abraham and Abimelech) and Genesis 26 (Isaac and Abimelech) is about 75 years. It is therefore unlikely that the two Abimelechs are the same person. Probably, we are dealing with a father and son, or even a grandfather and a grandson who have the same name.

father had given them. The covenant of peace that Isaac makes with Abimelech (Gen 26:26–33) is remarkably similar to the one his father had made many years earlier (see Gen 21:22–34).

Once again, God confirms his covenant with Isaac and once again the echoes of father Abraham run like a thread through the promise God makes:

> *And the* LORD *appeared to him the same night and said, "I am the God of Abraham your father. Fear not, for I am with you and will bless you and multiply your offspring for my servant Abraham's sake." So he built an altar there and called upon the name of the* LORD *and pitched his tent there. And there Isaac›s servants dug a well. (Gen 26:24–25)*

It's tough to be a son. And it's especially tough to be the son of a *great* father. Isaac must have often wondered if he would ever be anything more than an echo of his father's life. His story seemed to be a repetition of the same promises, issues, neighbors, wells, and temptations that his father experienced. It seemed that everything he was and all that he had was because of his father, whose influence continued to overshadow everything in his life. Was he to be a son forever? Would he ever be taken seriously as an adult? Would the son ever become a father himself?

More than any other character in the Bible, Isaac teaches us what sonship is all about. Just as Abraham is the quintessential father, so Isaac is the quintessential son. Eventually, he will succeed in passing the baton of the covenant to his own son. But the real message of Isaac's life, as told in Genesis, is not his fatherhood, but his sonship. The narrative in Genesis introduces us not only to the blessings of being a son, but also to its challenges and dangers. Overshadowed by his father, pampered by his mother, and manipulated by his wife (see the next chapter), Isaac spends most of his life reacting to what happens rather than acting. He illustrates how difficult it is to be the man in the middle. Although Isaac's race may have been short, routine, and to some degree forgettable, he succeeds in the one thing that really matters: passing the baton to the next generation. This is what qualifies him to be a patriarch. And this is what makes him a hero we should all aspire to imitate!

The Family Tree

One of the greatest messages of the book of Genesis is found not in the details of the lives of its characters but in the overall big picture when viewed as a whole. When seen from 10,000 feet, the earth reveals patterns, shapes, and connections that are unnoticed from ground level. In a similar manner, Genesis 12–50, looked at as a whole, from 10,000 feet as it were, reveals a panoramic grand narrative that traces the transmission of the faith from one generation to the next. Abraham, Isaac, Jacob, and Joseph are not separate, disconnected stories. No, seen together, these four men are relay runners on a *single* team, running in a *single* race, seeking to win a *single* prize.

The big story in Genesis is how Abraham passed the baton of faith to Isaac who passed the baton to Jacob who passed the baton to Joseph. Genesis is relevant for us today because the same principles that were at work in the transmission of the faith in the time of the patriarchs are at work today. In our families, churches, and institutions, we too are part of a relay race. Those before us passed the baton of faith to us who, in turn, are expected to pass the baton to the next generation. Will the transmission of faith be successful, or will someone drop the baton? Will the faith be diluted or deformed in the process? These are questions of great importance! The future of the world hangs in the balance on how these questions are answered.

In closing, let's take a quick survey of Genesis 12–50 and summarize what Abraham, Isaac, Jacob, and Joseph teach us about the transmission of the faith. Representing four different generations, these men help us to better understand the typical way that the faith is diluted and deformed as it is passed from father to son. But one must never assume that such downward generational drift is inevitable. The progression outlined here is not a fixed formula, thanks be to God! Genesis reminds us that the general tendency, over time, is that faith will diminish, commitment will waver, convictions will be compromised, love will grow cold, and fire will go out. This is a frightful reality we dare not ignore. But the fact that Scripture warns us about these things gives us the reassurance that God stands ready to help us work against this downward pull.

Abraham—First-generation Faith

Abraham is a powerful illustration of what it is like to turn from unbelief to faith, from death to life, from the kingdom of darkness to the kingdom of light. Born into paganism and idolatry, Abraham's conversion was dramatic and clear. His choice to put his trust in God was an adult decision, freely made after maturely considering the matter. One day he was an unbeliever, then, suddenly, he believed. Life was never again the same. As a result, Abraham's faith was passionate, bold, and intense. Everyone knew he was a believer; some probably thought he was a fanatic. His faith was a whole-hearted love relationship with the God who had called him out of bondage into glorious liberty. His life was one of full and complete surrender to the will of God. Perhaps the best symbol of Abraham's life is an altar. It seemed that wherever he went, he built an altar where he could sacrifice, give thanks, and commune with God: at Shechem (Gen 12:6–7), at Bethel (Gen 12:8), at Hebron (Gen 13:14–18), and most famously at Mount Moriah (Gen 22:9).

Isaac—Second-generation Faith

How different Isaac's spiritual journey was compared to that of his father. While Abraham made an adult choice to enter a covenant relationship with God, Isaac was born into a family where this choice had already been made for him! Circumcised when he was an infant, no one asked Isaac if he wanted to be part of God's covenant family. He was expected to simply go along with the plan. While Abraham was raised in a pagan environment of idolatry and sin, Isaac was raised in a godly home with praying parents, where worship and faith were the norm. Abraham obtained God's blessing through the obedience of faith. Isaac simply inherited those blessings and enjoyed the benefits! While the symbol of Abraham's life was an altar, perhaps the best symbol of Isaac's life was a well, representing worldly prosperity and wealth. Wherever he went, he dug a well: at Esek, Sitnah, Rehoboth, and Beersheba (see Gen 26:17–25, 32).

It is significant that Isaac's story, as told in Genesis, contains no account of a deeper work of grace. There is no indication that he ever came to a spiritual crisis where the faith of his childhood became the faith of a man. We saw that Abraham had a deeper experience later in life when he met God in such a new and profound way that God changed his name to commemorate the moment (see Gen 17). We will learn in future chapters that Jacob, Isaac's son, also had a transformative experience of grace. Beyond his initial encounter with God when he had a vision of a ladder reaching to heaven (see Gen 28:10–22), Jacob had a deeper experience when he wrestled with the angel (see Gen 32:22–32). This second encounter with God was so profound that he too received a new name, Israel. Thus, it seems significant that Isaac, the man in the middle, had no such testimony. Although he had an authentic relationship with God, there is no indication that he ever came to a place of full surrender and complete trust. Unlike his father and his son, he never received a new name.

Jacob—Third-generation Faith

Growing up with a father like Isaac, a nice man who was nominally religious and moderately spiritual, Jacob apparently failed to see the vital importance of personal faith and total consecration. His father's home was a place of lukewarm religious respectability. He concluded that the faith of his fathers could be placed in a compartment labeled "religion." Jacob therefore had no trouble calling himself a believer while living in disobedience to God's will. Filled with selfish ambition, Jacob's goal was to look out for number one. If he could use God to further his own agenda, so much the better.

Abraham built altars and Isaac dug wells. Jacob's life is perhaps best characterized by the pillars he erected. Although these shrines looked somewhat like an altar, they were not at all the same thing! At Bethel, Jacob erected a pillar to commemorate his dream of the stairway to heaven (Gen 28:16–22) and later set up a second pillar at the same location when God met him there a second time (Gen 35:9–

15). He erected another pillar at Mizpah/Gilead to commemorate the covenant he made with Laban (Gen 31:43–49) and yet another one in Bethlehem to mark the grave of his wife Rachel (Gen 35:16–20). Third-generation believers are quick to respect history and tradition but typically stop short of whole-hearted devotion.

Fourth-Generation Faith and Beyond

Although Jacob is the last of the three patriarchs, the book of Genesis does not stop there. By telling how the faith was transmitted to Joseph, the book ends on a note of hope that all future generations will have the capacity to be part of God's covenant family. Genesis devotes fourteen chapters to telling the amazing story of Joseph (Gen 37–50). A fourth-generation believer, Joseph recaptures the first-generation passion and authenticity of his great grandfather, Abraham. With Joseph, the story of the transmission of the faith has come full circle. The author of Genesis is assuring us that, even when spiritual drift is at its worst and it appears that true faith is about to vanish from the earth, God can raise up a Joseph generation to revive his work and restore his church.

Abraham, Isaac, Jacob, and Joseph; together they compose an amazing relay team. And what a race they ran! None of them ran perfectly. Sometimes they stumbled. Occasionally, they struggled to hold on to the baton. But in the one thing that ultimately mattered, each runner was successful: he received the baton of faith and then, when the time was right, passed it on to the next runner. In this, they are all heroes, and their lives are to be emulated.

So even to old age and gray hairs,
O God, do not forsake me,
until I proclaim your might to another generation,
your power to all those to come. (Ps 71:18)

GENERATIONAL DRIFT

The chart attempts to summarize what typically happens to the faith when it is transferred from one generation to the next.

	First Generation	Second Generation	Third Generation
Person	Abraham	Isaac	Jacob
Symbol	Altar	Well	Pillar
God	Has a relationship	Has a religion	Performs duties
Heart	Whole-hearted	Half-hearted	Hard-hearted
Character	Holy	Nice	Selfish
Passion	Seeks the blessing	Enjoys the blessing	Feels entitled to the blessing
Experience	Knows God	Knows about God	Doesn't know God
Focus	To please God	To please others	To please self
World	Lives for the kingdom of God	Tries to live in two worlds at same time	Lives for the kingdom of this world

QUESTIONS FOR DISCUSSION

1. The author compares the four main characters of Genesis to runners in a relay race. Explain in your own words what he means and why this is relevant for us today.
2. Describe what, for you, is the hardest part about being a son (or a daughter).
3. Isaac lived in the shadow of his father. In many ways, his life was an echo of his father's life. Is this a good thing or a bad thing? Explain.
4. Isaac repeated the sins of his father when he tried to protect himself by claiming his wife was his sister. Are there sins in your family that are passed from one generation to the next? What would it take to break the cycle?
5. Think about the generations in your own family. As you look at the chart, which generation best describes you? What lessons have you learned from this study?
6. Think about your children and your grandchildren (if you have them). What is the Lord saying to you about them?

21
Jake the Snake
Genesis 25:19–34; 27:1–28:9

He is called Jacob for a reason! The name describes his character. Born grasping the heel of his twin brother, who came out of the womb first, the Hebrew term *yakob* was given to him, meaning "he takes by the heel" (see Gen 25:26). Figuratively, the word thus describes someone who "trips from behind," "cheats," and "deceives." Genesis makes it clear that Jacob deserves his name. Constantly in conflict with someone, he uses deception and trickery to subdue his opponents. Jacob's life is a lengthy litany of competition with one rival after another.

Perhaps the best way to capture the essence of Jacob's life and character is to picture him as a professional wrestler. Yes, I'm talking about those wild and crazy musclemen with names like Hulk Hogan, Andre the Giant, and The Undertaker, who compete with one another in events like Royal Rumble, WrestleMania, and SmackDown. Everybody knows these guys don't fight fairly! They choke, bite, pull hair, break arms, and bribe the officials. Supposedly, this all makes for great entertainment. One of the most famous wrestlers of recent memory is a fighter named Jake Roberts, better known as Jake the Snake. Often bringing a python into the ring, this rascal was notorious for being deceptive and fighting unfairly. Somehow, the moniker "Jake the Snake" seems appropriate for Jacob, the third patriarch of Israel.

Jacob's life is characterized by a series of conflicts. One after another he steps into the ring to wrestle with an opponent whom he intends to pin to the mat one way or another. First, we find Jacob wrestling with his elder, twin brother Esau (Gen 25–28). He wins this match only by trickery and deception. The second wrestling match is between Jacob and his father-in-law, Laban (Gen 29–31). This competition has no clear winner. The important thing to notice, however, is that Jacob gets a taste of his own medicine. Laban is a trickster himself who doesn't fight fairly, and the deceiver is deceived. In the third match, Jacob wrestles with God (Gen 32). At last, Jacob meets his true "Adversary." Here he discovers that, all along, his real struggle in life has been not with his brother and not with his father-in-law, but with God. Ironically, Jake the Snake wins this match by losing it!

In this chapter, we will examine Jacob's first wrestling match, the one with his brother Esau (Gen 25:19–34; 27:1–28:9). We could say that this match has three rounds: wrestling in the womb (Gen 25:19–28), wrestling for the birthright (Gen 25:29–34), and wrestling for the blessing (Gen 27:1–28:9).

Wrestling in the Womb

In answer to Isaac's prayer, God enables his wife, barren for twenty years, to become pregnant. Though the promise of new life must have brought great joy, Isaac and Rebekah soon discover that the Lord has answered their prayer in a way they could have never imagined. Rebekah conceives twins and the pregnancy is very difficult.

> *The children struggled together within her, and she said, "If it is thus, why is this happening to me?" So she went to inquire of the* Lord. *And the* Lord *said to her, "Two nations are in your womb, and two peoples from within you shall be divided; the one shall be stronger than the other, the older shall serve the younger." When her days to give birth were completed, behold, there were twins in her womb. The first came out red, all his body like a hairy cloak, so they called his name Esau. Afterward his brother came out with his hand holding Esau's heel, so his name was called Jacob. Isaac was sixty years old when she bore them. (Gen 25:22–26)*

The author of Genesis talks about Esau and Jacob in the womb as if they are *already* members of the human family. They are treated as persons, not "fetal tissue." Today, in a culture that routinely denies legal status to the unborn, this biblical perspective is a powerful reminder of how God thinks about those in the womb.

The hardest thing to understand about Rebekah's pregnancy, however, is not the pain involved in bearing twins, but the prophetic announcement: "the older shall serve the younger" (Gen 25:23). In choosing the second-born to have senior status, God is going against cultural norms. Though this is perhaps a surprise, it is not that unusual. There are numerous occasions in the Bible when God choses a younger brother to take the place of his older sibling: Isaac over Ishmael, Ephraim over Manasseh, David over his brothers, Solomon over Adonijah, etc. God's ways are often contrary to man's ways. The problem that many have is that God seems to impose his will on these two boys while they are still in the womb! Paul states the issue this way: "though they were not yet born and had done nothing either good or bad," God declared that the older would serve the younger (Rom 9:11–12). For many people, this seems unfair and smacks of divine favoritism. It appears that God has predetermined what will happen to each twin and nothing they do can change it. Their fate is sealed. Do Jacob and Esau have no say in their own destiny? Does God's sovereign plan for their lives rob them of their own free will? Although this is not the place to have an extended discussion of the doctrines of election and predestination, a few comments are in order.

First, notice that in speaking about the future, God is forecasting *the roles* that Jacob and Esau will play, not predetermining their eternal salvation. In choosing Jacob over Esau, God is not talking about final destinies. He is simply announcing his decision to use Jacob, and not his brother, to be the one through whom the nation of Israel and the Messiah will come. God also has a plan for Esau and his descendants, the Edomites. But Edom is just another nation in history, one among hundreds. Though God loves the Edomites, they are *not* his chosen people. That honor belongs to Israel alone. To pretend that this passage refers to a sovereign, unchangeable decree that Jacob will go to heaven and Esau will go to hell is to read a meaning into the text that is simply not there!

As the author of human history, God is proclaiming the roles and functions that he has established for two of his characters to play. This does not mean Jacob and Esau are puppets, or that they have no say in their own lives and destinies. As their stories unfold in Genesis, we learn that both men make many choices, some good and some bad. God holds them both fully responsible for their actions. It is true that they cannot change the roles they have been assigned to play. Jacob's lineage, not Esau's, is where God will work out his covenant purposes for the world. This is fixed and unchangeable. Regardless of how Jacob and Esau may feel about this or how hard they may try to change it, God's will cannot be altered. But when it comes to their personal lives and individual destinies, both Jacob and Esau have the freedom and the responsibility to make their own choices.

God tells us in Malachi 1:3, echoed by Paul in Romans 9:10–13, "I have loved Jacob, but Esau I have hated." In saying that he "loves" Jacob, God is not expressing favoritism! He is explaining rather his election of Jacob and his descendants to be the channel through whom his covenant purposes will be worked out in the world. In saying that he "hates" Esau, God is not expressing animosity or ill will. The strong words imply rather, that in comparison to God's amazing purpose for Jacob and his descendants, his plan for Esau seems negligible.

Secondly, when God says that the older son will serve the younger, we need to understand that the words apply to much more than single individuals. In choosing Jacob, God is choosing his descendants, the nation of Israel, the Jewish people. God is speaking corporately, not individually. The election of Jacob in Rebekah's womb is about the nation that will come from his lineage, the chosen people. God wants everyone to understand that his purposes for the world can only be understood through the people he has chosen. And God specifically wants his people to know that they belong to him not because they are racially or morally superior to others, but because, in the divine mystery of his sovereign will, he chose them. Before they had done anything good or bad, God decided that he would work in them and through them to show his redemptive plan to the entire world. One misunderstands what the Bible has to say about election and predestination when one thinks only in terms of individuals and their eternal salvation.

Finally, the fact that God predicts what will happen in the lives of Jacob and Esau in the future does not mean that he *causes* these future events to happen. To know that something will happen does not make it happen. Foreknowledge is not foreordination. Every parent understands this! When I was a spiritually lost teenager, my father prophesied what would happen if I went to the beach on spring break. His prediction came true. But he certainly wasn't the cause of my stupid choices! His ability to foresee events in my future was based on the simple fact that he knew me well and loved me deeply.

With God, our heavenly Father, the issue of foreknowledge is even more complex. Because he is eternal and lives outside of time, in an eternal now, God sees and experiences all events concurrently—past, present, and future. So, one can honestly ask: Is God's foreknowledge of Jacob and Esau's behavior the cause or the effect of their future choices? Do the boys do what they do because they were predestined to do it or do their actions (foreknown by God) cause God to foretell their choices? In other words, are our actions determined by God's prophetic word or is God's prophetic word determined by what he already knows we will do? Which comes first, the chicken or the egg?

God knows the future and our role in it and yet he has given us free will. We decide whether we will follow God's plan for our lives or not. Though God is sovereign, we have a will of our own. Those who choose to trust in God prove that they are chosen. Those who turn their backs on God's free offer of salvation prove only that they are guilty of a great sin.

To be sure, none of us will ever be able to fully comprehend or explain how divine sovereignty and human freedom work together. After three chapters of wrestling with these questions in Romans,

Paul concludes by saying: "Oh, the depth of the riches and wisdom and knowledge of God! How unsearchable are his judgments and how inscrutable his ways!" (Rom 12:33).

Genesis 25:19–28 is important not only because of its treatment of divine foreknowledge and predestination but also because of the insight it gives into the troubling dynamics at work in the family of Isaac and Rebekah. The sibling rivalry going on in the womb will only get worse as the story unfolds. But it is the marital discord seen in parental favoritism that the author of Genesis highlights in the next verses. Although Isaac and Rebekah had a marriage made in heaven, their relationship was visibly dysfunctional.

> *When the boys grew up, Esau was a skillful hunter, a man of the field, while Jacob was a quiet man, dwelling in tents. Isaac loved Esau because he ate of his game, but Rebekah loved Jacob. (Gen 25:27–28)*

Jacob and Esau are not identical twins. Not only is their appearance different, but so are their temperaments. Esau is the macho, outdoors type while Jacob is more of a homebody. Rebekah seems to prefer Jacob because of God's prophetic announcement that the second-born would have prominence over the first-born. But Isaac's preference for Esau is harder to understand. Had he heard God's prophecy? Had he, in old age, perhaps forgotten it? Did he think he could ignore it or change it? The only explanation given for his favoritism is that he loved the way Esau cooked. In other words, Isaac prefers the wrong son for a bad reason! This is going to cause great problems in the family as we are about to see.

Wrestling for the Birthright

The second round of Jacob's wrestling match with his brother occurred this way:

> *Once when Jacob was cooking stew, Esau came in from the field, and he was exhausted. And Esau said to Jacob, "Let me eat some of that red stew, for I am exhausted!" (Therefore his name was called Edom.) Jacob said, "Sell me your birthright now." Esau said, "I am about to die; of what use is a birthright*

> *to me?" Jacob said, "Swear to me now." So he swore to him and sold his birthright to Jacob. Then Jacob gave Esau bread and lentil stew, and he ate and drank and rose and went his way. Thus Esau despised his birthright. (Gen 25:29–34)*

Although Jacob's actions are cruel, cold, and calculating, he does nothing deceitful here. Perhaps his mother had told him that one day the birthright would be his. If so, his manipulative actions express his attempt to do God's will man's way. Once again, Genesis teaches us that the consequences are always devastating when we seek to do the work of the Spirit in the power of the flesh.

Esau is depicted as a slave to his appetites, fixated on immediate gratification. Like a brute, he points and grunts: "Red stuff; eat!" As in the Garden of Eden, the temptation comes through food. Esau is more interested in short-term satisfaction than long-term joy. The text specifies that he was both tired and hungry. Recovery groups often use the acronym HALT to help people recognize when sin is crouching at the door. If one is feeling Hungry, Angry, Lonely, or Tired—be careful, watch out! These conditions make one especially vulnerable to temptation and making choices one will later regret.

It is frankly hard to tell whose actions are worse: Esau's or Jacob's. Jacob was cruel and manipulative, but he did not steal the birthright; he purchased it. To his credit, he strongly desired something of great value; he wanted to have something that was worth having. His methods for obtaining the prize, however, were unscrupulous and wrong. But Scripture seems to hint that Esau is guilty of the greater sin. He sold his birthright for a bowl of porridge! A commentary has been added to the text: "Thus Esau despised his birthright" (Gen 26:34). This is the only occasion in the entire book of Genesis when the author feels compelled to pronounce judgment on someone's actions. The word means that he had a flippant attitude toward his birthright and considered it worthless.

Although Jacob won this second round of the wrestling match with his brother, he destroyed their relationship. The price of victory was a deep and bitter animosity that continued to fester between the two brothers for years to come. The competitive nature of their relationship would spill over into the decisive third round of their wrestling match.

WRESTLING FOR THE BLESSING

Now that Jacob has the birthright (*bekorah*), he and his mother (*Rebekah*) conspire to steal the blessing (*beraka*). In Hebrew, the repetition of similar sounds has a pleasing effect on the ear as the story is told. For Jacob to be recognized as Isaac's heir, the recipient of the Abrahamic covenant, and the third patriarch of Israel, he needs more than the *bekorah*. He needs his father's *beraka* as well. It is important to notice that Rebekah is more concerned than Jacob that this second step be taken. She is willing to do whatever it takes to ensure that God's covenant promise falls fully on her favorite son.

Isaac, however, is focused on giving his blessing to Esau, his favorite son. He puts in motion a plan that will make the wrong son the rightful heir. Rebekah is horrified that her husband, the head of her home and the second patriarch of Israel, is about to make a tragic mistake. But what can she do? Should she quietly submit to his misguided leadership? Should she usurp authority and act in his place? Should she leave? File for divorce? Her options are few. In such a desperate situation, Rebekah chooses the only path she believes is open to her: deception. Enlisting Jacob's help in her conspiracy, she implements a plan that, in her opinion, will save the day. Preparing Isaac's favorite meal, she has Jacob dress in his brother's clothing and pulls off one of the greatest scams in the Bible. Amazingly, it works! Blind Isaac, tricked by his own wife and son, gives his blessing to Jacob, making him the legitimate heir of the family.

When Esau discovers what has happened, he is enraged and tries desperately to reverse his father's decision. But it is too late. The blessing, once given, cannot be revoked. With bitter hatred and a desire for revenge, Esau vows to kill his brother after his father dies. Rebekah, realizing that things at home are deteriorating rapidly, sends Jacob far away to her brother Laban for safety. He will remain there for twenty long years. She will never see her favorite son again.

This sad story ends, however, on a positive note. These events, troubling as they are, have caused Isaac to finally come to his senses. In this closing episode, he finally manifests the dignity and authority of a true patriarch! With full awareness of what he is doing and why he is doing it, he reaffirms his blessing to Jacob and instructs him to go to Mesopotamia and find the right kind of wife. If there was any question concerning his first blessing of Jacob, when he was deceived, there is no question now! In terms of his role as the third patriarch of Israel, this was Isaac's finest hour!

> *Then Isaac called Jacob and blessed him and directed him, "You must not take a wife from the Canaanite women. Arise, go to Paddan-aram to the house of Bethuel your mother's father, and take as your wife from there one of the daughters of Laban your mother's brother. God Almighty bless you and make you fruitful and multiply you, that you may become a company of peoples. May he give the blessing of Abraham to you and to your offspring with you, that you may take possession of the land of your sojournings that God gave to Abraham!" Thus Isaac sent Jacob away. (Gen 28:1–5)*

DYSFUNCTION JUNCTION

Before closing this sad chapter, it will be helpful to examine more closely the four characters in this story one at a time. Each bears a measure of responsibility for the sin and dysfunction that is tearing this family apart. As we better understand what they did wrong in their family so long ago, perhaps it will help us to protect our families today from similar types of destructive family dynamics.

Esau

At first glance, some may feel pity for Esau. He was victimized by his own mother and sabotaged by his twin brother. We may be tempted to say, "Poor boy; it's so unfair that those awful people ganged up on you like that." Although the Scripture makes no attempt to minimize the wrongs that were committed against him, the text is quick to remind us that Esau is by no means innocent and pure. Perhaps the clearest revelation of his true character is seen in the way he "despised" his birthright (see Gen 25:29–34). Controlled by his appetites and living for the present moment, Esau only wanted worldly pleasures and had no interest in spiritual realities. And though he swore an oath to the validity of the transaction when he sold the birthright to his brother, we soon learn that, when it came time for the paternal blessing, he still claimed to be the rightful heir.

Our worst fears about Esau's worldly, rebellious character are confirmed when we learn of his multiple marriages. In ugly defiance of his parents' desire, he married two Hittite women; Judith and Basemath (see Gen 26:34–35; 27:46). These marriages brought great grief to Isaac and Rebekah and made life bitter for them. Later, trying to repair the damaged relationship with his parents, Esau married a cousin, a daughter of Ishmael named Mahalath (see Gen 28:6–9). His lame attempt at restitution, however, did little to mend the breach. Like closing the barn door after the horses have already escaped, his effort was too little, too late.

The New Testament confirms Esau's wicked character, using him to illustrate the danger of worldliness and sin that can take root in the heart of members of God's covenant family.

> *See to it that no one fails to obtain the grace of God; that no "root of bitterness" springs up and causes trouble, and by it many become defiled; that no one is sexually immoral or unholy like Esau, who sold his birthright for a single meal. For you know that afterward, when he desired to inherit the blessing, he was rejected, for he found no chance to repent, though he sought it with tears. (Heb 12:15–17)*

Esau's sin was far more serious than a lapse of judgment or an unfortunate mistake. He willfully, knowingly, and continually rejected God's plan for his life to such a degree that genuine repentance became impossible. He reached the point of no return. The author of Hebrews is warning Christians to beware, lest they too fall from grace in such a way that their condition becomes irremediable.

Isaac

Isaac's performance as a patriarch is, well, a big disappointment. As we saw in the last chapter, he struggled with his calling to be "the man in the middle." Though he had a relationship with God, he never quite managed to discover that whole-hearted, full-throttle passionate commitment that we see in both his father and his son. Isaac tended to be passive in his faith. Rather than *make* things happen, he was inclined to *let* them happen. But in this passage (Gen 27) he becomes surprisingly proactive and intentional. He looks like a leader as he makes plans to pass on the paternal blessing to the next generation. But alarmingly, he has chosen the wrong son, for a bad reason!

The text indicates that Isaac's main problem was that he was relying on his five senses to tell him what he should do rather than trusting in the revealed will of God.

- *His sight was defective.* Because he was blind (see Gen 27:1), he had to rely on his other four senses to discern reality.
- *His touch was defective.* Jacob had put the skins of young goats on his hands, arms, and neck so that if his father touched him, the hairy skin would make Isaac think he was Esau. The plan worked (see Gen 27:21–23).
- *His taste was defective.* Rebekah prepared domesticated goat meat for Isaac's meal but when he ate it, he thought it was wild game that had been hunted and prepared by Esau (see Gen 27:3–4, 9, 25).
- *His smell was defective.* Because Jacob had dressed in his brother's clothes, he smelled like Esau (see Gen 27:27). It is interesting to note that Isaac trusted his nose, perhaps the most animalistic of all the sense organs, more than any of his other senses. It was when he smelled the clothing of Esau, that he made the decision to give the blessing.
- *His hearing was surprisingly good.* "The voice is Jacob's voice." (Gen 27:22). It is significant that Isaac's hearing was the only one of his five senses that was providing him with accurate information. Yet this was the one sense organ he chose to ignore!

The writer of Genesis is telling us that all of Isaac's senses led him astray *except* his sense of hearing. And yet he refused to heed the one sensory organ that was most reliable for pointing him to the truth. This was a tragic mistake. He trusted the information that he should have doubted. He doubted the information that he should have trusted. Is the author of Genesis suggesting that of all our five senses, our hearing is perhaps the most reliable when it comes to discerning the will of God? "So faith comes from hearing, and hearing through the word of Christ" (Rom 10:17).

Rebekah

It would be wrong to attribute Rebekah's preference for Jacob to ugly favoritism alone. She knew that God had clearly foretold that the elder twin would serve the younger. In giving preferential treatment to Jacob, she was cooperating with the will of God. Her actions may have been questionable, but her intentions were pure, right, and good.

Rebekah illustrates the dilemma faced by people who find themselves under the leadership of someone who is leading badly, whether it is a husband, pastor, boss, or president. What should one do when the captain of the ship is steering the vessel toward destruction? How should you respond when the God-ordained authority in your life is making choices that are not God's will; choices that will have catastrophic consequences for everyone? This was the situation in which Rebekah found herself. It is worthwhile to think through the possible options that she could have, theoretically, taken.

1. *Submission.* Rebekah could have kept her mouth shut and simply submitted to Isaac's authority. After all, he was the God-ordained head of the family and thus responsible for decisions like this.
2. *Domination.* When she recognized that Isaac was about to make a terrible decision, Rebekah could have usurped his authority and taken charge of the family. Because he was old, blind, and incompetent, she could have easily justified such a move.
3. *Confrontation.* Rebekah could have sat down with Isaac and confronted him about his lack of leadership. She could have demanded they see a counselor. If the situation got worse, she might threaten to call a lawyer.
4. *Deception.* If Rebekah felt that options one, two, and three would be ineffective and that time was running out, then her

only recourse was to trick Isaac into doing the right thing. Using deception and lies, she would manipulate things so that the old geezer would, unknowingly, make a good decision.

Rebekah chose the fourth option. It is interesting that the Bible does not pronounce a judgment on her actions, either good or bad. The narrative simply tells what she did and then leaves it up to us to determine whether she did the right thing. Though her behavior is certainly questionable, when compared to the actions of Isaac, Esau, and Jacob, Rebekah seems to be the least guilty of the bunch. Leon Kass believes that, in context, she did the right thing.

> The true hero of the story is the courageous, tactful, and above all, lovingly prudent Rebekah, who conducts affairs always with circumspection, often behind the scenes, but in full view of the readers. Thanks to Rebekah, the new way survives a most severe test; thanks to Rebekah and the generations of women who, inspired by her example, followed in her footsteps, it survives at least to the present day.[1]

Jacob

In this third round of the wrestling match with his brother, we see the true character of Jake the Snake. The portrait painted in Genesis depicts him as egotistical and proud, a scheming, deceitful, manipulative controller. But at least he wants the right things (the birthright, the father's blessing). His methods may be questionable, but his desires, in contrast to his brother's, are fixed on what is good.

At this point in his story, Jacob knows that he is the child of promise and a patriarch in Israel, but he has no clue what this means. He still believes that he can accomplish the work of the Spirit in the power of the flesh and appears to lack any self-awareness of his own glaring character flaws. In the next chapters, we will learn that it will take two works of grace, one at Bethel and a second at Peniel, to transform Jake the Snake into Israel.

---

1   Kass, *The Beginning of Wisdom*, 401.

QUESTIONS FOR DISCUSSION

1. Can one be a member of God's family and at the same time be a manipulative, heel-grabbing deceiver?
2. Describe a family you know (no names, please!) where parental favoritism is evident. Now, describe a situation where there is sibling rivalry. What are the consequences when these kinds of dysfunction are at work in a family?
3. Have you ever been in a situation, like Rebekah, where the leader made terrible decisions? How did you handle the situation?
4. Do you consider Rebekah a heroine? Why or why not?
5. What lessons should we learn from Isaac's five senses?

22
Heaven's Gate
Genesis 28:10–22

Authors and movie directors have long understood how a door (or gate) is a powerful metaphor that can greatly enhance the story they are telling. When standing open, a door suggests opportunity and promise; when closed, hopelessness and despair. Serving as a passageway that provides a link between two otherwise separate places, a door suggests the possibility of transition and change. Doors can even evoke emotions such as anxiety, joy, depression, or hope. Whether we are talking about C. S. Lewis' wardrobe door in *The Chronicles of Narnia*, the song *Love Is an Open Door* in the movie *Frozen*, or the dramatic ending to the movie *Titanic* where the main character, Rose, is saved from drowning by clinging to a floating door, we are all captured by the metaphorical power of doors to speak deeply to our innermost souls!

My personal favorite illustration of how doors are used symbolically in literature comes from *Les Misérables* by Victor Hugo. Early in the story, having just been released from prison, Jean Valjean trudges into a village where he hopes to find food and shelter. Knocking on one door after another, he seeks a place to rest. Because of his status as an ex-prisoner, no one will receive him. The inn, the tavern, a farmhouse, and even a kennel for dogs, all slam their doors in his face. As night falls, he curls up on a stone bench in the town square. He is angry, hungry, depressed, and cold.

Just then an old woman came out of the church. She saw the man lying there in the dark and said: "What are you doing there, my friend?"

He replied harshly, and with anger in his tone: "You see, my good woman, I am going to sleep." . . .

"Upon that bench?" she said.

"For nineteen years I have had a wooden mattress," said the man. "Tonight, I have a stone one." . . .

"Why don't you go to the inn?"

"Because I have no money."

"Alas," she said. . . . "You cannot pass the night so. You must be cold and hungry. (The inn) should give you lodging for charity."

"I have knocked at every door. . . . Everybody has driven me away."

The good woman touched the man's arm and pointed out to him, on the other side of the square, a little low house beside the bishop's palace. "You have knocked at every door?" she asked.

"Yes."

"Have you knocked at that one there?"

"No."

"Knock there."[1]

Everything changed for Jean Valjean when he knocked on the door where the woman pointed. Welcomed inside by the priest, the visit in this home led to a radical transformation of character which is the subject of the remainder of this literary classic. It all began when he found the right door—and knocked.

Not surprisingly, the Bible has a lot to say about doors. On many occasions it simply describes a physical door, gate, or opening that provides access to a tent, temple, city, sheepfold, or tomb. But it is when the Bible uses doors figuratively that we discover the real power of this symbol to convey the Good News of the gospel. At times, it may

---

1   Hugo, *Les Misérables*, 10–11.

simply indicate that a divine opportunity is at hand, as when Paul spoke of the "wide door for effective work" that God had opened before him (see 1 Cor 16:9). But it is when the Bible uses a "door" or "gate" to describe the passageway leading from earth to heaven, the link that gives sinners access to God, that we see this metaphor's greatest importance. In fact, one could summarize the message of the Bible by saying it is all about helping sinners find the doorway that leads to God. The difference between salvation and damnation, life and death, heaven and hell, is ultimately the difference between those who find the door, and those who don't.

The prophet Isaiah cried out in anguished desperation, "Oh that you would rend the heavens and come down" (Isa 64:1). He is pleading with God to rip open a hole in the wall that separates us from him and invade our world. In other words, he is begging God to make a door where there is no door, so that we can have access to him, and he can have access to us.

The Good News of the gospel is that God has answered Isaiah's prayer. He has torn open a hole in the heavens and made a door! Not only has God walked through it to enter our world, but he invites us to walk through this door and enter his. The vocabulary used in Scripture may vary, but the concept of a passageway that provides a link between the kingdom of man and the kingdom of God is a theme found throughout the Bible. In fact, this gate connecting earth and heaven, man and God, is one of the primary themes in Scripture.

Consider, for example, how the book of Genesis introduces us to this door that connects us to God. When Adam and Eve sinned, they were expelled from the Garden of Eden. Though the word "door" or "gate" is not specifically used in the text, we learn that the entrance to Paradise was shut and guarded by an angel with a flaming sword. The doorway to God's dwelling place was closed tight and locked from the inside! Adam and Eve, and all their descendants, must now live "east of Eden," with no possibility of access to God (see Gen 3:24). Turning to the story of Noah, we are struck by the significance of the single door leading into the ark. Those who entered by it were saved, those on the outside perished. It is important to notice that God himself is the one who shut the door (see Gen 7:16). The story of the Tower of Babel takes on new meaning when one realizes that the word *babel* comes from an Akkadian word meaning "gate of god." The tower was more than an egotistical monument to human achievement. It was an attempt to reach heaven's door. But it didn't work, and the construction project was a spectacular fiasco. Babel's tower is a permanent reminder of the futility of every human effort to reach God. The distance is too great; the wall of separation is too impenetrable.

As we read through the Bible, we discover how different people occasionally got a glimpse through the door and were able to see what was happening on the other side. Elisha (2 Kgs 6:17), Ezekiel (Ezek 1:1), Stephen (Acts 7:56), Peter (Acts 10:11), and John (Rev 4:1) each had a moment when the doorway to heaven was opened and they got to look inside. Their descriptions of what they saw tell of a world of beauty, love, joy, and holiness.

In the New Testament, when Jesus was baptized, announcing the beginning of his public ministry, "the heavens were opened" and the Spirit descended on him like a dove (see Matt 3:16–17). The coming of Jesus meant that the doorway between earth and heaven was now fully open. Though he sometimes pointed to the door and urged his listeners to enter (see Matt 7:7–8), it was the way he identified himself as the door that was one of the most shocking things he ever said. "I am the door. If anyone enters by me, he will be saved and will go in and out and find pasture" (John 10:9).

One might say that the climactic moment of human history, as told in the book of Revelation, will occur when this doorway between heaven and earth is finally opened in such a way that everyone everywhere will see it and understand what is happening. Jesus will come again, in power and glory, at the head of an army of saints on white horses charging through the door. Then the kingdoms of this world will become the kingdom of our Lord and of his Christ, and he shall reign forever and ever (see Rev 11:15).

Then I saw heaven opened, and behold, a white horse! The one sitting on it is called Faithful and True, and in righteousness he judges and makes war. His eyes are like a flame of fire, and on his head are many diadems. . . . And the armies of heaven, arrayed in fine linen, white and pure, were following him on white horses. . . . On his robe and on his thigh he has a name written, King of kings and Lord of lords. (Rev 19:11–16)

Yes, there is a door and it is open. Proclaiming this Good News is what the message of the Bible is all about.

Surprisingly, the honor goes to Jacob for being the first person who actually saw the door and grasped its meaning. Genesis 28:10–22 tells the story. Most treatments of this passage focus on the ladder, or stairway, that leads to heaven. I want to suggest, however, that it is the doorway standing open at the top of the stairs, not the stairway itself, that is the real point of the story! Jacob himself makes this clear when he summarizes his experience by saying, "this is the gate of heaven" (Gen 28:17).

JACOB'S FIRST ENCOUNTER WITH GOD

How ironic that God would choose Jake the Snake to be the first person in history to see the door that leads to heaven and experience the grace and power that flow through it! As we have seen, Jacob is a self-absorbed, deceitful manipulator. Circumcised as a child, he had a nominal faith and an intellectual understanding of the covenant and the role he was called to play in it. But he has not yet had a personal encounter with God. He has a religion, not a relationship, head knowledge, not heart experience.

Jacob has two reasons for leaving home and traveling five hundred miles to Haran: to flee his brother's wrath and to find a suitable wife. Unlike Abraham's servant who had traveled this same road decades earlier in a caravan of ten camels (see Gen 24), Jacob is alone. He is filled with fear and anxiety as he faces a very uncertain future. There is no indication that Jacob is looking for God. Yet, we soon realize that God is looking for him!

> *Jacob left Beersheba and went toward Haran. And he came to a certain place and stayed there that night, because the sun had set. Taking one of the stones of the place, he put it under his head and lay down in that place to sleep. And he dreamed, and behold, there was a ladder (or, flight of steps) set up on the earth, and the top of it reached to heaven. And behold, the angels of God were ascending and descending on it! And behold, the* Lord *stood above it (or, beside him) and said, "I am the* Lord*, the God of Abraham your father and the God of Isaac. The land on which you lie I will give to you and to your offspring. Your offspring shall be like the dust of the earth, and you shall spread abroad to the west and to the east and to the north and to the south, and in you and your offspring shall all the families of the earth be blessed. Behold, I am with you and will keep you wherever you go, and will bring you back to this land. For I will not leave you until I have done what I have promised you." Then Jacob awoke from his sleep and said, "Surely the* Lord *is in this place, and I did not know it." And he was afraid and said, "How awesome is this place! This is none other than the house of God, and this is the gate of heaven."*
>
> *So early in the morning Jacob took the stone that he had put under his head and set it up for a pillar and poured oil on the top of it. He called the name of that place Bethel (Hebrew, house of God), but the name of the city was Luz at the first. (Gen 28:10–19)*

Jacob's conversion occurred when his life was in ruins. Hated by his brother, sent away by his parents, lonely, guilt-ridden, and confused, he sets out on a journey of five hundred miles to live with relatives he has never met in the hopes of finding a wife. Jacob's encounter with God occurred when he was desperate and miserable, when he had hit rock bottom.

> It is a poor thing to strike our colors to God when the ship is going down under us; a poor thing to come to him as a last resort, to offer up "our own" when it is no longer worth keeping. If God were proud, he would hardly have us on such terms: but he is not proud, he stoops to conquer. He will have us even though we have shown that we prefer everything else

to him and come to him because there is "nothing better" now to be had.[2]

The stone that Jacob used for his pillow, he also used to construct a memorial shrine, or pillar, to commemorate his conversion. Twenty years later, when he returns home, he will revisit this site and renew his vows to God (see Gen 35:9–15). During his lifetime, Jacob will erect several pillars to commemorate other important events (see Gen 28:18–22; 31:43–49; 35:16–20). It is interesting to note that Jacob's grandfather, Abraham, was known for building altars (see Gen 12:6–8; 13:14–18; 22:9). Though altars and pillars, both made of piles of stone, look somewhat similar, they have two very different purposes. Pillars celebrate the past and tend to honor the individual who built them. Altars honor God and are a place for worship and sacrifice. Jacob understands that something significant has happened to him at Bethel, but he doesn't yet know that full-throttle devotion and warm-hearted passion that characterized the faith of his grandfather. He now has a personal faith, but his character remains largely unchanged. Though he has taken a huge step in the right direction, Jake the Snake still needs a deeper work of grace.

The Hebrew term used to describe the "ladder" occurs only here in the Bible. Most scholars believe that it probably refers to a flight of steps, a stairway, like those running up the sides of a ziggurat. If it had been a ladder with rungs, it is hard to see how the angels could be ascending and descending at the same time, as indicated in the text (see Gen 28:12).

Genesis 28:13 is difficult to understand because the Hebrew is unclear. This is reflected in translations that are exactly opposite to one another. Some indicate that God is standing *at the top* of the stairway while other translations picture him standing by Jacob's side *at the bottom*. Arguments can be made for both interpretations. Leon Kass writes insightfully:

> The position of the Lord is, in fact, unclear. The Hebrew prepositional phrase . . . could mean "upon it (the ladder)" or

---

[2] Lewis, *The Problem with Pain*, 77–78.

"beside him (Jacob)." The ambiguity is, in a way, perfect, for it hints that the Lord can be—is—at once both near and far.... I prefer the more remote positioning of God. That he would be in the picture at all, and speaking with Jacob, is nearness enough for those who wish to stress God's proximity to man.[3]

Perhaps the best way to understand the real significance of Jacob's vision of the stairway to heaven is to compare it to the Tower of Babel built so many years earlier. The ziggurat at Babel also had a flight of steps leading upward. Its builders hoped that they could reach heaven's gate. Although we have compared and contrasted Babel's Tower and Jacob's Stairway on an earlier occasion, it is worthwhile to review and summarize what has been said. Few messages in Genesis are more important than this.

Babel's Tower (Gen 11:1–9)	Jacob's Stairway (Gen 28:10–22)
Made by man	Made by God
Man reaching up	God reaching down
Began in pride, ended in confusion	Began in confusion, ended in trust
Failure—does not reach heaven's gate	Success—heaven and earth are linked
Story ends in judgment	Story ends in blessing

Before moving on from our discussion of Jacob's "ladder," a word of warning about mystical interpretations is in order. Neglecting completely the context, many have seen "Jacob's ladder" as a means of self-improvement. The idea is, that by human effort, one can climb higher and higher toward perfection until finally God is reached at the top.[4] This is a gross perversion of what the passage actually says. Jacob is not being encouraged to "try harder." Rather, he is given the opportunity to freely receive God's grace and favor. God is the one who has taken the initiative, not man. Rather than teaching man's ascent to God, the story teaches God's descent to man.

---

3   Kass, *The Beginning of Wisdom*, 414.
4   Such false doctrine of works righteousness has unfortunately crept into some of the church's music. See, for example, the old spiritual "We Are Climbing Jacob's Ladder."

Jacob's Vow

What Jacob *saw* in his dream, the stairway to heaven and the open door at the top, was only part of Jacob's conversion experience. What he *heard* composed the rest. His conversion would have been little more than pious intentions motivated by vague hopes had not God spoken to Jacob in a way that he could clearly understand. It wasn't the stairway that transformed Jacob's life. It was the Word of God! "The entrance of your words gives light" (Ps 119:130 NKJV).

> *I am the LORD, the God of Abraham your father and the God of Isaac. The land on which you lie I will give to you and to your offspring. Your offspring shall be like the dust of the earth, and you shall spread abroad to the west and to the east and to the north and to the south, and in you and your offspring shall all the families of the earth be blessed. Behold, I am with you and will keep you wherever you go, and will bring you back to this land. For I will not leave you until I have done what I have promised you. (Gen 28:13–15)*

Surprisingly, God does not rebuke Jacob for his past deceitful behaviors. Instead, he proclaims a series of unconditional promises. "I will give to you . . . I will keep you . . . I will bring you back . . . I will not leave you." In substance, God is repeating to Jacob the covenant promises that he had earlier made to Abraham and to Isaac. God's promises centered on three primary realities:

- *The land of Canaan.* Though Jacob is now poor and owns nothing, all the land around him will one day belong to him and his descendants forever.
- *Descendants.* Though Jacob is now unmarried and has no children, one day his offspring will be as numerous as the dust of the earth.
- *To be a blessing to the whole earth.* Though Jacob, until now, has only wanted to take the blessing and grasp it for his own enjoyment, one day he will be the channel through whom God's blessings go forth to the entire world.

When God gave these amazing covenant promises to Abraham and Isaac, we saw how they responded with worship, gratitude, and faith. Not so with Jake the Snake! He responds to God's promises by making the first vow recorded in the Bible. But as Leon Kass astutely observes; the vow's "character reflects the calculating character of its maker."[5] Although God's promises to Jacob had been unconditional, Jacob's vow is anything but!

> *Then Jacob made a vow, saying, "If God will be with me and will keep me in this way that I go, and will give me bread to eat and clothing to wear, so that I come again to my father's house in peace, then the* LORD *shall be my God, and this stone, which I have set up for a pillar, shall be God's house. And of all that you give me I will give a full tenth to you." (Gen 28:20–22)*

Jacob is negotiating with God, hedging his bets. His intent is to make God an offer he can't refuse. Despite having just experienced one of the most dramatic visions in the history of the world, Jacob is not quite sure about this God who has come through the door and revealed himself to him. Though Jacob has been converted, it is obvious that his character remains largely unchanged. He continues to be shrewd, conniving, and self-reliant.

The first thing one notices about Jacob's vow is the repetition of first-person singular pronouns. "If God will be with *me* and will keep *me* in this way that *I* go, and will give *me* bread . . . so that *I* come again to *my* father's house in peace . . ." At least ten times in three verses we hear him say either "I", "me", or "my." Jacob has an "I" problem. His egocentrism seems as prominent *after* his conversion as it was before! Tragically, Jacob's new faith now allows him to cloak his self-absorption in a mantle of piety. Though Jacob could now confess his faith his God, his self-centered nature remains unchanged. It's still all about me.

It is difficult to determine whether Jacob's vow is a prayer or not. At first, he talks *about* God, as if he were conducting negotiations with some corporation. He speaks of God in the third person (see Gen 28:20–22a). "If God will do such and such, then I will do such and such." But then, at the end, he awkwardly switches to the second

---

5 Kass, *The Beginning of Wisdom*, 417.

person and addresses God directly. He talks *to* God. "And of all that you give me I will give a full tenth to you" (Gen 28:22b). Though we can rejoice in the fact that Jacob is in personal communication with God, it is obvious that the relationship is one-sided, distant, formal, and unhealthy.

The most shocking part of Jacob's vow is its conditional nature. The "if . . . then" wording is, frankly, offensive. Jacob is saying, "OK God, *if* you come through for me and do all the things you have promised, *then* I'll let you be my God. I'll even start tithing!" One can only marvel at the brazen audacity of a man who would talk to God like this! The promise to start tithing if God keeps his end of the bargain qualifies as one of the most callous attempts to manipulate God in the entire Bible.

Although Jacob's encounter with God at Bethel is an authentic conversion, it is obvious that his character remains basically unchanged. He is still the heel-grabbing, manipulative, deceitful controller that he has always been. But now, his egocentrism is camouflaged under a cloak of pious spirituality. Jacob's first encounter with God is a strange mixture of divine grace and selfish ambition.

Is That All There Is?

Jacob's conversion experience at Bethel leaves us with two equal and opposite reactions. On the one hand, we can rejoice that this rascal has finally met the living Lord. The prodigal son has returned. He who was lost has now found the way. Yes, the fact that Jake the Snake got saved is worthy of a hearty "Hallelujah! Praise the Lord!" This is good, really good.

On the other hand, the same Biblical text that tells us about Jacob's conversion reveals that his character has not been changed at all. He is still Jacob, the heel-grabber, a conniving trickster and self-centered manipulator. Now, he is even trying to use the God of the promises to advance his own egocentric career! This is troubling, really troubling.

Although Bethel is a good place for Jacob to *begin* his spiritual journey, it is only that, a beginning. It will take a second work of grace, recorded in Genesis 32, to bring Jacob to a deeper experience with

God that will transform his character. This will happen at Peniel when he has his famous wrestling match with God (see chapter 24, "The Magnificent Limp"). Jacob named the place of his first encounter with God "Bethel," meaning "house of God." But Jacob will name the place of his second encounter "Peniel," meaning "face of God." Entering God's house caused Jacob to make a few adjustments to his lifestyle but seeing God's face will completely transform his soul! At Bethel, Jacob received a new status. At Peniel, he will receive a new nature, and God will give him a new name, Israel. At Bethel God did a great work *for* Jacob. At Peniel he will do a great work *in* Jacob. No longer will Jacob say, "It's all about me." Now, Israel will exult: "It's all about the Lord! It's all about others!" At Bethel, Jacob was justified; at Peniel, he will be sanctified.

Jacob's life perfectly matches the description of a believer's spiritual progress outlined by Charles Williams in his book *He Came Down from Heaven*. Williams says there are three degrees on the journey of salvation, which I have listed below, adding a short sentence to explain how Jacob's life provides a classic illustration.

1. *The old self in the old way.* Before Jacob left home, his life was marked by sin and selfishness. He was lost, arrogant, manipulative, and deceitful (see Gen 25–27).
2. *The old self in the new way.* At Bethel, he met the living God and was converted. Now his life had meaning, purpose, and direction. However, it was soon obvious that though he was on a new path, Jake the Snake was still very much alive and well (see Gen 28–31).
3. *The new self in the new way.* At Peniel, Jacob had his ultimate wrestling match—with God. He won the fight by losing! The encounter transformed his character and God gave him a new name. Though still human and flawed, Israel loved the Lord with all his heart. Humbled and filled with love for others, Israel became a channel of grace to those around him (see Gen 32–36).

QUESTIONS FOR DISCUSSION

1. What were you thinking as the author described how "doors" have been used as a metaphor in books, movies, and the Bible? How does this add meaning to Jesus' statement, "I am the door"?
2. What theological truths did you gain from comparing Jacob's Stairway to Babel's Tower?
3. What is the difference between a pillar (memorial shrine) and an altar? Why is this important?
4. Can one be truly converted and yet manifest one's old sinful nature? Can one be justified but not sanctified? What does this mean?
5. Look again at Charles William's three degrees on the journey of salvation. Think about how Jacob's life illustrates each degree. Now think about your own life. What is the Holy Spirit saying to you?

Nearer, My God, to Thee
Sarah Flower Adams (1841)

Nearer, my God, to thee, nearer to thee!
E'en though it be a cross that raiseth me,
Still all my song shall be,
Nearer, my God, to thee;
Nearer, my God to thee, nearer to thee!

Though like the wanderer, the sun gone down,
Darkness be over me, my rest a stone;
Yet in my dreams I'd be
Nearer, my God, to thee;
Nearer, my God, to thee, nearer to thee!

There let the way appear, steps unto heaven;
All that thou sendest me, in mercy given;
Angels to beckon me
Nearer, my God, to thee;
Nearer, my God, to thee, nearer to thee!

Then, with my waking thoughts bright with thy praise,
Out of my stony griefs Bethel I'll raise;
So by my woes to be
Nearer, my God, to thee;
Nearer, my God, to thee, nearer to thee!

23
The Deceiver Is Deceived
Genesis 29–31

This chapter is about deception. Specifically, it is about being deceived: believing something that just ain't so. If you think this topic doesn't relate to you, that may only indicate how deceived you are! People who are deceived, by definition, don't know they are deceived. *That* explains why the issue is so serious. Deception occurs when one has been led to accept as true something that is false. It takes lies, distortions, secrets, innuendos, and half-truths to make deception work. Few spiritual conditions are more deadly than this. Hell will be populated by people who never imagined they would end up there!

We have seen how Jacob, the third patriarch of Israel, was a master deceiver. In fact, his name describes his character: one who supplants, trips from behind, cheats, and deceives. When he couldn't get what he wanted fairly, he resorted to tricks, treachery, and lies. In "Jake the Snake" on page 303, we saw how he deceived his own father so that he could receive the paternal blessing. Family dynamics became so strained that Jacob had to flee far away to Haran where he lived with his uncle Laban and married two of his daughters.

Genesis 29–31 describes the twenty years that Jacob lived with and worked for his uncle. Deception is the primary theme of these three chapters. But in Haran, Jacob meets his match! Laban is also a master deceiver and on numerous occasions he cheats his son-in-law. On his wedding night, Jacob was shocked to learn that his uncle had tricked him, giving him Leah as a wife rather than Rachel. "Why have you *deceived* me?" he cried (see Gen 29:25). During the years that Jacob worked for his uncle, Laban "cheated" him by changing his wages ten times (see Gen 31:7, 41). The theme of deception took a new twist when Jacob's own wife Rachel, without his knowledge, stole her father's household gods and took them with her back to Canaan (see Gen 31:19, 32). In Haran, Jacob got a taste of his own medicine. The deceiver is deceived!

These chapters make it clear, however, that though Jacob had had a conversion experience at Bethel and now had a relationship with God, his nature remained unchanged. And though the abusive treatment he received in Haran may have sobered and humbled him, he still deserved his name. He was still Jake the Snake. His deceitful character is seen in the way he "tricked" his father-in-law by not telling him about his plans to leave, and then slipped secretly away, heading back to Canaan (see Gen 31:20).

The Mosaic law states that sinners will eventually experience the bitter fruit of their own wicked deeds. Liars, cheats, and con artists will not get away with their evil schemes forever. God's moral law is emphatic: "Be sure your sins will find you out" (Num 32:23). It was as Jacob found himself on the receiving end of deception and got a taste of his own medicine that he was being prepared for a deeper work of God's grace. Though his experience in Haran was certainly painful, it was, in reality, a great blessing! For the first time in his life, Jacob became self-aware, awake to his own despicable nature. God, in his sovereign plan, was preparing him to face the most spiritually transformative experience of his life (see Gen 32).

A Night to Remember

In a manner reminiscent of Abraham's servant finding a wife for his master (see Gen 24), Jacob meets his future wife at a well. He is smitten the first time he lays eyes on Rachel. It is love at first sight. We might say that Jacob is the first person in the Bible to "fall in love." In a show of heroic strength and machismo, he single-handedly rolls the great stone away that covers the mouth of the well, a stone that normally required several men to move. Then, before he even speaks to Rachel, he kisses her!

Rachel takes Jacob home and introduces him to her father and the rest of her family. Laban welcomes his kinsman and immediately invites Jacob to stay and work for him, permitting him to name his own wages. "I will serve you seven years for your younger daughter Rachel," Jacob says (Gen 29:18). The plot thickens, however, when we learn that Rachel has an elder sister, Leah. Because it was not customary for the younger daughter to be married first, this created a problem for Laban. But rather than discussing the issue openly, he keeps his dilemma a secret and decides on a path of deception.

The Biblical description of the two sisters is brief but poignant: "Leah's eyes were weak, but Rachel was beautiful in form and appearance" (Gen 29:17). The *New Living Translation* puts the verse this way: "Leah had pretty eyes, but Rachel was beautiful in every way, with a lovely face and shapely figure." The word used to describe Leah's eyes is somewhat ambiguous but probably means "gentle," "tender," or "delicate." In contrast to her sister's glamourous face and curvaceous body, the dominant characteristic of Leah's appearance was her eyes. Leon Kass sees great significance in this emphasis and believes that the ambiguity of the term that describes Leah's eyes is part of the message.

> Do they reveal her to be weak, or tender? Is she the maternal, nurturing, or householdly sort? Could she be more discerning, a better "looker" than her better-looking sister? However suggestively the text might invite such thoughts, it surely forces *us* to look searchingly into her eyes and into what lies behind them and within. But Jacob has eyes only for Rachel.[1]

Without even being aware of what is happening, Jacob has been put in a situation where he must choose between a woman with beautiful eyes (inviting him to look into the depths of her soul) and a woman with a curvaceous body (inviting him to sensual pleasure). It took no time at all for Jacob to decide what he wanted: he "loved

---

[1] Ibid., 424.

Rachel more than Leah," indeed, he "hated" Leah (Gen 29:30–31). His passion for Rachel was such that he worked seven years in order to marry her, "and they seemed to him but a few days" (Gen 29:20).

Jacob offers a classic picture of the battle that every male must face in his relationship with women. Will he be captured by outward beauty or inward character? Will his marriage be defined by *eros* (desire and pleasure) or *agape* (other-oriented affection, selfless devotion)? The way these questions are answered will shape our lives and legacies.

Driven by his passionate love (lust?) for Rachel, Jacob eagerly anticipates his wedding day. This is the moment he has been waiting for.

> *Then Jacob said to Laban, "Give me my wife that I may go in to her, for my time is completed." So Laban gathered together all the people of the place and made a feast. But in the evening, he took his daughter Leah and brought her to Jacob, and he went in to her. . . . And in the morning, behold, it was Leah! And Jacob said to Laban, "What is this you have done to me? Did I not serve with you for Rachel? Why then have you deceived me?" Laban said, "It is not so done in our country, to give the younger before the firstborn. Complete the week of this one, and we will give you the other also in return for serving me another seven years." Jacob did so, and completed her week. Then Laban gave him his daughter Rachel to be his wife. (Gen 29:23–28)*

It is hard to imagine how a man, on his wedding night, could fail to discern the identity of the woman at his side! Perhaps it was just too dark to see. Perhaps the bride was wearing a veil. Perhaps Jacob was drunk. No explanation is given in the text and once again, the reader must provide his own interpretation. Perhaps the author's point is to show that Jacob, dominated by selfish desire and passion, has lost all his powers of discernment. Driven by lust, all women are the same in the dark.

Let's pause and examine more closely the character qualities of these two sisters. The Bible seems intent on suggesting that though Rachel was outwardly beautiful, her inner character qualities were unimpressive. By contrast, Leah, though humbler in appearance, was a woman of inner strength and beauty. It shouldn't surprise us that Jake the Snake preferred Rachel.

Leah's character is seen most clearly in the names she gives to the children born to her (and her servant Zilpah). Scripture is intent on letting the reader know that it was the mother who named the children and why each name was chosen.

- Reuben—The Lord has seen my affliction (Gen 29:32).
- Simeon—The Lord has heard that I am hated (Gen 29:33).
- Levi—Now my husband will be attracted to me (Gen 29:34).
- Judah—I will praise the Lord (Gen 29:35).
- Issachar—God has given me my wages (Gen 30:17–18).
- Zebulun—God has endowed me with a good endowment (Gen 30:19–20).
- Gad (through Zilpah)—Good fortune has come to me (Gen 30:10–11).
- Asher (through Zilpah)—Happy am I (Gen 30:12–13).

These names reveal that Leah, though far from perfect, is a strong and authentic worshipper of Jacob's God. Her trust is squarely in the God of Abraham. Furthermore, God's favor on Leah is shown in the fact that two of her sons will provide the most influential leadership in the future nation of Israel: Levi (the priesthood) and Judah (the kingship through David, and eventually the Messiah).

Rachel, on the other hand, is depicted in a more ambiguous light. On the outside, she is beautiful and charming, and her husband loves her dearly. But on the inside, we see someone who is competitive, vindictive, manipulative, superstitious, and who still practices idolatry! For example, when God blesses Leah and gives her children, rather than rejoicing with her, Rachel becomes envious (see Gen 30:1). From this point forward, a spirit of competition will define the sisters' relationship: Who will have the most babies? Who is the most loved? Whose kids will get the best treatment?

The names that Rachel gives to the children born to her and her servant Bilhah, rather than reflecting gratitude and praise, seem to be tainted with spite and a competitive spirit:

- Dan (through Bilhah)—God has vindicated me (Gen 30:5–6 NIV).
- Naphtali (through Bilhah)—I have wrestled with my sister and prevailed (Gen 30:7–8).
- Joseph—God has taken away my reproach; may the Lord give me another (Gen 30:22–24).

Further questions about Rachel's character are raised in the story of the mandrakes (see Gen 30:14–18). We wonder if she has any trust in the God of Abraham at all. Apparently, Rachel had a superstitious belief in the magical powers of the fruit of the mandrake plant as a kind of aphrodisiac. The narrative, however, makes clear that God alone, not some magical plant, is the source of fertility.

Perhaps the most troubling story relating to Rachel's character is her theft of her father's household gods (see Gen 31:19, 30–35). At least three very serious sins are evident in this action. First, she *stole* something of value that was not hers. Second, she *deceived* her husband. She did not ask his counsel before her action and kept it a secret afterward. Third, and most troubling of all, she apparently *practiced idolatry*. Why else would she have stolen the household gods if she did not believe, to some degree, in their power to protect and provide?

Though Rachel would easily win a beauty contest, the Genesis narrative wants us to understand that, on the inside, she is a seething cauldron of envy, vindictiveness, competitiveness, manipulation, superstition, thievery, and idolatry. It almost makes one smile to imagine what her marriage to Jake the Snake was really like.

WRESTLING LABAN

If Jacob's marriage to Rachel was difficult, think what his relationship with his father-in-law must have been like! For twenty long years, these two controllers lived together, deceiving and being deceived. Jacob had truly met his equal. The very first words that Laban spoke to his nephew were truer than either of the men realized: "Surely you are my bone and my flesh!" (Gen 29:14). Oswald Chambers writes: "The humor of God is sometimes tragic; he engineers across our path the kind of people who exhibit to us our own characteristics—not very flattering, is it?"[2]

Just as the Bible highlights the character qualities of Leah and Rachel, so it provides plenty of information about Laban so that the reader is able to discern just what sort of man he really is. He not only deceived Jacob on his wedding night by giving him Leah rather than Rachel, but he used this event to coerce his son-in-law to work an additional seven years in his employment (see Gen 29:18–30). While in his service, Laban cheated Jacob by changing his wages ten times (see Gen 31:7, 41).

We get further insight into Laban's dubious character by learning that he practices divination (an occult activity) and worships other gods (see Gen 30:27; 31:19, 30). In other words, he is a sorcerer and an idolater. When the two men agree on Jacob's severance package (the spotted and striped lambs), Laban then proceeds to secretly remove the spotted and striped males from the flock (see Gen 30:34–36). Most tellingly, Laban's own daughters clearly see the abusive and manipulative ways of their father. They have no desire to live near him any longer. "Are we not regarded by him as foreigners? For he has sold us, and he has indeed devoured our money" (see Gen 31:14–16). Finally, the speech Laban gives when he says goodbye to Jacob and his family is one of the most sanctimonious, self-righteous, and hypocritical speeches in the whole Bible (see Gen 31:25–30).

Why would God, in his sovereign wisdom and love, arrange things so that Jacob had to live with a rascal like Laban for two solid decades? What was it that the Lord wanted to teach him during those years in Haran? That is a very good question! Let's enumerate three vitally important lessons that God wanted Jacob to learn while living with Uncle Laban.

First, God wanted Jacob to learn what it feels like to be deceived, manipulated, and used. There was little chance that Jake the Snake would ever change if he never understood in a personal way the damage and pain caused by deceit. Though he may have had an abstract

---

[2] Chambers, *Our Portrait in Genesis*, 972.

awareness of how his behavior deeply wounded his brother Esau, he had no clue what that meant in actual experience. In an amazing act of grace, God gave Jacob the privilege of tasting his own medicine and experiencing firsthand what it feels like to be used and abused.

Second, the years in Haran made Jacob self-aware. Living with his uncle was like living with a mirror. Jacob knew what a no-good, low-down, dirty rotten bum his uncle was. Recognizing that he was one, too, was one of the greatest discoveries of Jacob's life! Few things motivate sinners to change more than getting a glimpse of who they really are. It is only when we see our sin in all its ugliness that we begin to long for the kind of transformation that only grace can make possible.

Third, the twenty-year experience in Haran made Jacob aware of his need for a deeper work of grace. Although he had had an authentic encounter with the living Lord at Bethel, when he dreamed of the stairway to heaven, he now knew that this was not enough. God had changed his status, but could God change his heart? The Lord had done great things *for* him, but could God do great things *in* him? Could God transform Jake the Snake into a new creation?

SELF-DECEPTION

Prior to Jacob's sojourn in Haran, he had been the *subject* of deception. He had deceived others. He was the deceiver. But now, during the years with his Uncle Laban, he has become the *object*. The deceiver is deceived. The perpetrator becomes the victim, not only by the dishonest tricks of his uncle, but also by the hidden secrets of his wife. In Haran, Jacob had the privilege of experiencing the bitter taste of deceit.

But something else was happening, something deeper and much more important. For the first time in his life, Jacob discovered who his own worst enemy really was: himself! In Haran, he discovered that his greatest problem came neither from his uncle's tricks or his wife's secrets. No, *self*-deception, *that* was the real problem. Jacob realized that he believed things about God, others, and himself that just weren't so. He slowly became aware of his own damnable ability to deceive, mislead, and manipulate himself. Yes, he was his own worst enemy!

Through the lies, half-truths, and distortions that he told himself, Jacob came face-to-face with the reality of his own capacity for self-destruction. It took twenty years, but when he left his uncle's house Jacob was a humbled man, blessed with self-awareness. He wasn't yet a transformed man, but he had taken a huge step in the right direction.

A case could be made that, in spiritual terms, self-deception is the deadliest of all sins—not because it is somehow "worse" than other sins, but because it is unrecognized. Those who are self-deceived, by definition, don't know they are. And because they can't see their own sin, they have no motivation to confess, repent, and seek forgiveness. This means their sins will cling to them forever! In this respect, the sin of self-deception is similar to the sin against the Holy Spirit; it is unforgiveable.

It is terrifying to realize that self-deception is perhaps the easiest of all sins to fall into! In studying the third chapter of Genesis, we saw how Eve tried to justify her sin by saying, "The serpent *deceived* me, and I ate" (Gen 3:13). This is where the sin problem typically begins: the tempter deceives us and then we deceive ourselves. We become so good at this that we deceive ourselves into thinking we are not deceived!

As children of Adam and Eve, we are born with an inherent predisposition to self-deception; we assume that our motives are pure, our actions are right, and our thinking is clear. We reject any evidence that suggests we are trusting in lies and half-truths. The prophet Jeremiah reveals the sober truth about our capacity for self-deception when he writes: "The heart is deceitful above all things, and desperately sick; who can understand it?" (Jer 17:9)

Self-deception is a terrible thing, of course, wherever it is found, but it is a tragedy of epic proportions when it is found in the church, among the people of God! In John's description of the seven churches of Asia (see Rev 2–3), we have two illustrations of people who considered themselves to be Christians but who were clearly deceived. To the members of the church in Sardis, the risen Christ said, "You have the reputation of being alive, but you are dead" (Rev 3:1). The members of Sardis Community Church genuinely believed they were an authentic expression of the true church. They confessed the creeds, said the prayers, and went through all the right motions. Yet Jesus himself tells them they are spiritually dead! They were deceived about their spiritual condition.

For the members of the church in Laodicea, the situation was similar. They too fancied themselves as true believers. When they compared themselves to other churches, they concluded that they were doing fine. But Jesus saw things differently. "You say, I am rich, I have prospered, and I need nothing, not realizing that you are wretched, pitiable, poor, blind, and naked" (Rev 3:17). They too were deceived.

SEVEN QUESTIONS FOR SELF-EXAMINATION

Paul encouraged the Christians in Corinth to examine themselves. He knew this church well and suspected that some among the membership were deceived about their true spiritual condition. But rather than sending them to a religious professional or a spiritual director, he told them to conduct their own self-examination.

> *Examine yourselves, to see whether you are in the faith. Test yourselves. Or do you not realize this about yourselves, that Jesus Christ is in you?—unless indeed you fail to meet the test! (2 Cor 13:5)*

In closing this chapter, I want to encourage us to do what Paul asked the Corinthians to do: examine ourselves. I'm suggesting a very simple method to help us. If we give ourselves diligently to this, I believe we will never be deceived about our true spiritual status.

On seven different occasions, the New Testament specifically alerts its readers to the danger of self-deception. These warnings seem to highlight those situations where Christians are most susceptible to believe something that just ain't so. When put into the form of a question, we have the tools with which we can conduct a thorough self-examination.

> **"Let no one deceive himself.** *If anyone among you thinks that he is wise in this age, let him become a fool that he may*

become wise. For the wisdom of this world is folly with God."
(1 Cor 3:18–19, emphasis added)

A first question for self-examination is this: *Do I consider myself to be smart?* Even a pagan philosopher like Socrates understood that the first mark of wisdom was recognizing what a fool one was! Those who claim to have the Christian walk figured out are more likely to be deceived than almost anyone else. God promises wisdom to those who know they are fools; strength to those who know they are weak; fullness to those who know they are empty; holiness to those who know they are sinners; and he'll show the way home only to those who know they are lost.

> *Or do you not know that the unrighteous will not inherit the kingdom of God?* **Do not be deceived**: *neither the sexually immoral, nor idolaters, nor adulterers, nor men who practice homosexuality, nor thieves, nor the greedy, nor drunkards, nor revilers, nor swindlers will inherit the kingdom of God. And such were some of you. But you were washed, you were sanctified, you were justified in the name of the Lord Jesus Christ and by the Spirit of our God. (1 Cor 6:9–11, emphasis added)*

A second question for self-examination is this: *Is there any unconfessed sin in my life?* The Bible makes it very clear that one cannot live in willful, habitual, blatant disobedience to the known will of God and still be in a right relationship with him. You can be sure deception is at work when someone who claims to be a Christ follower is not following Christ. This does not mean that Christians do not sin. It means, rather, that when Christians do sin, they confess, repent, receive forgiveness and ask for strength to be victorious when temptation comes again.

> **Do not be deceived**: *"Bad company ruins good morals."*
> *(1 Cor 15:33, emphasis added)*

Here we see yet another question useful for self-examination: *Are my friendships and relationships spiritually healthy?* Many Christians assume they can remain in worldly company without becoming worldly. They imagine themselves obeying Jesus' command to be salt and light among unbelievers. Yet often these Christians are naïve to the seductive power of sin and fail to recognize that the world is having more influence on them than they are having on the world.

> **Do not be deceived**: *God is not mocked, for whatever one sows, that will he also reap. For the one who sows to his own flesh will from the flesh reap corruption, but the one who sows to the Spirit will from the Spirit reap eternal life. (Gal 6:7–8, emphasis added)*

A fourth question for self-examination is this: *Do I think I am immune from the consequences of sin?* Many Christians mistakenly believe that, somehow, the sins they refuse to give up will not have negative consequences. They think they are immune from penalty and the verses that talk about this don't apply to them. When it comes to their sins, thy think that God will make an exception.

> *But be doers of the word, and not hearers only, **deceiving yourselves**. (Jas 1:22, emphasis added)*

A fifth question for self-examination can be stated this way: *Am I living in the known will of God or are there areas where I have given myself permission to live in disobedience?* Many people in church seem to believe that doing God's will is optional. Some think they can disregard his commands and yet somehow be pleasing to him. This is delusional thinking indeed.

> *If anyone thinks he is religious and does not bridle his tongue but **deceives his heart**, this person's religion is worthless. (Jas 1:26, emphasis added)*

A sixth question for self-examination is this: *Is my tongue under control?* The Bible often emphasizes the importance of the tongue for the simple reason that what comes out of the mouth reveals what is in the heart. James' words are a wake-up call to those who see no relationship between their spiritual condition and how they use their tongues.

> *If we say we have no sin, **we deceive ourselves**, and the truth is not in us. If we confess our sins, he is faithful and just to forgive us our sins and to cleanse us from all unrighteousness. (1 John 1:8–9, emphasis added)*

A seventh question for self-examination can be asked this way: *Do I pretend to be sinless?* We saved this verse for last because John not only warns us about self-deception, but far more importantly, he tells us what to do if, in fact, we discover self-deception in our own hearts: we confess our sins. Confession is simply agreeing with God, facing reality, acknowledging the truth. Confessing sin brings light, truth, and freedom. The power of deception is broken! God steps in and forgives our sin and cleanses our heart.

QUESTIONS FOR DISCUSSION

1. Give an example of someone you know whose sin caught up with him/her. How does this illustrate Numbers 32:23: "Be sure your sin will find you out"?
2. Have you ever been tricked, deceived, or treated unfairly? How did you react? How did it feel? Did this experience cause you to wonder if you had ever treated others in a similar manner?
3. What lesson do you think God wants us to learn from Jacob's preference for Rachel (gorgeous face and body) over Leah (beautiful eyes)?
4. Have you ever awakened to the fact that you were deceived about something? What enabled you to see the truth?
5. Of the seven questions for self-examination, which one spoke most powerfully to you? Why?

24
The Magnificent Limp
Genesis 32:1–33:20

When we think of spiritual warfare, we typically imagine demons, devils, and the powers of darkness fighting to conquer someone's soul. The story of Jacob, however, teaches us that the ultimate spiritual warfare is not the soul's battle with Satan, but rather with God! The greatest crisis of Jacob's life was not his struggle with the devil, the flesh, or the world. Neither was it his conflict with his brother Esau or his father-in-law, Laban. No, his greatest battle was with God himself! Until his will was fully surrendered, it often must have seemed to Jacob that his worst enemy was God. Yes, as he desperately struggled to maintain control of his life and get what he wanted, he learned that his fiercest opponent was the very One he claimed to worship! At Peniel, Jacob finally came to the end of himself. Here he made the most important discovery of his life: victory comes through surrender!

Genesis 32–33 tells the dramatic story of Jacob's return to Canaan. During his twenty years in Haran, God had blessed him with a large family and great wealth. But now, it is time to go home and assume his role as the third patriarch of Israel. We remember that when Jacob had left his home twenty years earlier, he was not only looking for a wife, he was fleeing his brother's wrath. The last glimpse we had of Esau was of an angry man vowing vengeance. But now, Jacob's options have run out and he knows he must return to Canaan and face his ugly past and his unresolved conflict with his brother. As he makes the long journey, Jacob is filled with fear and dread. This is the hardest thing he has ever done! Leon Kass observes:

> But confronting Esau is more than a practical inevitability; it is also a moral imperative. Failure to settle accounts with Esau and to make amends for his conniving past would leave a permanent blot on Jacob's supremacy. It would also cast grave doubts on his fitness as the next patriarch under the covenant.[1]

These two chapters in Genesis make clear that for Jacob to get right with his brother, he must first get right with God. The inspired author skillfully places these two stories side by side: Jacob's wrestling match with God told in Genesis 32 and Jacob's reunion with his brother told in Genesis 33. The reader understands that one story is impossible without the other. Jacob's decision to make things right with Esau leads inevitably to his spiritual crisis with God. Then, his crisis with God prepares him to meet his brother. In other words, for Jacob, reconciling with Esau and reconciling with God are two sides of the same coin. The two events are distinct, yet inseparable. Jacob's vertical relationship with God and his horizontal relationship with his brother are intimately connected. What God has joined together, let no one separate!

The author weaves these two stories together by his masterful use of the word *face*, which introduces us to the primary motif in the narrative. The Hebrew term *panim* occurs sixteen times in these two chapters.[2] English translations have a difficult time in conveying this emphasis because the word *face* also carries the connotation of "in the presence of," "in front of," "before," "beside," and "ahead." We get a good idea, however, of what these two chapters are about by looking at those verses where the word *panim* is used most distinctively.

- "[Jacob] thought, 'I may appease him [appease his face] with the present that goes ahead of me [before my face], and afterward I shall see his face. Perhaps he will accept me [lift my face].' So the

---

1   Kass, *The Beginning of Wisdom,* 446.
2   Genesis 32: verses 3, 16, 17, 20 (four times), 21, and 30 (two times). Genesis 33: verses 3, 10 (two times), 14 (two times), and 18.

present passed on ahead of him [before his face], and he himself stayed that night in the camp." (Gen 32:20–21)
- "So Jacob called the name of the place Peniel [face of God], saying, 'For I have seen God face to face, and yet my life has been delivered.'" (Gen 32:30)
- "Jacob said, 'No, please, if I have found favor in your sight, then accept my present from my hand. For I have seen your face, which is like seeing the face of God, and you have accepted me.'" (Gen 33:10)

In other words, Jacob is terrified of facing up to his sinful past and facing his estranged brother. But when he sees God face to face, he has the courage to face the future. When he finally sees Esau, he recognizes the face of God in the face of his brother.

PLEASE, LORD, DELIVER ME

As Jacob returns home, he is met by a company of angels (see Gen 32:1–2). Twenty years earlier, as he was leaving home, he had a similar encounter with celestial beings when he had his vision of the stairway and saw angels ascending and descending, going back and forth between earth and heaven (see Gen 28:12). God apparently wants to encourage Jacob by reassuring him that the stairway to heaven is still there! The connecting link between earth and heaven, between sinners and God, is still working. For a rascal like Jacob, what a comfort this must have been as he prepared to face the greatest challenge of his life.

When he learns that Esau is coming to meet him with four hundred men, Jacob is "greatly afraid and distressed" (Gen 32:7). Assuming that his brother's intentions are violent, he divides his family and possessions into two camps, thinking, "If Esau comes to the one camp and attacks it, then the camp that is left will escape" (Gen 32:8). Then he prays as he has never prayed before:

> O God of my father Abraham and God of my father Isaac, O LORD who said to me, 'Return to your country and to your kindred, that I may do you good,' I am not worthy of the least of all the deeds of steadfast love and all the faithfulness that you have shown to your servant, for with only my staff I crossed this Jordan, and now I have become two camps.

> *Please deliver me from the hand of my brother, from the hand of Esau, for I fear him, that he may come and attack me, the mothers with the children. But you said, 'I will surely do you good, and make your offspring as the sand of the sea, which cannot be numbered for multitude.'" (Gen 32:9–12)*

Compared to how Jacob prayed at Bethel twenty years before (see Gen 28:20–22), this is a remarkable improvement! His earlier conversation sounded more like a self-centered attempt to manipulate God than an authentic prayer. But here, as he faces the greatest crisis of his life, he truly prays to God. Humbly acknowledging his unworthiness, Jacob makes sure that God understands that he is in this situation only because he has obeyed the divine summons to return home. Quoting God's own words, Jacob reminds God of his covenant promises. But at its heart, his prayer is a cry for help: "Please deliver me from the hand of my brother!" As the narrative unfolds, we discover this is a prayer that God both hears and answers.

How are we to understand the lavish gift Jacob sends to his brother? Whatever its motivation, the gift itself is impressive: two hundred female goats, twenty male goats, two hundred ewes, twenty rams, thirty milking camels and their calves, forty cows, ten bulls, twenty female donkeys, and ten male donkeys (see Gen 32:14–15). Some see these five hundred and fifty animals as Jacob's desperate attempt to try to buy his brother's favor. According to this interpretation, Jacob continues to act like a snake, trying to manipulate the situation by bribing his brother. But seen in the context of how God has been working in Jacob's life, humbling him by making him aware of his deceitful heart, a better way to understand the gift is to see it as a form of restitution for the sins he has committed against his brother, namely, extorting the birthright and stealing the paternal blessing. The gift is Jacob's way of acknowledging his past sins, expressing regret for his hurtful behavior, and seeking to make amends.

Wrestling with God

Jacob's all-night wrestling match with the angel of the Lord is unique in the Bible. The closest parallel is Jesus' tortuous prayer in the

Garden of Gethsemane. There, literally sweating blood, Jesus had his own "wrestling match" with God: "Father, if you are willing, remove this cup from me." It is instructive to note that Jesus found victory only through surrender: "Not my will, but yours, be done" (see Luke 22:39–46). Jacob's wrestling match with God is similar, yet distinct.

> *The same night he arose and took his two wives, his two female servants, and his eleven children, and crossed the ford of the Jabbok. He took them and sent them across the stream, and everything else that he had. And Jacob was left alone. And a man wrestled with him until the breaking of the day. When the man saw that he did not prevail against Jacob, he touched his hip socket, and Jacob's hip was put out of joint as he wrestled with him. Then he said, "Let me go, for the day has broken." But Jacob said, "I will not let you go unless you bless me." And he said to him, "What is your name?" And he said, "Jacob." Then he said, "Your name shall no longer be called Jacob, but Israel, for you have striven with God and with men, and have prevailed." Then Jacob asked him, "Please tell me your name." But he said, "Why is it that you ask my name?" And there he blessed him. So Jacob called the name of the place Peniel, saying, "For I have seen God face to face, and yet my life has been delivered." The sun rose upon him as he passed Peniel, limping because of his hip. Therefore to this day the people of Israel do not eat the sinew of the thigh that is on the hip socket, because he touched the socket of Jacob's hip on the sinew of the thigh. (Gen 32:22–32)*

Almost everything about this wrestling match is mysterious. Who is this "man" that wrestles with Jacob? And why does he attack? Why did he wait so long to use his miracle powers of dislocating Jacob's hip? Who won the match? Is Jacob's limp permanent? What does this story mean? Perhaps the real genius of the inspired narrative is that we, the readers, must provide our own interpretation both for what this wrestling match meant for Jacob—and what it means for us today.

The first thing to notice is that this is a *wrestling* match. It is not a fist fight. There are no knives, spears, swords, or slings. The purpose of a wrestling match is not to kill or maim your opponent, but to dominate him, to gain control over him, to pin him to the ground and force him to say "uncle." Of all the many different forms of combat, wrestling is perhaps the most "intimate"; it is up close and personal. The combatants experience full-body contact; they literally get in each other's faces.

Though Jacob has picked many fights in his life and has been the cause of many conflicts, *this* is a battle that he does not start! A mysterious "man" attacks him in the night and will not let him go. Who is he and what does he want? And why won't he reveal his name? During the fight, Jacob is obviously ignorant of who his adversary is but by the time it is all over, he has no doubt about his assailant's true identity: "I have seen God face to face," he gasps.

The prophet Hosea gives further insight into the identity of this mysterious stranger. He calls the divine wrestler both "God" and an "angel".

> *In the womb (Jacob) took his brother by the heel, and in his manhood he strove with God. He strove with the angel and prevailed; he wept and sought his favor. (Hos 12:3–4)*

On numerous occasions in the Old Testament, God is pictured as coming to earth in physical, bodily form.[3] These theophanies have provoked endless theological discussion. How can God, who is Spirit, take on physical form? If he is one being, how can he be in heaven and on earth simultaneously? How can the Creator become part of the created order? The texts that describe these appearances of "the angel of the Lord" at times speak as if the personage were an angel, a messenger from God, and at other times as if he were God himself, in bodily form. With whom is Jacob really wrestling? The question is worth asking. Answering it takes us into the deepest mysteries of the being and nature of God. Perhaps the best answer is to identify the "man" who fought with Jacob as a preincarnate manifestation of the Second Person of the Trinity.

It may seem strange that Jacob's assailant asks him his name. We should not imagine that the questioner does not know the answer. The question's significance begins to emerge when we remember that

---

3   See for example Genesis 16:7–14; 18:1–33; 22:11–15; Exodus 3:2–4; Numbers 22:22–38; Judges 2:1–3; 6:11–23; 13:3–22; etc.

twenty years earlier, Jacob's blind father Isaac had asked him a similar question: "Who are you, my son?" On that occasion, Jacob, disguised as his brother, had answered the question deceitfully: "I am Esau, your firstborn." (Gen 27:18–19). This posture of pretending to be someone he wasn't served as a very apt description of Jacob's devious character. Now, as Jacob wrestles with God in the greatest crisis of his life, he is finally ready to acknowledge the truth about himself.

In voicing his name, Jacob he is doing much more than sharing a piece of information. He is confessing the truth about his identity: "I am Jacob; a cheater, deceiver, liar, manipulator. *That* is who I am." This was a life-changing moment for Jacob. Finally, self-aware, he embraces the truth about himself. Prior to this moment, he believed that he was a sinner because he occasionally sinned. But now, for the first time, he comes to the terrifying recognition that he sins because *he is a sinner*. This defines not just his behavior but his core identity. The problem is not just with the naughty things he has done. The problem goes much deeper than that! The problem is with his heart, his nature, his innermost person. He is Jacob!

Amazingly, when he confesses the truth about himself by acknowledging his deceitful nature, he opens the door for God's grace to do a work of transformation in his heart he never dreamed possible. As his wrestling match with God comes to an end, Jacob realizes that God wants to do more than forgive his sinful actions and help him modify his behavior. God has come to transform his heart. In giving him a new name, God is making him a new creation.

As the morning breaks and it appears the wrestling match will end in a draw, Jacob's assailant resorts to a new tactic. He uses his miraculous power to dislocate Jacob's hip! No longer able to fight effectively, all Jacob can do is cling to his opponent and hold on. But this technique seems to be more effective than all of Jacob's previous efforts combined and he "wins" the wrestling match by losing it! He receives both a new name and a divine blessing.

There is no indication that Jacob's wound ever healed. His limp became his most distinctive physical trait for the rest of his life.

Jacob's handicap carried such meaning that the nation of Israel made it a dietary regulation to refrain from eating "the sinew of the thigh that is on the hip socket" (Gen 32:32). God's people understood that something of eternal significance had happened at Peniel, and they wanted to ensure that they would never forget.

To enable us to better grasp the significance of Jacob's wrestling match, it is helpful to compare it to his first encounter with God. Twenty years earlier, at Bethel (see Gen 28:10–22), he had experienced an authentic conversion when he had a vision of the stairway to heaven. But in Genesis 32, at Peniel, this initial experience is deepened and enriched. Putting the two experiences side by side helps us to see Jacob's growth in spiritual maturity.

Genesis 28:10–22	Genesis 32:2–32
Bethel—House of God	Peniel—Face of God
This is easy—only believe	This is hard—a wrestling match
A change of status	A change of nature
What God does *for* Jacob	What God does *in* Jacob
Still the old Jacob	A new creation—Israel
Justification	Sanctification

Reconciling with Esau

Now that Jacob has seen God's face, he is ready to see Esau's face. Having settled things vertically with God, he is prepared to do all that he can to work things out horizontally with his brother. As he arrives with his four hundred men, we discover that God has been working in Esau's heart too! When he sees his brother walking toward him limping, bowing to the ground seven times, twenty years of hostility and hatred just melt away. The reunion of the two brothers is one of the most moving passages in all Scripture.

> *And Jacob lifted up his eyes and looked, and behold, Esau was coming, and four hundred men with him. So he divided the children among Leah and Rachel and the two female servants. . . . He himself went on before them, bowing himself to the ground seven times, until he came near to his brother. But Esau ran to meet him and embraced him and fell on his*

> *neck and kissed him, and they wept. And when Esau lifted up his eyes and saw the women and children, he said, "Who are these with you?" Jacob said, "The children whom God has graciously given your servant." . . . Esau said, "What do you mean by all this company that I met?" Jacob answered, "To find favor in the sight of my* LORD.*" But Esau said, "I have enough, my brother; keep what you have for yourself." Jacob said, "No, please, if I have found favor in your sight, then accept my present from my hand. For I have seen your face, which is like seeing the face of God." (Gen 33:1–10)*

The tearful reunion causes Jacob to see something he could have never seen before. Esau's face bears a distinct resemblance to the One he had wrestled with the night before!

Though reconciled, the brothers recognize they represent two very different ways of life and so agree to an amicable separation. Esau will live in Seir. His descendants will become the Amalekites, future enemies of the Jews. Jacob, now called Israel, will live in Shechem where he buys some land (see Gen 33:12–20).

It is noteworthy that, after his safe and peaceful return to the land of promise, Jacob, for the first time in his life, builds an *altar* (see Gen 33:20). Earlier, at Bethel, he had erected a *pillar* to celebrate his conversion (see Gen 28:18). Such a shrine, a type of memorial plaque, was intended to commemorate someone's achievement and bring glory to their memory. But at Shechem, rather than erecting a pillar, Jacob builds an altar. Here we have tangible evidence that the transformation that took place at Peniel is for real! Naming his altar *El-Elohe-Israel* (God, the God of Israel), his intention is to give glory and thanks to the One he knows face to face.

WALKING WITH A LIMP

It appears that, for the remainder of Jacob's life, he walked with a limp. Perhaps he used a cane. But rather than being embarrassed by his handicap or angered by his diminished mobility, it is easy to imagine that Jacob's limp became the singular most distinguishing characteristic of the aging patriarch's life. Now known as Israel, we can picture him hobbling through life with a curious smile on his face.

When someone would ask, "What happened? Why do you limp?", his eyes must have twinkled as he responded, "Sit down, my friend, and let me tell you a story."

In his book *Leading with a Limp*, psychologist Dan Allender describes what he calls the paradox of leadership:

> To the degree you attempt to hide or dissemble your weaknesses, the more you will need to control those you lead, the more insecure you will become, and the more rigidity you will impose. . . . So do yourself and your organization a favor and don't go there. Prepare now to admit to your staff that you are the organization's chief sinner. What I am calling you to is far more than the mere acknowledgment of your shortcomings. . . . I'm suggesting an outright dismantling of them—in the open and in front of those you lead.[4]

Using Jacob as one of his main examples, Allender insists that great leaders are effective not in spite of but *because of* their weaknesses, flaws, and sinful pasts! It is their authenticity in leading with a limp that inspires others to follow them. Flawed leaders are successful because they are not preoccupied with protecting their image. Because they have known failure, they are prepared to take risks and to trust in God. "Nothing succeeds like imperfection," Allender writes.[5]

Think about what it meant for Jacob, the third patriarch of Israel, to walk with a limp. One doesn't need a degree in psychology to realize that Jacob's limp accounts for his greatest successes as a leader.

- It was *visible* for all to see. Though some deformities and handicaps are hidden, not so Jacob's limp. This was a debilitating condition that everyone could see.
- It was *humbling*. His limp made it physically impossible to strut about in arrogant self-confidence. It was a constant reminder of his past, his brokenness, and his need for help.
- It was *painful*. Living with a low level of daily pain must have worked to soften Jacob's heart and make him more aware of the sufferings and difficulties of those around him.

---

4 Allender, *Leading with a Limp*, 3.
5 Ibid., 49.

- It *slowed him down*. No longer would Jacob's life be defined by busyness, deadlines, and frantic schedules. Traveling slowly enabled him to deepen relationships and enjoy blessings along the path that those in a hurry completely miss.
- It was *permanent*. At some point Jacob stopped praying "Lord, heal me" and started praying "Lord, give me grace to live with this limp." Accepting his disability was one of the greatest secrets of his success as a leader.
- It made him *approachable*. In his youthful arrogance, no one wanted to get close to Jake the Snake. He was unsafe. His limp, however, signaled that he was vulnerable, safe, easy to approach, and delightful company.

The more we understand the Gospel, the more we learn that *all* God's saints walk with a limp. It seems hard to find an exception. God apparently delights in working through the lives of men and women who are flawed. Rather than hiding these handicaps and deformities, God tends to highlight them! We have already looked at the troubling flaws in the lives of Adam, Noah, Abraham, and Isaac. But this pattern is repeated throughout the Biblical story: Moses, David, Elijah, Jeremiah, Peter, Paul, etc. Dan Allender says it well: "It seems God loves to use troubled, odd, unpredictable people to not only lead others but also to make the gospel known."[6]

The story of Jacob teaches us that, rather than hiding our deformities, wounds, and past sins, we should prayerfully consider how to use them as an integral part of our life story.

Making it Personal

Our examination of Genesis 32–33 must not end without asking the question "So what?" Are there lessons here for us today? Jacob's wrestling match with God and his reconciliation with his brother are stories intended to do more than teach history. Here are a few eternal principles that are relevant for us today.

---

6 Ibid., 53.

- *My real struggle in life is with God.* Like Jacob, we may imagine that our most significant life issues are the struggles we have with other people, the challenging circumstances we face, or even the temptations that come to us through the world, the flesh, and the devil. Jacob's story reminds us that our ultimate battles are not to be found there. Our real conflict is with God! As the sovereign ruler over all creation, he alone is ultimately responsible for all that happens. So, if life is not turning out the way you had hoped, get alone with God and fight it out.
- *Getting right with God precedes getting right with my brother.* Jacob needed to figure out his vertical relationship with God before he could figure out his horizontal relationship with Esau. When relationships with others become frayed and broken, the first priority is to get face to face with God and come to a place of full surrender. Then, and only then, one is ready to look into the face of an estranged brother or sister and try to make things right.
- *Victory comes through surrender.* When it comes to our struggle with God, we win the battle by losing. Not my will but yours be done! Jacob's victory came not by wrestling but by clinging. The Bible warns us that no one can see God's face and live (see Exod 33:20). We might say, then, that when he saw God's face, the old Jacob died and Israel was born.
- *Justification is incomplete without sanctification.* Jacob's conversion experience at Bethel was authentic and indispensable, but incomplete. Visiting God's house (Bethel) is a great place to begin. But seeing God's face (Peniel) is what salvation is all about.
- *Walking with a limp is a badge of honor.* Jacob's life became meaningful and influential only because we know the ugliness of his sinful past and the deceitfulness of his wicked heart. His witness was powerful and his leadership effective because he led with a limp. My life will be useful to God and to others only when I begin to let others know what grace can do in the life of

someone as broken and sinful as me. As Dan Allender puts it: "The older I become, the more I am utterly amazed that anyone as screwed up as I am is allowed to be in the ministry at all."[7]

QUESTIONS FOR DISCUSSION

1. Have you ever been put in a situation where you had to face up to something in your past that you had hoped could be forgotten? What happened?
2. Why did Jacob need a deeper work of grace? Why wasn't Bethel's experience sufficient?
3. Is Jacob's deeper experience at Peniel normative for all Christians? Discuss this.
4. What is the difference between "the house of God" and "the face of God"? How many people who visit God's house see God's face?
5. Have you ever seen God's face in the face of someone else?
6. Do all God's saints walk with a limp? Do you? Describe your limp.

---

[7] Ibid., 152.

Come, O Thou Traveler Unknown ("Wrestling Jacob")

Charles Wesley (1742)

Come, O Thou Traveler unknown,
Whom still I hold but cannot see;
My company before is gone,
And I am left alone with Thee;
With Thee all night I mean to stay,
And wrestle till the break of day.

I need not tell Thee who I am,
My sin and misery declare;
Thyself hast called me by my name,
Look on Thy hands, and read it there;
But who, I ask Thee, who art Thou?
Tell me Thy name, and tell me now.

In vain Thou strugglest to get free;
I never will unloose my hold;
Art Thou the Man that died for me?
The secret of Thy love unfold;
Wrestling, I will not let Thee go,
Till I Thy name, Thy nature know.

Yield to me now, for I am weak,
But confident in self-despair;
Speak to my heart, in blessings speak,
Be conquered by my instant prayer;
Speak, or Thou never hence shalt move,
And tell me if Thy name be Love.

'Tis Love! 'tis Love! Thou diedst for me,
I hear Thy whisper in my heart;
The morning breaks, the shadows flee:
Pure, universal Love Thou art;
To me, to all Thy mercies move;
Thy nature and Thy name is Love.

Lame as I am, I take the prey;
Hell, earth, and sin, with ease o'ercome.
I leap for joy, pursue my way,
And, as a bounding hart, I run,
Through all eternity to prove
Thy nature and Thy name is Love.

25
#MeToo[1]
Genesis 34:1–31

Genesis 34 is a troubling story about rape, violence, mass murder, and plunder. There is no mention of God anywhere in the text and the author makes no attempt to draw a moral lesson from the sordid events recounted here. The main character, Dinah, never speaks. Thus, we can only guess what she is thinking and feeling. The narrative leaves the reader feeling confused and unclean. One wonders how a story like this ended up in the Bible. What is its purpose? Why is it here?

I'm so glad you asked!

Genesis 34 is a sober reminder that the Bible deals with real sins, committed by real people, in a complex and confusing world. At times, the narrative seems to blur the distinction between guilt and innocence, perpetrator and victim, and the text is full of moral ambiguities. If the story of Dinah's rape and her brothers' murderous rampage to get revenge leaves you feeling disoriented and confused—welcome to the real world. As Christians, we should rejoice that our sacred book contains stories like this because it reminds us how messy life can be in a fallen world.

Perhaps the first thing to be said about this troubling narrative is that it is not unique. As difficult as it may be to understand why this

---

1   *#MeToo* is the name of a movement against sexual harassment and assault of women. Its goal is to encourage and empower women, especially the young and the vulnerable, to speak up about harmful incidents they may have experienced at work, home, school, the gym, etc.

story is in the Bible, the difficulty is only heightened when we learn there is another story in Scripture that is remarkably similar. II Samuel 13 describes how Tamar, the daughter of King David, is raped by her half-brother Amnon. When her father the king does nothing to address the injustice, her full brother Absalom steps in and gets revenge by murdering the rapist. When the story of Dinah is compared to that of Tamar, we see similar themes running through both narratives:

- A young woman is raped.
- A father is emotionally detached and passive.
- A brother (or brothers) step in to take violent revenge.

Because these stories are in the Bible, we can assume that God *wants* us to talk about such matters. The nature of these behaviors (sexual sin, harassment, rape, etc.) causes many to feel embarrassment when such topics are brought into the light. Consequently, they would prefer to keep these matters hidden. But this is precisely what we must *not* do! The fact that these stories make us uncomfortable is the very reason they are included in God's Word. Sexual harassment, assault, and rape have been an unfortunate part of human history since the beginning of time. Not only are these sins found among pagans and unbelievers, but, as these stories in Scripture remind us, they are sometimes encountered in the family of God. When these ugly behaviors are denied or hidden, the consequences only get worse.

No two situations of sexual assault are alike. What happened to Dinah and Tamar will never again be repeated in quite the same way. And yet, the themes we see in their stories recur from one generation to the next. The recent high-profile examples of sexual predatory behavior of men with power, status, and wealth have made us hypersensitive to the issue of sexual harassment and assault. The *#MeToo* movement has helped to bring needed attention to a dirty secret in our culture, even though it has at times overstated the issue. Examining Genesis 34 can provide helpful guidelines to enable us to both discuss and take action on a very troubling social issue of our day.

DINAH IS DEFILED

> *Now Dinah the daughter of Leah, whom she had borne to Jacob, went out to see the women of the land. And when Shechem the son of Hamor the Hivite, the prince of the land, saw her, he seized her and lay with her and humiliated her. And his soul was drawn to Dinah the daughter of Jacob. He loved the young woman and spoke tenderly to her. So Shechem spoke to his father Hamor, saying, "Get me this girl for my wife." (Gen 34:1–4)*

The story begins by telling us that Dinah, a single teenage girl, wanders off, alone and unprotected, in a dangerous city. She initiates contact with a group of young women, most notably those who live in Shechem.[2] We can only imagine what her intentions are. Is she lonely? Curious? Bored? Looking for fun? Flirtatious? Merely to ask such questions hints at the possibility of "blaming the victim." While the biblical narrative is clear that Shechem is a rapist, fully responsible for his violent act, it does not camouflage the reality that Dinah's behavior is naïve, careless, and dangerous. We would be justified in "blaming" her for what happened only if Dinah had sought to seduce Shechem in some way, which she didn't, or if she had deliberately gone against the warnings of her family, none of which were given. Leon Kass notes that "actions taken in innocence are often far from innocent, both in their inner meaning and in their outcome."[3]

The verbs used to describe Shechem's behavior in Genesis 34:2 are carefully chosen to convey the horrible reality of Dinah's defilement.

- He *saw* her. For men, sexual sin almost always begins with wandering eyes and a lustful look. This was certainly true for Samson (see Judg 14:1–3, 7; 16:1, 21). It was this struggle with lust that prompted Job to say, "I made a covenant with my eyes not to look lustfully at a young woman" (Job 31:1 NIV).
- He *seized* her. Far from being a tender touch of endearment, Shechem's embrace is forceful and violent. From this point

---

2 Shechem, the young man who rapes Dinah, has the same name as the city where he lives and where his father is the "mayor."
3 Kass, *The Beginning of Wisdom*, 479.

forward the encounter is non-consensual. Today, we would probably call what happened between Shechem and Dinah "date rape."

- He *lay with* her. Hebrew scholars note that the word "with" is not present in the text. A more accurate way, perhaps, to describe the event would be to say crudely that Shechem "laid" her.
- He *humiliated* her. The same word describes Amnon's behavior with Tamar (see 2 Sam 13:12, 14, 22, 32). Shechem's sexual assault on Dinah shames her and treats her as if she were a prostitute (see Gen 34:31). Elsewhere in the chapter, Shechem is said to have "defiled" Dina (see Gen 34:5, 13). This is a strong word that has the sense of making her contaminated, polluted, and unclean.

Rape is far more than a physical violation of a woman's body. It is just as profoundly a violation of her soul, her spirit, her person. It is important to remember that rape also has a profoundly destructive impact on the rapist. For both the victim and the perpetrator, things are never the same again after the rape as they were before. For Amnon, the rape causes his affection for Tamar to turn suddenly to hatred.

> *Then Amnon hated her with very great hatred, so that the hatred with which he hated her was greater than the love with which he had loved her. And Amnon said to her, "Get up! Go!" (2 Sam 13:15)*

With Shechem, however, the rape seems to have the exact opposite effect. "And his soul was drawn to Dinah. . . . He loved (her) and spoke tenderly to her" (Gen 34:3). We may struggle to understand the psychology of what happens in a man's soul when he sexually violates another human person, but whether he feels closer to the woman or is repulsed by her, the result is equally evil. On the surface, Shechem may appear to be a better man than Amnon because of his continuing love for Dinah, but don't be fooled. A man who rapes a woman and then sweet talks her is still a rapist.

It is worthwhile to remember that the Bible often speaks of sexual relations in terms of "knowing" one another. "Now Adam *knew* Eve, his wife, and she conceived" (Gen 4:1). "Cain *knew* his wife, and she conceived" (Gen 4:17), etc. The term refers to the beauty and intimacy of sexual relations between a husband and wife. It recognizes that two persons are freely disclosing themselves to one another in the most intimate of all possible forms of knowledge. It is noteworthy that in the description of the sexual relationship between Shechem and Dinah the term "to know" is missing! For Shechem, Dinah is not a person to know but an object to use for his own selfish pleasure.

In telling his father, Hamor, "Get me this girl for my wife" (see Gen 34:4), Shechem is seeking approval for his promiscuity and asking his father, the "mayor" of the city, to legitimize his predatory and violent treatment of Dinah. In giving his blessing to the proposed marriage, Hamor is in fact normalizing sexual harassment and assault and giving cultural affirmation to the abusive mistreatment of women.

JACOB IS SILENT AND PASSIVE

> *Now Jacob heard that he had defiled his daughter Dinah. But his sons were with his livestock in the field, so Jacob held his peace until they came. And Hamor the father of Shechem went out to Jacob to speak with him. The sons of Jacob had come in from the field as soon as they heard of it, and the men were indignant and very angry, because he had done an outrageous thing in Israel by lying with Jacob's daughter, for such a thing must not be done. (Gen 34:5–7)*

On learning of his daughter's rape, the text curiously notes that Jacob "held his peace" (see Gen 34:5). *The New Living Translation* says that he "did nothing." Ostensibly, he was waiting for his sons to arrive so that together they could prepare a plan of action. But the broader context provides a fuller understanding. Jacob's failure to respond immediately by providing strong and decisive leadership meant that others rushed in to fill void. Though he was the father, the leader of his clan, his delay meant that he lost control of the situation.

We can only guess what caused Jacob's reluctance to step boldly forward and lead his family. Was he in shock over what had happened? Was he in too much grief to think clearly? Was he paralyzed by fear?

Was he so emotionally detached from his daughter that he simply failed to grasp the significance of what had happened to her? Though we will never know what caused Jacob's passive response, we do know the tragic results: his hot-headed sons, notably Levi and Simeon, became the *de facto* leaders of the family. Livid with rage over what had happened to their sister, they provided the leadership that Jacob failed to give. Unfortunately, they led the family down a path of treachery, deceit, violence, and revenge.

It is interesting to note that the story of Tamar's rape also emphasizes her father's passivity and failure to act. David was not only Tamar's father, he was also the king of Israel. It was preeminently his responsibility to establish justice in the land. But when he learned of Tamar's rape, his only response was to become "very angry" (2 Sam 13:21). Though emotionally upset over what had happened, there is no indication that he took any disciplinary action against Amnon. Perhaps the memory of his own sin with Bathsheba made it difficult for him to enforce justice on others who were guilty of sexual misconduct. Whatever the reason, David failed, both as a father and a king, to provide the leadership that was needed. It was his inaction that created the opportunity for Absalom to step forward and take charge. The tragic consequences of David's abdication of leadership almost destroyed the nation.

Looking again at the story of Dinah, one can only wonder what would cause a father to be so emotionally detached when his own daughter is raped. Compared to how Jacob reacts years later when he is told (falsely) that his favorite son, Joseph, has been killed by a wild animal, his passive reaction to learning of Dinah's rape is all the more disturbing. On hearing the news of Joseph's death, Jacob tears his garments, puts on sackcloth, and weeps for many days, refusing to be comforted (see Gen 37:34–35). Parental favoritism, as we have seen on other occasions in Genesis, can make family dynamics a very toxic environment. One wonders if Dinah's decision to visit the Shechemites was not an unconscious search for the love and affirmation she had never found at home.

Jacob may be slow in recognizing the gravity of what has happened, but his sons are not! Although they are certainly wrong in what they do (mass murder, plunder, etc.), they are right in their understanding that a great injustice has been committed and the offense must be addressed. Shechem has done an "outrageous thing," something that should never happen in Israel (see Gen 34:7). It is interesting to note that the same vocabulary is used in II Samuel 13 when Tamar pleads with Amnon not to rape her: "No, my brother, do not violate me, for such a thing is not done in Israel; do not do this outrageous thing" (2 Sam 13:12). The brothers rightly understand that Shechem's behavior is not only a crime against their sister; it is a frontal assault on the entire nation!

SIMEON AND LEVI GET REVENGE

> *But Hamor spoke with them, saying, "The soul of my son Shechem longs for your daughter. Please give her to him to be his wife. Make marriages with us. Give your daughters to us, and take our daughters for yourselves. You shall dwell with us, and the land shall be open to you. Dwell and trade in it, and get property in it." Shechem also said to her father and to her brothers, "Let me find favor in your eyes, and whatever you say to me I will give. Ask me for as great a bride-price and gift as you will, and I will give whatever you say to me. Only give me the young woman to be my wife."*
>
> *The sons of Jacob answered Shechem and his father Hamor deceitfully, because he had defiled their sister Dinah. They said to them, "We cannot do this thing, to give our sister to one who is uncircumcised, for that would be a disgrace to us. Only on this condition will we agree with you—that you will become as we are by every male among you being circumcised. Then we will give our daughters to you, and we will take your daughters to ourselves, and we will dwell with you and become one people. But if you will not listen to us and be circumcised, then we will take our daughter, and we will be gone."*
>
> *Their words pleased Hamor and Hamor's son Shechem. And the young man did not delay to do the thing, because he delighted in Jacob's daughter. Now he was the most honored*

> *of all his father's house. So Hamor and his son Shechem came to the gate of their city and spoke to the men of their city, saying, "These men are at peace with us; let them dwell in the land and trade in it, for behold, the land is large enough for them. Let us take their daughters as wives, and let us give them our daughters. Only on this condition will the men agree to dwell with us to become one people—when every male among us is circumcised as they are circumcised. Will not their livestock, their property and all their beasts be ours? Only let us agree with them, and they will dwell with us." And all who went out of the gate of his city listened to Hamor and his son Shechem, and every male was circumcised, all who went out of the gate of his city.*
>
> *On the third day, when they were sore, two of the sons of Jacob, Simeon and Levi, Dinah's brothers, took their swords and came against the city while it felt secure and killed all the males. They killed Hamor and his son Shechem with the sword and took Dinah out of Shechem's house and went away. The sons of Jacob came upon the slain and plundered the city, because they had defiled their sister. They took their flocks and their herds, their donkeys, and whatever was in the city and in the field. All their wealth, all their little ones and their wives, all that was in the houses, they captured and plundered.*
>
> *Then Jacob said to Simeon and Levi, "You have brought trouble on me by making me stink to the inhabitants of the land, the Canaanites and the Perizzites. My numbers are few, and if they gather themselves against me and attack me, I shall be destroyed, both I and my household." But they said, "Should he treat our sister like a prostitute?" (Gen 34:8–31)*

When Hamor comes to Jacob to discuss the possible marriage of their children, there is no hint of an apology for the way Dinah had been treated, no acknowledgement that a wrong had been committed in the way this marriage was being arranged. One gets the idea that this sort of thing (date rape, premarital sex, violence against women, etc.) went on all the time in the city of Shechem. This was normal operating procedure.

Moving beyond the specific marriage proposal between Shechem and Dinah, Hamor suggests that the two tribes make an agreement to practice intermarriage, that they become one people. The financial advantages of such a deal seems to be his primary point. But Jacob's sons recognize this invitation for what it truly is: the annihilation of God's covenant people on planet earth. The Shechemites were seeking to absorb Israel, assimilate them, so that they no longer had a distinct identity as the people of God. Nothing the sons of Jacob could imagine would be more tragic than this! Hamor's offer may have sounded good and reasonable on the outside, but in reality, it was a diabolical attempt to destroy the people of God and divert them from their divine mission.

The brothers, knowing that Dinah is held in Shechem's home, perhaps against her will, and that an armed attack against the city would be suicidal, resort to deception (see Gen 34:13). Just as their father Jacob was a master of deceit, duplicity, and manipulation (see Gen 25:26; 27:24, 35–36), so are his sons. In making circumcision the condition for marriage, they are potentially asking the Shechemites to convert to a new religion. Amazingly, the leaders of the city agree. In using the most sacred ceremony of their faith to help them accomplish their murderous agenda, the brothers add blasphemy to their lengthy list of sins. They have profaned that which is holy.

Not only do Simeon and Levi brutally murder all the men, but they also plunder the city, callously taking the dead men's wives, children, and possessions. Their actions are clearly barbaric, cruel, and sinful. There is no suggestion that this was God's will. Years later, Simeon and Levi will be cursed by their father for their wicked actions.

> *Simeon and Levi are brothers;*
> *weapons of violence are their swords.*
> *Let my soul come not into their council;*
> *O my glory, be not joined to their company.*
> *For in their anger they killed men,*
> *and in their willfulness they hamstrung oxen.*
> *Cursed be their anger, for it is fierce,*
> *and their wrath, for it is cruel!*
> *I will divide them in Jacob*
> *and scatter them in Israel. (Gen 49:5–7)*

Once the killing and plunder has ended, Jacob rebukes Simeon and Levi for their murderous rampage. However, his concern at this time is not focused on their violent behavior, but the fact that their actions have exposed the family to danger. The brothers defend themselves simply by saying, "Should he treat our sister like a prostitute?" (Gen 34:31). Jacob's silence indicates that, even after all that has happened, as the leader of his family, he still has no better solution to offer for dealing with the outrageous defilement committed against his daughter.

Lessons Learned

Yes, Genesis 34 is a troubling story. None of us enjoy reading about rape, violence, mass murder, and plunder. But it is not just the actions in this melodrama that are troubling, it is the people involved. The narrative is a masterful description of the dysfunction, flaws, and sins that shape the personalities and influence the decisions of the major players in this sad story. This is a group of really messed-up people! As we close this chapter, let's look at them again, one by one, this time imagining how they might appear today.

A teenage girl named *Dinah*, feeling bored and neglected at home, wanders off wanting to experience the joys and excitement of city life. Naïve, gullible, and foolish, she and her girlfriends go places young girls should never go. Flirtatious and charming, she strikes up a relationship with the son of the mayor, a boy named Shechem. At first, she hangs out with him in the safety of the group, but then he coaxes her into going where they can be alone together. First using sweet talk, and then becoming physically aggressive, Shechem wants to have sex with her. Dinah protests but he is too strong and rapes her. Though obviously traumatized and hurt by the experience, Dinah never talks about it. We can only guess what she is thinking and feeling.

Shechem feels he has done nothing wrong. After all, Dinah is his friend and seems to enjoy his company. Sure, he may have been a little rough with her and a bit forceful, but that's not unusual in this town. Everyone he knows behaves like this. So, what's the big deal? Besides, he is in love with Dinah and wants to marry her. That makes it all legitimate, right? Among his friends, his actions would never be classified as "rape." Shechem talks Dinah into moving in with him and they live together in an unmarried state. When he tells his parents of his desire to tie the knot, his father is very supportive and promises to help arrange the marriage.

Hamor, Shechem's father, following cultural protocol, goes to Jacob to discuss the possibility of marriage between their children. When he discovers that Jacob is upset over his son's behavior with his daughter, he seeks to downplay the incident by saying, "Kids will be kids." To sweeten the deal, Hamor proposes that the marriage of their children be the first of many marriages between the two tribes. He hopes that the two groups can become one new people.

Dinah's father, *Jacob*, is bewildered by the whole situation. "Let's wait and see," he says. He recognizes that Shechem has mistreated his daughter but does nothing to address the injustice, fearing that it might escalate into an international incident. Being emotionally detached from his daughter, he fails to grasp the gravity of the situation and does nothing to help Dinah process the traumatic experience of sexual assault.

When *Dinah's brothers* realize their father is confused and dragging his feet, they huddle together and form a plan of their own. Livid with rage over what Shechem has done to their sister, they want only one thing: vengeance. Not once do they pray or seek counsel. Using deception, treachery, and lies, they implement their plan of genocide against the city where Shechem has taken their sister hostage. They succeed in making a bad situation worse.

But where is *God* in all this? He is not mentioned in the narrative at all—not even once. He is conspicuous only by his absence. We get the impression that the tragic events of this horrible story happen only because no one has invited him into the drama!

Before closing this sad chapter, let's highlight four lessons that we can learn. Hopefully, this will enable us to bring some moral clarity to an otherwise senseless story.

Lesson 1. Do not love the world.

The trouble began when Dinah was drawn to her pagan neighbors and wanted to be like them. Perhaps she was perturbed, even embarrassed, by her Jewish identity and how it made her different from all her friends. This posture of loving the world opened the door to trouble. "Do you not know that friendship with the world is enmity with God?" James asks (Jas 4:4). While God commands us to love our neighbors, we must beware of the seductive power of their worldly ways (cf. 1 John 2:15–17). This is especially true when it comes to sexuality. God's people are called to very different standard. Leviticus 18, perhaps the most important chapter in the Bible on sexual ethics, begins with these words:

> *And the* LORD *spoke to Moses, saying, "Speak to the people of Israel and say to them, I am the* LORD *your God. You shall not do as they do in the land of Egypt, where you lived, and you shall not do as they do in the land of Canaan, to which I am bringing you. You shall not walk in their statutes. You shall follow my rules and keep my statutes and walk in them. I am the* LORD *your God." (Lev 18:1–4)*

Lesson 2. Get things in their proper order.

Earlier in our study of Genesis, we learned that, when it comes to love, sex, and marriage, God has given specific instructions concerning the sequence of events: "Therefore shall a man leave his father and his mother and shall cleave (hold fast) unto his wife: and they shall be one flesh" (Gen 2:24 KJV).

- *First*, there is a leaving. Before establishing a home of his own, a future spouse is expected to leave his own family of origin. Whether the departure is physical, financial, or emotional, or all three, the break with mom and dad is the first prerequisite for successful homebuilding.
- *Second*, there is a cleaving. Marriage is to be built on the loving attraction that draws the man and the woman together. This union of love is formalized in a public wedding ceremony when the couple makes vows to one another.

- *Third*, having left their parents and entered a covenant of marriage, the couple is now free to enjoy the beauty and intimacy of sexual union.

A huge part of the problem in Genesis 34 is that Shechem has completely rearranged God's sequence of events! First, he had sex. Then, he fell in love. The *King James Version*, picking up the vocabulary of Genesis 2:24, says that "his soul clave unto Dinah" (see Gen 34:3). Finally, he wanted to marry her. We are never quite sure if he ever succeeded in doing the first thing necessary to make marriage work: separate from his parents. His difficulty in distancing himself from his father's dominant influence is seen throughout the narrative. This story teaches us that when God's plan for love, sex, and marriage is ignored, then sexual harassment and assault come in like a flood.

Lesson 3. How to respond rightly when we learn of sexual abuse.

How should we respond when we learn that a woman has been sexually abused, assaulted, or raped? While Genesis 34 does not offer a divine prescription that will fit every situation, it does describe three very bad responses to sexual abuse.

- *Normalize the abusive treatment of women.* Hamor and Shechem do not see sexually predatory behavior against females as a problem. This is simply how women are treated in their city. This is normal behavior.
- *Do nothing.* Jacob knows that what happened to his daughter is wrong but does nothing to address the situation. He is emotionally detached, silent, and passive. He lives in denial.
- *Violence.* Dinah's brothers respond with vigilante justice. They rightly recognize the seriousness of the issue but their response (revenge, murder, plunder, etc.) only makes a bad situation worse.

Because each situation of sexual abuse is unique, we can be thankful that the author of Genesis does not conclude the story of Dinah's rape by stating how it *should* have been handled! The three inappropriate responses in themselves have great pedagogical value.

It is precisely in imagining how the story *could* have been handled differently that the reader is prepared and equipped to face similar situations in the contemporary world.

Lesson 4. Sexual relations are never just between two people.

Many people flippantly profess to believe that what two people do in private is nobody else's business. This is simply not true. What happened privately between Shechem and Dinah became an international incident! Dinah's brothers rightly discerned that what had happened to their sister affected them all. Though sexual relationships should be personal, intimate, and private, the implications of what is happening have ramifications for the entire community. This is precisely why God wants us to talk candidly about these matters and seek his wisdom for how best to respond.

QUESTIONS FOR DISCUSSION

1. How do you feel about the *#MeToo* movement? Has it been a good thing for our country or a bad thing?
2. Describe what Dinah may have been thinking as she sought friendships with pagan neighbors. If you had been her dad or mom, how might you have counseled her?
3. Why does the Bible prohibit sexual relations outside of marriage? What's wrong with premarital sex?
4. When he learned that his daughter had been raped, Jacob did nothing; he was silent and passive. What happens when a person in authority fails to provide strong leadership when an injustice has occurred?
5. Have you ever been part of a community when a situation of sexual abuse came to light? How was it handled? What did you learn?

26
The Pits
Genesis 37:1–36

The last section of Genesis is devoted to the life of Joseph, the eleventh son of Jacob. It takes fourteen chapters, roughly one-third of the entire book, to tell his story (Gen 37–50). The narrative reads like a short novel, beginning with Joseph as a boy and ending with his death. There is a discernible plot that follows the theme of conflict among brothers who, in the end, are finally reconciled. It is a family story that deals with joy and sorrow, love and hate, poverty and wealth, sin and forgiveness, good and evil.

Though he is not one of the patriarchs, Joseph's life obviously has tremendous significance in the eyes of the author of Genesis. His story serves as a transition from the age of spiritual giants like Abraham, Isaac, and Jacob to a four-hundred-year period when God seems to be silent. The story of Joseph explains how Israel came to live in Egypt and grew from a small family into a great nation. It illustrates how God's people can have hope in the midst of adversity and how they can be a blessing to the nations.

In stark contrast to the sin-prone lives of the three patriarchs, Joseph is a sterling example of godliness, piety, and moral integrity. It is difficult to find a single character flaw in his life. With the possible exception of being a "spoiled brat" as a youth, the lengthy narrative of his life reveals no obvious instances of sin, hypocrisy, or moral failure. This is remarkable! In terms of godly character and righteous behavior, Joseph stands head and shoulders above every other major figure in the book of Genesis.

Joseph was neither a prophet nor a priest. He was a shepherd, a businessman, and a government worker. Yet his life had as great an influence in shaping the identity of the people of God as almost anyone else in Scripture. Joseph can be compared to Daniel, who lived many centuries later. Both men lived in a foreign land, interpreted dreams, served pagan rulers, held powerful positions in the government, and were unjustly thrown into prison. They were both laymen whose spiritual witness changed history.

Joseph's life can be outlined as a series of reversals:

- From being the eleventh-born son to being his father's favorite (Gen 37:1–11).
- From being his father's favorite to being thrown into a pit (Gen 37:12–36).
- From being in a pit to being elevated to the role of master steward in Potiphar's house (Gen 39:1–6).
- From being master in Potiphar's house to being thrown unjustly into prison (Gen 39:7–23).
- From being in prison to being elevated to the role of Prime Minister over all of Egypt (Gen 40–41).

Such sudden and unexpected reversals of fortune may, at first, appear to be random and haphazard. But a closer reading of the text reveals that God was providentially at work in each situation. While these abrupt reversals were taking place, it was difficult, if not impossible, for Joseph to see God's gracious hand at work. From his perspective, it must have seemed only painful, chaotic, capricious, and senseless. But near the end of his life when he looked back across the years, he could clearly see the amazing plan that God was bringing to fruition. In the rear-view mirror, it all made sense! Speaking to his brothers about how they had mistreated him, Joseph summed up his life in one, succinct sentence: "You meant evil against me, but God meant it for good" (Gen 50:20). Genesis 50:20 is to the Old Testament what Romans 8:28 is to the New Testament: "And we know that for those who love God all things work together for good, for those who are called according to his purpose."

Another way to understand the significance of Joseph is to see how his life foreshadows that of Jesus Christ. It takes only a little creativity to retell the story so that the parallels are obvious.

> Once upon a time, there was a father who had a beloved son who worked as a shepherd. He clothed him with a robe of majesty to show how much he loved him. But the father also had other children, and they had wandered far away. Calling his beloved son, the father said; "My children are lost, and I'm deeply concerned about them. I'm sending you to seek them, to find them, and to bring them home." "Yes, I'll go," said the obedient son.
>
> When the beloved son found his brothers, they did not welcome him or treat him kindly. In fact, they hated him and, conspiring together, they stripped him, beat him, and sold him for twenty pieces of silver. Throwing him into a pit, they thought they had destroyed him forever. But, to their shock and dismay, they later discovered that he had risen out of the pit and was very much alive! In fact, he was now sitting at the right hand of the king, ruling over all the earth in power and majesty.
>
> Years later, a terrible famine came to the land. The wicked brothers knew they would all die if they did not find help. Unaware that the Prime Minister was their brother, they bowed before him seeking to buy the food he had in abundance. Amazingly, the beloved son, rather than seeking revenge, lavishly gave them all the food they needed—for free! He graciously forgave them for the evil they had committed against him and invited them to come and live with him in security and peace.
>
> Moral: The father loved the world of sinful brothers so much that he gave his beloved son, so that whoever believes in him, will not perish, but will have abundant and eternal life.

DYSFUNCTION JUNCTION

Our first glimpse of Joseph leaves us feeling a bit confused. Is he a child prodigy with a divine destiny? Or is he a spoiled brat? Could it be possible that he is both, at the same time? The nuances and subtleties of the text are surely intended. Once again, the reader must interpret the narrative and discern its meaning. While the obvious purpose of the text is to introduce us to Joseph, the main character, its secondary purpose is to remind us that he is part of a very dysfunctional family.

> *Joseph, being seventeen years old, was pasturing the flock with his brothers. He was a boy with the sons of Bilhah and Zilpah, his father's wives. And Joseph brought a bad report of them to their father. Now Israel loved Joseph more than any other of his sons, because he was the son of his old age. And he made him a robe of many colors. But when his brothers saw that their father loved him more than all his brothers, they hated him and could not speak peacefully to him. (Gen 37:1–4)*

Of all people, Jacob should have been alert to the long-term damage that can be caused in a family by parental favoritism and sibling rivalry. We have seen how his own parents, Isaac and Rebekah, were guilty of letting the toxic vapors of favoritism bring catastrophic results to his own family. "Isaac loved Esau . . . but Rebekah loved Jacob" (Gen 25:28). This blatant, ugly favoritism on the part of the parents only exacerbated the sibling rivalry that was already evident between the twin brothers.

The reader is left feeling completely perplexed that Jacob would allow the poison of parental favoritism to be repeated in his own family! Didn't he know where this would lead? But rather than seeking to control and diminish his personal bias, he flaunted it! By giving Joseph a lavishly colored tunic,[1] Jacob proclaimed to the whole world that he loved Joseph the most. Jacob's favoritism only worked to enflame the jealousy that Joseph's brothers already had toward him.

Undoubtedly, the ugly examples of favoritism found in the book of Genesis help to explain the Bible's frequent warnings against this damnable sin. Whether expressed by parents, teachers, government leaders, judges, bosses, or pastors, prejudice is a grievous sin that is strongly condemned. We can be profoundly thankful that "God does

---

[1] The meaning of the Hebrew term is uncertain but different translations show possible meanings: "a richly ornamented robe" (NIV), "a long robe with sleeves" (RSV), "a varicolored tunic" (NASB).

not show favoritism" (Rom 2:11 NLT). Because we are created in his image, we must not show it either (see Lev 19:15; 1 Tim 5:21; Jas 2:9; etc.).

Though we sometimes make jokes about parental favoritism and sibling rivalry, the Bible reminds us that these kinds of family dysfunction are no laughing matter. Over and over again in the book of Genesis we have seen how conflict between siblings is not only ugly, it often leads to tragic consequences. Cain and Abel, Isaac and Ishmael, Jacob and Esau, Rachel and Leah, and Joseph and his brothers—one could almost say that sibling rivalry is what the book of Genesis is all about.

I Have a Dream

> *Now Joseph had a dream, and when he told it to his brothers, they hated him even more. He said to them, "Hear this dream that I have dreamed: Behold, we were binding sheaves in the field, and behold, my sheaf arose and stood upright. And behold, your sheaves gathered around it and bowed down to my sheaf." His brothers said to him, "Are you indeed to reign over us? Or are you indeed to rule over us?" So they hated him even more for his dreams and for his words.*
>
> *Then he dreamed another dream and told it to his brothers and said, "Behold, I have dreamed another dream. Behold, the sun, the moon, and eleven stars were bowing down to me." But when he told it to his father and to his brothers, his father rebuked him and said to him, "What is this dream that you have dreamed? Shall I and your mother and your brothers indeed come to bow ourselves to the ground before you?" And his brothers were jealous of him, but his father kept the saying in mind. (Gen 37:5–11)*

What are we to make of a seventeen-year-old boy dreaming dreams like this? Is Joseph experiencing delusions of grandeur? Does he suffer from a messiah complex? And why does he share these dreams with his brothers? To be sure, many interpret these verses to mean that Joseph is arrogant, brash, narcissistic, and consumed with selfish ambition. However, not everyone sees it this way. For example, Victor Hamilton gives very different interpretation.

> Joseph's behavior is not unlike that of the youthful David who is willing take on Goliath (1 Sam 17:26, 31), over the protestations of his older brothers and Saul. The dreams are from God. To teen-age Joseph the revelation means at least one thing: God has a plan for this young man's life, and that plan includes some type of leadership. Here then is a teenager with a sense of destiny, divine destiny. The fact is shared out of enthusiasm, not out of brashness. "Here I am, Lord, send me." But the brothers cannot tolerate this.[2]

When one knows the rest of the story, one realizes that Joseph's dreams are prophetic and describe a future that God himself will bring about. His brothers give no credence whatsoever to his dreams and conclude that their kid brother is an arrogant, megalomaniacal narcissist. The text does not tell us why Joseph wanted to share his dreams with his family. Was he bragging? Was he flaunting his status as the favored son? Was he looking for help in determining what the dreams meant? Or perhaps, in his youthful enthusiasm, was he simply naïve in thinking that his siblings would be excited, too? If there is any mistake or sin on Joseph's part, it is not in the content of what he dreamed but in his rash desire to share it with those who were not able to handle it. Perhaps this is an Old Testament illustration of Jesus' warning: "Do not give dogs what is holy, and do not throw your pearls before pigs, lest they trample them underfoot and turn to attack you" (Matt 7:6).

In the light of the horrible crimes these brothers are about to commit (assault and battery, kidnapping, conspiracy to commit murder, human trafficking, obstruction of justice), it is important to understand their motive. What could provoke such horrific atrocities? One assumes that the provocation will match the crime. The text, however, suggests that the motives are surprisingly mundane and routine; the types of relational challenges that go on in every family. In other words, Joseph may be difficult to live with, but he has done

---

2   Hamilton, *Handbook on the Pentateuch*, 129–130.

nothing to deserve this! The text offers three reasons to "explain" the brothers' murderous hatred. In their opinion, Joseph is:

- *A tattletale.* We can only guess what prompts Joseph to bring a "bad report" to his father concerning his brothers (see Gen 37:2). Is he a legitimate "whistle-blower," reporting something that his father needs to know? Or is he perhaps an opportunist, looking to score points with his dad? Though we don't know what motivates Joseph to bring the report, we *do* know how his brothers feel about it: they are livid and hate him for it!
- *A spoiled brat.* The favoritism Jacob shows for Joseph infuriates the brothers (see Gen 37:3–4). Their blind rage, however, causes them to fail to realize that their real problem is with their father, *not* with their brother!
- *A braggart.* In the opinion of his brothers, Joseph's dreams are evidence of narcissism and megalomania, perhaps a messiah complex. They never pause to consider, however, that God might actually be speaking to their baby brother. How different the story would have been if the brothers had been humble enough to ask if these revelations just might be true.

The story of Joseph teaches us that normal families dealing with normal challenges, when not handled properly, are capable of horrific atrocities.

Joseph's Terrible, Horrible, No-Good, Very Bad Day

> *Now his brothers went to pasture their father's flock near Shechem. And Israel said to Joseph, "Are not your brothers pasturing the flock at Shechem? Come, I will send you to them." And he said to him, "Here I am." So he said to him, "Go now, see if it is well with your brothers and with the flock, and bring me word." . . . . So Joseph went after his brothers and found them at Dothan.*
>
> *They saw him from afar, and before he came near to them, they conspired against him to kill him. They said to one another, "Here comes this dreamer. Come now, let us kill him and throw him into one of the pits. Then we will say that a fierce animal has devoured him, and we will see what will*

become of his dreams." But when Reuben heard it, he rescued him out of their hands, saying, "Let us not take his life." And Reuben said to them, "Shed no blood; throw him into this pit here in the wilderness, but do not lay a hand on him"— that he might rescue him out of their hand to restore him to his father. So when Joseph came to his brothers, they stripped him of his robe, the robe of many colors that he wore. And they took him and threw him into a pit. The pit was empty; there was no water in it.

Then they sat down to eat. And looking up they saw a caravan of Ishmaelites coming from Gilead, with their camels bearing gum, balm, and myrrh, on their way to carry it down to Egypt. Then Judah said to his brothers, "What profit is it if we kill our brother and conceal his blood? Come, let us sell him to the Ishmaelites, and let not our hand be upon him, for he is our brother, our own flesh." And his brothers listened to him.

Then Midianite traders passed by. And they drew Joseph up and lifted him out of the pit, and sold him to the Ishmaelites for twenty shekels of silver. They took Joseph to Egypt. . . .

Then they took Joseph's robe and slaughtered a goat and dipped the robe in the blood. And they sent the robe of many colors and brought it to their father and said, "This we have found; please identify whether it is your son's robe or not." And he identified it and said, "It is my son's robe. A fierce animal has devoured him. Joseph is without doubt torn to pieces." Then Jacob tore his garments and put sackcloth on his loins and mourned for his son many days. All his sons and all his daughters rose up to comfort him, but he refused to be comforted and said, "No, I shall go down to Sheol to my son, mourning." Thus his father wept for him. Meanwhile the Midianites had sold him in Egypt to Potiphar, an officer of Pharaoh, the captain of the guard. (Gen 37:12–36)

When you use your imagination to try to visualize the cold, calculated cruelty that the brothers utilize against Joseph, you begin to see the horrific wickedness of what is happening here. Far from being a crime of passion when emotions flare and people do unfortunate things, this was a premeditated crime that was carefully planned in advance. When we remember that Joseph is seventeen years old, a "minor" by today's legal standards, we understand that the crimes committed against him (kidnapping, attempted murder, human trafficking, etc.) appear in an even more sinister light.

The fact that Reuben and Judah make feeble attempts to mitigate the situation reveals that the brothers are not in full agreement with what is happening. Some of them, apparently, want more time to think it over and would like to rationally discuss possible alternative plans. But this is not permitted. In the end, all ten brothers act as a group, each one bearing his own measure of guilt and responsibility. "Group think" is the phenomenon that occurs when a body of people reaches consensus without the benefit of critical reasoning, an evaluation of the consequences, or a discussion of alternatives. Decisions are made based on peer pressure, political correctness, and the desire not to upset the balance of the group. Such a process helps to explain not only how brothers from a religious family could kidnap Joseph and sell him into slavery, but how the nation of Germany became complicit in the anti-Semitism of the 1930s and thus made possible the Holocaust.

Although this passage makes no mention of how Joseph responded to what was happening, we learn later that he was very vocal in begging and pleading with his brothers throughout the ordeal. Years later, when the brothers are trying to understand why so many misfortunes have befallen them, they conclude that they are reaping the consequences of their evil deeds. Their guilty consciences remember especially the way Joseph pled for mercy when they threw him into the pit and sold him as a slave:

> *Then they said to one another, "In truth we are guilty concerning our brother, in that we saw the distress of his soul, when he begged us and we did not listen. That is why this distress has come upon us." (Gen 42:21)*

To cover up their evil deeds, the brothers fabricate a lie and deceive their father into thinking that Joseph has been killed by a wild animal. Once again, the theme of deception is woven skillfully into the narrative. We have seen how, on numerous occasions, Jacob has been both the subject and the object of deception. This deception, however, when Jacob is led to believe that his favorite son is dead, is the cruelest of all.

THE PURPOSE OF PITS

The author of Genesis highlights the trauma of Joseph's treatment by his brothers by repeating the word "pit" seven times in this short narrative (see Gen 37:20, 22, 24, 28, 29). He wants us to recognize the crucial importance of Joseph's "pit experience" as one of the most formative events of his life. But this is not the only time Joseph will be thrown into a pit. When Potiphar puts him in prison (see Gen 39:20), Joseph will once again find himself in a deep, dark place, one from which escape is impossible. These "pit experiences" in Joseph's life are not random, meaningless events; nor do they indicate that God has abandoned him. Au contraire! These dark and painful moments are part of God's providential plan in preparing Joseph for leadership and for unimaginable blessings. What the brothers meant for evil, God was going to use for good (see Gen 50:20).

The Bible has a lot to say about pits. In English, the term translates several different Hebrew words that refer to things like a hole, a cistern, a well, a dungeon, an animal trap, Sheol, a grave, and even a prostitute. Little wonder that the word "pit" began to be used metaphorically to describe a situation that is very difficult and painful. If someone says their life is in "the pits" we understand immediately how the word is being used.

Numerous characters in the Bible, like Joseph, had "pit experiences" that were both literal and metaphorical. Though the reasons for being in a pit varied greatly, God delivered them all: Jeremiah (Jer 38:6), David (1 Sam 22:1–2; 24:1–3; Ps 57, 142), Elijah (1 Kgs 19:9–10), Jonah (Jonah 2:2–6), and Paul and Silas (Acts 16:23–24). It is interesting to note, that according to some traditions Jesus was both born and buried in a cave (a type of pit).

In Psalm 40, David talks about a "pit experience" in his life. Like Joseph, he made the sublime discovery that his time in the pit, though painful, was part of God's providential plan for his life. The education he received at Pit State University was the best leadership training he ever experienced.

> *I waited patiently for the* LORD;
> *he inclined to me and heard my cry.*
> *He drew me up from the pit of destruction,*
> *out of the miry bog,*
> *and set my feet upon a rock,*
> *making my steps secure.*
> *He put a new song in my mouth,*
> *a song of praise to our God.*
> *Many will see and fear,*
> *and put their trust in the* LORD. *(Ps 40:1–3)*

David's testimony is recorded so that anyone, anywhere, who finds himself in a pit can receive comfort, strength, and hope from these words. When you look at the pit experiences of David and Joseph, you can discern six directions to follow whenever you find yourself in a dark, painful, impossible situation.

Step 1. Confess the truth: "I am in a pit."

Sadly, many people are unable to get out of their pits for the simple reason they deny they are in one! But admitting reality and facing the truth is often harder than we think. We are not sure whether the "pit" David refers to in Psalm 40 is physical or metaphorical, or both; but one thing is certain: David found deliverance only when he confessed the truth.

Step 2. Acknowledge your inability: "I cannot save myself."

When Joseph was thrown into the pit, we can imagine that, at first, he feverishly tried every imaginable method he could think of to get out: jumping, climbing the walls, making a rope, screaming, etc. Nothing worked. David must have discovered that when the pit is a "miry bog," the harder you try to escape, the deeper you sink. Before a pit dweller can be delivered from his predicament, he must come to the place where he humbly recognizes that he cannot save himself.

Step 3. Cry out to God in prayer: "Lord, help!"

At some point, for both Joseph and David, all efforts to save themselves ceased, and they began to pray. Only God could save them now. Amazingly, God *wants* us to cry out to him for help. He invites us to pray (see 2 Chr 7:14; Jer 33:3; Matt 7:7–11; etc.). The story of blind Bartimaeus is recorded to encourage everyone in desperate situations to cry out to the Lord unceasingly until he comes to their aid (see Mark 10:46–52).

Step 4. Wait.

"I waited patiently for the Lord," David said (Ps 40:1). This is undoubtedly the hardest part about being in a pit. In the Bible, "waiting" on God is evidence of faith, hope, and confident expectation (see Ps 27:14; Isa 40:31; etc.). But be forewarned: God's deliverance may look very different than you expect! When Ishmaelite slave traders "delivered" Joseph from his pit, he must have wondered if God had heard his prayer at all!

Step 5. Love your enemies and pray for those who persecute you.

Perhaps the greatest danger in a pit is not the pain and loss we may experience, but rather the temptation to become bitter, cynical, and consumed with a desire for vengeance. If we become filled with hate, our enemy wins twice! Learning to love your enemies and eventually to forgive them is part of what the pit experience is all about.

Step 6. When God delivers you—tell the world!

David wrote Psalm 40 because he wanted everyone everywhere to know how God had delivered him. He hoped that his story would cause many others to "see and fear, and put their trust in the Lord" (Ps 40:3). The story of how God brought Joseph from the pit to the palace has encouraged millions of people for over 3,500 years.

Joseph got his best education at Pit State University. Here he learned humility, trust, patience, forgiveness, and how to love his enemies. These were precisely the qualities needed to make him great in the Kingdom of God. A. W. Tozer famously said: "It is doubtful whether God can bless a man greatly until He has hurt him deeply."[3] God permits pits and painful circumstances in our lives for a reason. He is training us in godliness, preparing us for leadership, and equipping us to be great in the Kingdom of God.

Russian Orthodox Christian Alexander Solzhenitsyn (1918–2008) was an outspoken critic of Communism and helped to raise global awareness of human rights abuses in the Soviet Union. His years as a prisoner in Soviet concentration camps, rather than making him cynical and bitter, deepened his faith and softened his heart. Looking back on his "pit experience" in the gulag, he was able to express gratitude for the transformative truths that he could have learned nowhere else.

> It was only when I lay there on rotting prison straw that I sensed within myself the first stirrings of good. Gradually, it was disclosed to me that the line separating good and evil passes not through states, nor between classes, nor between political parties either—but right through every human heart—and through all human hearts. . . . And that is why I turn back to the years of my imprisonment and say, sometimes to the astonishment of those about me: "Bless you, prison, for having been in my life!"[4]

QUESTIONS FOR DISCUSSION

1. Have you ever thought of Joseph's life as foreshadowing Jesus' life? Describe the parallels. What should we learn from this?
2. Did your parents show favoritism for one child over another? If you are a parent, do you tend to prefer one of your children over the others? What happens in a family when parents show partiality?
3. Have you personally experienced sibling rivalry? Describe what you have learned from this.
4. What do you think Joseph must have felt when he was thrown into the pit?
5. Describe a pit experience in your own life. What did you learn?

---

[3] Tozer, *The Root of Righteousness*, 137.
[4] Solzhenitsyn, *The Gulag Archipelago*, 312–313.

27
Here's to You, Mrs. Potiphar
Genesis 39:1–23

Baby Boomers will remember Simon and Garfunkel's Grammy Award-winning song "Mrs. Robinson." Written for the movie *The Graduate* (1967), the lyrics allude to the sordid story of a middle-aged woman, Mrs. Robinson, who seduces a twenty-one-year-old college graduate named Benjamin Braddock (played by Dustin Hoffman). The song and the movie are classic examples of the self-absorbed hedonism that so often characterized the Me Generation.[1]

Genesis 39 introduces us to the "Mrs. Robinson" of the Old Testament. We don't even know her name. All we know is that she is married to a prominent Egyptian official named Potiphar. Unlike the fictional Mrs. Robinson, this woman is all too real. She, like the woman in the movie, is famous for only one thing: seduction. She is a temptress. However, unlike Mrs. Robinson, Mrs. Potiphar fails in her objective. Her most seductive enticements are unable to lure young Joseph into her deadly embrace.

This is Joseph's second "pit" experience. Though very different from his first experience in a pit (see chapter 26), this one is just as

---

1   I'm struck by the similarities between Mrs. Potiphar of Genesis 39 and Mrs. Robinson of *The Graduate*. But I'm even more struck by the differences between Joseph and Benjamin Braddock! Joseph resisted the temptress. Benjamin did not. Taking liberties with the original lyrics sung by Simon and Garfunkel, I offer my own rendition of the song, making it fit the story of Joseph (see page 401).

dangerous—maybe more so. "A prostitute is a deep pit; an adulterous woman is treacherous. She hides and waits like a robber, looking for another victim." (Prov 23:27 NLT). God is not finished with the leadership training program he has prepared for Joseph. Learning how to remain pure in a sexually obsessed culture is part of the core curriculum at Pit State University.

This passage is not just about sexual temptation, however. The bigger issue is whether Joseph can maintain his Jewish identity while living in a foreign land. He is not just being seduced *in* Egypt; he is being seduced *by* Egypt. Alone, and far from his family, his culture, and his religious practices, Joseph finds himself at the epicenter of one of the greatest civilizations in human history. This is a classic story of a country boy coming for the first time to the big city. Joseph's eyes must be wide with wonder as he sees the wealth, beauty, power, and cultural sophistication of all that is Egypt. His own humble upbringing in Canaan must seem simplistic, backward, and provincial in comparison. As he adjusts to his new surroundings, Joseph can perhaps identify with Dorothy when she suddenly found herself in the land of Oz: "Toto, we're not in Kansas anymore."

Mrs. Potiphar's attempt at seduction is merely sexual. She wants to capture Joseph's body. The glittering allure of Egypt, however, confronts Joseph with a temptation that is far more sinister and deadly, a seduction that aims to capture Joseph's mind and heart. Succumbing to the charms of an adulterous woman may cause Joseph to lose his job. But if the young man from the country embraces the seductive pleasures of worldliness, he will surely lose his soul.

How will Joseph fare in such an environment? Will he be ashamed of his past and deny his identity as a Jew? Will he begin to think and act like an Egyptian? Will he assimilate into the culture? Or will Joseph learn how to live out his identity and faith as an alien in a foreign land? Will he find a way to live in Egypt without become Egyptian? These are the questions that provide the foundation for understanding the Joseph story. It is one thing for Joseph to be in Egypt. God obviously wants him there. But it is another matter entirely if Egypt should ever get in him! God has called Joseph to Egypt to be in the world, but not of it!

> No place exemplifies more successfully or more fully the way of the world than does Egypt. In no place is assimilation to the way of the world more tempting. . . . From Joseph's first Egyptian encounter we begin to see how Israel differs from Egypt. We wonder: Can Israel survive the encounter? Can and will Joseph preserve his identity? Can and will he be able to safeguard his people? With our eyes adjusted to this larger horizon, we are ready to look closely at the details of the story itself.[2]

RISING IN POWER

> *Now Joseph had been brought down to Egypt, and Potiphar, an officer of Pharaoh, the captain of the guard, an Egyptian, had bought him from the Ishmaelites who had brought him down there. The* LORD *was with Joseph, and he became a successful man, and he was in the house of his Egyptian master. His master saw that the* LORD *was with him and that the* LORD *caused all that he did to succeed in his hands. So Joseph found favor in his sight and attended him, and he made him overseer of his house and put him in charge of all that he had. From the time that he made him overseer in his house and over all that he had, the* LORD *blessed the Egyptian's house for Joseph's sake; the blessing of the* LORD *was on all that he had, in house and field. So he left all that he had in Joseph's charge, and because of him he had no concern about anything but the food he ate. (Gen 39:1–6)*

Four times in this narrative we are told that "the Lord was with Joseph" (Gen 39:2, 3, 21, 23). The word used here is *Yahweh*, the personal name of God. The author wants to assure us that the One who is accompanying Joseph in Egypt is not some vague, generic deity but rather the very same personal God who revealed himself to Abraham, Isaac, and Jacob.

There is no indication in the Joseph narrative that he ever experiences a physical manifestation of God's presence, as was true of the patriarchs before him, when God came in some tangible manner to

---

2   Kass, *The Beginning of Wisdom*, 538–539.

speak and act. Such theophanies become rare in biblical history once the age of the patriarchs ended. But this does not mean that God is now absent. Far from it! The story of Joseph introduces us to how God will typically be present in the lives of those who come after the patriarchs. The author of Genesis wants us to know that though Joseph may not experience God's presence physically and dramatically as the patriarchs did, he nevertheless enjoys *Yahweh's* authentic presence, even in Egypt! This makes all the difference.

When God first called Abraham, part of his covenant promise was that "all the families of the earth" would be blessed through him and his descendants (see Gen 12:1–3). Ironically, when he visited Egypt and pretended that Sarah was his sister, resulting in her being taken into Pharaoh's harem, Abraham brought not blessings but curses to that land. "The Lord afflicted Pharaoh and his house with great plagues because of Sarai, Abram's wife" (Gen 12:17). Joseph's godly example succeeds where Abraham's ungodly one did not! "The Lord blessed the Egyptian's house for Joseph's sake; "the blessing of the Lord was on all that he had, in house and field" (Gen 39:5). The Joseph story is the first installment of God's promise to bless the entire earth through his covenant people.

Potiphar may be a pagan idolater, but he is not dumb. He knows that the blessings and prosperity he is enjoying are because of Joseph. And he further understands that the secret to Joseph's life is found, not in gifting, talent, or hard work, but in the God he worships. Potiphar is convinced that his prosperity is directly tied to Joseph's God. But on what basis does he know this? Even if Joseph has told Potiphar about the God of Abraham and given him credit for all the good things that are happening, this alone does not account for Potiphar's awareness of God's hand of blessing in his life. How *does* Potiphar know?

Perhaps he recognizes that Joseph's religion, so foreign to Egyptian understandings of piety, is the cause of his righteous character and moral integrity. Unlike his other workers, Joseph is honest, diligent, industrious, prompt, obedient, and reliable. He can be trusted even when no one is watching. He isn't a drunkard, a womanizer, or a gambler. He always tells the truth, doesn't cheat on his expense reports, and treats the other slaves kindly and fairly. Such character qualities in the Chief Steward cannot help but have a positive impact on the overall welfare of his estate. Perhaps Potiphar recognizes God's hand of blessing by the simple fact that Joseph's religion is the explanation for his moral integrity and sterling character.

But there is more going on here than how personal character qualities affect business success, as important as that may be. Potiphar knows that the real explanation for his well-being is not Joseph but God! Even as a pagan unbeliever, he recognizes that the God of Abraham is at work both in Joseph and through him. This is a fact he simply cannot deny. Centuries later, God will reveal to Moses that this is exactly the kind of reaction that one can expect when his people obey their covenant mandate in the world.

> *If you fully obey the* Lord *your God and carefully keep all his commands that I am giving you today, the* Lord *your God will set you high above all the nations of the world. You will experience all these blessings if you obey the* Lord *your God:*
>
> *Your towns and your fields will be blessed. Your children and your crops will be blessed. The offspring of your herds and flocks will be blessed. Your fruit baskets and breadboards will be blessed. Wherever you go and whatever you do, you will be blessed. . . .*
>
> *Then all the nations of the world will see that you are a people claimed by the* Lord, *and they will stand in awe of you. . . . If you listen to these commands of the* Lord *your God that I am giving you today, and if you carefully obey them, the* Lord *will make you the head and not the tail, and you will always be on top and never at the bottom. (Deut 28:1–14 NLT)*

Resisting Temptation

Perhaps we could say that Joseph's first temptation in Egypt was the worldly seduction of material wealth and power. Would his success and prosperity as the Chief Steward in Potiphar's house cause him to forsake his identity as a child of Abraham and conform to Egyptian ways? His second temptation comes on the heels of the first: sexual immorality. Often, it seems, these two temptations come together.

> *Now Joseph was handsome in form and appearance. And after a time his master's wife cast her eyes on Joseph and said, "Lie with me." But he refused and said to his master's wife, "Behold, because of me my master has no concern about anything in the house, and he has put everything that he has in my charge. He is not greater in this house than I am, nor has he kept back anything from me except you, because you are his wife. How then can I do this great wickedness and sin against God?" And as she spoke to Joseph day after day, he would not listen to her, to lie beside her or to be with her.*
>
> *But one day, when he went into the house to do his work and none of the men of the house was there in the house, she caught him by his garment, saying, "Lie with me." But he left his garment in her hand and fled and got out of the house. And as soon as she saw that he had left his garment in her hand and had fled out of the house, she called to the men of her household and said to them, "See, he has brought among us a Hebrew to laugh at us. He came in to me to lie with me, and I cried out with a loud voice. And as soon as he heard that I lifted up my voice and cried out, he left his garment beside me and fled and got out of the house." Then she laid up his garment by her until his master came home, and she told him the same story, saying, "The Hebrew servant, whom you have brought among us, came in to me to laugh at me. But as soon as I lifted up my voice and cried, he left his garment beside me and fled out of the house." (Gen 39:7–18)*

There is nothing subtle about Mrs. Potiphar's strategy of seduction: "Lie with me." (Gen 39:7). And when her method fails, she tries it again; "Lie with me!" (Gen 39:12). We tend to think of sexual harassment as originating with the male, as when Shechem raped Dinah (see Gen 34:1–3). Contemporary social movements like *#MeToo* often create the impression that sexual predators are all men, and victims of sexual assault are all women. But in Genesis 39, it is Mrs. Potiphar, a woman of power, wealth, and influence, who is the aggressor, and Joseph, her employee (slave), is the victim. The Bible shows us that sexual harassment is far more complex than we may at first imagine.

Mrs. Potiphar's twice-repeated proposition is short, steamy, and to the point: "Lie with me!" Joseph offers two reasons why having sex is a bad idea. First, this would be a sin against Potiphar, who has put him in charge of everything he owns and held back nothing except his wife. Perhaps Joseph, in the heat of the moment, is talking to himself as much as he is to Mrs. Potiphar. The point he labors to make is that having sex with her would be a brazen betrayal of trust.

If the first reason for resisting sexual temptation is Potiphar, Joseph's second reason is God. "How can I do this great wickedness and sin against God?" he asks (Gen 39:9). Joseph knows that more is involved in adultery than betraying a spouse. Fundamentally, adultery is a sin against God. It violates the boundaries God has established for sexual expression (see Gen 2:24–25). David makes the same point when he reflects on his adulterous relationship with Bathsheba in Psalm 51. Worse than his sin against Uriah, Bathsheba's husband, is his offense against God. "Against you, you only, have I sinned and done what is evil in your sight," David groans out to God in prayer (Ps 51:4). Although Joseph lived centuries before the Ten Commandments were given, he knows adultery is a deadly sin. Though he is living in Egypt and far from home, he has no doubt that "the eyes of the Lord are in every place, keeping watch on the evil and the good" (Prov 15:3).

The English playwright William Congreve, in his play *The Mourning Bride* (1697) wrote, "Hell hath no fury like a woman scorned." One could easily imagine that he had Mrs. Potiphar in mind because his words describe so perfectly her reaction to Joseph's rejection. Calling first the other servants, and then her husband, she falsely accuses Joseph of trying to rape her. She even has his garment to prove it! With deceptive cunning, the perpetrator takes the role of victim. No one, not even her husband, dares to challenge her.

When we analyze her words, we begin to realize the diabolical web of deceit Mrs. Potiphar is weaving and the devious ingenuity she uses to manipulate and control other people. She begins by blaming

Potiphar for what happened! This servant "that *you* brought among us" has tried to rape me, she tells him (see Gen 39:17). This would have never happened, she seems to be saying, if my husband had been the man he ought to be!

Then, in a tactic that reveals even more about the sinister evil residing in her heart, Mrs. Potiphar plays the race card. Refusing to use his name, she twice calls Joseph a "Hebrew" (Gen 39: 14, 17). By calling him a Jew, she seeks to enflame the latent racism in her Egyptian environment. She will win her argument, not by an appeal to the facts, but by racial slurs and innuendos. Masterfully, she changes the focus of attention from the facts of what actually happened to Joseph's race, ethnicity, skin color, accent, religion, and country of origin. Joseph clearly has no chance of a fair trial in a place like this!

CONTINUING EDUCATION AT PIT STATE UNIVERSITY

> As soon as his master heard the words that his wife spoke to him, "This is the way your servant treated me," his anger was kindled. And Joseph's master took him and put him into the prison, the place where the king's prisoners were confined, and he was there in prison. But the LORD was with Joseph and showed him steadfast love and gave him favor in the sight of the keeper of the prison. And the keeper of the prison put Joseph in charge of all the prisoners who were in the prison. Whatever was done there, he was the one who did it. The keeper of the prison paid no attention to anything that was in Joseph's charge, because the LORD was with him. And whatever he did, the LORD made it succeed. (Gen 39:19–23)

When Potiphar learns from his wife about the incident, "his anger (is) kindled" (Gen 39:19). But at whom is he angry? The text leaves us guessing. If Potiphar really believed that Joseph had sexually assaulted his wife, he would surely have had him put to death immediately. The fact that he chooses to put Joseph in the prison where he himself is the warden, a prison for political prisoners, not criminals, makes us wonder what is really going on (see Gen 37:36; 39:20; and 40:3). Could it be that Potiphar is suspicious of his wife's description of what happened? He knows her well. He also knows Joseph well. Perhaps his anger is directed, not against Joseph, but against the manipulative way his wife has pushed him into a corner, forcing him to take actions he does not want to take, actions that he knows, in his heart of hearts, are unjust.

Joseph makes no effort to speak up in his own defense. He knows such an attempt would be futile and only make things worse. He chooses rather, to trust in God and let him work things out. Subjected unjustly to yet another "pit" experience, Joseph once again discovers the reality of God's presence in a very difficult situation. "But the Lord was with Joseph and showed him steadfast love" (Gen 39:21). The way Joseph responds to unjust treatment once again foreshadows the life of Jesus. Perhaps Peter was thinking of the similarity when he wrote:

> *Servants, be subject to your masters with all respect, not only to the good and gentle but also to the unjust. For this is a gracious thing, when, mindful of God, one endures sorrows while suffering unjustly. For what credit is it if, when you sin and are beaten for it, you endure? But if when you do good and suffer for it you endure, this is a gracious thing in the sight of God. For to this you have been called, because Christ also suffered for you, leaving you an example, so that you might follow in his steps. He committed no sin, neither was deceit found in his mouth. When he was reviled, he did not revile in return; when he suffered, he did not threaten, but continued entrusting himself to him who judges justly. (1 Pet 2:18–23)*

THE FIRE WITHIN

As we close this chapter, let's look again at the subject of sexual temptation and how Joseph resisted and remained morally pure. In a world like ours, this is a story that needs to be told again and again.

Mrs. Potiphar is a classic illustration of the seductive temptress who lures young men into her embrace by promising them unrestrained sexual expression. She is beautiful, wealthy, and self-confident. Reading between the lines, we can imagine that she is pampered, bored, and perhaps trapped in a loveless marriage. Joseph is young and single. He is handsome "in form and appearance" (Gen 39:6). The wording means that he well-built, buff. He got his good looks from his mother Rachel, whose appearance is described in the very same words: beautiful "in form and appearance" (Gen 29:17).

Though sexual temptation can be strong in almost any setting, here in the home of Mrs. Potiphar the lure of sin is especially hard to resist for several different reasons. For one thing, she is Joseph's social superior. She has status, wealth, and power. And her attempt at seduction is not just a one-time affair. She keeps "putting pressure on him day after day" (Gen 39:10 NLT). When she makes her moves, she always ensures that she and Joseph are alone, that no one else is in the house (see Gen 39:11).

And think of the long list of justifications that Joseph could have come up with to rationalize giving in:

- No one will know.
- She's my boss. It's my job to do what she tells me to do.
- If I refuse, I might be fired.
- I didn't start this, she did.
- Life's been hard lately. I deserve a little fun.
- This may advance my career.
- There's no law against this.
- People do this all the time in Egypt.
- Even if I do something questionable, what's the big deal? My family has a long history of sexual misconduct.[3] I might as well join them.

Yes, Joseph is a remarkable young man. When the moment of temptation comes, he is ready. Only a foolish soldier would wait until the battle starts to check his equipment: Is my rifle working properly? Do I have enough ammunition? etc. The key to victory in combat is being prepared. So is it with sexual temptation. Looking at Joseph's example, as well as others in the Bible who experienced moral failure

---

[3] His great-grandfather Abraham slept with one of his slaves and twice put his wife in a pagan king's harem. His grandfather Isaac also put his wife in a pagan king's harem. His distant cousin Lot committed incest with his two daughters. His brother Ruben committed incest with his stepmother. His brother Judah committed incest with his daughter-in-law. And numerous family members had multiple wives and concubines.

in this area (notably Samson and David), we can enumerate five things we can do to prepare for battle with sexual temptation.

1. Cultivate and maintain a vital relationship with the Lord Jesus.

Don't miss the fact that the story of Joseph's victory over sexual temptation includes the repeated reminder that the Lord was with him (see Gen 39:2, 3, 21, 24). God's presence is the key to victory. For Joseph, this was a blessed reality that started long before he began working at the Potiphars' home. Had he waited to develop a relationship with the Lord until the moment Mrs. Potiphar walked into the room in her night gown, it would have been too late! Joseph had victory because he had cultivated and maintained a daily walk with the Lord long before the temptation came. Paul expresses this truth in these words: "Walk by the Spirit, and you will not gratify the desires of the flesh" (Gal 5:16). The old gospel song says it well:

> *I need Thee every hour,*
> *Stay Thou nearby.*
> *Temptations lose their power,*
> *When Thou art nigh.—Annie S. Hawks*

2. Make a covenant with your eyes.

For men especially, the battle with sexual temptation is, first of all, a struggle with the eyes. Both Samson (Judg 14:1; 16:1) and David (2 Sam 11:2) let their eyes wander, and this is where their troubles began. As the children's chorus reminds us: "O be careful little eyes, what you see; for the Father up above, is looking down in love; O be careful little eyes what you see." This explains why Job said, "I made a covenant with my eyes not to look lustfully at a girl" (Job 31:1 NIV). In a culture like ours where we are constantly bombarded with visual stimuli of a sexual nature (billboards, magazines, TV ads, internet, etc.), it may not be possible to control the first look, but it is possible to control the second. Martin Luther quipped: "I cannot stop the birds from flying over my head, but I can stop them from building a nest in my hair."

3. Run.

When Mrs. Potiphar propositions Joseph, he runs like a jack rabbit (see Gen 39:12). He doesn't pause to pray about what he should do. He doesn't try to witness to her or share his testimony. He skedaddles out of the house as fast as he can go! With most temptations, the Bible urges us to stand and fight. But when it comes to sexual temptation, the most spiritual thing we can do is to turn and run! Every second counts. "Flee sexual immorality" (1 Cor 6:18). "Flee youthful passions" (2 Tim 2:22).

The Bible tells us that we should flee adultery not only because it is sinful, but also because it is dumb! Adulterers are not just sinners, they are fools. They have embarked on a path that will bring about their own destruction. This is the point made repeatedly in the book of Proverbs. Chapter 7, for example, gives a graphic description of how a young man "who lacks common sense" is seduced by an adulterous woman. Luring him into her home, she invites him into her bedroom, saying:

> *Come, let's drink our fill of love until morning.*
> *Let's enjoy each other's caresses,*
> *for my husband is not home.*
> *He's away on a long trip. . . .*
>
> *So she seduced him with her pretty speech*
> *and enticed him with her flattery.*
> *He followed her at once,*
> *like an ox going to the slaughter.*
> *He was like a stag caught in a trap,*
> *awaiting the arrow that would pierce its heart.*
> *He was like a bird flying into a snare,*
> *little knowing it would cost him his life. (Prov 7:18–19, 21–23 NLT)*

The author's purpose in giving such a graphic description of seduction is to warn his own son to flee from the adulterous woman because "she has been the ruin of many . . . her bedroom is the den of death" (Prov 7:27 NLT). Therefore, run, my son; yes, run!

4. Be accountable.

Joseph's victory is even more remarkable when we realize that he had no family, no wife, no small group, or no church where he could openly discuss these kinds of temptations and find support. Real victory in dealing with sexual temptation often comes only when we find a safe place to talk openly about such matters, study what the Bible has to say, and hold one another accountable. "Confess your sins to one another and pray for one another, that you may be healed" (Jas 5:16).

5. Fight fire with fire.

Gaining victory over sexual temptation requires more than behavior modification. The best way to control the raging passion of lust is to find another passion that burns even hotter. There is only one: the fire of Pentecost, the Holy Spirit. When we are filled with the Spirit's fire, we begin to experience what Thomas Chalmers (1780–1847) calls "the expulsive power of a new affection." When our passion for the things of God burns brighter and hotter than all other passions, then, and only then, are we prepared to face sexual temptation.

Greek mythology contains two very different stories of men who sought to sail safely past the Island of the Sirens, where beautiful women, using their seductive charms and voices, sought to entice passing sailors to come and visit them. But when the ships drew close to shore, they crashed upon the rocks and all on board would perish.

One story tells how Ulysses ordered his men to put wax in their ears so they could not hear the women singing. He made them tie him to the mast, leaving his own ears unstopped because he longed to hear the music. As the ship passed the island, he begged his men to untie him so he could sail closer to shore and answer the siren call. Fortunately, they refused. The ship got safely past the temptresses, but only because of the wax in the ears and the physical restraint of the ropes. The outward actions of Ulysses and his men were impressive, but their inner hearts remained polluted, filled with the passions of carnal lust.

A second myth tells how Jason, and his men (the Argonauts), found a much better method for sailing past the island. Calling the musician Orpheus on deck to make music with his magic harp, the melodies he produced were sweeter and more enticing than the songs of the sirens.

The power of seduction was broken, and the ship sailed safely past the island because the melodious music of Orpheus' harp was so much preferable to the harsh and discordant music of the sirens.

The gospel offers victory over sexual temptation not by forceful willpower or techniques of behavior modification, but by the transformation of the heart. When our loves are rightly ordered and our passions burn for God and his holiness, then, and only then, are we prepared to face sexual temptation. The Lord Jesus does not want to extinguish our passions—he wants to sanctify them!

> *For this is the will of God, your sanctification: that you abstain from sexual immorality; that each one of you know how to control his own body in holiness and honor, not in the passion of lust like the Gentiles who do not know God. . . . For God has not called us for impurity, but in holiness. Therefore whoever disregards this, disregards not man but God, who gives his Holy Spirit to you. (1 Thess 4:3–8)*

QUESTIONS FOR DISCUSSION

1. What is the appeal of movies like *The Graduate* and chapters of the Bible like Genesis 39? Why are stories like this important?
2. Joseph is being seduced not just *in* Egypt, but *by* Egypt. Discuss this.
3. When was the last time you heard a sermon on the sin of worldliness? Why has this topic become so rare in the American church?
4. With most temptations the Bible encourages us to stand and fight. With sexual temptation it encourages us to turn and run. Talk about this.
5. What is the meaning of the phrase "the expulsive power of a new affection"? How does it relate to sexual temptation?
6. When it comes to sexual temptation, do most people today follow the Ulysses model or the Jason model? Discuss this.

Mrs. Potiphar[4]

Stan Key

And here's to you, Mrs. Potiphar,
Jesus loves you more than you will know. Wo, wo, wo.
Turn from your sin, Mrs. Potiphar
There's still time to change your ways and pray. Hey, hey, hey. (2X).

We'd like for you to know what God thinks of someone like you.
We'd like to help you change your ways.
For women who seduce and capture young men in their arms;
May have some fun, then both will lose.

Koo-koo-ka-choo, Mrs. Potiphar,
Beneath your plastic face and painted eyes. Wo, wo, wo.
We see the slut that you really are,
Lusting like a spider for some prey. Hey, hey, hey. (2X).

What's that you say, Mrs. Potiphar;
Your marriage stinks, your husband's far away? Wo, wo, wo.
And so you think, Mrs. Potiphar,
You have the right to make your bed and play. Hey, hey, hey. (2X).

Sitting here in church on Sunday morning in these pews,
Listening to the preacher, preach the Word;
Will I laugh or will I cry? Oh, how will I respond?
Every way I look, I have to choose!

Where have you gone, Joseph, Jacob's son?
Our nation wonders if there is a man. Wo, wo, wo.
Who can withstand Mrs. Potiphar,
Resist her charms and turn and run away. Hey, hey, hey. (2X).

Jesus Christ can cleanse a heart and make it strong and pure,
He can take a man and make him new!
So, if Mrs. Potiphar is knocking at your door,
Let Jesus go and answer it for you!

---

[4] Key, *Face to Face*, 348–349. Modified.

28
Faith@Work
Genesis 40:1–41:57

In the last chapter we saw how Joseph, after being falsely accused of attempted rape, was thrown into prison. The closing paragraph of Genesis 39 emphasized two realities about this second "pit experience." First, the Lord was with him (see Gen 39:21, 23). Though his circumstances were tragic and painful, the God of Abraham was present there in the prison with Joseph to encourage and strengthen him. Second, in all that he did, Joseph prospered. The keeper of the prison could see that God's hand of blessing was upon him, so he put him in charge of everything (see Gen 39:22). And whatever Joseph did, "the Lord made it succeed" (Gen 39:23).

Before looking at the next phase of Joseph's story, let's pause to recognize the pattern that is developing in his life. First seen when his brothers threw him into a pit and sold him as a slave, then in Potiphar's house where he was unfairly accused and thrown into prison, the pattern is clear:

- Joseph is treated unfairly and descends into a pit.
- God is with him in the pit so that he blesses him and everyone around him.
- Joseph ascends out of the pit in power and majesty.

We can only wonder how much of this pattern Joseph understood while the tumultuous events of his life were happening. Did he see God's providential hand at work? Did he have peace in the midst of turmoil? Søren Kierkegaard famously said, "Life must be lived forward, but understood backwards."[1] While he was living forward, there must have been moments when Joseph scratched his head, wondering how the pieces of the puzzle could possibly fit together. But at the end of his life, looking back, it all made perfect sense. God was at work in the good moments and the bad, orchestrating each step, bringing about his beautiful plan not only for Joseph, but also for the world (see Gen 50:20).

ONCE AGAIN IN A PIT

Genesis 40–41 tells the dramatic story of Joseph's miraculous transition from the prison to the palace, from being a prisoner to being the Prime Minister. But this didn't happen immediately. Two long years had to pass before deliverance came. When he interprets the dreams of two of his fellow prisoners, it appears that he is about to receive a get-out-of-jail free card. However, as with so many other situations in his life, things are going to get worse before they get better.

> *And one night they both dreamed—the cupbearer and the baker of the king of Egypt, who were confined in the prison—each his own dream, and each dream with its own interpretation. When Joseph came to them in the morning, he saw that they were troubled. So he asked Pharaoh's officers who were with him in custody in his master's house, "Why are your faces downcast today?" (Gen 40:5–7)*

The story of Joseph's dramatic rise to power begins so simply we might not even notice it: he realizes that his fellow prisoners are troubled. He can read the distress and anxiety on their faces. He cares enough about them to notice their emotions. He takes the time to look them in the eye and ask, "What's wrong? Why the long faces?" (Gen 40:7 MSG).

When you pause to think about it, this is remarkable. Few people know how to read body language or interpret facial expressions. Most people simply don't care. They are too consumed with their own affairs to start a conversation aimed at discovering what someone else may be thinking or feeling. The fact that Joseph notices and takes the

---

1   Kierkegaard, *Provocations*, 263.

time to tactfully ask a heart-felt question reveals much about his true greatness as a leader.

> *They said to him, "We have had dreams, and there is no one to interpret them." And Joseph said to them, "Do not interpretations belong to God? Please tell them to me." (Gen 40:8)*

The vivid dreams Joseph had as a youth cause him to be particularly sensitive to the dreams of others. He knows from his own experience how God sometimes speaks prophetically through dreams, enabling the dreamer to better anticipate the future. His response to his fellow prisoners tells us a lot about Joseph's inner character. He is sensitive to their emotional state, confident that God will respond to their needs, and humble enough to give God credit for making the interpretation possible. The combination of these three traits simultaneously working together reveals Joseph's amazing giftedness as a leader.

> *So the chief cupbearer told his dream to Joseph and said to him, "In my dream there was a vine before me, and on the vine there were three branches. As soon as it budded, its blossoms shot forth, and the clusters ripened into grapes. Pharaoh's cup was in my hand, and I took the grapes and pressed them into Pharaoh's cup and placed the cup in Pharaoh's hand." Then Joseph said to him, "This is its interpretation: the three branches are three days. In three days Pharaoh will lift up your head and restore you to your office, and you shall place Pharaoh's cup in his hand as formerly, when you were his cupbearer. Only remember me, when it is well with you, and please do me the kindness to mention me to Pharaoh, and so get me out of this house. For I was indeed stolen out of the land of the Hebrews, and here also I have done nothing that they should put me into the pit."*

> *When the chief baker saw that the interpretation was favorable, he said to Joseph, "I also had a dream: there were three cake baskets on my head, and in the uppermost basket there were all sorts of baked food for Pharaoh, but the birds were eating it out of the basket on my head." And Joseph answered and said, "This is its interpretation: the three baskets are three days. In three days Pharaoh will lift*

> up your head—from you!—and hang you on a tree. And the birds will eat the flesh from you."
>
> *On the third day, which was Pharaoh's birthday, he made a feast for all his servants and lifted up the head of the chief cupbearer and the head of the chief baker among his servants. He restored the chief cupbearer to his position, and he placed the cup in Pharaoh's hand. But he hanged the chief baker, as Joseph had interpreted to them. Yet the chief cupbearer did not remember Joseph, but forgot him. (Gen 40:9–23)*

Note that in Genesis 40:15 Joseph calls his place of confinement a "pit." The word is used again in Genesis 41:14. This is the same word that was used in Genesis 37 to describe the hole in the ground where Joseph was thrown by his brothers (see Gen 37: 20, 22, 24, 28, 29). While outward circumstances differ considerably, Joseph realizes that his prison experience has many similarities to his earlier pit experience with his brothers. "I've been here before," he must have thought.

The Lord enables Joseph to give accurate interpretations for both of his fellow prisoners. The baker's dream is a frightful omen of his execution. The cupbearer's dream foretells a blessed return to Pharoah's favor and service. Joseph asks him to plead his case before the king when he is released. But the cupbearer either refuses to do so, or simply forgets.

For the third time, Joseph suffers a devastating, unfair setback. It is one thing to suffer because one has done something wrong. But when one has faithfully tried to do what is right and yet is punished again and again, it is very hard to see God's gracious hand in what is happening. For the next two years, Joseph must learn once again to cope with being the victim of injustice. Though the Scripture assures us that God was with him, one can easily imagine that Joseph must have felt that God was nowhere around!

FROM PIT TO PALACE

> *After two whole years, Pharaoh dreamed that he was standing by the Nile, and behold, there came up out of the Nile seven cows, attractive and plump, and they fed in the*

> reed grass. And behold, seven other cows, ugly and thin, came up out of the Nile after them, and stood by the other cows on the bank of the Nile. And the ugly, thin cows ate up the seven attractive, plump cows. And Pharaoh awoke. And he fell asleep and dreamed a second time. And behold, seven ears of grain, plump and good, were growing on one stalk. And behold, after them sprouted seven ears, thin and blighted by the east wind. And the thin ears swallowed up the seven plump, full ears. And Pharaoh awoke, and behold, it was a dream. So in the morning his spirit was troubled, and he sent and called for all the magicians of Egypt and all its wise men. Pharaoh told them his dreams, but there was none who could interpret them to Pharaoh. (Gen 41:1–8)

Pharaoh's dream is more like a nightmare. It is obviously ominous, foretelling something sinister, and Pharaoh's spirit is "troubled". Calling all the magicians and wise men of Egypt, he is desperate to find someone who can tell him what it means, but no one can help. This prompts the cupbearer to remember how, two years earlier when he was in prison, a "young Hebrew" (Gen 41:12) had accurately interpreted two different dreams. On learning this, Pharaoh immediately summons Joseph to appear before him.

However, before leaving the prison for his audience with Pharaoh, we are told that Joseph shaves and changes his clothing (see Gen 41:14). Why would the author of Genesis include this seemingly trivial piece of information? Leon Kass suggests what may be the significance of Joseph's behavior.

> Change of clothing to improve one's appearance is, of course, entirely appropriate when one is called into the royal presence. But change of clothing also represents change of custom. Joseph not only adopts Egyptian dress. He also adopts the peculiarly Egyptian practice of shaving. The Egyptians alone among the peoples of the ancient Near East shaved their faces and also their heads, and Joseph here for the first time acquires a fully Egyptian appearance. Is he thus trying to hide his Hebrew identity, or is he rather revealing his true, "Egyptian" nature? One cannot tell.[2]

---

2   Kass, *The Beginning of Wisdom*, 563.

In putting aside the customs and dress that mark him as a Hebrew, Joseph seems to be assimilating himself into Egyptian culture. His Egyptianization becomes even more pronounced when Pharaoh gives him his signet ring, new clothing, a gold chain, a chariot, an Egyptian name (Zaphenath-paneah), and an Egyptian wife (Asenath) (see Gen 41:42–45). Joseph seems to have taken on a new identity. The old has passed away. All things have now become Egyptian.

In seeking to understand Joseph's adaptation of Egyptian culture, we must remember that, just as he had no choice in coming to Egypt in the first place, so he has no choice concerning Pharaoh's effort to turn him into an Egyptian. We can only guess what Joseph may be thinking and feeling as the king of Egypt unilaterally bestows on him a completely new identity. So successful are his efforts, that, when Joseph's own brothers stand before him, they will see only a foreign government official. His Hebrew identity is completely hidden beneath an Egyptian exterior. His language, his diet, his dress, his shaven face and head, his mode of transport, his mannerisms, and his lifestyle all seem to indicate that Joseph has become an Egyptian.

However, a careful reading of the narrative suggests that Joseph may not be as "Egyptian" as he appears to be. For one thing, though he has been given an Egyptian name, it is never used in the biblical text; not even once; not even by Pharaoh who named him. But it is in the naming of his two sons that we have the strongest indication that Joseph remains conscious of his true identity. The names Manasseh and Ephraim are Hebrew, not Egyptian! We have seen elsewhere in Genesis how mothers are often involved in giving names to their children, so we can imagine that Asenath, Joseph's Egyptian wife, must have approved of these foreign names for her children. Does this hint that she may have become a convert to Joseph's God? One Jewish tradition suggests that this was indeed the case.

Pharaoh asked Joseph if he could interpret his dream. He did *not* ask him for advice concerning what he should do. But Joseph seized the occasion to counsel the most powerful man in the land on what he should do next.

> God has shown to Pharaoh what he is about to do. There will come seven years of great plenty throughout all the land of Egypt, but after them there will arise seven years of famine . . . it will be very severe. And the doubling of Pharaoh's dream means that the thing is fixed by God, and God will shortly bring it about. Now therefore let Pharaoh select a discerning and wise man, and set him over the land of Egypt. Let Pharaoh proceed to appoint overseers over the land and take one-fifth of the produce of the land of Egypt during the seven plentiful years. And let them gather all the food of these good years that are coming and store up grain under the authority of Pharaoh for food in the cities, and let them keep it. That food shall be a reserve for the land against the seven years of famine that are to occur in the land of Egypt, so that the land may not perish through the famine. (Gen 41:28-36)

The fact that God has given Pharaoh a prophetic look into the future, means that he now can get ready for what is coming. On the spot, Pharaoh makes Joseph Prime Minister (vizier) over all the land of Egypt and gives him authority to make preparations for what is about to happen.

> And Pharaoh said to his servants, "Can we find a man like this, in whom is the Spirit of God?" Then Pharaoh said to Joseph, "Since God has shown you all this, there is none so discerning and wise as you are. You shall be over my house, and all my people shall order themselves as you command. Only as regards the throne will I be greater than you." And Pharaoh said to Joseph, "See, I have set you over all the land of Egypt." Then Pharaoh took his signet ring from his hand and put it on Joseph's hand, and clothed him in garments of fine linen and put a gold chain about his neck. And he made him ride in his second chariot. And they called out before him, "Bow the knee!" Thus he set him over all the land of Egypt. . . . And Pharaoh called Joseph's name Zaphenath-paneah. And he gave him in marriage Asenath, the daughter of Potiphera priest of On. . . . Joseph was thirty years old when he entered the service of Pharaoh king of Egypt. (Gen 41:38-46)

Pharaoh recognizes that Joseph's ability to interpret dreams is a gift of God. It cannot be explained by natural talent, education, or training alone. This kind of wisdom and counsel can come only from

God (see Gen 41:38). Centuries later, another pagan king, Belshazzar, will say something similar about Daniel when he is called in to interpret the mysterious handwriting on the wall: "I have heard of you, that the Spirit of God is in you, and that light and understanding and excellent wisdom are found in you" (Dan 5:14 NKJV).

What are we to make of Joseph's marriage to the Egyptian Asenath? When his great grandfather Abraham took Hagar the Egyptian as a concubine, it brought only trouble into the covenant family. And on numerous occasions in the book of Genesis we have seen the divine mandate to marry within the faith strongly enforced. So how are we to understand Joseph's Egyptian wife? Her name, Asenath, probably means "she who belongs to the goddess Neit." Her father is a prominent priest of the god On. His name, Potiphera, means "he whom Ra, the sun god, has given." Joseph has obviously married into a non-Jewish family that practices and promotes idolatry. John Lennox comments on this troubling situation.

> Joseph was now son-in-law to a man who was, presumably, a high-ranking and influential pagan priest. The marriage raises obvious questions. Was it right for Joseph as a believer to marry an unbeliever from a foreign nation? However, we are given no more information as to the status of her belief; she may even have been a convert to Joseph's God, as one Jewish tradition has it. In any case, even if she was not (yet) a believer, Joseph does not appear to have had any choice in the matter, and there is no criticism of him in the text for having married her. Maybe the lesson we need to learn is that though it is God's stated ideal—indeed, command—that a believer should not marry an unbeliever, he, in his merciful providence, can help people to overcome even in a situation that is far from ideal that may be none of their own making.[3]

Joseph was seventeen years old when he was sold into slavery by his brothers (see Gen 37:2) and thirty years old when he became Prime Minister of Egypt (see Gen 41:46). This means he endured thirteen years of hardship, setbacks, frustration, and pain as a slave and prisoner. During that period, he must have often felt that his life

---

3   Lennox, *Joseph*, 158–159.

was meaningless, and the years wasted. But looking back on Joseph's life, we now realize that these thirteen years at Pit State University were not wasted. Far from it. God was training him for leadership. Without his education at PSU, Joseph's elevation to Prime Minister would have been disastrous!

The names Joseph gives his two sons are rich with meaning and give us a glimpse of what is going on in his soul. He names his firstborn *Manasseh* because "God has made me forget all my hardship and all my father's house" (see Gen 41:51). There are several ways this name can be understood. On the one hand, it may indicate that Joseph has experienced emotional healing from the trauma of his past and the name celebrates freedom and victory. But on the other hand, the name could reflect his desire to disassociate from his birth family and forge a new life and identity in Egypt. A third possibility is that the name is a strange mixture of both meanings together, indicating that Joseph still doesn't know how to deal with his tortuous past. Regardless of what Joseph may have meant by the name, there is a comic irony about his choice. By naming his son "Forget" he will be constantly reminded of what he doesn't want to remember! Manasseh's daily presence in his life will force Joseph to remember his true identity and his God-ordained mission. *Ephraim*, his second son, is so named because "God has made me fruitful in the land of my affliction" (Gen 41:52). Joseph realizes that Egypt, the place of his suffering, has now become the place of his greatest fruitfulness. God has turned poverty into abundance, defeat into victory, weakness into strength, bondage into freedom, suffering into triumph, and sorrow into joy.

During the seven years of abundance, Joseph gathers huge quantities of surplus food and stores them in the major cities of Egypt. The grain is so plenteous that it cannot be measured (see Gen 41: 49). Then, comes the seven years of hardship.

> *When all the land of Egypt was famished, the people cried to Pharaoh for bread. Pharaoh said to all the Egyptians, "Go to Joseph. What he says to you, do." So when the famine had spread over all the land, Joseph opened all the storehouses and sold to the Egyptians, for the famine was severe in the*

land of Egypt. Moreover, all the earth came to Egypt to Joseph to buy grain, because the famine was severe over all the earth. (Gen 41: 55-57)

The famine creates the opportunity for Joseph to establish policies in Egypt that centralize power and consolidate Pharaoh's reign. Genesis 47:13-26 explains what happens next. To buy bread, the people first give Pharaoh their money. Then, when their money is gone, they turn over their livestock in exchange for food. When their flocks and herds are gone, they give Pharaoh their land. Finally, when they have nothing else to give, they give themselves as slaves to Pharaoh, if only he will give them food to eat. Joseph makes it a rule in Egypt that the people will perpetually give Pharaoh twenty percent of all their harvests. Rather than begrudging their plight, the Egyptians thank Joseph for what he has done! "You have saved our lives; may it please my lord, we will be servants to Pharaoh" (Gen 47: 25). It may be difficult to understand the spiritual significance of Joseph's Big Government policies, but the Scripture is clear that the actions were never coercive but were taken only with the full consent of a grateful nation.

BUSINESS AS MISSION

In seeking to determine an overall theme for Genesis 40–41, most commentaries tend to focus on unjust suffering, the rewards of faithful living, or perhaps the meaning of dreams. This study, however, will focus on the theme of work. Joseph gives us one of the most important pictures in all the Bible of what godliness looks like in the workplace. He is the first and most compelling demonstration of business as mission. It would be difficult to name someone in history who had more influence as a godly witness than Joseph. And yet, he never preached a sermon, performed a miracle, or led a worship service. He was not a patriarch, prophet, priest, apostle, or missionary. The Genesis narrative tells us that Joseph held four different "jobs."

During his youth, he was a *shepherd* (see Gen 37:2). Apparently, God considers taking care of sheep to be superb training for future leaders. Think of the spiritual giants in Scripture who got their start as shepherds: Jacob, Joseph, Moses, David, Amos, etc. Jesus chose this line of work as a metaphor to explain his own understanding of messianic leadership: "I am the good shepherd. The good shepherd lays down his life for the sheep." (John 10:11)

The next job Joseph had was a *manager*. Potiphar made him the "overseer" in his house, putting him in charge of everything he owned (see Gen 39:4-6). Joseph's job was to take care of that which belonged to someone else. As manager of Potiphar's estate, he would have needed to learn a host of basic skills related to domestic affairs: maintenance, food service, agriculture, animal husbandry, budgets, construction, staffing, etc.

In prison, Joseph served as a kind of *executive director*. He was "in charge of all the prisoners" and "whatever was done there, he was the one who did it" (Gen 39:22-23). This took the leadership skills he had learned in Potiphar's house to a whole new level. Here he would have learned additional skills such as human resources, staff management, conflict resolution, legal and judicial issues, etc.

Finally, Joseph became *prime minister* (Gen 41:40-44). As the Grand Vizier of Egypt, only Pharaoh was higher in rank. This was the position for which all his previous work experience had been preparing him. In this role, he not only saved hundreds of thousands of people from starvation, but he preserved the covenant family of God for their future ministry to all the world.

Whether Joseph was in a prison or a palace, serving as a slave or a prime minister, the quality of his work was always the same. He lived by the creed that the apostle Paul would give voice to centuries later: "Whatever you do, work heartily, as for the Lord and not for men, knowing that from the Lord you will receive the inheritance as your reward. You are serving the Lord Christ." (Col 3:23-24).

Those around him recognized there was something different about how he worked. Though he had obvious gifts and talents for leadership, they knew that his abilities were more than human. Even pagans recognized that the Lord was with him. Often this brought a very positive response as when Potiphar, the head jailer, and

Pharaoh experienced blessings and prosperity under his leadership. But sometimes it brought persecution, as when Mrs. Potiphar falsely accused him of attempted rape and had him thrown into prison. Thus we learn that godly leadership can sometimes bring favor and at other times adversity.

Joseph may be one of the best examples of "faith at work" in the Bible but he certainly is not the only one. If space and time permitted, it would be helpful to examine the lives of other notable examples of godly workers in the Bible, such as:

- Bezalel, the artisan (Exod 31:1-6; 35:30-35).
- Daniel, the government leader in Babylon (book of Daniel)
- Paul, the tent maker (Acts 18:3; 20:34-35; 1 Thess 2:9-10; 2 Thess 3:7-12).
- Dorcas, the seamstress (Acts 9:36-43).
- Jesus, the carpenter. Don't forget that he worked as a carpenter for eighteen years before serving as a preacher for three (Mark 6:3).

As we close this chapter, let's summarize Joseph's work ethic in eight statements. What was true for Joseph, can also be true for you!

First, he submitted to the leadership training program God had for him at Pit State University. Before he could be entrusted with a significant leadership position, Joseph first needed to learn how to be faithful in the hidden places, the hard places, the unfair places, the small places, the painful places, the places where no one knows or cares what you do—except God. A. W. Tozer said, "God rarely uses a man greatly, until he hurts a man deeply."

Second, Joseph was a faithful witness for the Lord everywhere he went. Not only did he bear witness to his faith by silently doing his work with integrity, but he also gave verbal expression to what he believed. Everyone around him knew that Joseph worshiped the God of his fathers, not one of the deities of Egypt. His witness was tactful and showed respect for others, but it was crystal clear.

Third, he had moral integrity. He was not swayed by bribes or temptations. His superiors as well as his colleagues knew that he could be trusted. He was consistently honest, fair, gentle, loving, and diligent, whether in public or private.

Fourth, he showed compassion for others. He genuinely cared about the people around him, whether over or under him in the social order. Slave or free, male or female, rich or poor, Egyptian or foreigner, he treated everyone equally, as persons of worth and value, not as means to an end.

Fifth, Joseph was humble. As a youth, he seemed cocky and arrogant as he told others about his dreams. But his years of training at Pit State University made him humble, ready for service. He refused to take credit for what God had made possible, always giving him the glory for the good things that happened.

Sixth, he was faithful in the small things, even when no one was watching. Whether taking care of his brothers' sheep, Potiphar's estate, or his fellow prisoners, Joseph always performed his work with diligence and with excellence. His life proves the truth of Jesus' statement: "You have been faithful over a little; I will set you over much" (Matt 25:23).

Seventh, he knew how to be content. Rather than grumbling about his circumstances, Joseph quietly put his trust in the promises of God. His contentment came from within, not from outward perks, position, promotion, or paycheck. His education at Pit State had taught Joseph how to find contentment in God alone. With Paul he could say:

> *I have learned in whatever situation I am to be content. I know how to be brought low, and I know how to abound. In any and every circumstance, I have learned the secret of facing plenty and hunger, abundance and need. I can do all things through him who strengthens me. (Phil 4:11-13)*

Eighth, he learned to see God's providential hand in every situation. Whether Joseph was in a pit or in the palace, suffering or rejoicing, in need or in abundance, Joseph knew that God was in charge, working out his gracious plan. When he was the victim of injustice, rather than giving in to bitterness and revenge, he chose to trust in God and forgive those who had wronged him. "As for you, you meant evil against me, but God meant it for good" (Gen 50:20).

QUESTIONS FOR DISCUSSION

1. Give some examples of men and women you have known who were powerful witnesses for Christ "at work." What made their witness so effective?
2. From your own experience, what is the hardest part about being an effective witness at work?
3. Why do you think shepherding is such good training for leadership?
4. Jesus made cabinets and tables as a carpenter for eighteen years. Discuss what you think his work ethic was like.
5. Does the church do enough to help Christians in the workplace? What should the church be doing?
6. Look again at the eight elements of Joseph's work ethic. Which one spoke most powerfully to you? Why?
7. What one thing have you learned in this lesson that you want to begin doing in your own work environment?

29
Finding the Way Home
Genesis 42:1–44:34

Up until this point, the story of Joseph has focused on events in Egypt. Joseph now has a new country, a new name, a new family, and a new future. The family of Abraham, the land of Canaan, and the promises of God seem far away, perhaps forgotten. But in Genesis 42 the scene suddenly changes, and we are back in the Land of Promise with Jacob and his eleven sons. This reminds us of the Big Story that God is writing, the one about his covenant promises to Abraham, Isaac, and Jacob. As we pick up the main storyline again, we wonder if these promises of God are any closer to fulfillment? Are Abraham's descendants as numerous as the stars? Has the covenant family taken ownership of the Promised Land? Have the Hebrews been blessed in such a way that they are a blessing to all the nations? Has the seed of the woman, the serpent crusher, been born yet?

Genesis 42 plays a very important function: it ties together the Joseph story in Egypt with the Jacob story in Canaan. When Joseph was sold as a slave and taken to Egypt, it seemed that the two stories were on very divergent paths. What happened to Joseph in Egypt had no relevance to what was happening back in Canaan to the family of Abraham. Or so it seemed. Who could have ever imagined that the two stories would ever intersect again?

The closing paragraph of Genesis 41 sets the stage.

The seven years of plenty that occurred in the land of Egypt came to an end, and the seven years of famine began to come,

> as Joseph had said. There was famine in all lands, but in all the land of Egypt there was bread. . . . Moreover, all the earth came to Egypt to Joseph to buy grain, because the famine was severe over all the earth. (Gen 41:53-54, 57)

The famine that Joseph had predicted was no ordinary food shortage. Lasting seven long years and affecting "all the earth," this was a global crisis of catastrophic proportions. For Jacob and his family living in Canaan, however, the famine provoked a much bigger problem than physical hunger. This was not just a crisis of food; it was a crisis of faith that confronted them with two profoundly difficult *theological* questions.

First, how should one respond when the Promised Land resembles Death Valley and is not able to sustain human life? As they remembered the covenant promises, Jacob and his sons must have scratched their heads: Is *this* the inheritance God intends to give us? Is *this* the Land of Promise? What kind of God would treat us like this? And why, oh why, is there prosperity and an abundance of food in Egypt, a land full of idols, but poverty and starvation here in the Promised Land?

Later in the story, when God explicitly tells Jacob to pack his bags and move to Egypt (see Gen 46:3), this question becomes even more perplexing. *Leave* the land that God has promised us? *Move* to Egypt? *Settle* there? Jacob knew that the sojourn in Egypt would last much longer than the famine. He would have likely known what God had said to his grandfather Abraham many years earlier: "Know for certain that your offspring will be sojourners in a land that is not theirs and will be servants there, and they will be afflicted for four hundred years." (Gen 15:13).

Four hundred years? In Egypt? Here we see the *second* difficult theological question the people of God must answer: Can the Hebrews maintain their identity and their faith while living in a foreign land for four centuries? Is it possible to be an Israelite without Israel? Can the people of God live in Egypt without becoming Egyptian and being assimilated into Egyptian culture?

These are two of the most important questions the people of God will ever have to answer. Not only do they trouble the minds and hearts of Jacob's family long ago, but they continue to have great significance for followers of Christ today.

- As a member of God's covenant family, why does suffering come? If I'm walking in faith and obedience, why do tragic things happen?
- Can I maintain my faith while living in a hostile environment? Can I be in the world without becoming worldly?

Hopefully, this chapter will help to answer both questions.

A Drama in Four Acts

Let's examine the passage of Scripture before us by dividing it into four acts.

Act 1. Joseph's brothers' first trip to Egypt.

Reluctantly, Jacob finally agrees to allow ten of his sons to go to Egypt to buy bread. He refuses, however, to send his youngest son, Benjamin, "for he feared that harm might happen to him" (Gen 42:4). Benjamin is the son of Rachel, Jacob's favorite wife, who had died in childbirth (see Gen 35:16-20). Because he believes that Joseph is dead, it now appears that Benjamin, Joseph's full brother, has become Jacob's favorite son.

Arriving in Egypt along with many other foreigners seeking food, the brothers find themselves in the presence of the Egyptian governor.

> *Now Joseph was governor over the land. He was the one who sold to all the people of the land. And Joseph's brothers came and bowed themselves before him with their faces to the ground. Joseph saw his brothers and recognized them, but he treated them like strangers and spoke roughly to them. "Where do you come from?" he said. They said, "From the land of Canaan, to buy food." And Joseph recognized his brothers, but they did not recognize him. And Joseph remembered the dreams that he had dreamed of them. (Gen 42:6-9)*

What a rush of emotions and flood of memories Joseph must have experienced as his brothers bowed before him! We can only imagine all he must have felt in that moment. The text tells us only that he remembered his dreams. Over twenty years have passed since his family dismissed his dreams as childish bravado, megalomania. But now, those dreams have come true in a way that no one could have ever imagined. It is interesting to note that in Joseph's original dream, he saw *eleven* stars bowing down (see Gen 37:9). But here in Egypt, only ten brothers are prostrate before him. Perhaps this helped to alert Joseph to the fact that the dream wasn't yet completely fulfilled.

Although Joseph recognizes his brothers, they do not recognize him. As he is dressed in Egyptian clothing with a shaven face and head, having an Egyptian name, and speaking through an interpreter, the brothers naturally assume he is an Egyptian official. They have no clue that this is their long-lost brother.

We might wonder why Joseph doesn't immediately reveal himself to his brothers. Why does he delay? Why the charade? And why does he speak and act so roughly? We can perhaps better understand Joseph's harsh treatment of his brothers when we remember the final moments he had with them twenty years earlier. Ganged up on and bullied by his ten older siblings, Joseph knew he was about to be killed. Though he cried out in protest and begged for mercy, they callously sold him into slavery. His last memory of them was their hardened faces, filled with hatred and contempt, looking on in silence as he was led off into slavery. An awareness of the brutality involved in human trafficking enables us to better understand why Joseph chose to remain incognito and play his hand cautiously, slowly, and carefully. Joseph knew that *he* had changed through the years, but had *they*? Were they still the cruel, competitive, hard-hearted bullies that they were twenty years ago? Joseph wants to know. So, he decides to put his brothers through a series of tests to determine whether or not they have changed. First, he accuses them of being spies.

> *And he said to them, "You are spies; you have come to see the nakedness of the land." They said to him, "No, my lord, your servants have come to buy food. We are all sons of one man. We are honest men. Your servants have never been spies." He said to them, "No, it is the nakedness of the land that you have*

> *come to see." And they said, "We, your servants, are twelve brothers, the sons of one man in the land of Canaan, and behold, the youngest is this day with our father, and one is no more." But Joseph said to them, "It is as I said to you. You are spies. By this you shall be tested: by the life of Pharaoh, you shall not go from this place unless your youngest brother comes here. Send one of you, and let him bring your brother, while you remain confined, that your words may be tested, whether there is truth in you. Or else, by the life of Pharaoh, surely you are spies." And he put them all together in custody for three days. (Gen 42:9-17)*

Joseph must have silently laughed in cynicism when the brothers piously said, "We are honest men" (Gen 42:11). "Yeah, right," he must have thought. "You sold your brother into slavery and lied to your father claiming that he had been killed by a wild beast. Honest men? Give me a break." To prove their honesty, Joseph demands that one brother return to Canaan while the nine other brothers are held captive in Egypt. But three days later, he changes his mind and agrees to keep only one brother hostage while the nine others return to Canaan with food (see Gen 42:18-20).

The brothers, shocked by the unexpected rough treatment, conclude that God is punishing them for their sinful past. They have a theology of retribution that believes God will balance the scales, treating people in accordance to how they have treated others. An eye for an eye. Because they sold a brother into slavery, God is now demanding another brother to even the score. What goes around, comes around.

> *Then they said to one another, "In truth we are guilty concerning our brother, in that we saw the distress of his soul, when he begged us and we did not listen. That is why this distress has come upon us." And Reuben answered them, "Did I not tell you not to sin against the boy? But you did not listen. So now there comes a reckoning for his blood." (Gen 42:21-22)*

The brothers have admitted their guilt! Speaking in Hebrew to one another, they never imagine that Joseph understands what they are saying. Their conversation reveals that they have lived with a guilty conscience for twenty years. Time does *not* heal all wounds! Remorse and regret have haunted them for two decades. The transparent honesty of his brothers' confession moves Joseph deeply. He must hide his face to conceal his emotions as he weeps uncontrollably (see Gen 42:24).

Taking Simeon as a hostage, Joseph sends the nine brothers back to Canaan with their bags of grain. Secretly, however, he instructs his servants to "replace every man's money in his sack" (Gen 42:25). We can only guess what prompted Joseph to return the money. Was this a sinister trap to prove that the brothers were *not* honest men? Or was he expressing love and grace to his brothers by giving them the grain at no cost? Or was Joseph's action a strange mixture of both motivations reflecting the fact that he simply doesn't yet know how to respond to this incredible situation. Should he hug his brothers in love or kill them in revenge? Joseph hasn't yet sorted out his emotions and doesn't yet know what he should do. Wisely, he decides to give the matter more time.

When the brothers return to the land of Canaan, they give a full report of all that has happened to their father Jacob. They are shocked to discover that their money has been returned to each of them! What can this mean? Jacob is grieved that Simeon has been kept as a hostage in Egypt. But he is especially troubled by the demand that Benjamin must now be taken to Egypt as proof of the brothers' honesty. This is something that Jacob cannot allow!

> *And Jacob their father said to them, "You have bereaved me of my children: Joseph is no more, and Simeon is no more, and now you would take Benjamin. All this has come against me. . . . My son shall not go down with you, for his brother is dead, and he is the only one left. If harm should happen to him on the journey that you are to make, you would bring down my gray hairs with sorrow to Sheol." (Gen 42:36-38)*

This is the first time Jacob has accused the brothers of wrongdoing. You have "bereaved" me of Joseph, he says. Jacob seems to be saying that he may know more about what really happened to Joseph than he had let on.

Act 2. Joseph's brothers' second trip to Egypt.

It doesn't take long for Jacob's family to consume all the provisions they brought from Egypt. Because there is no end in sight to the famine, they begin to discuss the possibility of another trip to Egypt to buy more grain. The brothers refuse to go without Benjamin. They remember that this was the condition set by the Egyptian official when they visited the first time. Only if Benjamin goes with them will they be able to get Simeon out of prison and purchase more food. Judah steps forward to speak for the brothers and vows to take special care of Benjamin. It appears that Judah is emerging as the next leader of the family. His speech is convincing, and Jacob reluctantly agrees to let Benjamin go.

> *And Judah said to Israel his father, "Send the boy with me . . . I will be a pledge of his safety. From my hand you shall require him. If I do not bring him back to you and set him before you, then let me bear the blame forever." (Gen 43:8-9)*

Arriving in Egypt bearing gifts and twice the amount of money needed, the brothers once again stand before Joseph asking for food. Joseph invites the brothers to join him in his own house for a special meal. Simeon is released from prison and joins them for the banquet. To the brothers' amazement, they are treated royally. Once again, they bow before him. On seeing his full brother Benjamin, Joseph is overcome with emotion and seeks a private place where he can weep freely (see Gen 43:29-30).

The brothers marvel that they are seated at the table according to their birth order (see Gen 43:33). Henry Morris notes that the odds of seating eleven men in the right birth order by chance is roughly 40 million to one! They are again surprised to find that Benjamin's food portion is "five times as much as any of theirs" (Gen 43:34). Though Joseph is seated at a separate table, the atmosphere during the meal is festive and happy (Gen 43:34).

Act 3. Joseph devises a final plan to test his brothers.

As the brothers prepare to return home to Canaan, Joseph once again orders that each man's money be put in the mouth of his sack. This time, however, he has an additional instruction for his servant: "and put my cup, the silver cup, in the mouth of the sack of the youngest" (Gen 44:2). His plan sounds devious. Joseph will let the brothers begin their journey and then send men to arrest them, accusing them of stealing his personal property (the silver cup). What's going on here? Does Joseph want reconciliation or revenge? He seems conflicted. And why doesn't he reveal his identity? What is he waiting for?

The incident with the silver cup seems to be a test that Joseph has devised to see if his brothers will treat Benjamin as they treated him twenty years earlier? Will they turn on the favored son and abandon him when he is caught in the trap? Or will they come to his defense? The test will reveal the truth of whether or not his brothers have had a genuine change of heart.

When the cup is discovered in Benjamin's sack, the brothers are overcome with dismay. There is no suggestion that they think Benjamin has been framed. It seems almost that they assume he is guilty of the theft. Once again, they conclude that this unfortunate situation is part of God's retributive justice. Speaking for the group, Judah explains to Joseph, "God has found out the guilt of your servants" (Gen 44:16). None of this, however, dampens the commitment of the brothers to stand together in solidarity and support their little brother. In unison, they load their donkeys and return to Egypt.

Arriving at Joseph's house, Judah steps forward and gives one of the most remarkable speeches in the entire Bible.

> *Then Judah went up to him and said, "Oh, my lord, please let your servant speak a word in my lord's ears, and let not your anger burn against your servant, for you are like Pharaoh himself. My lord asked his servants, saying, 'Have you a father, or a brother?' And we said to my lord, 'We have a father, an old man, and a young brother, the child of his old age. His brother is dead, and he alone is left of his mother's children, and his father loves him.' Then you said to your servants, 'Bring him down to me, that I may set my eyes on him.' We said to my lord, 'The boy cannot leave his father, for if he should leave his father, his father would die.' Then you*

said to your servants, 'Unless your youngest brother comes down with you, you shall not see my face again.'

"When we went back to your servant my father, we told him the words of my lord. And when our father said, 'Go again, buy us a little food,' we said, 'We cannot go down. If our youngest brother goes with us, then we will go down. For we cannot see the man's face unless our youngest brother is with us.' Then your servant my father said to us, 'You know that my wife bore me two sons. One left me, and I said, "Surely he has been torn to pieces," and I have never seen him since. If you take this one also from me, and harm happens to him, you will bring down my gray hairs in evil to Sheol.'

"Now therefore, as soon as I come to your servant my father, and the boy is not with us, then, as his life is bound up in the boy's life, as soon as he sees that the boy is not with us, he will die, and your servants will bring down the gray hairs of your servant our father with sorrow to Sheol. For your servant became a pledge of safety for the boy to my father, saying, 'If I do not bring him back to you, then I shall bear the blame before my father all my life.' Now therefore, please let your servant remain instead of the boy as a servant to my lord, and let the boy go back with his brothers. For how can I go back to my father if the boy is not with me? I fear to see the evil that would find my father." (Gen 44:18-34)

Judah's speech is a masterpiece of persuasive rhetoric, emotional honesty, and theological wisdom, setting him apart as the obvious leader of the family. His willingness to serve as a substitute, to give his life so that Benjamin might live, shows that he has a profound understanding of the ways of God. Leon Kass has this to say about his amazing speech:

> This is, without a doubt, Judah's finest moment. Judah volunteers to be "the ram"—"instead of the lad" (see Gen 22:13). His magnanimous and self-sacrificing offer to remain as Joseph's slave in Benjamin's stead is unparalleled in the book of Genesis; in the Torah, it is surpassed only by Moses' plea to God to forgive Israel for the golden calf, asking to be

erased from God's book should He refuse to forgive his people for their sin.[1]

From this point on in the Genesis narrative, Judah is clearly God's choice to lead the covenant family. Not Ruben (the first born), not Simeon (the second born), and not even Joseph will be the recognized leader of the Hebrew people. Judah will be the father of David and ultimately through his lineage will Jesus Christ be born, God's promised Messiah. He will be the father of the promised Seed of the Woman, the serpent crusher (Gen 3:15). As Jacob foretold in his final prophecy: "The scepter shall not depart from Judah" (Gen 49:10). Judah's mother had named him well: "Praise the Lord!"

Act 4. Reconciliation.

Judah's speech strikes home! Joseph now has no doubts about what he should do. Bursting with emotion, he reveals himself to his brothers in one of the most dramatic scenes in the entire Bible.

> *Then Joseph could not control himself before all those who stood by him. He cried, "Make everyone go out from me." So no one stayed with him when Joseph made himself known to his brothers. And he wept aloud, so that the Egyptians heard it, and the household of Pharaoh heard it. And Joseph said to his brothers, "I am Joseph! Is my father still alive?" But his brothers could not answer him, for they were dismayed at his presence. So Joseph said to his brothers, "Come near to me, please." And they came near. And he said, "I am your brother, Joseph, whom you sold into Egypt. And now do not be distressed or angry with yourselves because you sold me here, for God sent me before you to preserve life." (Gen 45:1-5)*

In blurting out, "I am Joseph!" Joseph suddenly switches from Egyptian to flawless Hebrew, his native tongue. The interpreter is no longer needed. It is now crystal clear that he really does want to be reunited with his brothers. He wants reconciliation, not revenge. More than that, he longs to be reunited with his father. In asking if his father is still alive, Joseph is doing more that seeking information

---

1 Kass, *The Beginning of Wisdom*, 502.

about Jacob's physical well-being. He is asking if he still has a place in his father's heart. *Am I still a son of Jacob? Do I still belong to the covenant family of Abraham?*

The eleven brothers are not only shocked by this revelation, they are terrified! Joseph immediately reassures them by explaining that this is all part of God's sovereign and gracious plan. "God sent me before you to preserve life" (Gen 45:5).

We can only guess at what point in his life's journey Joseph became aware that his experience of being sold into slavery was really part of an amazing divine plan to save the world. But step by step, the staggering truth slowly dawned on Joseph that God, not his brothers, was the real Author of his life's script. He slowly came to realize that all things really had worked together for good, even the bad things—*especially* the bad things! It took over twenty years to grasp the reality but now it was gloriously clear: "You meant evil against me, but God meant it for good" (Gen 50:20). Though full reconciliation with his brothers would take time, the wounds and divisions in the family had finally been addressed. Now the healing could begin.

The Path toward Reconciliation

Before offering an abstract theological definition of a doctrine, the Bible often tells a story, giving a flesh-and-blood illustration of what the doctrine looks like in real life. The Joseph narrative gives us a beautiful illustration of the doctrine of reconciliation. The word refers to the doing away with enmity and the reuniting of persons who were formerly hostile to one another. It describes the restoration of friendly relations, the settlement of a disagreement, the resolution of a dispute. To be reconciled is to live in harmony with someone who was once an enemy. It describes how the animosity between adversaries is dissolved, how wounds are healed, and how unity is restored. The story of how Joseph and his brothers are reunited is a classic illustration of reconciliation. Though the steps involved typically follow a certain order, this is not always the case. But when reconciliation occurs, you can be sure that the following ingredients are involved.

A Sense of *Guilt*

Over twenty years have passed, and no one knows of the sinister deed the ten sons of Jacob have perpetrated against their brother. They have committed the perfect crime. Their secret will never be known. But no cover-up operation can ease the torment of their guilty consciences. Time does *not* heal all wounds! "Be sure your sin will find you out" (Num 32:23). The text gives multiple indications of the brothers' on-going struggle with guilt (see Gen 42:21-22, 28; 44:16). They simply cannot escape the haunting memory of what they have done.

For enemies to be reconciled, at least one of the parties must feel some guilt and take some responsibility for what has happened to cause the broken relationship. When functioning properly, a guilty conscience is a very good thing. Like the flashing "Check Engine" light on the dashboard of your car, its message must not be ignored. Jesus explained that this sense of guilt in a person's soul is preeminently the work of the Holy Spirit: "When the Holy Spirit comes, he will convict the world concerning sin" (John 16:8).

A Verbal *Confession*

As long as enemies suppress their guilt, deny their responsibility, rationalize their behavior, and blame the broken relationship on someone else, the wounds that cause the rupture will continue to fester. It is only when one of the parties humbly confesses the truth about their own sinful behavior that reconciliation becomes possible. In Greek, the word "confess" literally means "to say the same thing," "to agree." To confess is to simply acknowledge the truth: "What I did was wrong." It is not enough to confess our sins privately to God. The Bible urges us to find the appropriate context and confess our sins to one another (see Jas 5:16). Especially, we should acknowledge our sins to the person we have offended. To be effective, the confession should be succinct, specific, emotionally honest, and purged of all attempts to rationalize or justify one's behavior. In Psalm 32, David gives us an illustration of what this looks like:

> *For when I kept silent, my bones wasted away*
> *through my groaning all day long.*
> *For day and night your hand was heavy upon me;*
> *my strength was dried up as by the heat of summer.*
>
> *I acknowledged my sin to you,*
> *and I did not cover my iniquity;*
> *I said, "I will confess my transgressions to the* LORD,*"*
> *and you forgave the iniquity of my sin. (Ps 32:3-5)*

Heart-felt *Repentance*

Confession alone, however, is not enough. It is possible that the one who confesses is merely expressing sorrow that he got caught. Or perhaps he regrets that he has behaved so stupidly. Unless confession leads to repentance, genuine reconciliation simply cannot occur. To repent means more than feeling remorse for what happened. Judas felt remorse for what he had done in betraying Jesus. In returning the blood money to the Jewish leaders, he confessed his wrongdoing: "I have sinned by betraying innocent blood" (see Matt 27:3-5). But his confession did not lead to repentance (see 2 Cor 7:10). He therefore remained unreconciled.

The Greek word for repentance implies a change of mind and heart. More than simply feeling bad about what happened, repentance means that the behavior has been renounced; it will never happen again. When possible, the guilty party offers to do whatever he can to make restitution. The test Joseph devises with the silver goblet hidden in Benjamin's sack reveals that his brothers have indeed changed. Rather than abandoning Benjamin as they had abandoned Joseph, they stand in solidarity with him. There is simply no substitute for repentance. Without it, reconciliation is impossible. No one stated this truth more strongly than Jesus: "Unless you repent, you will all likewise perish" (Luke 13:3-5).

Substitutionary Suffering

In offering himself as a guarantee for Benjamin's well-being, Judah illustrates the principle of substitution. He is ready to take the punishment that someone else deserves. In freely choosing to act as a substitute for his brother, Judah is giving up his life so that Benjamin can go free. Judah's offer is not coerced. It is freely motivated by love. The principle of substitution affirms the theological truth that sin cannot be overlooked. Unjust behaviors cannot be swept under the carpet: "Don't worry about it; it's nothing." No. Something *did* happen, something awful. No amount of denial or pretending can erase the damage done. A price must be paid if reconciliation is to occur.

Reconciliation becomes possible only when a substitute steps forward and freely offers to accept the penalty that the sinful action deserves. Though he himself is not guilty of the crime, he is willing to take the punishment. The price for sin will indeed be paid, but by a substitute. In Genesis 22, we saw how God accepted a ram as a substitute sacrificial offering for Isaac (Gen 22:8, 13). But Judah is not offering an animal as a substitute for his brother, he is offering himself.

The ultimate substitute is, of course, the Lamb of God, Jesus Christ. As the father of the tribe from which Jesus will come, Judah's gracious offer of substitution prefigures what Jesus will do on Calvary many centuries later. On the cross, Jesus makes a free and gracious choice to die in the place of guilty sinners. In taking on himself the penalty for sin, he has become the sinner's substitute. He dies in our place.

> *Surely he has borne our griefs*
> *and carried our sorrows;*
> *yet we esteemed him stricken,*
> *smitten by God, and afflicted.*
> *But he was pierced for our transgressions;*
> *he was crushed for our iniquities;*
> *upon him was the chastisement that brought us peace,*
> *and with his wounds we are healed.*
> *All we like sheep have gone astray;*
> *we have turned—every one—to his own way;*
> *and the* Lord *has laid on him*
> *the iniquity of us all. (Isa 53:4-6)*

Joseph's reconciliation with his brothers becomes possible only when Judah freely steps forward and offers to be a substitute for Benjamin. This is the key that opens the door to forgiveness and restoration.

Gracious *Forgiveness*

Ultimately, the only way to bring healing to a broken relationship is through forgiveness. To be reconciled with his brothers, Joseph will have to forgive them for what they have done. In the next chapter we will discover how all these elements come together in a way that makes forgiveness and reconciliation possible.

QUESTIONS FOR DISCUSSION

1. This chapter suggests that two questions must be answered by every disciple of Jesus: 1) When I try to do right, why do bad things happen? 2) As a Christian, can I live in the world without becoming worldly? Which question is most challenging for you?
2. Look again at the five elements that define the path to reconciliation (guilt, confession, repentance, substitution, forgiveness). Which one seems most important to you?
3. Why did the author entitle this chapter "Finding the Way Home"?
4. Think of broken relationships in the world today (racism in the U.S., Arab-Israeli conflict, political divisions, etc.). What can be done? What should the church be doing?
5. Think of a broken relationship in your own life. As you look at the five elements that define the path to reconciliation, what is the Holy Spirit saying to you?

Come, Ye Sinners, Poor and Needy
Joseph Hart (1759)

Come, ye sinners, poor and needy,
Weak and wounded, sick and sore.
Jesus ready, stands to save you,
Full of pity, love, and power.

Refrain:
I will arise and go to Jesus,
He will embrace me in his arms.
In the arms of my dear Savior,
O, there are ten thousand charms.

Come, ye weary, heavy laden,
Lost and ruined by the fall;
If you tarry 'till you're better,
You will never come at all.

Let not conscience make you linger,
Nor of fitness fondly dream;
All the fitness he requireth
Is to feel your need of him.

30
Eden's Gates
Genesis 45:1-15; 50:15-21

In October of 2006, a crazed gunman entered an Amish one-room schoolhouse in Nickel Mines, Pennsylvania, taking as hostage ten young girls, ages six to thirteen. He brutally shot eight of them, killing five. The shooter, a local resident, then took his own life. In a nation habituated to the tragedy of mass shootings, this murderous rampage stood out from the rest. For days, the horror of the event captured national attention and was the subject of every major news outlet. The cold-blooded murder of innocent Amish girls was beyond anyone's ability to comprehend.

Soon after the killings, however, a second news item began to circulate. In some ways this follow-up story was even more shocking and difficult to understand than the murders themselves. It was this second story that fixed the massacre at Nickel Mines in our corporate memory. Almost immediately after the attack, members of the local Amish community extended forgiveness to the dead murderer and reached out in love to his widow and three children. They went so far as to set up a charitable fund for the shooter's family. The widow was one of the few outsiders invited to attend the funeral of one of the victims. National news struggled to determine which of these two stories was more newsworthy. Violence, unfortunately, is a rather routine occurrence in America today. But forgiveness—*that* is something rare indeed!

Perhaps no single word captures the essence of the Gospel more than the word forgiveness. Whether we are talking about the killing of Amish schoolgirls, the selling of Joseph into slavery, or some other grievous act of wickedness, we all understand that injustice cannot be swept under the carpet or ignored. Something terrible has occurred and human relationships are violently torn asunder. Our hearts immediately cry out for justice! The perpetrator must be punished, the wrong must be corrected, and the moral balance must be reestablished.

But how? Few questions in all of life are more important than this! This chapter will examine the dynamics of forgiveness. When practiced as God intended, not only does forgiveness restore justice and reestablish the moral balance but it makes possible authentic reconciliation. Those who were once at enmity now have the genuine opportunity to restore their relationship; *not* as it was before with all its dysfunctionality and sin, but as it ought to be, based in the liberating reality of God's truth. But for such reconciliation to occur with one another, we must first be reconciled with God. The horizontal dimensions of grace are rooted in the vertical dimensions. The story of how Joseph and his brothers were finally reconciled introduces us to the glorious reality of forgiveness. Through their lives we get a glimpse of the gates of Eden and the home we lost so long ago.

THE CRY FOR JUSTICE

Revenge is perhaps the oldest and most common way humans have used to deal with an offense. The goal is to make the guilty party suffer. "You hurt me; therefore, I will hurt you." Typically, the one who has been hurt feels the need to inflict a punishment that is *worse* than the one they received. Only in this way do they feel avenged. "You killed my son; therefore, I am going to kill your family." Which typically is met with the response, "You killed my family; therefore, we are going to destroy your village." The escalating cycle of violence ends only when one side brutally crushes the other, forcing them into submission. Might makes right. In such a situation, the victor may feel a measure of "satisfaction," but this approach does nothing to heal the wounds that caused the conflict or to bring about reconciliation between the warring parties.

Retributive justice is a much better response to an offense than revenge. Whereas the goal of revenge is to get even by inflicting pain on the perpetrator, the goal of retributive justice is to be fair and just in one's treatment of the offender. The guilty party must indeed pay a price for what he has done, but the punishment must fit the crime. As opposed to revenge, retributive justice is not personal, and those enforcing the punishment take no pleasure in what they are doing. Rather, every effort is made to ensure that proper procedures are employed, and that the retribution is proportionate to the offense. "You stole my cow; therefore, I am going to take your cow and charge you a fee to cover my lost income."

As its name implies, retributive justice is all about *justice*. The Latin term that describes this way of handling social crimes and relational sins is *lex talionis*: the law of retaliation. Once again, it is important to notice that the goal is *not* to heal past wounds or restore broken relationships. The purpose, rather, is to re-establish justice, to restore the moral order. This, of course, is a worthy goal. Human history would be very different if this principle had been followed consistently through the ages. In fact, so important is retributive justice that it is endorsed by God himself and enshrined in the Mosaic Law:

> *Whoever takes a human life shall surely be put to death. Whoever takes an animal's life shall make it good, life for life. If anyone injures his neighbor, as he has done it shall be done to him, fracture for fracture, eye for eye, tooth for tooth; whatever injury he has given a person shall be given to him. (Lev 24:17-20)*

Think how different the Joseph story would have been if Joseph had done nothing more than employ the principle of retributive justice (*lex talionis*). In such a case, when he finally revealed his identity to his brothers, he might have said something like this: "You sold me into slavery as a teenager. Therefore, to settle the score, I am going to take from each of you one of your children and sell them into slavery. Only then will I consider the case closed. An eye for an eye." Such an approach would conceivably have brought a measure of "satisfaction" to Joseph, knowing that the moral order had been re-established. But it would have done nothing to heal past wounds or restore ruptured relationships in the family. For reconciliation to occur, something more than retributive justice is needed. To be reunited with his brothers, Joseph is going to have to forgive them for the terrible things they have done.

The Ministry of Reconciliation

The book of Genesis repeatedly underscores the fact that one of God's primary attributes is justice. In casting Adam and Eve out of the Garden of Eden, in sending a flood on the sinful earth, and in forcefully stopping the builders of the tower at Babel, we see God's passionate commitment to the moral order, to justice. Sin will not be tolerated! And when it occurs, it must be condemned and punished.

And yet God is interested in more than justice—much more. He takes no pleasure in the death of the wicked. He longs to heal the wounds and restore the broken relationships caused by sin. He wants reconciliation, not just justice. First, he makes possible a way for sinners to be reconciled with himself so that there can once again be unbroken fellowship between God and man. Then, he sends his people into the world so that they can now be agents of reconciliation, helping those with broken relationships to be reconciled with one another. God's passionate purpose in Genesis is to repair the damaged relationships caused by sin, both vertically and horizontally. Mending broken relationships on earth is dependent on first mending our broken relationship with God. The former simply cannot occur without the latter.

In this life, however, it remains impossible to return to our original garden paradise and we must live "east of Eden." But God's work of reconciliation puts us close enough to home to see the garden gates! We can now, once again, live in the reality of unbroken fellowship with our Creator and Redeemer, enabling us to be agents of reconciliation throughout the world. The apostle Paul speaks about this ministry of reconciliation in his second letter to the Corinthians.

> *Therefore, if anyone is in Christ, he is a new creation. The old has passed away; behold, the new has come. All this is from God, who through Christ reconciled us to himself and gave us the ministry of reconciliation; that is, in Christ God was reconciling the world to himself, not counting their trespasses against them, and entrusting to us the message of reconciliation. Therefore, we are ambassadors for Christ, God making his appeal through us. We implore you on behalf of Christ, be reconciled to God. For our sake he made him to be sin who knew no sin, so that in him we might become the righteousness of God. (2 Cor 5:17-21).*

This amazing passage of Scripture reveals that the great purpose of God in redemption is not, as many American evangelicals seem to believe, taking us to heaven when we die. That may be one aspect of salvation, but this passage says there is so much more. God's purpose in redemption is to recreate us so that the original purposes of creation can be lived out in us! Not only are we reconciled with God through Christ, but we are called to be God's ambassadors, agents of reconciliation in the world. Because our own ruptured relationship with God has been decisively healed, we are now able to help others experience reconciliation as well; both vertically and horizontally. None of this would be possible, Paul explains, without the substitutionary work of God's own Son, Jesus Christ, who took on himself the sins of the world. He who knew no sin, became sin himself, "so that in him we might become the righteousness of God" (2 Cor 5:21).

Joseph Reconciles with His Brothers

The moment when Joseph revealed his identity to his brothers is perhaps the climactic scene in the entire book of Genesis. Few passages in all the Bible are more dramatic than this.

> *Then Joseph could not control himself before all those who stood by him. He cried, "Make everyone go out from me." So no one stayed with him when Joseph made himself known to his brothers. And he wept aloud, so that the Egyptians heard it, and the household of Pharaoh heard it. And Joseph said to his brothers, "I am Joseph! Is my father still alive?" But his brothers could not answer him, for they were dismayed at his presence. So Joseph said to his brothers, "Come near*

> to me, please." And they came near. And he said, "I am your brother, Joseph, whom you sold into Egypt. And now do not be distressed or angry with yourselves because you sold me here, for God sent me before you to preserve life. For the famine has been in the land these two years, and there are yet five years in which there will be neither plowing nor harvest. And God sent me before you to preserve for you a remnant on earth, and to keep alive for you many survivors. So it was not you who sent me here, but God. He has made me a father to Pharaoh, and lord of all his house and ruler over all the land of Egypt. Hurry and go up to my father and say to him, 'Thus says your son Joseph, God has made me lord of all Egypt. Come down to me; do not tarry. You shall dwell in the land of Goshen, and you shall be near me, you and your children and your children's children, and your flocks, your herds, and all that you have. There I will provide for you, for there are yet five years of famine to come, so that you and your household, and all that you have, do not come to poverty.' And now your eyes see, and the eyes of my brother Benjamin see, that it is my mouth that speaks to you. You must tell my father of all my honor in Egypt, and of all that you have seen. Hurry and bring my father down here." Then he fell upon his brother Benjamin's neck and wept, and Benjamin wept upon his neck. And he kissed all his brothers and wept upon them. After that his brothers talked with him. (Gen 45:1-15)

The text leaves us wondering whether Joseph forgave his brothers *before* this moment of self-disclosure or whether the forgiveness welled up in him *during* the encounter itself. The moment in time when forgiveness was granted may remain a mystery but there is no doubt at all about the fact! Joseph's words, emotions, and actions testify to the reality that he bears no grudge and carries no animosity toward those who have treated him so cruelly. There is not a trace of bitterness or hatred, no hint of vengeance. Judah's speech and his offer to serve as a substitute for Benjamin is the key that unlocked the door holding back Joseph's emotions. As he reveals his identity to his brothers he unleashes a torrent of mercy, grace, and love.

Three times Joseph affirms that God, *not* his brothers, is responsible for sending him to Egypt (Gen 45:5, 7, 8). The brothers are certainly guilty of brutality, abuse, and human trafficking, but Joseph has come to see that beyond their malicious cruelty the sovereign hand of God has been at work all the time. "A man's heart plans his way, but the Lord directs his steps" (Prov 16:9 NKJV). Joseph has made the revolutionary discovery that the evil deeds of men cannot thwart the good and gracious will of God. This awareness changes everything! The lessons that Joseph has learned at Pit State University are paying rich dividends. He has become a theologian—a *good* theologian!

Although Joseph has forgiven his brothers for their wicked deeds, he is not yet ready to be reconciled with them. Forgiving an offense is one thing. Reestablishing a relationship is another. Though many seem to believe that forgiveness and reconciliation are synonymous actions, Joseph astutely recognizes that these are two distinct steps, both theologically and psychologically. In forgiving the sin, Joseph is purging his soul of the poison that comes from hatred and bitterness. This means that he no longer carries a grudge nor feels the need to punish his brothers for what they have done. He is letting them off the hook. But forgiveness alone, as important as it is, does not restore a relationship. It is possible to forgive someone yet keep them at arm's length. For reconciliation to occur, the victim must have assurance that the perpetrator has changed, that he is now safe to be with. Before Joseph can be reconciled with his brothers, he needs to know whether they can be trusted. This will take some time.

The importance of Joseph's forgiveness of his brothers is so significant that the author of Genesis returns to it again at the very end of the book.

> *When Joseph's brothers saw that their father was dead, they said, "It may be that Joseph will hate us and pay us back for all the evil that we did to him." So they sent a message to Joseph, saying, "Your father gave this command before he died: 'Say to Joseph, "Please forgive the transgression of your brothers and their sin, because they did evil to you."' And now, please forgive the transgression of the servants of the God of your father." Joseph wept when they spoke to him. His brothers also came and fell down before him and said, "Behold, we are your servants." But Joseph said to them, "Do not fear, for am I in the place of God? As for you, you meant evil against me, but God meant it for good, to bring it about*

that many people should be kept alive, as they are today. So do not fear; I will provide for you and your little ones." Thus he comforted them and spoke kindly to them. (Gen 50:15-21)

Joseph reassures his brothers of his forgiveness and once again emphasizes God's sovereign plan. Human sinfulness is a serious reality that must be dealt with decisively, but no wicked schemes of men are able to thwart the gracious plan of God. "You meant evil against me, but God meant it for good" (Gen 50:20). These words remind us of the tree in the Garden of Eden named "the tree of the knowledge of good and evil" (Gen 2:17). Adam and Eve fell into sin and lost their home in paradise because in eating the forbidden fruit they failed to discern the difference between good and evil. Believing that God's prohibition from eating the fruit was something "bad" and Satan's enticement to eat was something "good," they got things exactly backward! In calling good evil and evil good, Adam and Eve took their first step on the downward path of sin, and human history began its tragic journey moving from one catastrophic decision to another. But here, at the end of the Genesis story, Joseph finally gets it right! With divine insight, he discerns correctly that what seemed to be evil was in reality something good. This provides a fitting conclusion to the book of Genesis and prepares us for the next chapter of the story God is writing: the book of Exodus.

What Forgiveness Is Not

In summarizing the Joseph story, it will be helpful to sharpen our definition of forgiveness. The reason many struggle today with both forgiving others and being forgiven is because they have never paused to think carefully about what forgiveness is and what it is not. Let's begin by stating clearly what forgiveness is not.

Forgiveness Is Not Forgetting

We may scratch our theological heads when the Bible tells us that God "forgets" our sins when he forgives them. How can the One who is omniscient and knows everything from beginning to end forget anything? And yet Isaiah hears God himself declare that he "will not remember" our sins (Isa 43:25). And the prophet Micah proclaims that God "will cast all our sins into the depths of the sea" (Mic 7:19). Regardless of how one may explain the "forgetfulness" of God when it comes to forgiveness, we need to remember one very important fact: *we* are not God! What may be possible for him is impossible for us. We are not computers equipped with a "delete" button so that painful memories can be erased. Forgiveness is not pretending the events of the past did not occur. Rather, it is making a choice to live with the consequences of what happened and not to allow poison and bitterness to infect our lives.

During a marriage counseling session, a husband, in great frustration, blurted out to the counselor; "Every time my wife and I fight, she gets historical." The counselor, not quite sure he had heard correctly, said; "I think you must mean she gets hysterical." "No," said the husband. "My wife gets historical. She begins to recite from memory all the mistakes I've made during the entire thirty years we have been married." Obviously, the wife had not forgiven her husband. Her poisonous memory and her readiness to exploit it was proof that she continued to hold a grudge against her husband. Forgiveness means that the victim has made a conscious choice to never again use the past as a weapon against the offender. The memory may remain, but the poison has been extracted.

Forgiveness Is Not Condoning

Many people have the strange idea that to forgive something means to disregard it, to shrug it off, to excuse it. They seem to believe that if they forgive some terrible deed, they are saying that it was OK that it happened, or perhaps that it really wasn't that bad. When Joseph forgave his brothers, he was certainly *not* condoning child trafficking! God never asks us to excuse the inexcusable!

It is possible to forgive someone and, at the same time, agree that the offender should be held accountable for his actions (be fined, fired, arrested, etc.). The Bible is very clear that even forgiven sin may still have negative consequences. A forgiven and reformed alcoholic may still suffer and even die from cirrhosis of the liver. A forgiven murderer may still spend his life on Death Row in prison. A man who steals from his employer may be forgiven, yet still lose his job. Forgiveness does not mean that we pretend the offense wasn't offensive. Rather, it means that, in those areas where you are in charge, you will not press the matter further. It means that you are taking the offender off your hook and putting him on God's. Vengeance belongs to the Lord, not to us (Rom 12:19). And God's promise is that one day, he will settle all accounts justly and fairly!

Forgiveness Is Not Pretending

Many people, in a valiant effort to put a painful, abusive experience behind them, try to minimize what happened. Some live in the land of denial: "Oh, it didn't really hurt." Others, seek to be dismissive: "It was no big deal." Still others make excuses for what happened: "They didn't really mean to hurt me." Some people deal with their pain by extending the olive branch of forgiveness prematurely. They quickly offer to forgive the offender in the hopes that this will enable them to bypass the trauma of what happened. These approaches to relational pain are unhealthy and unwise. They do not bring genuine healing or make possible authentic reconciliation. The "forgiveness" offered is illusory. Pretending that the wounds have healed, when they haven't, that the perpetrator is trustworthy, when he isn't, or that the situation is behind us, when it isn't, is not only naïve, it may be dangerous.

Forgiveness Is Not Reconciliation

When we fail to distinguish between forgiveness and reconciliation, multiple problems arise in both our thinking and our actions. Many people seem to think that if they forgive someone, then they should be chummy again with the person that hurt them. Such muddled thinking can lead to foolish choices. To forgive an abuser doesn't mean that he should be invited back into the house. To forgive a thief doesn't mean that he should be made the treasurer of the company. Reestablishing a relationship must be based on trust, and trust must be earned. This takes time.

Forgiveness is a unilateral act. It can be offered regardless of the actions or inactions of the offender. To forgive is to get the poison out of our system before it hurts us! Reconciliation, on the other hand, is bilateral. It occurs when two persons, formerly at odds, reestablish a healthy and meaningful relationship. This can happen only when trust has been rebuilt and the relationship is safe and healthy. Joseph had clearly forgiven his brothers for what they had done. But was it safe to reestablish a relationship? Could they be trusted? Could they once again relate to one another as brothers, members of the same family? This was another matter entirely.

What Forgiveness Is

When we forgive someone, we give up the right to use what they did as a weapon against them. Joseph clearly had the right to have his brothers arrested and charged with kidnapping, child trafficking, slave trading, conspiracy, and obstruction of justice. When he forgave them, he gave up this right—forever. Like a sponge, he absorbed in his own person the horrific consequences of their actions. In doing so, he broke the cycle of retaliation. He emasculated sin, stripping it of its power. Because he took on himself their sin, they could be forgiven, and reconciliation became a real possibility.

But How Does Forgiveness Work?

First, Joseph learned to think theologically. To put it in gospel terminology, he learned to think with the mind of Christ. Typically, when someone is victimized and hurt, they think in terms of vengeance, legal action, or psychological care. But Joseph knew that, if the situation with his brothers was ever going to be made right, he would need more than lawyers and counselors. It is only when he invited God into the situation that he found the ability to think with the mind of Christ, to think redemptively. This changed everything.

> *And now do not be distressed or angry with yourselves because you sold me here, for God sent me before you to preserve life. . . . And God sent me before you to preserve for you a remnant on earth, and to keep alive for you many*

survivors. So it was not you who sent me here, but God. (Gen 45:5-8)

This mindset enabled Joseph to realize that though his brothers were *to blame* for what had happened to him, God was the one who was ultimately *responsible*! Reconciliation with sinners is only possible when we bow before a sovereign God and say, "Lord, what are *you* trying to do in and through this painful situation that *you* have allowed to happen?"

Secondly, Joseph stopped trying to be God's prosecuting attorney. He realized that it was not his job to be the ultimate judge of all the earth nor to make his brother's pay for the terrible things they had done. It was God's job to maintain the moral order, not his. Joseph realized that in forgiving his brothers, he was not pronouncing them innocent. No! He was simply taking them off his hook and putting them on God's. Joseph's treatment of his brothers is a classic illustration of what Paul was describing in his epistle to the Romans:

Beloved, never avenge yourselves, but leave it to the wrath of God, for it is written, "Vengeance is mine, I will repay, says the Lord." To the contrary, "if your enemy is hungry, feed him; if he is thirsty, give him something to drink; for by so doing you will heap burning coals on his head." Do not be overcome by evil, but overcome evil with good. (Rom 12:19-21)

Thirdly, Joseph absorbed the pain. The abuse that Joseph received from his brothers must have been incredibly painful, both physically and psychologically. But rather than lashing back in vengeance, Joseph chose to suffer. Like a sponge, he absorbed into himself the suffering caused by sin. This caused the sting of sin to lose its power.

C. S. Lewis famously said, "Everyone says forgiveness is a lovely idea, until they have something to forgive."[1] To forgive is costly indeed! Sin can be defeated only when someone absorbs its full impact. Jesus Christ is, of course, the ultimate expression of this world-changing truth. On the cross, he took onto himself the sins of the world, absorbing them into his own body. Indeed, he *became* sin (2 Cor 5:21).

---

1   Lewis, *Mere Christianity*, 115.

And in so doing, God gave up forever the right to use the evil things we have done as a weapon against us.

To a limited degree, when we forgive someone who has sinned against us, we do the same thing Jesus did on the cross. Paul alluded to the importance of this kind of suffering when he said, "Now I rejoice in my sufferings for your sake, and in my flesh I am filling up what is lacking in Christ's afflictions for the sake of his body, that is, the church" (Col 1:24). Only the sufferings of Christ have the power to forgive sin. In comparison to his divine work on the cross, any suffering we may take on is insignificant. However, when we suffer as he suffered, that is, when we absorb the pain of someone else's sin, then our sufferings are, in some small way, a participation in the sufferings of Christ. The redemptive power inherent in this gospel truth has the potential to reform the church and transform the world. Joseph's decision to suffer rather than retaliate was, on a small scale, a picture of what Christ did on the cross. It was his decision to absorb the pain of someone else's sin that made forgiveness and reconciliation possible.

Christ sends us into the world to minister in the same way that he did, though obviously not to the same degree. We are sent out as ministers of reconciliation. We are sent to lay down our lives for others, to absorb in our own selves the pain that has been caused by other people's sins. After his resurrection, Jesus visited his disciples and showed them his nail-pierced hands and said, "As the Father has sent me, even so I am sending you" (John 20:21). When his death is at work in us, then life can come through us to others (see 2 Cor 4:12).

QUESTIONS FOR DISCUSSION

1. Have you known someone who was consumed by the desire for revenge? Describe the situation and how it ended.
2. The author states that retributive justice (*lex talionis*) is a good thing, and yet it is limited. It is not enough. What does the author mean by this?
3. How is vertical reconciliation (with God) connected to horizontal reconciliation (with one another)?

4. Describe what it means to forgive. For God. For you.
5. Why is it important to distinguish between forgiveness and reconciliation?

31
The Last Words of Joseph
Genesis 46–50

What people say when they face death often reveals the deepest realities that have characterized their lives. A person's last words can sometimes summarize their life's message.

- Nathan Hale—"I only regret that I have but one life to give for my country."
- Admiral Nelson—"Thank God, I have done my duty."
- Thomas Jefferson—"Is it the fourth?"
- John Wesley—"The best of all; God is with us."
- Paul—"I have fought the good fight, I have finished the race, I have kept the faith."
- Jesus "It is finished."

As recorded by the author of Genesis, the last words of Joseph are equally powerful. They give us a glimpse of his deepest convictions. It is no accident that these words also serve as an ending to the book of Genesis.

> *And Joseph said to his brothers, "I am about to die, but God will visit you and bring you up out of this land to the land that he swore to Abraham, to Isaac, and to Jacob." Then Joseph made the sons of Israel swear, saying, "God will surely visit you, and you shall carry up my bones from here." So Joseph died, being 110 years old. They embalmed him, and he was put in a coffin in Egypt. (Gen 50:24-26)*

Taking his cue from this passage, the author of Hebrews summarizes Joseph's life in these words: "By faith Joseph, at the end of his life, made mention of the exodus of the Israelites and gave directions concerning his bones" (Heb 11:22).

Joseph had lived ninety-three years in Egypt, had an Egyptian wife, and an Egyptian name. He spoke, dressed, and shaved like an Egyptian. He worked for the Egyptian government. He loved Egypt and Egyptians. But deep in his heart, Joseph knew that he was *not* an Egyptian and that Egypt was *not* his home. In giving orders that his embalmed body should be placed in an unburied coffin and in making the sons of Israel swear that they would bury his bones in Canaan, Joseph was affirming in the strongest manner possible that his true identity was Hebrew, not Egyptian. He was a child of Abraham. And his true home was not Egypt, but Canaan.

Four hundred years would pass before this promise would be fulfilled but when the Hebrew people finally began their exodus out of Egypt, Scripture tells us that "Moses took the bones of Joseph with him" (Exod 13:19; see also Josh 24:32). Speaking about the significance of Joseph's bones, the Scottish Baptist minister Alexander Maclaren (1826–1910) wrote:

> He filled his place at Pharaoh's court; but his dying words open a window into his soul, and betray how little he had felt that he belonged to the order of things in the midst of which he had been content to live. Though surrounded by an ancient civilization; and dwelling among granite temples and solid pyramids and firm-based sphinxes, the very emblems of eternity; he confessed that he had here no continuing city but sought one to come.[1]

Survey of Genesis 46–50

Jacob, also known as Israel, has every reason to hesitate before moving his family to Egypt. God had promised to give the land of Canaan to his descendants. So why leave? Even though the famine was severe, shouldn't he remain in the Land of Promise and trust God to provide for the needs of his family? Undoubtedly, Jacob remembered the story of what had happened to his grandfather Abraham who, in

---

1   Quoted in F. B. Meyer, *From the Pit to the Throne*, 147–148.

a similar situation, had left Canaan and gone to Egypt for help. The results were not pretty (see Gen 12:10ff.). So, God makes a special visitation to Jacob to reassure him that in *this* situation, moving the entire family to Egypt is a good thing.

> *And God spoke to Israel in visions of the night and said, "Jacob, Jacob." And he said, "Here I am." Then he said, "I am God, the God of your father. Do not be afraid to go down to Egypt, for there I will make you into a great nation. I myself will go down with you to Egypt, and I will also bring you up again, and Joseph's hand shall close your eyes." (Gen 46:2-4)*

With such a clear understanding of God's will and the promise of his presence and favor, Jacob and his family (seventy persons) pack up all their belongings and move to Egypt. Because of the severity of the famine, they know that this will not be a short visit, but they would have been utterly shocked to realize that their descendants would live in the land of Pharaoh for the next four centuries!

The reunion of Jacob and his son Joseph is one of the most tender scenes in all of Scripture. Traveling to Goshen in his chariot, dressed in all his regal splendor, Joseph meets his father and welcomes him to the land of Egypt. The embrace between father and son is long and tearful (see Gen 46:29). Jacob exclaims, "Now let me die, since I have seen your face and know that you are still alive" (Gen 46:30). And yet the reunion must have also provoked inner turmoil in Jacob as he realizes that his son, a child of Abraham, has apparently taken on a new Egyptian identity. The shaved head, the royal clothing, the chariot, the new name, the Egyptian wife—is this still Joseph, the Hebrew, a circumcised member of the covenant family? Leon Kass makes more of this than is perhaps warranted, but his commentary on this reunion enables us to better imagine the conflicting emotions that must have flooded Jacob's soul as he reconnects with his long-lost son.

> Very likely, feelings of disbelief, joy, awe, repugnance, and sorrow trip over one another in his soul. Is this really Joseph? Look, how superbly he is bedecked and appointed! But where

is his beard, where his hair, and what mean these foreign trappings? Have I found him, or have I lost him?[2]

The text describes how Jacob and his family settle in the land of Goshen where they can keep their flocks and herds and explains why this location was chosen: because "every shepherd is an abomination to the Egyptians" (Gen 46:34). There was a clear social distinction between the upper-class Egyptians and the minority status Hebrews from the very beginning (see also Gen 43:32; Exod 8:26). The longer the Hebrews stayed in Egypt, the more pronounced this cultural divide would become. The list of Jewish practices that were offensive to Egyptian sensibilities grew longer and longer. Whether it related to occupations, diet, sexual conduct, sorcery, treatment of the dead, idols, or shaving the head, the tension between Egyptians and Hebrews could be felt at every level of society. It was in Egypt that the first expressions of antisemitism had their birth. Joseph, at least at first, tried to assimilate himself into Egyptian culture. His goal, it seems, was to soften the racial differences by taking on Egyptian customs. But his story was not repeated. Though the Hebrews lived in Egypt for four hundred years, they never took on local ways; they never became Egyptian; they never assimilated. They maintained their distinctive Jewish identity. This is truly remarkable.

The story of how Jacob blessed Pharaoh is one of the most poignant scenes in the entire book of Genesis (see Gen 47:7-12). We can only wonder what prompted the mighty Pharaoh to seek a blessing from his social inferior. But the moment provides a dramatic illustration of the fulfillment of God's promise to Abraham: "in you all the families of the earth shall be blessed" (Gen 12:3). Though Jacob shows respect for the ruler of Egypt, he is not bedazzled by his wealth or envious of his power. Jacob is secure in his humble identity as a member of God's covenant family.

When it comes time for Jacob to die, he gives a special blessing to each of his twelve sons. As the last of the patriarchs, he knows that his sons will be the heads of the twelve tribes that will compose the

---

2   Kass, *The Beginning of Wisdom*, 622.

future nation of Israel. He takes his patriarchal duties very seriously. When it comes to Joseph, however, Jacob does something remarkable. He decides that there will be no tribe named "Joseph." Rather, he "adopts" Joseph's two sons, Ephraim and Manasseh, as his own (see Gen 48:1-22). In treating them as his sons, rather than his grandsons, Jacob makes them fathers of two tribes in Israel. Because Levi would be set apart by Moses for priestly duties and thus would receive no share of the land in Canaan (see Josh 14:4), the total number of tribal allotments in Israel would remain the same: twelve.

Genesis 49 records the poetic blessing that Jacob gives to each of his sons, a blessing that extends to the tribes that descend from each of them. Though each blessing has important details, our interest lies mainly in the two longest blessings; the ones given to Judah (Gen 49:8-12) and Joseph (Gen 49:22-26). Joseph, one of the greatest heroes of faith in all the Bible, receives a special blessing simply because of the remarkable life he has lived and the way he has brought glory to God. Jacob's blessing emphasizes the fact that Joseph is "fruitful . . . fruitful" (Gen 49:22). The word is a pun on the name Ephraim, Joseph's son (see Gen 41:52). In adopting Ephraim and Manasseh as his own sons and making them the fathers of tribes, Jacob is bestowing on Joseph a double blessing.

The most surprising part of Jacob's final blessing, however, is what he has to say about his fourth-born son, Judah.

> *Judah, your brothers shall praise you;*
> *your hand shall be on the neck of your enemies;*
> *your father's sons shall bow down before you.*
> *Judah is a lion's cub;*
> *from the prey, my son, you have gone up.*
> *He stooped down; he crouched as a lion*
> *and as a lioness; who dares rouse him?*
> *The scepter shall not depart from Judah,*
> *nor the ruler's staff from between his feet,*
> *until tribute comes to him;*
> *and to him shall be the obedience of the peoples.*
> *Binding his foal to the vine*
> *and his donkey's colt to the choice vine,*
> *he has washed his garments in wine*

and his vesture in the blood of grapes.
His eyes are darker than wine,
and his teeth whiter than milk. (Gen 49:8-12)

We have seen in previous chapters how Judah, despite his birth order and questionable moral history, emerged as the spokesman for the brothers and became their acknowledged leader (see Gen 43:8-10; 44:14-34; 46:28). In offering to give his life in exchange for Benjamin, he exhibited both servant leadership and self-giving love. His older siblings, Reuben, Simeon, and Levi had proven that they were unworthy and had forfeited their right to leadership. Jacob, fully aware of these dynamics, pronounced his blessing on Judah, elevating him in prominence over all his brothers, even over Joseph. "Your father's sons shall bow down before you. . . . The scepter shall not depart from Judah. . . . To him shall be the obedience of the peoples" (Gen 49:8, 10). From Judah's descendants, kings will come who will rule not only over Israel, but over all the world. As God had chosen Isaac over Ishmael and Jacob over Esau, so he is choosing Judah over his brothers to be the channel through whom his special blessings will flow out to all the earth.

Jacob's prophetic blessing on Judah reminds us once again of the Seed Project that God had begun centuries earlier in the Garden of Eden. When God prophesied that the seed of the woman would crush the head of the serpent (see Gen 3:15), he was announcing in advance the arrival of a Savior who would deliver his people from Satan's evil power. The book of Genesis traces the lineage of this coming serpent crusher by indicating time and again where the seed of the woman was located. Not in Cain, but in Seth. Not in Ham or Japheth, but in Shem. Not in Ishmael, but in Isaac. Not in Esau, but in Jacob. Not in Reuben, Simeon, Levi, or Joseph, but in Judah. As the book of Genesis comes to a close, we realize that this Seed Project continues through Judah's descendants throughout the rest of Old Testament history. It can be traced, for example, through Perez (Gen 38:1-30), Rahab, Ruth, David, Solomon, Jehoshaphat, Uzziah, Josiah, and finally, through Mary. The Seed of the Woman, the serpent crusher, had its ultimate and final expression in the birth of Jesus in Bethlehem, of the tribe of Judah. John Lennox describes this amazing Seed Project in these terms:

> This is not simply a prediction that God will triumph, an issue that was never in doubt. It is a prediction that humanity will triumph. In the end it will be the "seed of the woman," a human being, that will conquer the enemy. Thus begins the story of the seed that, according to the New Testament, finds its ultimate focus in the One whom Paul calls the seed, or the offspring—that is, Jesus Christ (Gal 3:16). Genesis contains the account of the initial trajectory of the seed.[3]

ISRAEL IN EGYPT

The book of Genesis closes in a surprising manner. The covenant people of God find themselves in, of all places, Egypt! Although God has promised them the land of Canaan, the Hebrews find themselves living as exiles in a foreign country, where they will remain for four hundred years. Later in the Old Testament, and for very different reasons, Israel will again find herself far from home when she is exiled to Babylon for a period of seventy years. These seasons of exile confront us with a very significant problem: Can God's people maintain their covenant identity and preserve their faith when forced to live in a pagan environment? Is it possible to live in the world without becoming worldly? And what should be their attitude toward their pagan neighbors? Should they bless them or curse them? These questions raise some of the most important issues God's people will ever confront. Much of the Bible is devoted to helping us find answers to these difficult questions.

When forced into exile, whether Egypt, Babylon, or some other pagan environment, two basic choices confront the people of God. Will they *assimilate* with the culture around them, or will they *separate* themselves from it? Joseph, it seems, chose the path of assimilation. Jacob and his other sons opted for separation.

---

3   Lennox, *Joseph*, 24.

On the one hand, it makes sense to assimilate. As a minority group, there are many advantages to adapting to cultural norms. No one wants to be considered odd or seen as a social misfit. Not only will this be less painful by allowing God's people to minimize the differences between themselves and their unbelieving neighbors, but it will provide a bridge to the culture so that the truth of the gospel will perhaps be seen as relevant and meaningful by the pagan environment. By *being similar* to the world around them, God's people can contextualize the message of the gospel so that outsiders actually hear the Good News. Isn't this what the incarnation is all about? When Jesus became a man, he assimilated with our human condition so that we could understand both our need and God's provision. In the fourth century AD, Emperor Constantine believed that the Roman Empire could actually be Christianized. Culture and faith could become a single reality. This is how the mission of God is advanced in the world. Right?

On the other hand, a case can be made for separation. If God's people mingle with the wicked world around them, the risks of compromise are just too great. Rather than evangelizing the world, it is more likely that the world will contaminate the church. When this happens, members of the second and third generation covenant family often abandon the faith of their fathers completely. To preserve the faith, therefore, many believers think they should create a distinctive subculture. *Being different* is the key. Not only will this make survival more likely, but it will actually increase missional effectiveness. While many unbelievers will mock such nonconformity, some will find it highly appealing and will be drawn in and embrace the faith. The Amish, for example, have preserved their identity for centuries by following this pattern of separation.

Assimilation? Or separation? Both options have much that can be said in their favor. Both are fraught with dangers and problems. How can God's people preserve their identity and yet be culturally relevant? How can they be in the world without becoming worldly? How can they be faithful citizens of the City of God while living in the City of Man? Every member of God's family must wrestle with these questions. Finding the right answers requires both wisdom and courage. Historically, Christians have fallen into three basic categories.[4]

Opposition: Christ *Against* Culture

Some Christians believe that the best way to live out their faith and be an effective witness to the pagans around them is for them to oppose the culture. Whether it be Egypt, Babylon, or some other worldly environment, these believers view the culture as corrupt and irredeemable. The kingdom of God and the kingdoms of this world are like oil and water; they don't mix. They have nothing in common. Therefore, God's people must come out and be separate (see, for example, 2 Cor 6:14-18; 1 John 2:15-17; Jas 4:4).

Compromise: Christ *of* Culture

Rather than working in opposition to culture, these believers want to improve their surroundings, to Christianize the environment. They seek to use everything they can for Kingdom purposes: music, technology, the calendar, etc. These believers see culture as a potential ally. The goal is to redeem the culture, not condemn it. Therefore, these Christians work hard to elect government leaders who will promote moral values. They make their worship services as seeker-friendly as possible in the hopes that outsiders will feel welcome and comfortable. They believe that Christ is most glorified, and their witness is most effective, when their pagan neighbors look on them with respect, not with mocking condescension.

Paradoxical Tension: Christ *Above* Culture

This position recognizes the complexity of the issue and therefore uses elements from both of the above positions. It recognizes the dangers and shortcomings of opting for a single approach. On the one hand, these Christians recognize the categoric distinction that exists between the Kingdom of God and the kingdoms of men. It knows that

---

[4] The classic presentation of this issue is H. Richard Niebuhr's book *Christ and Culture*. This is a must-read for those who think seriously about how Christians should interact with culture. My outline here is a much-simplified summation of Niebuhr's more detailed presentation.

cultures on earth can be modified and improved, but they can never be transformed by human effort so that they become the Kingdom of God. This will happen only when Christ returns at the end of the age. But on the other hand, these Christians understand their calling to love their neighbors, evangelize the lost, and do all they can to improve life on earth by reforming oppressive structures, redeeming the arts, practicing economic fairness, cleaning up the environment, and building hospitals and schools. They understand that God has not only given them the Great Commission to preach the gospel so that sinners can be saved, but he has also given the Great Commandment to love our neighbors and the Cultural Mandate to have dominion over all creation.

How Then Should We Live?

The Bible gives almost no information about how the Hebrews managed to preserve their identity as the covenant family of God during their long sojourn in Egypt. There was no Mosaic Law, no priesthood, and no synagogues. All they had was the covenant promise to Abraham and the sign of circumcision. And yet, this was enough to enable them to preserve their identity in a hostile environment for four hundred years. It seems likely that they adopted the mentality of opposition (Christ against culture). Isolating themselves in the land of Goshen and practicing a trade (shepherding) that was an abomination to the Egyptians, the Hebrews maintained their identity by emphasizing how different they were from the surrounding culture. This posture of separation, however, meant that they did little or nothing to share their faith with their pagan neighbors and their influence on the Egyptian culture appears to have been negligible.

Today, when it comes to living out our faith in the post-modern world of the 21st century, we can debate which approach to culture is best. Should we live in opposition to culture, perhaps establishing Christian communities where we separate ourselves from the evil society around us? Or should we embrace culture as much as we can, building bridges and points of contact where we can help postmodern men and women see the relevance of the Gospel? But how can we live in the world without becoming worldly? And what about our children? Should we raise them to be different and stand out from the crowd? Or should we equip them to go into the world as witnesses, able to relate to modern culture and speak its language? Finding answers to these questions is not easy. And the stakes are high!

In the sixth century before Christ, the Hebrew people found themselves once again in exile; this time, in Babylon for a period of seventy years. The prophet Jeremiah, living 800 miles away in Jerusalem, wrote them a letter. He knew how hard it was to maintain the faith in a pagan environment and so he wrote a sort of "Survivor's Guide" for believers in Babylon. Drawing from all three approaches to culture outlined above, Jeremiah's message is surprisingly relevant for contemporary Christians who are seeking to survive, thrive, and evangelize in the godless culture around them today.

> *Thus says the* LORD *of hosts, the God of Israel, to all the exiles whom I have sent into exile from Jerusalem to Babylon: Build houses and live in them; plant gardens and eat their produce. Take wives and have sons and daughters; take wives for your sons, and give your daughters in marriage, that they may bear sons and daughters; multiply there, and do not decrease. But seek the welfare of the city where I have sent you into exile, and pray to the* LORD *on its behalf, for in its welfare you will find your welfare. For thus says the* LORD *of hosts, the God of Israel: Do not let your prophets and your diviners who are among you deceive you, and do not listen to the dreams that they dream, for it is a lie that they are prophesying to you in my name; I did not send them, declares the* LORD.

> *For thus says the* LORD: *When seventy years are completed for Babylon, I will visit you, and I will fulfill to you my promise and bring you back to this place. For I know the plans I have for you, declares the* LORD, *plans for welfare and not for evil, to give you a future and a hope. Then you will call upon me and come and pray to me, and I will hear you. You will seek me and find me, when you seek me with all your heart. I will be found by you, declares the* LORD, *and I will restore your fortunes and gather you from all the nations and all the places where I have driven you, declares*

the LORD, and I will bring you back to the place from which I sent you into exile. (Jer 29:4-14)

We can summarize Jeremiah's message in six short exhortations. If you, dear reader, find yourself in a hostile environment and wonder if your faith can survive, these six commands are for you.

Remember Who You Are and Whose You Are

You may live in Babylon, but you are *not* a Babylonian. Your citizenship is in Jerusalem, the city of God. Don't let Babylon squeeze you into its mold. Be who you are: a child of God, a citizen of the kingdom of God. This is the message that Peter is passionate to communicate when he writes his first epistle. Addressing himself to "exiles of the Dispersion" (1 Pet 1:1), Peter reminds them of their true identity:

> *But you are a chosen race, a royal priesthood, a holy nation, a people for his own possession, that you may proclaim the excellencies of him who called you out of darkness into his marvelous light. Once you were not a people, but now you are God's people; once you had not received mercy, but now you have received mercy. Beloved, I urge you as sojourners and exiles to abstain from the passions of the flesh, which wage war against your soul. Keep your conduct among the Gentiles honorable, so that when they speak against you as evildoers, they may see your good deeds and glorify God on the day of visitation. (1 Pet 2:9-12)*

Bloom Where You Are Planted

Jeremiah urges the exiles in Babylon to build houses, plant gardens, and get married because they will be staying in this wicked city for a long time; a lifetime, in fact (seventy years). So, stop complaining and wishing you were back in Jerusalem! *This* is the place where God intends for you to live out your calling. As much as is possible, show respect for your environment and ask God for the strength to be a good witness. God has placed you in Babylon to be salt and light (see Matt 5:13-16). When you find it impossible to *do* witnessing, then you can discover that your most important task is to *be* a witness (see Acts 1:8). God is the one who planted you in this location, so bloom there!

Love Your Babylonian Neighbors

The word "welfare" in this passage (see Jer 29:7) comes from the Hebrew *shalom*. Rather than cursing Babylon and praying for its destruction, God wants us to seek the shalom (total well-being) of this pagan city! While this may at first seem startling, this merely underscores the reality that God loves sinners (see John 3:16; Rom 5:8; 1 Tim 1:15; etc.)! God sends us to Babylon so that he can love the Babylonians through us!

Choose Your Pastors Carefully

Unfortunately, some of the prophets in Babylon were preaching a false gospel. These preachers were promising that the exile would be short and in just two years the people would be back in Jerusalem. Naturally, the exiles were attracted to this kind of optimistic message and gave these preachers their fervent attention. Through the prophet Jeremiah, however, the Lord warned them not to be deceived, "for it is a lie that they are prophesying to you in my name; I did not send them" (Jer 29:9). Jeremiah goes so far as to name the names of these false prophets: Ahab, Zedekiah, Shemaiah, and especially Hananiah (see Jer 29:15-32 and Jer 28:1-17). In effect, he is telling the people not to go to the megachurches where these prosperity preachers are proclaiming a message of health, wealth, and happiness. Don't listen to their sermons, don't buy their books, and don't believe their promises. They are liars, frauds, deceivers, and false prophets. A child of God simply cannot survive in Babylon unless he finds a church community where the pastor preaches the pure, unadulterated Word of God!

Seek the Lord With All Your Heart

The great danger in Babylon is that the exiles will begin to seek the treasures and pleasures of this world. This temptation must be resisted at all costs. The only real security in Babylon is to seek the Lord with *all* your heart. The promises God gives are qualitatively different from the pious platitudes offered by the false prophets who speak only of a speedy return to the status quo, pain relief, and temporal happiness. God's promises are so much deeper and richer than that! As they love their pagan neighbors and seek the shalom of Babylon, God promises to fill his people's lives with peace and wellbeing, because in Babylon's welfare they will find their own welfare (see Jer 29:7). And though the exile will last a lifetime (seventy years), God promises to bring his people home and to restore their fortunes. But most of all, God promises to come and live among his people. He promises to give them himself. To have the Giver is a treasure infinitely greater than any of his gifts. Therefore, Jeremiah urges the exiles to seek the Lord with *all* their hearts. This effort will certainly be rewarded. "I will be found by you," God promises (Jer 29:14).

Be in the World but Not of It

Jeremiah refuses to offer a formula for how to survive in Babylon. He does not tell the people to separate from their sinful neighbors, nor does he tell them to assimilate to Babylonian culture. Rather, he urges them to live in the tension. At times, this may mean pulling back and emphasizing the differences between the people of God and pagans. It may mean practicing non-conformity and being counter-cultural. The goal will be to obey the biblical mandate to "be separate from them . . . and touch no unclean thing" (2 Cor 6:17). But at other times it may mean making friends with your Babylonian neighbors, building bridges, creating common ground, and working to make life better for all the citizens of Babylon. Here, one will be motivated by the example of the apostle Paul who wrote, "I have become all things to all people, that by all means I might save some" (1 Cor 9:22).

When it comes to surviving, thriving, and evangelizing in Babylon, there are no formulas. We are to be *in* the world but not *of* the world. It is a good thing when a boat is in water. That is what boats are made for. But it is a bad thing when water is in the boat! God wants his people to be in the world. But he does not want his people to become worldly. This may be the Christian's greatest challenge in life! No wonder, Jesus' final prayer for his disciples included these words:

> *I do not ask that you take them out of the world, but that you keep them from the evil one. They are not of the world, just as I am not of the world. Sanctify them in the truth; your word*

is truth. As you sent me into the world, so I have sent them into the world. And for their sake I consecrate myself, that they also may be sanctified in truth. I do not ask for these only, but also for those who will believe in me through their word, that they may all be one, just as you, Father, are in me, and I in you, that they also may be in us, so that the world may believe that you have sent me. (John 17:15-21)

QUESTIONS FOR DISCUSSION

1. Describe why Israel's sojourn in Egypt was so important.
2. As a Christian living in the world today, do you tend to assimilate with the culture or separate from it? Why? Does something need to change?
3. What about your church and your worship services? Does it tend more toward assimilation or separation?
4. What is the main thing you have learned from this lesson?
5. As you think about your own death, what would you like for your last words to be?

This World Is Not My Home

(from the southern African-American spiritual tradition)

This world is not my home, I'm just a passing through;
My treasures are laid up, somewhere beyond the blue.
The angels beckon me from heaven's open door
And I can't feel at home in this world anymore.

Refrain:
O Lord, you know I have no friend like you,
If Heaven's not my home, then Lord what will I do?
The angels beckon me from Heaven's open door,
And I can't feel at home in this world anymore.

Bibliography

Allender, Dan. *Leading with a Limp*. Colorado Springs: Waterbrook Press, 2006.

Andreades, Sam A. *enGendered*. Wooster: Weaver, 2015.

Blocher, Henri. *In the Beginning*. Downers Grove: InterVarsity Press, 1984.

Bonhoeffer, Dietrich. *The Cost of Discipleship*. New York: Macmillan, 1948.

Chaffey, Tim, ed. *Ark Signs that Teach a Flood of Answers*. Green Forest, AR: Master Books, 2017.

Chambers, Oswald. "Not Knowing Whither." In *The Complete Works of Oswald Chambers*. Grand Rapids: Discovery House, 2000.

_____. "Our Portrait in Genesis." In *The Complete Works of Oswald Chambers*. Grand Rapids: Discovery House, 2000.

Chesterton, G. K. *Orthodoxy*. San Francisco: Ignatius Press, 1986.

Clarke, Adam. *Commentary on the Bible*. 1811-1825. 6 vols. Reprint, Nashville: Abingdon, 1950.

Collins, C. John. *Genesis 1–4: A Linguistic, Literary, and Theological Commentary*. Phillipsburg: P&R Publishing, 2006.

Crabb, Larry. *The Silence of Adam*. Grand Rapids: Zondervan, 1995.

Dante, *The Divine Comedy*. Vol 1. *The Inferno*. New York: Penguin, 2003.

Ellul, Jacques. *The Meaning of the City*. Grand Rapids: Eerdmans, 1970.

Foster, Richard. *Celebration of Discipline*. New York: Harper and Row, 1978.

Gladwell, Malcolm. *The Tipping Point: How Little Things Can Make a Big Difference*. New York: Little, Brown, & Company, 2000.

Graham, Billy. *Just as I Am*. New York: Harper, 1997.

Hamilton, Victor. *The New International Commentary on the Old Testament: The Book of Genesis Chapter 1–17*. Grand Rapids: Eerdmans, 1990.

―――――. *The New International Commentary on the Old Testament: The Book of Genesis Chapter 18–50*. Grand Rapids: Eerdmans, 1990.

―――――. *Handbook on the Pentateuch*. Grand Rapids: Baker, 1982.

Hugo, Victor. *Les Misérables*. Translated from the French by Charles E. Wilbour. Abridged. New York: Fawcett, 1961.

Ingram, Chip. *Love, Sex, and Lasting Relationships*. Ada: Baker, 2003.

Jukes, Andrew. *Types in Genesis*. Grand Rapids: Kregel, 1976.

Kass, Leon R. *The Beginning of Wisdom: Reading Genesis*. Chicago: University of Chicago Press, 2003.

Kent, Jack. *There's No Such Thing as a Dragon*. New York: Dragonfly Books, 1975.

Key, Stan. *Face to Face*. Wilmore, KY: Francis Asbury Press, 2015.

―――――. *Marriage Matters*. Wilmore, KY: Francis Asbury Press, 2017.

Kierkegaard, Søren. *Fear and Trembling*. 1843. Reprint, New York: Penguin, 2003.

―――――. *Provocations*. Farmington, PA: Plough Publishing House, 1999.

Kinlaw, Dennis F. *Lectures in Old Testament Theology: Yahweh Is God Alone*. Wilmore: Francis Asbury Society, 2010.

Lennox, John C. *God's Undertaker: Has Science Buried God?* Oxford: Lion Hudson, 2009.

―――――. *Joseph*. Wheaton: Crossway, 2019.

―――――. *Seven Days that Divide the World: The Beginning According to Genesis and Science*. Grand Rapids: Zondervan, 2011.

Lewis, C. S. *Mere Christianity*. New York: HarperCollins, 1952.

―――――. *The Problem of Pain*. Glasgow: Fount Paperback, 1940.

―――――. *The Weight of Glory*. New York: Touchstone, 1949.

Meyer, F. B. *From the Pit to the Throne*. London: Elliot Stock, 1885.

Milton, John. *Paradise Lost*. New York: Penguin, 2000.

Morris, Henry M. *The Genesis Record: A Scientific & Devotional Commentary on the Book of Beginnings*. Grand Rapids: Baker, 1976.

Muggeridge, Malcolm. *Jesus Rediscovered*. Garden City, NY: Doubleday, 1969.

Niebuhr, H. Richard. *Christ and Culture. New York:* Harper & Row, 1951.

Packer, J. I. *Knowing God*. Downers Grove: InterVarsity Press, 1973.

Pascal, Blaise. *Pensées*. New York: Penguin, 1966.

Plato. *The Symposium*. New York: Penguin, 1951.

Postman, Neil. *Amusing Ourselves to Death: Public Discourse in the Age of Show Business*. London: Methuen, 2007.

Power, Mike. *Prayers for the Journey*. Wilmore, KY: Francis Asbury Press, 2021.

Richter, Sandra. *The Epic of Eden*. Downers Grove: IVP Academic, 2008.

Ross, Allen P. *Creation & Blessing: A Guide to the Study and Exposition of Genesis*. Grand Rapids: Baker, 1996.

Seuss, [Geisel] Theodor. *On Beyond Zebra*. New York: Random House, 1955.

Smith, James K. A. *You Are What You Love*. Grand Rapids: Brazos Press, 2016.

Spurgeon, Charles H. "Christ the Conqueror of Satan." Sermon, Metropolitan Tabernacle, London, England, November 26, 1876.

Strobel, Lee. *The Case for Faith*. Grand Rapids: Zondervan, 2000.

_____. *Inside the Mind of Unchurched Harry and Mary*. Grand Rapids: Zondervan, 1993.

Solzhenitsyn, Alexander. *The Gulag Archipelago*. Abridged by Edward E. Ericson. New York: HarperPerennial, 2007.

Tolkien, J. R. R. *The Return of the King. Boston:* Houghton Mifflin, 1955.

Tozer, A. W. *The Root of Righteousness*. Chicago: Moody, 1955.

Wesley, John. *The Works of John Wesley*. 3rd ed. Vol VI. Grand Rapids: Baker, 1978.

Wiesel, Elie. *Messengers of God: Biblical Portraits and Legends*. New York: Simon & Schuster, 1976.

Williams, Charles. *The Forgiveness of Sins.* 1942. Reprinted, Grand Rapids: Eerdmans, 1984.

_____. *He Came Down from Heaven.* 1938. Reprinted, Grand Rapids: Eerdmans, 1984.

Made in the USA
Columbia, SC
23 September 2024

42655065R10254